THE DEVELOPMENT OF AMERICAN PUBLIC POLICY

The Structure of Policy Restraint

THE DEVELOPMENT OF AMERICAN PUBLIC POLICY

The Structure of Policy Restraint

David Brian Robertson
University of Missouri, St. Louis

Dennis R. Judd
University of Missouri, St. Louis

Scott, Foresman/Little, Brown Series in Political Science
Scott, Foresman and Company
Glenview, Illinois   Boston   London

Library of Congress Cataloging-in-Publication Data

Robertson, David Brian, 1951–
   The development of American public policy : the structure of policy restraint / David Brian Robertson, Dennis R. Judd.
   p.   cm. — (Scott, Foresman/Little, Brown series in political science)
   Includes bibliographies and index.
   ISBN 0-673-39881-1
   1. Federal government—United States—History. 2. Political planning—United States—History. 3. Policy sciences. I. Judd, Dennis R. II. Title. III. Series.
JK311.R63 1989
321.02'0973—dc19
                                       88-23901
                                             CIP

1 2 3 4 5 6 7 8 9 10 -KPF- 94 93 92 91 90 89 88

Printed in the United States of America

Acknowledgments
Table 6.1 p. 193 From *Implementation of Civil Rights Policy*, by C.S. Bullock, III and C.M. Lamb. Copyright © 1984 by Wadsworth, Inc. Reprinted by permission of Brooks/Cole Publishing Company, Pacific Grove, CA 93950. (Original data for this table from various issues of *Statistical Summary and Southern Education Report*, Southern Education Reporting Service, Nashville.)

Table 10.1 p. 324 Gilroy and Shapiro, *Public Opinion Quarterly*. 50(2), (Summer, 1986): 270–279. Reprinted by permission of The University of Chicago Press.

Table 7.7 p. 238 Copyright 1984 by *National Journal, Inc.* All Rights Reserved. Reprinted by Permission.

Quotes excerpted on p. 274 Copyright 1986, *The Chronicle of Higher Education*. Reprinted with permission.

Table 9.4 p. 291 Adapted from Leo F. Schnore, Carolyn D. André, and Harry Sharp, "Black Suburbanization, 1930–1970," in Barry Schwartz ed., *The Changing Face of the Suburbs* (Chicago: University of Chicago Press, 1976), 80. Reprinted by permission.

Quote on p. 373 Copyright © 1982/86 by the New York Times Company. Reprinted by permission.

To Bryan Robertson

. . . D.B.R.

To Lawrence and Patty Mosqueda

. . . D.R.J.

PREFACE

The study of public policy has emerged as a separate field of inquiry only in the last two decades. The explicit study of policy processes and outcomes evolved because of the proliferation of government programs in the 1960s and early 1970s that aimed, among other goals, to reduce the incidence of poverty and unemployment, to improve education, to rebuild the cities, and to clean up the environment. The concerns motivating the new policy scholarship involved explanations of why programs were enacted, how they performed, and who benefited. By 1972 policy studies as a distinct field had progressed far enough to result in the founding of the interdisciplinary Policy Studies Organization, and in the same year one of the first public policy textbooks was published. Courses on public policy analysis and process have become standard items in the curriculum of most colleges and universities, and books and journals addressing a variety of policy issues are available to both popular and scholarly audiences. The number of academic journals devoted to public policy continues to grow, with, for example, the addition of the *Journal of Policy History* in 1989.

But unlike the older and well-established academic disciplines, a theoretical tradition has not yet emerged to guide policy analysis. Policy research often focuses on specific programs, so that one analyst's answer to the questions of "who gets what, how, and when" may seem utterly unrelated to explanations offered by other scholars. Anyone who reads public policy journal articles or books could easily conclude that American public policy is constructed of a crazyquilt of programs that bear little relationship to one another, that policy effectiveness cannot be reliably assessed, and that every imaginable cause of policy outcomes is equally important. For example, Thomas Dye's book, *Understanding Public Policy* (a sixth edition appeared in 1987), describes eight different models of public policy analysis and in effect invites readers to give all of them equal weight.

Though we agree that public policy can be examined in a variety of ways, it is imperative that an effort be made to identify the main undercurrents that push policy in one direction or another. Enough formal scholarship about public policy has accumulated to make it possible to explain its processes and outcomes coherently. In this book we undertake this task by tracing the development of policies over our national history and by comparing policies among the capitalist democratic nations.

vii

Our thesis is that America's policymaking structure always has fragmented and limited the development of effective and equitable policymaking effort in the United States. The unevenness and disorder of contemporary American public policy reflects the incapacity of our government institutions to design and implement coherent policies. Policymaking capacity—jurisdiction, revenues, expenditures, and professional personnel—has been vastly enhanced in this century. But policymaking incoherence—notably institutional fragmentation and rivalry within and among all levels of government—has not changed very much; instead, new agencies and programs seem to have increased rather than reduced policymaking incoherence. The story of American public policy is in large measure a struggle by policymakers to develop and implement effective programs within the context of an elaborate and resiliently incoherent government structure.

Like detectives following a new lead, this hypothesis led us to reexamine our own assumptions and to look at public policy in a new light. Indeed, we had to start from the beginning, investigating the evolution of government responsibility and specific policies over the past two centuries. We grew more confident of our thesis as our efforts led us into statutes, Congressional hearings, presidential documents, and other original sources as well as the writings of authorities in many fields.

We have placed the story of individual programs in historical and comparative context. We have painstakingly reconstructed the evolution of government capacity and coherence since the 1780s, demonstrating that choices made in one period constrained or dictated policy options available later. Policymaking has developed in four stages: a period of dividing policy responsibility among government institutions (1787 to the 1870s); state government activism (from the 1870s to 1933); national activism (from 1933 to 1961); and national standards (1961 to the present). In each stage, government grew more capable of making policy, but at each stage institutional fragmentation imposed significant obstacles to enacting and implementing equitable and efficient programs.

In August 1988, as we send this preface to our publishers, it appears that the nation may be entering a period of policy activism. A new fair housing bill has just been passed; the Democratic-controlled congress has passed plant-closing legislation, and President Reagan has admitted he cannot stop it; and concerted action on acid rain appears to be just around the corner. The Republican nominee for President, George Bush, has proposed national income supports for children and education tax credits. If Michael Dukakis wins the presidential contest, we may see a new round of social legislation, including a national health insurance initiative, welfare reform, and strengthened environmental standards.

In the past, spurts of reform often have been interpreted as radical departures. But there are narrow limits to how far and in what direction anyone can steer the American policy system. As policy scholars, we will be very surprised if national standards are soon imposed consistently and equitably across the nation. Consistent with the analysis offered in this book, we predict that the state-based politics in Congress, institutional fragmentation all through the intergovernmental system, and devolution of responsibilities to states, local governments, and private institutions, will continue to slow and fragment the implementation of national policy. If this proves not to be the case, then for public policy the past is not prologue, and the attempt to explain how our national political process changed so quickly and fundamentally will become a cottage industry for political pundits and policy scholars.

Policymaking structure fundamentally affects outcomes, and policymakers' ignorance of the roots of public policy and of the ways that other nations handle similar problems has contributed to a myopic quest for marginal change that too often yields results that satisfy virtually no one. All too often public policy in the United States has been judged a failure because the resources allocated to accomplish policy goals have become lost in a maze of institutions and governments pursuing conflicting and contradictory goals and priorities.

This book is designed both for advanced scholars and for students taking their first course. We have sought to write a readable and jargon-free scholarly contribution to the literature on public policy. We also present an account of policy development sufficiently coherent and comprehensive that we expect our book to be used as a textbook. A textbook should derive its strength from original scholarship and insight while thoroughly synthesizing the literature that defines a field of inquiry. The scholarly enterprise and a textbook project should not be mutually exclusive undertakings. Guided by that principle, we have combined both tasks.

David Brian Robertson

Dennis R. Judd

ACKNOWLEDGMENTS

As a last but important step in completing an undertaking of this scope, it is a special pleasure to express our appreciation to the many people who helped bring this book to fruition. We are lucky to be surrounded by such supportive and helpful colleagues and friends.

The University of Missouri-St. Louis provided important resources that helped us pursue our research. In particular, a research leave during the summer of 1986 and fall of 1987 had an especially salutary effect on Robertson's contributions. The staff of the Thomas Jefferson Library was extremely helpful. The Center for Metropolitan Studies at UM-St. Louis provided research and production assistance. The staffs in the Political Science Department and in the Center for Metropolitan Studies were singularly outstanding in their professional abilities, and remarkably patient with us. We owe a tremendous debt to Pam Vierdag, Lana Sink, Jan Frantzen, Sandy Overton-Springer, and Karen Griffith. We hope they never try to collect.

The *Journal of Policy History* has generously given permission to use material from Robertson's article. "The Bias of American Federalism: Political Structure and the Development of America's Exceptional Welfare State in the Progressive Era" (April 1989).

Ken Cook's contributions to this book were invaluable. He provided comment and direction to the general theme of the entire manuscript, and researched and authored Chapter 8, "Public Education: Opportunity and Its Limits." We thank him for his participation.

Eugene Meehan and Alfred Diamant stand out as two genuine scholars whose comments on the first draft of our argument helped us amplify its strengths and minimize its weaknesses. Thad Beyle of the University of North Carolina at Chapel Hill, and Michael Reagan of the University of California at Riverside examined a nearly final draft of the argument in exhaustive detail. We initially bridled at some of their criticism, finally saw that they had identified crucial deficiencies, and got on with the difficult task of making major revisions. Their meticulous reading of the manuscript changed it substantially, and for the better; we are very grateful for their help.

We want to thank several colleagues and friends who read and provided trenchant comments on the entire manuscript: Susan Fainstein, Gary Huxford, and Daniel Berman. We wish to thank Kay Gasen for her assistance on an early draft of Chapter 7, "American Welfare Policy: Fragmented Programs, Divided Constituencies." A number of our colleagues also read and commented on parts of the argument: Lawrence

Mosqueda, Lana Stein, Lance LeLoup, Fred Springer, Carol Kohfeld, Timothy Tilton, and Vernon Coleman. Several students at the University of Missouri-St. Louis helped us in this regard; Jayson Tipp and Carter Whitson gave especially detailed comments, and Stacey Barwick, Toby Paone, John Hancock, and Ken Westphal all provided suggestions. Students in the undergraduate public policy, comparative public policy, and public policy administration seminars discussed the book, and helped us refine our arguments.

As usual in a drama of this length, the families played an important offstage role. Cathleen Robertson appeared as the jack of all trades with effective comments, suggestions, editing, and typing. Bryan Robertson played the part of the infant and later the two-year-old hot dog with relish.

Two days after the final manuscript was sent to the publisher, Tracy and Linden Judd correctly complained to their father that he had been neglecting them. One suspects that they may come to regard the increased attention made possible by the completion of this book as a mixed blessing.

D.B.R.

D.R.J.

CONTENTS

Chapter 3

WHY DID THE UNITED STATES DIVERGE?
A COMPARATIVE VIEW

Chapter 4

THE FRAGMENTATION OF NATIONAL
ACTIVISM: THE NEW DEAL LEGACY

Chapter 5

ACTIVISM AND RESTRAINT: THE GRANTS STRATEGY, 1940S to 1989   125

Chapter 6

CIVIL RIGHTS AND THE STRUGGLE AGAINST "STATES' RIGHTS"   168

Chapter 7

AMERICAN WELFARE POLICY: FRAGMENTED PROGRAMS, DIVIDED CONSTITUENCIES

202

Chapter 8

PUBLIC EDUCATION: OPPORTUNITY AND ITS LIMITS   by Kenneth Cook   245

Chapter 9

NATIONAL URBAN POLICY: UNDERWRITING SEGREGATION AND FRAGMENTATION   279

Chapter 10

THE POLITICS OF NATIONAL STANDARDS: ENVIRONMENTAL PROTECTION

321

Chapter 11

POLICY PERFORMANCE AND STRUCTURAL REFORM

354

TABLES AND FIGURES

THE DEVELOPMENT OF
AMERICAN PUBLIC POLICY

The Structure of
Policy Restraint

Chapter 1

THE POLITICAL ECONOMY OF POLICY RESTRAINT

THE PUZZLE OF AMERICAN POLICY RESTRAINT

The United States has ranked among the world's wealthiest nations for all of this century. Considering the resources at its disposal, its capacity to provide for the well-being of its citizens has been unsurpassed. Yet, in comparison with almost all of the advanced capitalist democracies, it has exercised remarkable restraint in ensuring that its citizens receive a minimum level of the basics required for living a full life: health, housing, and income necessary to maintain daily existence. Governments in the United States do less to reduce the risks and to rectify the inequalities that result from market capitalism because they raise less revenues, spend less money, and impose fewer restrictions on the uses of property than do comparable nations.[1]

To explain the paradox of America's minimal government effort in the context of its vast resources is one of the most daunting but important tasks that can be undertaken by social analysts. Probably the most common popular explanation—and one scholars often invoke as well—is that Americans value individualism and equality of opportunity above all else and that they therefore distrust collective efforts promoted by government. They insist on political and legal processes that appear to treat each person the same way, instead of public policies that redistribute resources or that guarantee a minimum level of well-being as a right of citizenship.

It has often been said that this American definition of equality favors policies that promote individual competition and self-betterment at the same time that it militates against solidarity and universal social programs. This American notion of equality of opportunity might even, paradoxically, require material inequality for its fulfillment. According to the historian David Potter,

1

A European advocating equality might very well mean that all men should occupy positions that are roughly the same level in wealth, power, or enviability. But the American, with his emphasis upon equality of opportunity, has never conceived of it in this sense. He has traditionally expected to find a gamut ranging from rags to riches, from tramps to millionaires . . . Thus equality did not mean uniform position on a common level, but it did mean universal opportunity to move through a scale which traversed many levels . . .[2]

In this view, America's political culture suffices to explain the public policies it has pursued. From this perspective public policy in the United States is conservative, involving less public effort to accomplish more limited aims than in other nations, because Americans demand less from government.

The political ideas that Americans share may explain a great deal about American *society* today, and they help us to understand some of the unique features of American public policy. But for two reasons, it is insufficient to explain conservative public policies in the United States solely by reference to the values and beliefs making up its political culture.

First, American political culture has never been uniform in all times and places. In fact, the idea of a singular culture in such a diverse country is built upon an enduring mythology that the waves of immigrant groups and ethnic cultures somehow blended together and adopted values peculiar to the American nation. But in fact, powerful social and political movements demanding government intervention to accomplish public and community, as opposed to private, purposes have periodically exploded onto the American scene. These movements have been similar in intensity to those that have been mobilized in capitalist nations that have enacted far more encompassing public policies than has the United States. Nevertheless, despite the strength of these mass movements, governments at all levels in the United States have lagged far behind governments in other nations in enacting policies that inhibit private property rights in favor of collective protections or benefits.

Second, over a long period public opinion polls have indicated that Americans consistently support the expansion of specific public programs. Public opinion polls reveal that when they are asked broad questions about personal responsibility, the size of government, and equality of opportunity, Americans indeed seem more individualistic than citizens of other nations.[3] Although Americans are somewhat less receptive to the general notion of government guarantees of employment and health care than citizens in other Western democracies, they still favor such guarantees by large margins. For example, a 1987 poll of registered voters found that 78 percent agreed that "the Government in

Washington should guarantee medical care for all people."[4] And when Americans are questioned about more spending on *specific* health and other social programs, they respond favorably and in proportions similar to the responses of citizens of the United Kingdom and Sweden.[5] Though political culture seems to affect general beliefs about the role of government, citizens seem to express similar opinions about specific government activities whether they live in the United States, in Sweden, or in Britain. One can conclude that America's relatively conservative public policies cannot be explained solely by reference to cultural values.

In this book we offer an encompassing explanation for the character of public policy in the United States. Our central theme is this: the structure of government authority in the United States has repeatedly thwarted political movements that have demanded public policies intended to provide broad social benefits or to set limitations on the use of private property. The calculated complexity and incoherence of American government structure have placed obstacles in the path of social reformers fighting for well-financed, equitable, inclusive, and well-coordinated public policies.

America's policymaking structure divides responsibilities among several institutions at the national level, and the same fragmentation exists in the states. In addition, most policies are decentralized through the federal system. This structure impedes efforts to secure the necessary public capacity for achieving policy objectives equitably and efficiently across the nation. The fragmentation of decisionmaking authority that characterizes the American political system has, over the long run, become a vehicle for frustrating policy reforms.

American history and civics texts never fail to recount the advantages of the government plan that the founders produced. There were checks and balances among several branches of government, each responsive to their own constituencies, to keep popular majorities from trampling on the rights of smaller political factions. With only the House of Representatives elected by the people directly—and even then, with each legislator representing a small geographic constituency—republican government provided a powerful check on the sudden passions and impulses of the mass electorate.

The founders were also politically shrewd enough to design a *federal* republic, and they could scarcely have done otherwise: the Constitution would not have been ratified without agreement by the states. Despite the extensive powers left to the states in the document, ratification by the states was far from certain.

This fragmented political structure has continued to regulate and channel social and political change. In many areas of concern, government efforts can be so diverse and uncoordinated that experts question whether any welfare, health, civil rights, or other "policy" exists at all. Most of the time, American policy seems very *incoherent*—that is, it lacks national consistency, order, and uniformity. America has no easily recognizable labor market policy, for example. Instead, labor market policies emerge from a century of accumulated national, state, and local statutes, court decisions, administrative actions, and "seat of the pants" initiatives.[6] Much the same can be said of most other policies as well.

ANALYZING PUBLIC POLICY: OUTCOMES, DEMANDS, AND POLICYMAKING STRUCTURE

The object of our study, "public policy," is very difficult to define with precision, as is illustrated when textbook definitions are attempted. In his leading text, Thomas R. Dye concluded simply that "public policy is whatever governments choose to do or not to do."[7] James Anderson and his colleagues stated that a public policy involves a "purposeful course of action" (although its effects may not be anticipated), that it is based on law and thus backed up by the police power of government (although many policies may not be enforced), and that government's refusal to act when called upon to do so is a form of policy.[8]

Figure 1.1 illustrates the distinction between what causes issues to reach the policymaking agenda (policy demands) and what government does in response (policy outcomes). This schema distinguishes between policy causes (or "inputs") that originate in society and those elements of the policymaking structure that amplify some of these demands, repress others, and add demands of their own.[9] Much of the policy literature has assumed that government functions basically as an impartial umpire among contending interests. In our analysis we bring government back in as an independent agent in the policymaking process.[10]

How Is Policy Made?

The outcomes of government action are difficult to define and analyze, and the process of arriving at policy results is not much clearer. Nevertheless, there are distinct stages that can be identified. Though he warns that it is a drastic oversimplification, John Kingdon has asserted that

> public policy making can be considered to be a set of processes, including at least (1) the setting of the agenda [the list of subjects or problems to which government officials, and people outside of government closely associated with those officials are paying some serious attention at any given time], (2) the specification of alternatives from which a choice is to be made, (3) an authoritative choice among those specified alternatives, as in a legislative vote or a presidential decision, and (4) the implementation of the decision.[11]

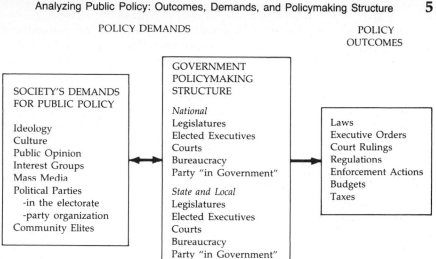

Figure 1.1. *Components of policymaking*

These stages in the policymaking process are far less easily distinguishable in practice than in theory because actual policymaking is an untidy affair in which the boundaries between these stages are hard to draw.[12]

Policy Demands

More important for our purposes is the distinction between the demands made upon government and the way in which government processes, alters, and sometimes ignores these demands as it produces public policy (Figure 1.1). The independent effect of the structure of government—the "black box" of the policymaking process—has been underappreciated in understanding American public policy. The boundary between government and society is reasonably clear, although a few influential policy experts routinely move back and forth between government and the private sector.

At each stage of policymaking, participants outside of government demand that issues of importance be brought to the public agenda and that their preferred alternatives be discussed, approved, and implemented according to their wishes. Opponents seek to prevent action or to substitute their preferences at each stage. These participants include interest groups, such as businesses, trade unions, labor, agricultural organizations, and "single" issue groups concerned with gun control, abortion, government reform, or any of hundreds of other issues. Individual experts, such as academics and professional consultants, also shape agendas and alternatives.

Public opinion can set the bounds of what is and is not an appropriate problem for government to solve and what solutions are considered appropriate, but only in some instances are issues put on the policy agenda. Newspapers and television publicize problems, solutions, and dramatic events such as disasters. Political party leaders outside of government try to capitalize on these forces by pressuring their elected or appointed colleagues in government.[13] As an example, in the early 1980s several well-publicized tragedies mobilized some citizens to create new interest groups such as Mothers Against Drunk Driving (MADD), and American state and national governments reacted to these pressures by increasing penalties for drunk driving and raising the minimum age for purchasing liquor.

Most American policy studies since the 1940s have assumed that such demands from outside of government predominantly account for policy outcomes.[14] According to Theda Skocpol,

> "Government" was viewed primarily as an arena within which economic interest groups of normative social movements contended or allied with one another to shape the making of public policy decisions. Those decisions were understood to be *allocations* of benefits among demanding groups. Research centered on the societal "inputs" to government and on the distributive effects of governmental "outputs." Government itself was not taken very seriously as an independent actor . . .[15]

Policy analysts have frequently disagreed about the relative influence of various "inputs" to government policy. For example, a classic debate about urban policy turned on whether local elites determined policy outcomes[16] or whether outcomes reflected the balance of group competition.[17]

Policymaking Structure

Most policy scholars have acknowledged that such features of the American policymaking structure as federalism and checks and balances complicate the American policy process,[18] and they often have described how structure affects policy results. An oft-cited example is the fact that federalism permits enormous variations in expenditure on education, welfare, and other policies across the American states.[19] And a large number of policy studies have relied on case studies of institutional battles pitting one branch of government against another, the result usually being policy proposals delayed or side-tracked altogether. Yet authors who acknowledge the importance of structural features seldom generalize about the effects of the policymaking process as a whole on policy outcomes. They note that even in individual policy enactments the forces that contributed to the policy are so varied and interdependent that none can be isolated. Or they describe the effects of structural factors in specific cases of policy development, such as the role of the filibuster in delaying civil rights legislation of the 1950s and 1960s and the effect of congressional fragmentation on the incoherence of energy policy in the late 1970s.

We employ a more inclusive concept of public policymaking structure that emphasizes the independent effect of government on policy outcomes *as well as its influence on the way policy demands are expressed* (thus, arrows in Figure 1.1 point in both directions away from "policymaking structure").[20] Europeans are more familiar than Americans with the notion that government plays an independent role in their lives. European analysts use another word—the *State*—to refer to the "continuous administrative, legal, bureaucratic and coercive systems that attempt not only to structure relationships *between* civil society and public authority in a polity but also to structure many crucial relationships within civil society as well."[21]

There are two important ways that government affects public policy, independent of "inputs" or outside pressures. First, its policymaking rules (how laws are made, what jurisdiction an agency enjoys, what powers a court exercises) present a set of opportunities for or obstacles to achieving specific policy outcomes. These formal and informal rules have a profound impact on the goals, strategies, and tactics of government officials. For example, if a legislator is required to stand for election periodically and has the opportunity to vote for increases in government benefits (social security payments, veterans' benefits, or new construction projects in the legislators' constituency), these circumstances encourage a positive vote just before a reelection campaign, regardless of whether citizens' demands for those benefits change.[22] In addition, administrators in defense, social security, or other government agencies share an incentive to expand the budget, power, and responsibilities of their agencies regardless of external demands (though a claim to external support is crucial for their ultimate success).[23]

Second, government rules affect the way that groups and citizens interact with one another and with government. This contradicts the commonly held view that government acts as a neutral umpire in social and political conflicts. Through election, lobbying, and regulatory laws, governments determine the circumstances under which citizens can organize into groups and demand policy change. Political conflict will be targeted toward the institutions or levels of government most capable of responding to demands. If local governments are constitutionally empowered to regulate business, for example, then demands for regulation will concentrate on the local level and move to the national level only when local governments are unresponsive to or ineffectual in solving the problems in question. If courts are more responsive to racial minorities than a legislature, proponents of expanded civil rights laws will tend to focus on the courts. And thus with all political conflicts.

Once established, these rules and patterns of organizational behavior are hard to change.[24] Public agencies develop routines and constituencies better suited to their original purposes than to new problems or changed priorities. For example, such agencies as the Federal Housing Administration and the United States Employment Service, established to help the middle class recover from the Depression of the 1930s, resisted pressures to help poor minorities in the 1960s, because these agencies had learned how to seek political support from middle-class client groups.

Over time, public officials, citizens, interest groups, and political parties adapt to these rules and learn how to take advantage of them. Political battles are as often fought over long-standing procedural rules as over substantive policy changes, a recognition that procedures make a difference in determining future policies. For example, during the 1950s and the early 1960s many liberals in Congress battled for the reform of the House of Representatives' Rules Committee and the Senate filibuster rule, which southern members of Congress had long used to bury effective civil rights legislation. In turn, in the 1980s liberals often tried to use congressional procedures to obstruct and blunt the conservative initiatives sponsored by the Reagan administration.

Of course, it is obvious that the institutions making up a policymaking structure are affected by external social and political pressures. Prevailing beliefs about the appropriate role and structure of government shape laws and especially constitutions, as beliefs in the sanctity of private property and limited government shaped the American constitution. Changing economic conditions, popular beliefs, political party coalitions, and interest group power can exert irresistible pressures on government, forcing even the most rigid institutions to change their priorities.

One interest—business—deserves special mention. Business has a "privileged position" in policymaking in every capitalist democracy, including the United States.[25] Policymakers' political futures depend on the economic well-being of their constituents, and in all capitalist economies that well-being depends most of all on the performance of business, particularly its ability to provide employment and income for citizens and taxes for government. Business is probably no more selfish or venal in the United States than anywhere else; indeed, some American businesses have pioneered social protections for their own employees.[26] However, in comparison to other Western democracies, America's political structure made American policymakers especially reluctant to intrude on business, more willing to accommodate business needs, and more cautious about initiating public programs to rectify the risks and inequalities that result from market capitalism.

THE STRUCTURE OF POLICY RESTRAINT: CAPACITY AND COHERENCE

The effects of policymaking structure accumulate and magnify over time. Two characteristics of American government have most profoundly shaped policy development in the United States: limited policymaking capacity and the absence of policymaking coherence.

Policymaking Capacity

A government's policymaking *capacity* can be defined as its ability to entertain a variety of responses to social and economic problems, to enact or reject authoritative solutions, and to implement its decisions. Indicators of government capacity include the scope of government authority, taxes and expenditures, and the level of its commitment and resources to formulate and implement policy on a continuing basis.

First, a government's capacity to consider a variety of responses to social and economic problems is defined by the formal boundaries established for legitimate state intervention. For example, the United States constitution more narrowly circumscribes the government's ability to interfere in religious matters than is true in many other countries. Often, the boundaries defining legitimate action are disputed and they change. Until the 1930s federal courts interpreted government powers to regulate commerce very narrowly, effectively prohibiting national regulation of business in most (but not all) sectors of the economy. But since 1937, the Supreme Court has tended to uphold broad national powers to govern the economy, such as the regulation of minimum wages, environmental quality, and product safety standards.

The Western democracies draw boundaries between government and the market in different ways. There are no economies that are either fully nationalized or left entirely in the hands of the free market. Within that range, most capitalist democracies rely more on government than does the United States to provide goods and services.[27] The United States has opted to regulate but to leave in private hands railroads, banks, airlines, television, and other major social and economic activities.[28]

A second indicator of a government's capacity is its ability to raise taxes and fund policy initiatives. In most nations, government taxing and spending have tended to increase steadily in this century.[29] However, arbitrary rules may inhibit the growth of taxes and government spending. Most American state constitutions require that state expenditures not exceed state tax receipts in a budget year, and the states impose similar limits on city governments. Such pervasive and automatic restrictions on capacity do not exist in other nations.

Third, policymaking institutions differ in the workload they are capable of undertaking. American governments in the early eighteenth century possessed very little capacity to implement policies of any kind because legislatures met infrequently (every other year for brief sessions) and officials were usually untrained amateurs. Over time, Congress and state legislatures, the president and state governors, and bureaucracies at all levels of government have grown larger, and more professional. State legislatures, for example, now meet more frequently and for longer sessions than in the past, and legislators and elected executives are allocated vastly more professional staff assistance. And merit requirements have reduced (but not eliminated) the tendency to fill administrative posts with inexperienced but politically loyal officials. The policymaking capacity of the executive branch, and particularly of the executive agencies, has indisputably outpaced the capacity of other government institutions at all levels.[30]

All else being equal, public policymaking capacity increases in step with the scope, taxes, spending, and institutional workloads of governments. However, even if policy effort expands, the result is not necessarily coherent, and policy incoherence impedes policy development almost as much as a lack of capacity.

Policymaking Coherence

Policymaking *coherence* describes the degree to which the various policymaking institutions align their efforts in a consistent policy direction. Coherence is a function of the number of government units involved in policymaking and the ability or motivation of these units to stop or alter policy in the agenda-setting, formulation, enactment, and implementation stages. When government is extremely fragmented, consistent policy that is efficiently implemented becomes a rarity.

Within a government, a one-house legislature is more likely to arrive at coherent policy than a two-house legislature. A parliamentary system (such as that at the national level in Britain or Sweden or at the subnational and national levels, as in Canada and Australia) is more likely to arrive at a coherent policy than the American system of separate executive and legislative powers. Policy approval does not require the separate consent of the executive in a parliamentary system but it does require such consent in the United States, where the president can veto acts of Congress.

The national government of the United States distributes authority among several institutions. The lower and upper houses of Congress are coequal branches (while the upper house in contemporary parliamentary systems usually has a limited power to stop the initiatives of the dominant lower house). Both the U.S. Senate and the House of Representatives are internally fragmented institutions in which centrifugal forces overwhelm the weak centralizing force of party discipline. Additionally, the federal courts have used their power to strike down legislation at least as actively as any such courts elsewhere.[31]

In American states this extreme division of authority is even more pronounced. Many executive leaders, such as lieutenant governors, attorneys general, secretaries of state, and state auditors, are elected independently of one another. In Texas, for example, voters elect nine executive officers and the state maintains two separate supreme courts, one for civil cases and one for criminal appeals.

A second dimension of policy incoherence in the United States is the considerable degree of autonomy possessed by independent governments. By definition, a federal system distributes governing power so as to "recognize the sovereignty of a central authority while [subunits retain] certain residual powers of government."[32] Although the U.S. national government's authority has expanded in this century, state governments continue to exercise a great deal of independence in policymaking. This is the case even when states implement programs that originated at the national level. For example, states are permitted to set benefit levels, eligibility standards, and other key features of a wide range of social programs. In other federal systems, such as in Australia, Canada, and the Federal Republic of Germany, there is much more constancy in these programs.

The degree of fragmentation within government increases the likelihood that policy design will be illogical and prone to failure because (1) it increases veto points; (2) it allows formal and informal changes in policy goals; and (3) it produces the need for expedient compromises. Senate and House leaders, presidents and administrators, and state and local officials are always trading off one policy goal in order to protect another. This is built into a highly fragmented process, and the institutional actors understand up front that this will happen. The best known examples are the "pork-barrel" bills that strategically locate defense, highway, river and harbor improvements, or expensive projects in particular Congressional districts in order to "logroll" support or expand the size of the legislative coalition, regardless of demonstrated need or objective locational considerations. Other less obvious tradeoffs also undermine policy coherence by creating policy designs that are logically inconsistent—such as the Model Cities Program of 1967, with ambitious goals for urban revitalization in a few "demonstration" cities, but, ultimately, a dispersal of funds to all too many cities (pork-barrel politics) for the funds allocated.

Policymaking Incoherence Limits Policymaking Capacity

The framers of the American constitution understood that fragmentation tends to impede policymaking capacity. The fragmentation of American national government was a deliberate effort to make positive, decisive governmental action difficult. The founders were concerned about protecting citizens from the oppressive and arbitrary use of government power. They wanted to ensure that public power would not be abused by the national government. The checks and balances established by provisions for two houses of Congress, a separate executive branch and a presidential veto, and a federal court system all weakened the national government's ability to act decisively on behalf of popular majorities or well-organized political movements. With the Bill of Rights, Americans came to enjoy unprecedented legal rights of free speech, freedom of the press, freedom of religion, and fair legal processes. Though political hysteria has swept the United States periodically and has often enough resulted in effective organized repression of some ideas and groups, American government provided no easy way to engineer an antidemocratic takeover of policymaking such as the one that succeeded in Nazi Germany in the 1930s. It is important to note this as a significant feature of a fragmented government structure.

The bias against policy activism also has worked to limit public policies of an entirely different sort. As we detail in Chapter 3, turn-of-the-century social policies that advanced in Britain foundered in the United States. The U.S. government lacked the administrative and political capacity to manage a welfare state, and when it tried to erect a few national standards (such as a prohibition of child labor) the Supreme Court struck down such efforts. Social policy in the states met with numerous structural obstacles: the need to amend state constitutions to permit the administration of social welfare programs, the veto ability of a few legislative leaders at all levels whose cooperation was necessary for enactment, and the use of judicial review by both the federal and state courts. A crucially important obstacle to policy activism at the state level was the perception held by state officials that activism would harm the ability of their states, in competition with other states, to attract and keep industry.

Interstate Economic Competition and Policy "Drag"

Unlike national officials in small countries,[33] American state and local officials cannot use currency devaluations, targeted subsidies, preferential tariffs, or other tools to benefit businesses within their borders as compensation for the taxes needed to fund social programs. Since they have virtually no power to limit the movement of business out of their jurisdictions, they are especially reluctant to intrude on business, more willing to accommodate its needs, and more cautious about initiating public programs to rectify the risks and inequalities that result from market capitalism.

The historically large economic disparities among the states, combined with the states' dependence on whatever revenue they can collect within their own boundaries, has accentuated economic competition among them. States often have promoted lower wages, discouraged unionization, and kept taxes low as a means to attract business investment. When these states appear successful, states disposed to regulate business more closely or to adopt generous social policies come under pressure to "hold the line" on offering progressive policies.

State policymakers act *as if* generous social policies and relatively restrictive business regulations diminish the attractiveness of their state to business, even though little evidence supports the assumption that such policies consistently affect actual business decisions.[34] First, anecdotes drawn from throughout American history confirm that businesses occasionally respond to lower taxes and wages, weaker unions, and fewer restrictions on business. Second, elected officials are extremely vulnerable to charges that they are unfriendly to business. If business leaves or the local economy deteriorates, politicians become handy scapegoats. At the other extreme, elected officials are quick to take credit for business expansion in their jurisdictions, regardless of their actual role in attracting new business.[35] This was evident in Massachusetts governor Michael Dukakis's campaign for the Democratic presidential nomination in 1988. Third, businesses can easily threaten to leave one jurisdiction and relocate elsewhere in order to get favorable policies enacted. This logic tends to infuse state (and local) policy debates with an overriding concern about the consequences of public policy for the business climate.

The high priority placed on the health of the business climate has not invariably imposed a straightjacket on state policy effort. The states always have differed in social policy spending and innovation. Such states as New York, Wisconsin, Massachusetts, and California consistently have offered far more generous social welfare benefits and enacted more restrictive regulatory policies than such states (for example) as Texas, Mississippi, and Wyoming. Innovative state education and environmental initiatives sometimes have sparked international interest.[36] Even in laggard states there have been political leaders who pressed for more governmental effort.[37]

Yet no American state is willing to go as far as the most progressive states in other federal systems to provide a wide range of protections, and none matches, or can match, the effort of the most extensive national welfare programs adopted by other nations. Considering interstate resource limits and disparities, American state officials' un derstandable concern with the economic vulnerability of their states creates a drag on policy effort, innovation, and design.

How Coherent Policy Emerges in Fragmented Systems

Fragmented policy systems do not always prevent the enactment of coherent policy. There are at least two circumstances in which coherent policy can emerge from an incoherent policymaking structure. First, a powerful national mass movement mobilized in support of a policy remedy can simultaneously pressure all institutions in a fragmented system to align in support of uniform policy. Such movements facilitated the passage of the old age insurance title of the Social Security Act of 1935, the Civil Rights Act of 1964 and the Voting Rights Act of 1965, and the Clean Air Act and other environmental statutes of the early 1970s. Even in these cases, however (as described in subsequent chapters), coherent policy once enacted was often slowed or undermined when implemented through the fragmented political structure.

Second, the most favored political interest, business, may under some circumstances fight for uniform national standards. Business may seek to eliminate variations in state law (and also to evade more restrictive state regulations), as in the 1880s when the railroad industry successfully lobbied for national railroad regulation and in the 1980s when the trucking industry pushed for national rules permitting double-bottomed trucks (overriding laws in some states that prohibited such trucks). Or these laws may reflect a business faction's interest in maintaining a competitive position, as in the case of northern businesses that lobbied for national minimum wage laws in the 1930s in order to eliminate some of the southern factories' wage advantage.

The record of policy development in the United States reveals that such policy coherence is the exception rather than the rule. For instance, acid rain is an interstate pollution problem that ruins forests and lakes in New England. But the American policymaking structure is ill-equipped to solve the problem because it permits the Midwestern utilities that contribute to acid rain an effective way to block any policy solution that requires them to sustain significant expenses to reduce emissions.

POLICY DEVELOPMENT IN THE UNITED STATES

The history of policy development shapes contemporary policy choice. Policies enacted in one era structure reformers' choices in later eras. For example, American welfare policy today is the product of a tortuous evolution of programs, institutions, and choices made long ago. Today's Aid to Families with Dependent Children is a recognizable descendent of the states' Mother's Aid laws of the 1910s, and these laws in turn aimed to reform the states' Poor laws of the nineteenth century.

As reform followed reform, agencies, rules, habits, and commitments became ingrained, limiting the range of options available to each new generation of reformers. Inside and outside of government, groups developed a vested interest in protecting the mission and the independence of the agencies that were created, and these groups steered policy discourse away from any fundamental challenge to the assumptions on which their prerogatives were based. Thus, *ad hoc* remedies are far more common than new policy designs.

Figure 1.2 indicates four major periods of policymaking development in the United States. In this periodization, we generalize about policy trends, but the exceptions and patterns identified are not invariable. In a general sense this scheme organizes the chapters in this book. Chapters 2 (the "dividing policy responsibility" and "state activism" periods), 3 (state activism), 4 (national activism), and 5 (national standards) analyze the development of policymaking capacity. Chapters 6 through 10 analyze the effects of this development in five policy areas: civil rights, welfare, education, urban policy, and environmental protection.

In the "Dividing Policy Responsibility" period, (1787–1870s), government capacity remained limited and states dominated the development of public policy in nearly every area of political life, with the exception of war and international commerce. In the "State Activism" period (1870s–1933), states (especially where manufacturing was becoming dominant) expanded their social policy capacity, and for the first time there were efforts to persuade the states to bring more order to social policy by enacting uniform laws. In the "National Activism" period (1933–1961), national and state capacity expanded at an accelerated rate and the national government began more actively to encourage coherent policy. In the "National Standards" period (beginning in 1961), the concern with coherent policy has become pronounced, but the institutionalized solutions of the past have made it extraordinarily difficult or even impossible to achieve national standards for most policies.

Figure 1.2. *Stages of American policymaking development*

Dividing Policy Responsibility, 1787–1870s

The U.S. Constitution was designed to confer on the central government the capacity to govern commerce and defense, but to leave most of the everyday governing of life in the hands of the states.[38] The framers of the U.S. Constitution designed a *federal* republic for practical reasons: the Constitution could not have come into existence without approval by political leaders whose careers were identified with states. Despite the extensive powers left to the states in the document and the deliberate creation of state-based representation in both houses of Congress, three state legislatures voted for ratification only by the slimmest of margins. In the first several years after the Constitutional Convention, states in both the North and South threatened to secede. In 1798 both Thomas Jefferson and James Madison encouraged state legislatures to nullify federal laws within their boundaries. Movements to withdraw New England and other northern states from the Union were initiated after the presidential elections of 1804, 1808, and 1812.[39] The question of state secession was not definitively settled until the military victory of northern states in the Civil War.

The Founders, in effect, apportioned political power in the Constitution between the national government and the states so as to *minimize the ability of both levels of government* to engage in policy adventures that would intrude upon private property rights and to make it difficult for popular majorities to mobilize on the basis of shared political interests. They set out to subvert coalitions that were attacking creditors and propertied interests in Rhode Island, Massachusetts, and other states in 1787, as we detail in the first half of Chapter 2. Their scheme of a fragmented national government power remains intact, and even though since then all the branches of government have vastly increased policymaking capacity, all the policies that emerge at the national level must survive the policy gauntlet that was erected in 1787: approval by the House of Representatives, the Senate, the President, and often (after the assertion of judicial review in 1803) the U.S. Supreme Court. Additional complications, such as Congressional committees and subcommittees, were later elaborations on the basic structure.

At the state level, institutional fragmentation also prevailed, and along with it came uncertain fiscal capacity. The Constitution made no provision for national aid to state governments or for the leveling of state resources (in contrast to the Australian Constitution of 1901). National distribution of surplus revenues to the states in 1803 and 1837 reflected unique circumstances rather than reliable aid. In the aggregate, the differences in state policies grew more pronounced. Welfare, education, and economic development policies evolved in a crazy-quilt pattern, with occasional fads (such as the movement for asylums before the Civil War) sweeping most but not all of the states.

Interstate economic competition became institutionalized. In every historical period the states developed an elaborate set of policies for improving the "business climate" in order to attract business and prevent its departure. State-subsidized commercial improvements are a constant in American history, from port developments and canals in the early nineteenth century to highways in the twentieth century. Today the states have devised an even more elaborate array of "economic development" policies, such as tax exemptions and deductions, site development, and job training programs, all aimed to improve each state's "business climate." Chapters 2 and 3 illustrate how these pressures restrained and fragmented public policy and prevented the mobilization of the kinds of social reform movements that helped bring about social programs in other nations.

Reconstruction provided an opportunity to establish more coherent policies. With southern obstruction removed from the U.S. Congress, Radical Republicans enacted a set of regional protections for citizens that included not only the civil rights of blacks but a nationally administered welfare agency, the Freedmen's Bureau. But this embryonic policy vanished from the South along with the departure of the last remaining federal troops in 1877.

State Activism, 1870s–1933

In two ways, policymaking capacity increased markedly between the 1870s and the Great Depression. The Civil War, the Spanish–American War, and World War I caused federal revenues, expenditures, and the number of civilian employees to ratchet upward. States also added employees, and additional taxes multiplied state revenues more than twelvefold between 1902 and 1932.[40] Moreover, the activism of Presidents Theodore Roosevelt and Woodrow Wilson and of such progressive governors as Wilson, Robert LaFollette of Wisconsin, and Hiram Johnson of California began to shift policymaking leadership at the national level and in some states away from legislatures and toward elected chief executives.

But in this period the legacy of the past imposed two significant limitations on government capacity. First, after years of relying on political patronage to fill government jobs, neither the states nor the national government possessed experienced, professional administrators that could effectively design and implement new programs. Second, the dominance of the state and especially the federal courts in setting the limits of government intervention gave defenders of *laissez-*

faire an effective institutional bulwark against government regulation of business. Though some measures were upheld, the courts limited the jurisdiction of state governments to regulate commerce within their boundaries and sharply circumscribed Congress's attempts to regulate interstate commerce. The courts thus created an economic "no man's land" which left many business decisions beyond the reach of any governmental body.[41] By 1922 the U.S. Labor Department published a ninety-page volume listing over 300 labor laws that U.S. courts had declared unconstitutional.[42]

The policymaking incoherence of American government also slowed the expansion of social welfare policies by fragmenting the demands for policy intervention. The Constitution's allocation of power held pressures for business regulation in check during the period from Reconstruction to World War I, when economic disruption fueled widespread discontent and popular demands for the regulation of business and some remedies for the consequences of industrialization. The national government was virtually incapable of responding to these pressures, as a federal official observed in a 1924 assessment of the meager and convoluted tactics available for establishing a national minimum of safety in coal mining.[43]

Chapter 3 focuses on the unique aspects of the American welfare state in comparison with other industrialized democracies. The conservative and fragmented nature of American social policy was firmly established in the 1910s, when, despite a concerted campaign by reformers, no American state enacted a public health insurance plan (today only the United States fails to provide universal access to health care for all its citizens). Reformers were unable to mobilize the extraordinary support necessary to overcome the opportunities that the fragmented political system offered to opponents who sought to block the measure as it progressed from one policy bottleneck to the next.

The policy "drag" of interstate competition affected even the most progressive states. Although states such as Wisconsin, California, Massachusetts, and New York pioneered social protections that were eventually adopted by other states, important policy innovations were effectively blocked. The battle for unemployment compensation, for example, began in the mid-1910s, but not until 1932 did Wisconsin enact such a law—the only state to do so before the New Deal unveiled its plan for an unemployment insurance system.[44] At the national level, federal employment and economic planning agencies established during World War I were disbanded after the war, and the national government resumed its relatively passive role until the deepening economic disaster of the 1930s permanently altered the federal government's policy role.

National Activism 1933–1961

Chapter 4 examines the impact of the American policymaking structure during one of the two most intense periods of policy development in this century—the New Deal of the 1930s. The New Deal marked a turning point in American social policy, institutionalizing the active role of the national government and committing governments at all levels to respond more directly to social ills. The Supreme Court's dramatic reversal permitting extensive the national intervention in interstate commerce and economic regulation expanded the scope of the national government's authority.

The New Deal's strategy for implementing greater activism reinforced and strengthened fragmented and uneven policies. Because old age insurance (now equated with the term "Social Security") was backed by the most potent and unified national constituency and because no state had created such a program, national standards and management became possible (although business strenuously objected to increased taxes). But where the states already had established income maintenance programs, such as mother's aid, old age pensions, aid to the blind, and unemployment insurance, the New Deal in effect underwrote these programs without imposing standards of performance much beyond the merit selection of state personnel. Except for the Social Security Trust Fund, "national" social welfare policy became, in reality, a collection of programs administered by the states, with matching funds and some guidelines from Washington.

The late 1940s and 1950s marked a stalemate in policy development, with the Eisenhower administration resisting policy expansion and national standards and liberal Democrats in Congress developing an activist policy agenda. The Democratic presidential victory in 1960 aligned the executive and legislative branches for a new period of policy activism.[45]

National Standards, 1961 to the Present

Experiencing the most prosperous years in their histories from the 1960s to the mid-1970s, each of the industrial democracies, including the United States, expanded social policy dramatically. In the United States, national activism extended for the first time to primary and secondary education, long the exclusive domain of state and local government, and to health insurance, in the form of Medicare and Medicaid.

Unprecedented coherence was imposed on areas long the province of the states, such as civil rights policy, and on relatively new areas of public concern, such as environmental quality. New forms of national regulation, such as civil rights requirements, were added to all grants received by a government, offering a new way to impose policy standards nationwide. The federal courts ruled in favor of rigorous and nationally uniform standards in the areas of legislative representation, criminal justice, civil rights, environmental protection, and equity in housing, education, and other areas.

The states rapidly expanded their policymaking capacity.[46] Between the early 1950s and the mid-1970s, state revenues increased at a faster rate than federal revenues, and the number of state employees mushroomed. State legislatures became more representative and more professional. State governors expanded their staffs, their budgets, and their executive powers. Compared with the 1930s the extreme variations in state per capita income diminished, but significant differences persisted.[47]

Yet American policy expansion continued to lag behind comparable nations, a development partially attributable to the continued incoherence of the policymaking structure. The national government became even more fragmented as the authority of political parties and their legislative leaders dissipated, as congressional subcommittees proliferated and as incumbents' advantages in congressional elections increased.[48]

Federalism again slowed the adoption and implementation of national policies, for it favored the use of grant-in-aid programs that enhanced policy control exercised by states, localities, and private institutions. Social policy by "proxy"[49] consumed enormous administrative energy and created complicated, uneven programs. The complicated policy structure eroded the coherence, legitimacy, and popularity of national programs of all kinds.

In the 1980s the variations in state policy effort continued to undermine coherence in welfare, education, urban affairs, civil rights, and environmental policy. The Reagan administration advanced a case for a "new" federalism that sought to reduce government capacity at all levels and to diminish nationally imposed standards (but in practice, it championed nationally imposed conservative standards in some areas, as we point out in Chapter 11). Like the 1950s, the 1980s marked a period of policy stalemate. Unlike the 1950s, the budget and trade deficits of the decade foreshadowed a future of policy austerity rather than policy expansion.

JUDGING POLICY RESTRAINT

Independent of our scholarly analysis, we subscribe to some values that we wish to highlight. We believe that the relative absence of social policies that can mitigate disastrous life circumstances is unjustifiable.

We also assert that policies that underwrite more material inequality, such as the current educational finance system, constitute bad policy. And we believe that with respect to fundamental human needs, such as a subsistence level income (whether in the form of a job or an income transfer), access to adequate health care, education, and housing, universal and nationally consistent programs are superior to fragmented and variable policies.

Some readers will disagree with these value premises. But the analysis presented here does not require agreement about preferred policies. Instead, it describes the relationship between policy outcomes and the policy process in the United States. Those people who think that government should do less rather than more will find confirmation for their strategies to fragment authority among many public institutions and to decentralize policy responsibility through the federal system. Reformers who prefer greater and more uniform policy efforts should recognize that the American policymaking structure needs to be changed if it is to produce policy outcomes that are more equitable, efficient, uniform, and innovative.

The complicated policymaking structure in the United States will persist and, indeed, there are no simple solutions to the problem it creates. The disadvantages of centralized bureaucracy are well known, and the value of checks and balances has been made clear every time the national executive branch abuses its powers. The achievements of progressive states and provinces in federal systems suggests that decentralization is not inherently conservative under all conditions.[50] Some policies can profitably be nationalized and others probably are best when administered by the states and localities.

Its is essential that the capacity and coherence of American public policy be improved. The social and economic problems of the late twentieth century require it. In our concluding chapter, we indicate the reform strategies necessary for making America's public policies more equitable, responsive, and manageable.

NOTES

1. The literature outlining the differences between social policy in the United States and in other wealthy capitalist democracies is vast. The differences were recognized by American experts early in this century; for example, see the report of a special committee on Workingmen's Insurance and Old Age Pensions, *Proceedings of the National Conference of Charities and Corrections*, 1906. In the last few years American policy exceptionalism has been examined by, among others, Seymour Martin Lipset, *The First New Nation: The United States in Historical and Comparative Perspective* (New York: Basic Books, 1963); Andrew Schonfield, *Modern Capitalism: The Changing Balance of Public and Private Power* (New York: Oxford University Press, 1965); Anthony King,

"Ideas, Institutions, and the Policies of Governments: A Comparative Analysis," *British Journal of Political Science* 3:3–4 (June and October 1973), 291–313, 409–23; David Collier and Richard E. Messick, "Prerequisites versus Diffusion: Testing Alternative Explanations for Social Security Adoption," *American Political Science Review* 69:4 (December 1975): 1299–1315; Harold L. Wilensky, *The Welfare State and Equality: Structural and Ideological Roots of Public Expenditures* (Berkeley: University of California Press, 1975); Arnold J. Heidenheimer, Hugh Heclo, and Carolyn Teich Adams, *Comparative Public Policy*, 2nd ed. (New York: St. Martin's Press, 1983); Howard M. Leichter and Harrell R. Rodgers, Jr., *American Public Policy in a Comparative Context* (New York: McGraw-Hill, 1984); Theodore J. Lowi, "Why Is There No Socialism in the United States? A Federal Analysis," in Robert T. Golembiewski and Aaron Wildavsky, eds., *The Costs of Federalism* (New Brunswick, NJ: Transaction Press, 1984), 37–53; Ann Shola Orloff and Theda Skocpol, "Why Not Equal Protection? Explaining the Politics of Public Social Spending in Britain, 1900–1911, and the United States, 1880s–1920," *American Sociological Review* 49:4 (December 1984), 736; Margaret Weir, Ann Shola Orloff, and Theda Skocpol, *The Politics of Social Policy in the United States* (Princeton, NJ: Princeton University Press, 1988); Neil Gilbert and Ailee Moon, "Analyzing Welfare Effort: An Appraisal of Comparative Methods," *Journal Policy Analysis and Management* 7:2 (March, 1988), 326–40.

2. David M. Potter, *People of Plenty* (Chicago: University of Chicago Press, 1954), 91.

3. James A. Davis, "British and American Political Attitudes in 1985," (unpublished mimeo: National Opinion Research Center, February 1986).

4. E. J. Dionne, Jr., "Poll Finds Reagan Support Down But Democrats Still Lacking Fire," *New York Times*, 1 December, 1987, 1. In public opinion surveys dating back a quarter of a century, researchers observed the paradox that majorities of Americans are conservative in principle and liberal on specific issues; cf. Lloyd A. Free and Hadley Cantril, *The Political Beliefs of Americans: A Study of Public Opinion* (New Brunswick, NJ: Rutgers University Press, 1967).

5. Davis, "British and American Political Attitudes in 1985"; Richard M. Coughlin, *Ideology, Public Opinion, and Welfare Policy: Attitudes Toward Taxes and Spending in Industrialized Societies* (Berkeley, CA: Institute of International Studies, 1980), 18–9, 74–83.

6. David Brian Robertson, "Governing and Jobs: America's Business-Centered Labor Market Policy," *Polity* 20 (Spring 1988), 426-56.

7. Thomas R. Dye, *Understanding Public Policy*, 5th ed. (Englewood Cliffs, NJ: Prentice-Hall, 1984), 2.

8. James E. Anderson, David W. Brady, Charles S. Bullock III, and Joseph Stewart, Jr., *Public Policy and Politics in America*, 2d ed. (Monterey, CA: Brooks/Cole, 1984), 4.

9. This distinction corresponds to the components in systems theory labelled "inputs," "outputs," and the "black box." In this view inputs are the demands placed on government, outputs are policies, and the black box refers to the government participants and structures that translate demands into policy. See David Easton, *A Framework for Political Analysis* (Englewood Cliffs, NJ: Prentice-Hall, 1965) and Dye, *Understanding Public Policy*, 40-2.

10. Theda Skocpol, who is perhaps its leading American proponent, reviews much of this research in "Bringing the State Back In: Strategies of Analysis in Current Research," in Peter B. Evans, Dietrich Rueschmeyer, and Theda Skocpol, eds., *Bringing the State Back In* (New York: Cambridge University Press, 1985), 3–37. See also James G. March and Johan P. Olsen, "The New Institutionalism: Organizational Factors in Political Life," *American Political Science Review* 78:3 (September 1984), 734–49.

11. John W. Kingdon, *Agendas, Alternatives, and Public Policies* (Boston: Little, Brown, 1984), 3.

12. Ibid.; Charles E. Lindblom, *The Policy-Making Process*, 2d ed. (Englewood Cliffs, NJ: Prentice-Hall, 1980), 4–5.
13. Kingdon, *Agendas, Alternatives, and Public Policies*, p. 48–74.
14. Samuel H. Beer, "Political Overload and Federalism," *Polity* 10:1 (Fall 1977) 5–17. Eric A. Nordlinger synthesizes and critiques these views in *On the Autonomy of the Democratic State* (Cambridge, MA: Harvard University Press, 1981), 42–73.
15. Skocpol, "Bringing the State Back In," 4.
16. Floyd Hunter, *Community Power Structure: A Study of Decision Makers* (Chapel Hill: University of North Carolina Press, 1953).
17. Robert A. Dahl, *Who Governs? Democracy and Power in New Haven* (New Haven, CT: Yale University Press, 1961).
18. Anderson et al., *Public Policy and Politics in America*, 16–22; Clarke E. Cochran, Lawrence C. Mayer, T. R. Carr, N. Joseph Cayer, *American Public Policy: An Introduction*, 2d ed. (New York: St. Martin's Press, 1986), 8–10.
19. Dye, *Understanding Public Policy*, 279–97.
20. Cf. Hugh Heclo, *Modern Social Politics in Britain and Sweden: From Relief to Income Maintenance* (New Haven, CT: Yale University Press, 1974).
21. Alfred Stepan, *The State and Society* (Princeton, NJ: Princeton University Press, 1978), xii. Stepan's definition is quoted by Skocpol, in "Bringing the State Back In," 7.
22. Edward Tufte, *Political Control of the Economy* (Princeton, NJ: Princeton University Press, 1978).
23. Morton H. Halperin, *Bureaucratic Politics and Foreign Policy* (Washington, DC: Brookings, 1974); Martha Derthick, *Policymaking for Social Security* (Washington DC: Brookings, 1979); Francis E. Rourke, *Bureaucracy, Politics, and Public Policy*, 3d ed. (Boston: Little, Brown, 1984).
24. In this observation we are deeply influenced by such works as: Max Weber, "Bureaucracy," in H. H. Gerth and C. Wright Mills, eds., *From Max Weber: Essays in Sociology* (New York: Oxford University Press, 1946), 228–39; Anthony Downs, *Inside Bureaucracy* (Boston: Little, Brown, 1967), 5–23, 41–8, 158–66; Arthur L. Stinchcombe, "Social Structure and Organizations," in James G. March, ed., *Handbook of Organizations* (Chicago: Rand McNally, 1965), 142–93; James D. Thompson, *Organizations in Action* (New York: McGraw-Hill, 1967); and W. Richard Scott, *Organizations: Rational, Natural, and Open Systems*, 2d ed. (Englewood Cliffs, NJ: Prentice-Hall, 1987).
25. Charles A. Lindblom developed the concept of a privileged position of business in policymaking in *Politics and Markets: The World's Political Economic Systems* (New York: Basic Books, 1977) and "The Market as Prison," *Journal of Politics* 44:2 (May 1982): 324–36. See also Stephen L. Elkin, "Pluralism in Its Place: State and Regime in the Liberal Democracy," in Roger Benjamin and Stephen L. Elkin, eds., *The Democratic State* (Lawrence: The University Press of Kansas, 1985), 179–211. This view is critiqued from very different perspectives in G. William Domhoff, "State Autonomy and the Privileged Position of Business: An Empirical Attack on a Theoretical Fantasy," *Journal of Political and Military Sociology* 14 (Spring 1986), 149–62, and David Vogel, "Political Science and the Study of Corporate Power: A Dissent from the New Orthodoxy," Business and Public Policy Working Paper BPP-15, Center for Research in Management, University of California—Berkeley Business School, July 1986.
26. Edward Berkowitz and Kim McQuaid, *Creating the Welfare State: The Political Economy of Twentieth Century Reform* (New York: Praeger, 1980); Neil J. Mitchell, "Corporate Power, Legitimacy, and Social Policy," *Western Political Quarterly* 38:2 (June 1986), 197–212.
27. Lindblom provocatively analyzes the difference between political and market solutions to policy problems in his landmark *Politics and Markets*.
28. Michael D. Reagan, *Regulation: The Politics of Policy* (Boston: Little, Brown, 1987), 9–14.

29. Patrick D. Larkey, Chandler Stolp, and Mark Winer, "Why Does Government Grow?" in Trudi C. Miller, ed., *Public Sector Performance: A Conceptual Turning Point* (Baltimore: Johns Hopkins University Press, 1984), 65–101.

30. Mattei Dogan, ed., *The Mandarins of Western Europe* (New York: Halsted Press, 1975); Joel D. Aberbach, Robert D. Putnam, and Bert A. Rockman, *Bureaucrats and Politicians in Western Europe* (Cambridge, MA: Harvard University Press, 1981).

31. American bureaucracy is also very fragmented. Some agencies, such as the Federal Reserve Board and independent regulatory commissions, were designed so as to limit the control of other elected officials over their actions. Some agencies cultivated allies inside and outside of government and have exercised enormous power independent of their political superiors (J. Edgar Hoover's Federal Bureau of Investigation is the classic example).

32. Adapted from Deil Wright, *Understanding Governmental Relations*, 2d ed. (Monterey, CA: Brooks/Cole, 1984), 26. In the third edition of his book (1988), Wright provides an excellent analysis of the concept of federalism, particularly American federalism, in more detail (31–59). See also William Riker, *Federalism: Origin, Operation, and Significance* (Boston: Little, Brown, 1964).

33. See Peter J. Katzenstein, *Small States in World Markets: Industrial Policy in Europe* (Ithaca, NY: Cornell University Press, 1985).

34. Thomas R. Plaut and Joseph E. Pluta, "Business Climate, Taxes and Expenditures, and State Industrial Growth in the United States," *Southern Economic Journal* 50:1 (July 1983), 99-119. See also literature review in Michael Peter Smith, Dennis R. Judd, and Randy Ready, "Capital Flight, Tax Incentives, and the Marginalization of American States and Localities," in Dennis R. Judd, ed., *Public Policy Across States and Communities* (Greenwich, CT: JAI Press, 1985).

35. Barry Rubin and C. K. Zorn, "Sensible State and Local Economic Development," *Public Administration Review* 45:2 (March/April 1985), 333–9; Barry Bozeman and J. Lisle Bozeman, "Manufacturing Firms' Views of Government Activity and Commitment to Site: Implications for Business Retention Policy," *Policy Studies Review* 6:3 (February 1987), 538–53; Dennis O. Grady, "State Economic Development Incentives: Why Do States Compete?" *State and Local Government Review* 19:3 (Fall 1987), 86–94.

36. Ann O'M. Bowman and Richard C. Kearney, *The Resurgence of the States* (Englewood Cliffs, NJ: Prentice-Hall, 1986).

37. Cf. Peter J. Boyer, "The Yuppies of Mississippi," *New York Times Magazine*, 28 February, 1988, 24 ff.; David Osborne, *Laboratories of Democracy* (Cambridge, MA: Harvard Business School Press, 1988).

38. See Federalist Paper Number 45, in *The Federalist Papers* (New York: Mentor, 1961).

39. Lipset, *The First New Nation*, 34.

40. U.S. Bureau of the Census, *Historical Statistics of the United States, Colonial Times to 1970* (Washington, DC: GPO, 1975), 1102–4, 1129.

41. Cynthia Cates Colella, "The United States Supreme Court and Intergovernmental Relations," in Robert Jay Dilger, ed., *American Intergovernmental Relations Today: Perspectives and Controversies* (Englewood Cliffs, NJ: Prentice-Hall, 1986), 42-4.

42. U.S. Bureau of Labor Statistics, *Labor Laws That Have Been Declared Unconstitutional*, BLS bull. 321 (Washington, DC: GPO, 1922).

43. Frederick P. Lee, "Possibilities of Establishing a National Minimum of Safety in the Coal Industry," *American Labor Legislation Review* 14:1 (March 1924), 71–80.

44. Daniel Nelson, *Unemployment Insurance: The American Experience, 1915–1935* (Madison: University of Wisconsin Press, 1969).

45. James Sundquist, *Politics and Policy: The Eisenhower, Kennedy, and Johnson Years* (Washington, DC: Brookings, 1968).

46. Bowman and Kearney, *The Resurgence of the States*, 47–104.

47. The ratio of average personal income in the lowest income state to the highest income state was 1:4.33 (South Carolina to New York) in 1929, 1:2.32 (Mississippi to Connecticut) in 1960, and 1:1.89 (Mississippi to Connecticut) in 1984. The ratio of the average hourly earnings of production workers in the lowest to the highest paying states remained little changed from 1950 (1:1.85, Mississippi to Oregon) to 1985 (1:1.74, Mississippi to Michigan). U.S. Bureau of the Census, *Historical Statistics*, 243–5, and *State and Metropolitan Area Data Book, 1986* (Washington, DC: GPO, 1986), 558; U.S. Bureau of Labor Statistics, *Handbook of Labor Statistics, 1975—Reference Edition* (Washington, DC: GPO, 1975), 262-3, and *Employment and Earnings*, 22:8 (February 1986), Table C-8.

48. David Mayhew, *Congress: The Electoral Connection* (New Haven, CT: Yale University Press, 1974).

49. Donald F. Kettl, *Government By Proxy: [Mis?]Managing Federal Programs* (Washington, DC: Congressional Quarterly, 1988).

50. This is one of the most important distinctions between our view and Grant McConnell's thesis, stated in *Private Power in American Democracy* (New York: Alfred A. Knopf, 1966).

Chapter 2

THE LEGACY OF CONSTITUTIONAL DESIGN

POLITICAL STRUCTURE AND THE DISTRIBUTION OF POWER

A political crisis rooted in economic conflict motivated the adoption of a new constitution in the late 1780s. The new government emerged in part as a response to threats against property, wealth, and privilege. The American Constitution ingeniously distributed powers between the states and the national government in a way that reduced the chances that such threats could be carried out by government at any level. It did so by giving the national government the power to protect commerce and property, and at the same time it stripped the states of significant powers to restrict and regulate commerce and property. It created a series of checks and balances at the national level that among other purposes aimed to protect property rights.

Policymaking structure organizes the politics and shapes the policy outcomes long after it is put in place.[1] An important if unanticipated consequence of biasing the constitutional system in favor of property rights was that reformers who later fought for governmental protections against the problems created by industrial capitalism consistently found themselves handicapped by the American political structure. Why was this the case? The expanding industrial corporations discovered that a fragmented policymaking system designed to protect property often gave it a powerful advantage in battles over policy outcomes. The struggles for more active government and more coherent policy from the Civil War through the Progressive Era show that this policymaking structure served to fragment and frustrate efforts to regulate economic institutions and to expand the social responsibilities of governments.

26

DIVIDING POLICYMAKING POWER, 1787–1870s

The Backlash Against Propertied Interests in the 1780s

When the delegates to the Constitutional Convention gathered in Philadelphia during the summer of 1787, they represented independent commonwealths. The label "state" suggests that the colonies viewed themselves as sovereign as the states of Europe. Indeed, in the years since the Treaty of Paris had ended the Revolutionary War in 1783, rivalries and border disputes had become almost commonplace.[2] Connecticut imposed a tax on imports from Massachusetts, and Pennsylvania and Virginia fought a pitched battle over their western border. The states were tied together by only the weakest of compacts, the Articles of Confederation. The national government created by the Articles had little money and few powers. It could not even collect all of the taxes owed it by the states. The national government lacked the resources to mount an effective defense against military threats and economic reprisals from the European superpowers, Britain, Spain, and France. It was threatened from all sides. The new nation appeared too unstable to attract trade and investment from Europe.[3]

Deteriorating economic conditions and domestic unrest were as worrisome to elites as the threats from abroad. Instead of the prosperity that many people believed would follow independence, depression and economic hardship became the rule, especially for heavily indebted owners of small farms. Prices collapsed for important agricultural products, including rice, wheat, corn, and tobacco. Wholesale prices overall declined 50 percent between 1781 and 1785. Because state governments had run up huge debts to finance the war, high state taxes threatened to ruin small farmers. The situation was worst in New England, where farm foreclosures were common and farmers were frequently jailed for failing to pay debts.[4]

The farmers' frustration culminated in a political backlash against creditors and merchants. Many of them blamed their plight on the chronic shortage of currency, leading them to demand that state governments, through the simple expedient of printing money, induce inflation to relieve their debt burden. Merchants and creditors predictably opposed such a solution. In the spring of 1786, Rhode Island voters elected a legislature dominated by radical farmers, which promptly printed paper currency and passed a bill that specified criminal penalties for anyone refusing to accept the new money. (Subsequently, the state's highest court ruled that one of the provisions meant to enforce the law violated the state's constitution.) Later, in the debates in Philadelphia, the delegates reminded one other of the Rhode Island example. To them, it demonstrated that property rights had to be protected from excesses of popular democracy.[5]

Western Massachusetts farmers took a more militant approach than their counterparts in Rhode Island. Daniel Shays, a Revolutionary War veteran, organized a ragtag army of farmers and debtors that forced local courts to suspend foreclosure proceedings. Shays' group next intended to recapture farms that had already been foreclosed. In late 1786, his troops seized several towns and threatened to overrun the Springfield military garrison. An army hastily assembled by Boston's merchants finally routed Shays' volunteers, and his movement collapsed.[6] Shays' Rebellion sparked other revolts. Debtors rioted in Maryland. Farmers in Vermont surrounded the legislature. Merchants and creditors heard rumors of a plan to redistribute property and forgive debts.[7]

Erecting Structural Obstacles to Radical Policy

The delegates who convened in Philadelphia during the summer of 1787 agreed that there was an urgent need for a central government strong enough to contain popular pressures and protect property.[8] "Good God!" wrote George Washington in response to the bloodshed in Massachusetts, "[t]here are combustibles in every state, which a spark might light a fire to."[9] Though there was intense debate over the form a new republic should take, solid consensus existed on the need to achieve political and economic stability.[10]

The nation's founders were not motivated solely by a desire to protect their property and wealth. Though not all of them favored democracy, they shared an assumption that government ought to respect life, liberty, and property as basic human rights. They believed that, unless unified into a nation, the states would evolve into several impotent and impoverished commonwealths open to merciless exploitation by European powers. Within this context, nevertheless, it was taken as an article of faith that propertied interests should be granted a privileged position in the new political system.

The delegates to the constitutional convention faced two principal practical problems in designing a new government. First, they were obligated to seek ratification from state legislatures, and to accomplish this the states were granted significant autonomy in the new governing arrangement. This constraint was so obvious that it required little discussion at the Convention. Instead, debates turned on how to strengthen national institutions while reassuring the states that they would not sacrifice their political autonomy. Despite abundant assurances to this effect, the special state conventions narrowly voted to ratify the constitution in Massachusetts, New York, Virginia, and Rhode Island.

A second practical problem received careful attention. Even if a national government with sufficient powers emerged, it could not itself be allowed to endanger property or commerce. It would have contradicted the founders' purposes to establish a government that could be captured by radical elements such as those that had taken over the legislature of Rhode Island.

Apportioning National and State Powers in the Constitution

In most of its language the Constitution is artfully ambiguous. In contrast, provisions designed to allocate governmental powers to regulate commerce and property are very specific. The delegates went to considerable lengths to ensure that states could not easily override commercial and propertied interests. Under Article I, Section 10 the states were barred from concluding treaties with foreign powers, erecting tariffs, coining and printing money, or impairing contractual obligations (such as debt repayments). The national government was granted explicit authority to *promote* business and protect property. Article I, Section 8 permitted the national government to regulate commerce, establish a communications and transportation system (post offices and post roads), issue patents, punish pirates, and use military force to "suppress Insurrections and repel Invasions"—a thinly veiled reference to Shays' Rebellion as well as to the foreign powers beyond the national borders.

Though they removed some of the states' prerogatives to make economic policy, the framers could justifiably assure the states that the Constitution preserved their status as the primary locus of everyday governance. James Madison noted in *The Federalist* that the authority of the national government "will be exercised principally on external objects, [such] as war, peace, negotiation, and foreign commerce." In contrast, the states' power "will extend to all the objects which, in the ordinary course of affairs, concern the lives, liberties, and properties of the people, and the internal order, improvement, and prosperity of the State."[11] Madison had hoped that the Constitution would go further by allowing the federal government to veto radical state taxation and police (law enforcement) policies. Keenly aware that such a provision would reduce the chances that the states would ratify the Constitution, the delegates defeated Madison's proposal.[12]

Soon after the Constitution was ratified, the broad state policy role became fixed in American law. Added in 1791, the Tenth Amendment allocated to state governments "or to the people" those legal powers not delegated to the national government or not prohibited to the states—a provision Madison considered unnecessary but harmless. What Congress failed to do was just as important as passing the amendment. It did not attempt to build a new legal system from the ground up, as did Napoleon after France's revolution in the 1790s. Instead, national lawmakers left in place the existing body of state law as the framework for American policy. For all of U.S. history the states have been the principal source of laws and regulations governing corporations, banks, credit, communities, families, and crime and punishment.[13]

The Constitution thus sorted political conflicts into different jurisdictions. E. E. Schattschneider has observed that similar substantive conflicts fought in different political arenas may have widely varying outcomes, because the balance of power among contending political groups differs within each arena. Moving conflict from the state level to the federal level, for example, increases the number and variety of participants. A perceptive student of politics understands that "the most important strategy of politics is concerned with the scope of conflict."[14] Groups attempt to fight their political battles in the arena where the balance of power already favors their interests as much as possible. Any political interest that benefits from the absence of governmental intrusion will try to prevent conflict from reaching the government's agenda at all (that is, it will seek to keep the conflict private), or will try to confine the dispute to the institution or arena least capable of enforcing decisions that are reached. Civil rights leaders in the 1960s, for example, moved conflict over racial discrimination out of the southern states and into national politics. The scope of conflict thus expanded to embrace groups that favored desegregation and racial equality. The struggle to expand conflict, or to narrow it by locating it in states or localities, is a basic feature of many public controversies.

Madison possessed a sophisticated political sense of the significance of controlling the scope of conflict:

> The smaller the society, the fewer probably will be the distinct parties and interests composing it; the fewer the distinct parties and interests, the more frequently will a majority be found of the same party; and the smaller the number of individuals composing a majority, and the smaller the compass within which they are placed, the more easily will they concert and execute their plans of oppression. Extend the sphere and you take in a greater variety of parties and interests; you make it less probable that a majority of the whole will have a common motive to invade the rights of other citizens; or, if such a common motive exists, it will be more difficult for all who feel it to discover their own strength and act in unison with each other.[15]

Madison argued that the constitutional framework effectively addressed Washington's fears of popular majorities: a system of fragmented governmental power would guarantee that the radical ideas that grip one state "will be unable to spread a general conflagration throughout the other States." He assured readers of *The Federalist* that the states could successfully resist national laws to which they objected—but having adopted the Constitution, the states already would have surrendered the authority to take measures similar to Rhode Island's. A decentralized system was well suited to the "diversity in the faculties of men from which the rights of property originate."[16] In his most eloquent defense of the Constitution, Madison deftly argued that the new federal system would structure conflict so as to prevent radical policies that might endanger property rights.

One of the enduring consequences of the American federal structure is that policy conflicts tend to turn as much on jurisdictional questions as on the merits of policy alternatives. For example, since the 1930s conservatives opposed to new social welfare policies have seldom questioned the federal government's basic constitutional right to intervene in civil rights, welfare, education, and environment policy. But they have usually argued that control over social policies should be left to state governments. They understand that devolving policy responsibility to state governments will usually reduce the scope and effectiveness of public policies.

Interstate Competition and Policymaking in the States

By fragmenting political conflict, the Constitution channeled state activism away from the regulation of property and toward the promotion of private economic development. It did so by creating the world's largest "free trade" zone. The states could not prevent businesses from entering or leaving their borders. Nor did states have much latitude to enact legislation favoring in-state enterprises, in contrast to the national government's powers even in small nations.[17] Business has remained legally mobile throughout American history, free to abandon any political jurisdiction with which it grows disenchanted and to enter a jurisdiction offering a better environment. States always have been willing to lure business by providing an attractive "business climate," consisting of low taxes, few labor protections, and strategically designed business subsidies.

This system strongly encourages state policymakers to match the business concessions offered by the poorest states.[18] Any state that seems insufficiently friendly to business risks the loss of both tax payments and jobs. Incumbent public officials risk stinging criticism from political challengers. Concern for "business climate" thus pervades state-level policy decisions.[19] This interstate competition has sobered the states that might be favorably disposed to adopt strict regulatory, environmental, or labor policies and has energized states willing to offer generous public subsidies in an attempt to encourage business creation and expansion.[20] At the same time, state and local governments resist offering more attractive social benefits than other jurisdictions if such benefits require higher taxes or attract potentially dependent new residents who seek the benefits.[21] Under these conditions, states face a strong incentive to resist popular demands for individual protection from economic hardship when such protections appear to make the state deviate too far from other states.

These trends appeared even before the states ratified the Constitution, when their governments began to redouble their efforts to attract and promote business. Massachusetts, for example, had directly subsidized the production of hemp (grown in the state and used in shipping) in 1786 and enacted new subsidies in 1788 and 1791. In these years the state also granted new subsidies to manufacturers of sailcloth, duck, and twine and granted tax relief to brewers, glassmakers, and cotton factories.[22]

In the first half of the nineteenth century all the states entered into a frenzied period of public construction of roads and canals,[23] but the panic of 1837 drained the treasuries of the more interventionist states. By then state policymakers were already relying on relaxed business regulations to compete with one other. States enacted corporate charters that often protected companies from the public consequences of their actions. For example, a company chartered to build a canal might enjoy state protection from bearing the full responsibility for flood damage resulting from construction.[24]

Limited Policymaking Capacity and Coherence in National Powers

Congress. Madison and his colleagues believed that in a republic the legislature necessarily dominated policymaking (Madison personally helped build the House of Representatives into an effective legislative body).[25] Though the issue sparked controversy at the Convention, the delegates agreed to design a national legislature virtually incapable of overriding states' interests. As explained by Madison, "each of the principal branches of the federal government will owe its existence more or less to the favor of the State governments." The founders debated at length whether the states or the federal treasury should provide the salaries of the members.[26] The state legislatures selected members of the U.S. Senate. "Even the House of Representatives," argued Madison, "though drawn immediately from the people, will be chosen very much under the influence of that class of men whose influence over the people obtains for themselves an election into the State legislatures."[27] In the House, it was expected that delegations from each state would share interests. Madison soon discovered the accuracy of this assumption, when the first House of Representatives eliminated from his proposed Bill of Rights language prohibiting the states from violating freedom of speech, the press, conscience, and trial by jury.[28]

The members of Congress have remained keenly sensitive to the interests of the districts and states they represent. Even in the House of

Representatives, where few members must win statewide approval, members follow the lead of others who represent the same state and the same political party. A study of House votes in the late 1950s indicated that the shared interests of state party delegations accounted for most of the differences in votes among congressional representatives on social welfare, civil liberties, and government management issues.[29] Among the reasons for the close attention to state interests is that some members of the House aspire to higher offices, such as senator or governor, that are elected statewide.[30] Congressional rules and procedures, many of which are designed solely to protect the prerogative of groups of House members or senators from one or a few states, reinforce the conservatism of the policymaking process by adding opportunities to delay or derail policy initiatives opposed by a minority of states or congressional districts.

Congress always has been biased not only toward delay, but also toward *distributive* policies that allocate tangible benefits to large numbers of districts and states, and against redistribution proposals that aid some areas more than others. Like the states, the national government in the early nineteenth century considered building a system of canals and roads to promote commerce. Secretary of the Treasury Albert Gallatin's report on internal improvements, issued in 1808, was the first proposal for national economic development and planning at the national level. The need for congressional approval substantially altered Gallatin's recommendations, for he proposed to spend $3.4 million of the $20 million total to subsidize local projects that had no relationship whatever to the national transportation system. Gallatin evinced political shrewdness, for it was necessary to win the support of congressional delegations from states that would not receive a "fair share" of the federal subsidy if spending was restricted solely to projects integral to a national system. Later, President James Madison vetoed a more characteristically congressional plan that would have allocated internal improvement grants to each state without federal conditions or a national plan.[31] When the federal government expanded its role in social and economic policy in the 1930s, 1960s, and 1970s, it typically did so through loosely controlled grants-in-aid that contained generous subsidies for projects in almost every state.

Courts. Article III of the Constitution, which describes the national court system, has little to say about the specific structure and responsibilities of the courts. Two features of the federal court system contributed to the national government's arsenal of property protections, however: its reinforcement of state courts, and the existence of a federal Supreme Court.

First, by exercising its power to regulate the size and the jurisdiction of the federal court system, Congress strengthened the state court systems and added the federal courts as a check against property restrictions that might be permitted by those courts. The first Judiciary Act was a masterstroke of compromise that left significant discretion in state hands. It provided that in state matters (and thus in most social conflicts), the decisions ultimately handed down by state courts were final. Those conflicts that touched on the narrow jurisdiction of the national government could be appealed to the federal courts.[32] This dual court system effectively provided property owners with two chances to seek court intervention on their behalf. People seeking to limit property rights were denied the same opportunity. Congress refused to grant the federal courts the authority to hear cases in which *state* courts had struck down state regulatory actions, but cases could be brought before the federal courts if state courts had upheld restrictions on property rights. After the Civil War, when a multitude of fundamental economic conflicts were brought into the court system, Congress manipulated court jurisdiction in a way that protected business interests.

Second, the example of the Rhode Island Supreme Court had taught the founders the value of a judicial (and nonelected) bulwark against radicalism. They therefore advocated a court system protected from popular political pressures. Hamilton promoted the idea that the federal courts could judge congressional laws to be unconstitutional. Early Supreme Court decisions, particularly *Marbury* v. *Madison* (1803), asserted the political independence of the Supreme Court and its right to rule on the constitutionality of congressional acts. In these years the Court frequently struck down laws that regulated the use of private property. In *Dartmouth College* v. *Woodward* (1819), the Court ruled that a corporation was an individual in the eyes of the law and was entitled to the same liberties and constitutional protections as any citizen. This ruling provided a powerful protection for business against state law, one that was more fully elaborated in the latter years of the nineteenth century.

Some state court decisions also protected individuals in the economic system. Court decisions in the first half of the nineteenth century protected workers' rights to join unions, and the Massachusetts Supreme Court in 1842 ruled that workers could go on strike to force an employer to hire only union members.[33] But the unevenness of these protections were an inevitable outcome of contradictory decisions made by courts in different states.

The executive. Though the founders assumed that the president would provide leadership in the new government, they limited presidential powers significantly. Presidents would have to seek approval from

Congress not only for new initiatives but also for approval of budgets and key personnel appointments. Presidents adapted by negotiating with state congressional delegations on important decisions; an example is the tradition of senatorial courtesy, in which a president informally seeks the approval of the senators of his party before naming an appointee to the federal court in that state. The Constitution also tried to ensure that presidential selection would depend upon the states more than upon the popular will. The founders assumed that the state legislatures would select the "electoral college" that chooses the president. Though the electoral college has long reflected the desires of state voters rather than legislatures, its membership still is apportioned on the basis of state populations. Since presidential candidates must pay particular attention to the needs of contested large states, their policy positions are tempered by state interests.[34]

The fact that the president (elected for four years), and members of the Senate (elected for six years) and the House (elected for two years) each are subject to a different electoral calendar severely limits any president's role as a centralizing force in the fragmented national government. Every House member stands for reelection independent of the party's presidential nominee in every other election. Only a third of the senators are elected during a presidential contest, and none of those run with or against the president again. These different electoral cycles mean that in contrast to a British prime minister (for example), whose election is always concurrent with all members of the House of Commons, the president's electoral fate is largely independent of members of Congress, including members of his own political party. Most members of Congress calculate that loyalty to their local constituency is far more important to their careers than loyalty to president and party.

STATE ACTIVISM, 1870s–1933

The Backlash Against Industrialization from the 1870s to the 1920s

American life changed abruptly between the 1870s and the 1920s. Popular discontent with the excesses of capitalism was used to mobilize a backlash against propertied interests that was far more threatening than the antiproperty rebellions of the constitutional period. The government that the founders established to withstand the pressures of the earlier period proved to be remarkably well constructed to cope with the post-Civil War crises. Its bias toward the protection of wealth proved durable in an era when much of the wealth protected was held by powerful industrial firms. America's policymaking structure narrowed and fragmented popular demands for government protection against

Table 2.1. *Population and employment change in the United States, 1870–1920*

	Population		Employment (%)		
	Millions	%Urban	Agriculture	Industry	Services
1870	39.8	25.7	50.8	30.0	19.2
1880	50.1	28.2	50.6	30.1	19.3
1890	62.9	35.1	43.1	34.8	22.1
1900	76.0	39.6	38.1	37.8	24.1
1910	92.0	45.6	32.1	40.9	27.0
1920	105.7	51.2	27.6	44.8	27.6

Sources: U.S. Bureau of the Census, *Historical Statistics of the United States, Colonial Times to 1970*, vol. I (Washington, DC: GPO, 1975), 8, 11; Victor R. Fuchs, *The Service Economy* (New York: National Bureau of Economic Research, 1968), 24.

the effects of industrial capitalism, permitting reforms that were by the standards of northwestern Europe distinctly limited, uneven, and minimally intrusive on business.

Drastic changes altered American society between the Civil War and the end of World War I. Table 2.1 outlines these changes. Swollen by a high birthrate and a floodtide of immigrants, the nation's population tripled. Urbanization also changed the basic character of American society. Chicago, for example, grew from a town of 30,000 in 1850 to one of the world's largest cities, with 2.7 million inhabitants, by 1920. In the same period, St. Louis's population increased from 78,000 to over 772,000, and Philadelphia grew from 121,000 to 1.8 million people.[35] During the late 1700s, virtually all Americans had been farmers, and half of them still earned their living on farms even after the Civil War. But an expanding workforce earned wages in the nation's mines, mills, factories, and offices in the decades after 1870.

The nation's wealth increased dramatically. Measured by reference to the value of a dollar in 1929, the nation's gross product jumped from $9 billion a year (1869–1873) to $55 billion a year (1907–1922).[36] A few enterprising industrialists and bankers amassed huge fortunes. Many of them ostentatiously displayed their wealth. In once-radical Rhode Island, Newport became a resort haven dotted with the summer mansions of multimillionaires. Public libraries, symphonies, and art museums depended on gifts from wealthy benefactors, and eminent universities (Stanford, the University of Chicago, Cornell, Vanderbilt, Tulane) owed their endowments to railroad, oil, banking, and other fortunes. A sizable portion of the new wealth, however, was obtained through bribery, kickbacks, and extortion and was devoted to the acquisition of powerful monopolies on which many nineteenth-century American fortunes were based.[37]

The extremes of wealth and poverty produced smoldering resentment among millions of American workers. Wrenching economic changes, periodic business downturns and depressions, and dangerous working conditions left millions of people at the margin between subsistence and destitution. Periodically, popular demands were voiced for a fundamental redirection of policy away from the promotion of business and toward its restriction.

Although farmers in general grew more prosperous, those in the South and West often viewed themselves as defenseless and exploited pawns of railroad "robber barons." They resented the banker whose high interest rates squeezed them to the brink of bankruptcy. They complained bitterly that the grain processing and farm equipment monopolies made excessive profits at their expense. Falling farm prices in the nineteenth century exerted the same effect as in the 1780s. Heavily indebted farmers in the South and West lashed out against the banks that foreclosed farms and the railroads that charged exorbitant freight rates.[38]

Journalists of the 1890s coined the term "populism" to describe the political movement energized by these conditions. In 1892, their leaders convened in St. Louis, where the passions of the movement rang out in the words of speakers like Ignatius Donnelly:

> The fruits of the toil of millions are boldly stolen to build up colossal fortunes, unprecedented in the history of the world, while their possessors despise the republic and endanger liberty . . . We charge that the controlling influences dominating the old political parties have allowed the existing dreadful conditions to develop without serious effort to restrain or prevent them. . . . They propose to sacrifice our homes and children upon the altar of Mammon; to destroy the hopes of the multitude in order to secure corruption funds from the great lords of plunder.[39]

Their demands were as radical as their analysis. Like their forebears in New England, they sought an expanded money supply (now through the circulation of silver coins). They wanted government ownership of the railroad, telephone, and telegraph systems, a progressive income tax, shorter hours for labor, and restrictions on private banks.[40] Their political party, the People's Party, won a million votes in the presidential election of 1892.

Wages and working conditions generally improved between 1870 and 1920, but this improvement masked serious hardships for millions of workers. In Massachusetts, the most heavily industrialized state, 20 percent of the workforce suffered some unemployment during such prosperous years as 1890 and 1900. Their unemployment lasted an average of three to four months. Individuals' plights grew much worse during the frequent economic slumps (1873–1879, 1883–1885, 1893–1897, 1907–1909, 1914–1915). During recessions and depressions, approximately one out of three workers went jobless for at least three months.[41]

A federal study showed that in 1900 the U.S. workforce included over one and three quarter million children between the ages of ten and fifteen. Some industries depended heavily on child labor. For example, 13 percent of the cotton industry's workers (and as much as 23 percent in North Carolina) were children. According to cotton manufacturers' own records, these children (some as young as six years old) worked an *average* of eleven and a half hours a day.[42] Most of the cotton mills, north and south, were poorly ventilated, dimly lighted, and lacked rudimentary sanitation. Children and adults shared the risk of dismemberment in machines and of fire in factories filled with flammable materials and lacking adequate fire escapes. In most cotton mills clouds of toxic cotton dust filled the air.[43]

Working conditions were dangerous in most industries. Insurance companies estimated that 25,000–35,000 industrial accident deaths and more than 2 million serious injuries occurred *annually* for several years after 1900.[44] Accidents of disastrous proportions captured national attention. In Fairmont, West Virginia, on December 6, 1907, Monongah mines 6 and 8 exploded in a disaster that killed 361 miners.[45] On March 25, 1911, a fire engulfed the Triangle Shirtwaist Company, a "sweatshop" with a mostly female workforce on the top floors of a New York City loft building. One hundred forty-five young women died, trapped without a fire escape. Many were forced by the flames to jump to their deaths.[46]

When workers joined unions to win a measure of protection, business reacted viciously. A wave of strikes in 1877 led to bloody confrontations across the country. During a Chicago strike in 1886, a bomb exploded among police assigned to patrol a meeting in Haymarket Square. Police opened fire, killing ten workers and wounding fifty. Violence erupted in 1892 at Andrew Carnegie's steelworks in Homestead, Pennsylvania. A bitter, protracted strike against the Pullman sleeping car company in 1894 escalated into industrial warfare that cost thirty-four lives and damage in the millions of dollars. Violence in coalfields of southern Colorado peaked in 1914 with the Ludlow massacre, when police and the National Guard put the tent city of Ludlow to the torch and randomly shot scores of men, women, and children. Strikers retaliated with a rampage against the mining company.[47]

A few members of the business community sympathized with some of the demands for regulation. Indeed, in some cases business factions made a strategic decision to join with movements for specific reforms. Shippers and merchants, for example, were as vehemently opposed to high railroad rates as farmers, and in the Midwest in the 1870s they joined forces in a common drive for strict controls on the railroads. Economic rivalries pitted urban against rural economic interests, eastern and midwestern against western and southern interests, large corporations against small businesses.[48]

In Europe as well as in North America, social and economic changes sparked a backlash against unrestricted property rights.[49] But in contrast to the United States, many European governments laid the foundations for welfare state programs that eventually provided inclusive income, employment, housing, health, and other protections to citizens.

The Expansion of Policymaking Capacity and Protective Policy

In the United States, expanding revenues, spending, and personnel at all levels of government indicate the growth of government policymaking capacity in this period. Table 2.2 shows that public sector taxes and spending increased much faster than the growth of the population. State and local governments raised roughly twice as much money in revenues as did the federal government, and they spent vastly more than the federal government on social policies such as education, highways, welfare, hospitals, and police and fire protection. State and local governments largely controlled such policies.

Table 2.2 suggests several noteworthy patterns in government taxation and spending. First, state and local governments continued to rely very heavily on property taxes. Although state sales taxes began to produce substantial revenues in the 1920s, state income taxes produced relatively little revenue for these governments. Second, in a generation between the turn of the century and 1922, state and local governments had nearly quadrupled their per capita spending. They more than quintupled spending on highways and nearly quintupled spending on education, their two largest expenditure categories. Even the most traditionally backward states dramatically improved their efforts in these areas.[50] Spending on welfare, hospitals, public health, and police and fire services increased at a slower rate, and these remained relatively small expenditure categories. However, by 1932, after three depression winters, spending on welfare, police protection, and hospitals had increased markedly.

In 1900, government at all levels employed about 1 million Americans, and that figure tripled to just over 3 million by 1928. The fastest growth occurred in local government, which by 1928 had slightly more than 1 million workers. Another million were employed in local public educa-

Table 2.2. *Per capita government revenues and expenditures, 1902–1932*

	1902 ($)		1913 ($)		1922($)		1932($)	
	Federal	State and Local	Federal	State and Local	Federal	State and Local	Federal	State and Local
Taxes	6.48	10.86	6.81	16.55	30.63	36.49	14.51	49.33
Individual income	—	—	—	—	{17.62}	.39	3.24	.59
Corporation income	—	—	.36	—		.53	4.79	.63
Sales, customs	6.15	.35	6.29	.60	10.47	1.40	5.87	6.02
Property	—	8.92	—	13.70	—	30.18	—	35.91
Direct expenditures	7.14	12.80	9.85	21.23	33.04	47.41	31.88	62.15
Education	.04	3.22	.05	5.93	.07	15.49	.11	18.50
Highways	—	2.21	—	4.31	.02	11.76	.20	13.93
Welfare	.05	.47	.05	.53	.08	1.08	.01	3.55
Hospitals	.03	.54	.01	.81	.79	1.82	.90	2.79
Health	.01	.21	.04	.30	.06	.53	.11	.86
Police	—	.63	.03	.92	.13	1.73	.25	2.55
Fire	—	.51	—	.78	—	1.44	—	1.68

Source: U.S. Bureau of the Census, Census of Governments, 1967, vol. 6: Topical Studies, no. 5, *Historical Statistics on Government Finances and Employment* (Washington, DC: GPO, 1969), Table 1, 31–2.

tion. During this period state government employment (about 300,000 in 1928) grew faster than federal employment (561,000 in 1928).[51]

A lively climate of policy innovation touched government at all levels. Many states enacted worker's compensation, factory inspection, and wage and hour laws. Federal and state governments passed laws that regulated railroads, banks, and food and drug manufacturing. Antitrust laws were aimed at preventing the largest enterprises from abusing their economic power. Some industrial giants, such as Standard Oil and American Tobacco, were compelled to break up into smaller firms, although enforcement of antitrust laws was neither universal nor sustained.

Their innovative and relatively generous policies gave some states an especially progressive reputation. These included the industrialized states, such as Massachusetts, New York, Illinois, Michigan, and California. It also included Wisconsin, Minnesota, and other states that pioneered reforms in taxation, elections, regulation, and social policy. While the state of Arizona spent $.02 per capita on public welfare in 1902, Massachusetts spent $.80; while South Carolina spent $.35 per capita in 1912, Massachusetts spent $2.51; and while Arkansas spent $.55 per capita in 1932, New Jersey and New York spent more than $4.30.[52]

America's policymaking structure could not and did not prevent demands for more government action from stimulating policy expansion, but *it absorbed and moderated the backlash* against business. The federal government's policymaking capacity developed late and remained limited in scope, so that the backlash against industrialization yielded few national policy protections for individuals. This limited national capacity made states the battleground for most progressive causes. But the states resisted progressive legislation when such laws seemed to place them at an unsustainable competitive disadvantage compared with other states. Though some states far exceeded others in offering protections to labor and a few social benefits, interstate competition, combined with tortuous policymaking and constitutional limitations, placed a ceiling on state policy experimentation. No state was willing to match the protections against illness and unemployment offered in Britain and other industrialized nations.

When some states did manage to enact laws limiting corporate autonomy, industrial corporations frequently seized the opportunity to appeal to the national government for relief. Thus new national regulations were enacted that, in effect, moderated the more stringent laws of a few states. In these circumstances business could more easily win increases in government capacity for its ends than reformers could for theirs. Government fragmentation permitted various business sectors to pursue with success a variety of strategies for dealing with demands for regulation—some opposed all regulation, some preferred regulation at the state level, and some preferred national regulation.

National Policymaking: Late Development and Limited Scope

Throughout the period from the 1870s to 1933, and especially from 1901 to 1920, some national officials struggled to develop the capacity to govern an industrialized nation. Presidents Theodore Roosevelt and Woodrow Wilson invested tremendous energy in activating and professionalizing the national government.[53] The Sixteenth Amendment, approved by two-thirds of the states in 1913, permitted the federal government to tax individual and corporate incomes. The income tax provided the federal government with a permanent, relatively stable source of revenue that could increase in step with the nation's employment and wealth. By 1915 the income tax replaced customs duties as the most important source of revenue for the federal government.[54] However, the new federal policymaking capacity developed late and did little to overcome policymaking incoherence. In addition, Congress and the federal courts continued to limit national government protections for vulnerable citizens.

Congressional limits on executive activism. The U.S. Congress, still the most dominant national policy institution, amplified conservative interests.[55] The amendment requiring the direct election of senators took effect in 1913, just as the momentum of the Progressive movement began to flag. Most of the members of the House of Representatives previously had been state political leaders. In the House and the Senate, politicians usually championed the business needs of their home states. Some of them, such as Republican Senators Nelson Aldrich of Rhode Island and Henry Cabot Lodge of Massachusetts, became national spokesmen for the nation's biggest industries and banks.

On some issues, notably tariffs, the business interests of different states came into conflict, and in these cases congressional debates were intense and votes were close.[56] But on most issues large majorities in the Senate, and to a lesser extent the House, were unwilling to consider legislation that threatened John D. Rockefeller, J. P. Morgan, and business leaders with holdings and influence across many states. When they yielded to popular and political pressure, they enacted regulatory laws in the weakest possible form. Aldrich, Lodge, and their allies foreclosed Theodore Roosevelt's hopes of enacting strict federal antitrust legislation. The Senate significantly weakened President Woodrow Wilson's antitrust legislation, refused to confirm the appointment of a Federal Trade Commission nominee opposed by business, and altered the Federal Reserve Board to ensure its control by private bankers.[57]

Federal grants-in-aid to the states constituted a form of national government activism that legislators from every state could embrace. The enactment of a federal income tax gave Congress the opportunity to provide cash grants to the states for specific social and economic purposes. Because grants-in-aid permitted the states to make important decisions about the use of federal funds, the states and their representatives in Washington found them ideal for increasing federal action while retaining state power. In 1916, Congress passed the Federal Road Act, providing federal grants to state highway departments for the purpose of building and improving rural roads. In 1917, Congress passed the Vocational Education Act, which authorized the federal government to help pay teachers' salaries and other costs of state vocational education institutions. In 1920 Congress approved a vocational rehabilitation program to help retrain injured workers. These grant-in-aid programs remained small throughout the 1920s, amounting to $163 million by 1931, with 83 percent of the total sum devoted to highway grants. But they set the precedent for the design and administration of social programs adopted during the New Deal: the states would receive federal dollars and use their own personnel and administrative structures to implement the programs.[58]

The court system limits government scope. In the late nineteenth century, conservatives had little to fear from the state courts, for most of them had erected effective and creative barriers to reform laws. In the case of *Godcharles* v. *Wigeman*, for example, the Pennsylvania court declared "utterly unconstitutional and void" a state law requiring laborers to be paid in cash at regular intervals, for such a statute was an "insulting attempt to put the laborer under legislative tutelage," "degrading to his manhood," and "subversive of his rights." The Illinois supreme court quashed statute after statute, including laws establishing fair standards for wages in mines, a law requiring that workers be paid their wages, and a law limiting female factory workers' hours.[59] Yet there were signs that some of the state courts were bending under the weight of public opinion.

Since Congress controlled the size and jurisdiction of the federal judicial system, it enhanced the power of federal courts as a second line of legal defense against unwelcome regulatory policies. Following the Civil War, Congress vastly expanded the jurisdiction of the federal courts to encompass the fundamental property conflicts sparked by industrialization.

> The sweeping powers granted [to the courts] were an open invitation to the federal judiciary to assume the role of stern policeman for the new national economy. In 1890, the federal judicial structure itself was reinforced with the establishment of a national appellate court system. The

expansion of federal judicial power in the late nineteenth century was a natural response . . . to demands for national authority in the industrial age.[60]

The new national authority was peculiarly one-sided, for until 1914 Congress denied federal courts the right to hear appeals on regulatory laws declared unconstitutional by the state high courts.[61] This meant that when state courts invalidated a law meant to regulate business practices they had the final word, but when they upheld a law its opponents—usually employers—could appeal to the federal bench.

The Court contorted the commerce clause to enhance business power at unions' expense. The Court ruled that businesses could require that new workers promise not to join a union and that the federal government could make no law to the contrary (*Adair* v. *U.S.*, 1908). But the national government was allowed to stop a railroad strike, on the grounds that such union activities would disrupt the U.S. mail and interstate commerce (*In re Debs*, 1895). The Court turned the Sherman Anti-Trust Act of 1890, a law enacted to control monopolies, into a tool for breaking up unions. The Sherman Act did not allow the federal government to prevent a monopoly in sugar refining, because, the Court ruled, manufacturing is not commerce (*U.S.* v. *E.C. Knight Co.*, 1895), yet the Court agreed with business that unions were "monopolies" that restrained trade, and thus the Sherman Act was used to regulate union activities closely (*Lowe* v. *Lawlor*, 1908).[62]

Ultimately, both state and federal courts gave ground to the pressures for reform. The federal courts were much more willing to uphold the modest economic regulations enacted by Congress than the often stronger legislation enacted by the states.[63] But the Court was inconsistent. In 1898, the U.S. Supreme Court upheld a Utah statute setting a limit of eight hours for miners (*Holden* v. *Hardy*), but in 1905 it struck down a New York law establishing a ten-hour day for bakers (*Lochner* v. *New York*). In the wake of the 1916 reelection of Woodrow Wilson and a Democratic majority in Congress, the Court in 1917 upheld state laws that set a ten-hour workday in manufacturing (*Bunting* v. *Oregon*), a federal minimum wage and maximum hour law for railroad workers (*Wilson* v. *New*), a minimum wage law for women (*Stettler* v. *O'Hara*), and several workers' compensation laws. These victories came after long delays and were offset by other rulings. For example, the Court unanimously upheld a state law prohibiting child labor in dangerous occupations (*Sturges and Burn Manufacturing Company* v. *Beauchamp*, 1913) but invalidated both a national child labor prohibition (*Hammer* v. *Dagenhart*, 1918) and then a prohibitory tax on child labor (*Bailey* v. *Drexel Furniture Company*, 1922). When the federal child labor law was challenged by southern employers, the Court sustained their view that the Congress had unconstitutionally interfered with a state prerogative.[64]

The Limits of State Activism

In addition to its advantage in choosing national or state jurisdiction, business enjoyed an especially "privileged position"[65] in the state capitals. For example, reformers had made significant progress in child labor reform; between 1904 and 1914 nearly all the states moved to strengthen child labor laws or to improve educational opportunities. But reformers noted a "growing resistance to legislative progress in the states." Both legislation and enforcement had begun to vary significantly among the states, and the states with the most stringent protections began to anticipate the potential loss of business, jobs, and taxes that could follow from additional laws. "State legislatures were increasingly reluctant to make further reform advances at what seemed the expense of the industrial interests of the locality."[66]

By the 1870s, businesses had learned to manipulate the states in two ways. First, business put pressure on progressive states to relax their regulations by threatening to move to the states with beneficial laws. Second, business mobilized political resources across state lines to quell demands for reform as they emerged in state legislatures. Proponents of state business restrictions often lacked the power and the organizational coherence to match these business advantages. In this context the victories they won are all the more remarkable.

Industrialization encouraged the states to refine old methods of competing for business and to invent new ones. When big corporations formed in the years following the Civil War, the states tried to outbid one another in adopting the loosest laws governing corporate charters. New Jersey gained an early lead in the race, chartering more than half of the largest corporations between 1888 and 1904, but Delaware subsequently loosened its law still further, touting itself as the "Little Home of Big Business." In 1988 nearly eighteen thousand corporations held Delaware charters, including more than half of the five hundred largest industrial concerns in the country. The state "is the most important base of corporate law in the country, exceeding even the U.S. Supreme Court [as] the author of corporate jurisprudence for the country, and in many ways the world."[67] In 1985, the Morgan Guarantee Trust Company, the nation's fifth-largest bank holding company and New York City's tenth-largest employer, nearly abandoned New York to move to Delaware. Only when the state of New York agreed to a tax reduction worth $20 million to the company did Morgan Guarantee agree to build a new headquarters in the city.[68]

Such competition pressured the industrialized states to scale back the business regulations they had pioneered. The glass industry and other employers of children opposed state laws regulating child labor by arguing that such laws would force them to shut down and locate in more favorable states.[69] These pressures affected no state more dramatically than Massachusetts. At the turn of the century, the state's political leaders recognized that the existing corporate charters had resulted in a loss of business to other states. Consequently, in 1903 Massachusetts repealed many of its regulations. Among other changes, the state forfeited its right to determine the value of corporate property and the amount of stock that could be issued on it, and protected corporate officers from personal liability for corporate debts. These actions removed important protections against business fraud and malfeasance that the state had previously erected. Interstate economic competition had altered the notion of corporate responsibility in Massachusetts. Once viewed as organizations tolerated to serve the public, corporations were regarded before the law primarily as vehicles for private profit, and corporate regulations came to be seen as an excessive government interference with property rights.[70]

Given this climate and the complex structure of state policymaking, successful reforms proceeded slowly and unevenly. The New York legislature took up the issue of workers' compensation in 1898, but it took a dozen years for a statute to become state law. The state supreme court then declared the law unconstitutional. New York finally enacted a workers' compensation program in 1914, after amending the state constitution. In 1911, Wisconsin's workers' compensation law became the first to survive a court challenge. By 1914, nine states had enacted minimum wage laws for women, and five had limited the courts' use of labor injunctions. Yet almost without exception, "most of this type of legislation was passed in agrarian states where the need for it was far less pressing than in the more industrially mature commonwealths."[71] The pathbreaking social policy innovations of a handful of states did not spread uniformly across all the states.[72]

To bear a chance of being enacted by state governments, most social reforms had to gain the support of a portion of the business community and result in a net savings to affected businesses or to state budgets. Table 2.3 shows that innovative social programs spread at uneven rates from the 1910s up to 1935, when the national Social Security Act was passed. Workers' compensation laws were widely adopted in industrial states after 1911 because many manufacturers were persuaded that such laws would save them money. Paying a small insurance premium seemed preferable to going to court, where sympathetic juries sometimes forced individual employers to pay large settlements to injured workers. Thirty of the state workers' compensation laws permitted employers to choose not to carry insurance but to continue to be liable to

Table 2.3. *Number of states adopting selected social insurance and pension programs through 1934*

	Number of States Enacting Programs	
	Progressive Era (1911–1920)	Total, Through 1934
Perceived impact of state budget or business climate		
Positive fiscal or business climate impact		
Workers' compensation[a]	41	43
Mother's Aid[b]	40	45
Neutral fiscal or business climate impact		
Aid to the blind[c]	10	27
Old-age pensions[d]	0	28
Negative fiscal or business climate impact		
Unemployment insurance	0	1
Medical insurance	0	0

[a]Workers' compensation laws enacted in Kentucky (1914), Montana (1909), and New York (1910) were declared unconstitutional.

[b]In ten states with such laws, no families received aid as of 1921–1922. In addition to three states without laws, three states had discontinued Mother's Aid payments by the end of 1934.

[c]Three states enacted pension laws for the blind before 1911: Ohio (1898), Illinois (1903), and Wisconsin (1907).

[d]An old-age pension law enacted in Arizona in 1915 was declared unconstitutional; an old-age pension law enacted by the territory of Alaska in 1915 withstood a challenge to its constitutionality.

Sources: U.S. Bureau of Labor Statistics, *Workmen's Compensation Legislation of the United States and Canada, 1919*, Bull. 272 (Washington, DC: GPO, 1921); John R. Commons et al., *History of Labor in the United States*, vol. III (New York: Macmillan, 1935), 575–7; Robert H. Bremmer, ed., *Children and Youth in American: A Documentary History* (Cambridge: Harvard University Press, 1971) 393; U.S. Committee on Economic Security, *Report to the President* (Washington, DC: GPO, 1935) 68, 71; U.S. Bureau of Labor Statisitics, "Public Pensions for the Blind in 1934," *Monthly Labor Review* 41:3 (September 1935) 584–601; Daniel Nelson, *Unemployment Insurance: The American Experience, 1915–1935* (Madison: University of Wisconsin Press, 1969), 162–91.

civil suits brought by injured workers (with some employers' defenses removed).[73]

"Mother's Aid" laws also won rapid legislative approval, in part because they reduced public expenditures on the poor. Before these laws were enacted, local courts often had little alternative but to break up destitute families, sending mothers to the poorhouse and children to juvenile homes. Mother's Aid permitted the courts to grant a small pension to families so that they could sustain themselves in their own home rather than becoming expensive wards of the state. In line with this philosophy, New York's governor directed county officials to award pensions only where the alternative was institutional care.[74]

Other programs included aid to the blind and the aged, usually enacted by the less industrialized states outside the South. Like the Mother's Aid laws, these pension programs did not entitle anyone to benefits; instead, they allowed local officials to give cash assistance to the "truly needy." Unemployment and medical insurance threatened to strain the state budgets and the profits of some industries (especially the private insurance companies). As a consequence, when such programs were eventually created in the United States, they came about through federal and not state action.

The southern states were especially successful at resisting reforms that intruded on business freedom. When a member of the North Carolina legislature introduced a bill to outlaw the employment of children under twelve in the state's factories, the proposal created a storm of protest. One cotton manufacturer described the bill as

> A gross insult to every parent whose child labors for its daily bread in the cotton factories of North Carolina and to every president, manager, or stockholder of a mill. It . . . takes the management of their property out of their hands and puts it in the hands of [public officials] who know as much concerning the . . . best interests of a factory as a billy goat knows about fishing.[75]

During hearings on the bill, the only proponent spoke on behalf of a national child labor reform group. The several factory owners who spoke against the proposal seemed wounded that the state legislature would even consider the bill ("the manufacturers felt that this was a legislature they could trust"). The legislature proved its trustworthiness by tabling the proposal indefinitely.[76]

In contrast to their sensitivity to corporate interests, the states often tried to undermine the political demands put forth by trade unions. Unions were viewed as a liability in attracting corporations. State court rulings and state militias protected the rights of business against unions, often denying unions the right to organize. The courts frequently ruled that strikes were illegal (the most restrictive courts of all after 1900 were those in Massachusetts). Where strikes occurred, courts used injunctions to force strikers back to work. California upheld the right to strike but determined that all picketing was illegal; Massachusetts and other states followed suit. Though the federal Clayton Act of 1914 was viewed by many as guaranteeing trade union rights, this largely symbolic legislation left intact the fundamental imbalance observed by contemporary experts: "While the workingmen's right to strike is restricted, the employer's right to discharge is absolute."[77]

State militias provided an effective means for states to discourage union activity. In the late 1870s, the state militias were inept organizations that mainly provided political patronage for state politicians. But the massive railroad strike of 1877 infused new energy into militias. Between 1878 and 1892, every state revised its military code. New York, Massachusetts, Connecticut, New Jersey, and Pennsylvania invested huge sums to transform their militias into effective riot and strike control forces. Fortified armories were built in most northern cities. The business community often supplemented state funds for the militia, and after 1877 they provided most of the officers free of charge. By the turn of the century, the state militias had become fully vitalized as "a formidable internal police of over 100,000 men," more than 70 percent of whom were located in the industrial heartland.[78] At Homestead, Pullman, Ludlow, and other bloody landmarks in labor history, the state militias honed their skills in controlling labor.

Of course resistance to unions was not confined to the United States, but repressive laws in relatively centralized political systems were reversed more quickly than were laws in the fragmented American system. In Britain the House of Lords dealt a serious blow to unions in its Taff Vale decision of 1901, which made unions financially liable for the costs incurred by employers during strikes. This decision was short-lived. In 1903 the unions entered into an electoral alliance with the Liberal party, and when the party won the election of 1906 it enacted a Trades Union Dispute Act that nullified the Taff Vale decision.[79]

The perception of interstate competition increased state officials' sense of vulnerability and acted as a drag on business regulation and taxation in the average American state. New types of taxation tended to be enacted under conditions of severe fiscal stress and not in prosperity (a trend evident again in the 1980s).[80]

These pressures did not affect all states equally, and several states pioneered progressive legislation. Even in Wisconsin, however, conservatives effectively used business climate arguments to defeat the progressives in the mid-1910s.[81] When business climate concerns alone could not halt the advance of reform, business could seek less restrictive laws and more responsive regulatory agencies at the federal level.

Business' Advantages in the Distribution of Policymaking Power

The Constitution conferred on business a crucial political advantage in that it could narrow or broaden the scope of political conflict virtually at will. When a state or several states attempted to restrict their autonomy, some business interests turned to the national government to nullify or weaken state laws. Unions and social reformers had much more difficulty in finding a level of government that would or could respond to their demands. Thus, though the government's national policy capacity expanded through increases in revenues and personnel, its authority to limit property rights and corporate decisions remained restricted.

Railroad regulation offers an excellent example of the way in which the federal system worked to business' advantage. The midwestern farmers who regarded the railroads as the villains in the farm crisis of the 1880s managed to pressure several state legislatures to enact regulations of railroad freight charges. Several states (including Illinois, where Chicago was a key hub for the entire industry) created a railroad commission with the authority to control excessive freight rates. In response, railroad barons turned to the national government for protection against state regulation. In 1887 Congress created the first *national* regulatory agency, the Interstate Commerce Commission, to preempt the regulatory threat posed by the states.

> The hostility of workers and farmers, many of whom controlled state politics, pointed to the possibility of local attacks which threatened to dislocate railroad systems . . . Federal railroad regulation appeared to many railroad leaders as a safe shield behind which to hide from the consequences of local democracy . . . If [they] often disagreed on the details . . . the railroads nevertheless supported the basic principle and institution of federal regulation . . . And . . . they enthusiastically worked for its extension and for the supremacy of federal regulation over the states.[82]

The ICC helped the railroad interests by stabilizing railroad rates and ensuring that they would enjoy a comfortable profit margin under national government protection.

Similarly, coal mine owners sought federal involvement in mine safety. Soon after the Monongah mining disaster of 1907, Congress approved funds for scientific studies of mine safety, and it later created a separate U.S. Bureau of Mines to monitor the industry. Remarkably, neither miners' unions nor the public had clamored for such federal actions. Rather, Congress had acted at the request of mine operators, especially those located in West Virginia. At a January 1908 meeting with federal representatives, the mine owners passed a resolution "that the United States government should take the necessary steps to determine the causes [of mine accidents] before any attempt is made to apply legislative remedies." Among themselves, these owners admitted that they sought federal intervention to preempt "radical legislation" in the coal mining states, which they feared would be "drastic and burdensome if not almost prohibitive."[83]

The political struggle to regulate the insurance industry also illustrates how important the choice of jurisdiction could be for business. Like the coal mine operators, insurance companies sought federal relief from regulations imposed by a few states. After 1912, however, the insurance industry abruptly changed its view and opposed a national insurance law. The change of heart came after the election of Woodrow Wilson to the presidency. The industry recognized that Wilson valued the advice of Boston reformer Louis Brandeis. Since Brandeis had battled the insurance companies in Massachusetts and vigorously investigated their practices, the industry calculated that it would be better to accept relatively strict regulation in some states than to risk the possibility of tighter national control.[84]

Some industries, such as the meatpackers and the food processors, sought national government regulation when adverse publicity and public pressure threatened their sales at home and abroad. Following the 1904 publication of *The Jungle*, Upton Sinclair's exposé of the Chicago meatpacking industry, sales of meat and meat products fell 50 percent. The meatpackers lobbied heavily for federal legislation to restore the public's confidence and to bolster exports. The Pure Food and Drug Act of 1906, and especially the Meat Inspection Act of 1907, were passed more in response to pressure applied by H. J. Heinz and other large food industry magnates than to popular demands.[85]

In several decisions handed down after the Civil War the Supreme Court vastly enhanced business' advantages by creating a "no man's land" protecting property rights from federal or state interference.[86] The Fourteenth Amendment, ratified in 1866 specifically to protect the civil rights of southern blacks, stated that no state shall "deprive any person of life, liberty, or property, without due process of law; nor deny to any person within its jurisdiction the equal protection of the laws." This amendment would finally have extended national protections to individuals against arbitrary state government actions, language that was dropped from the original Bill of Rights. But the federal courts, rather than using the amendment to protect the rights of southern blacks, used it to strengthen the property rights of corporations (as legal "individuals"). As early as 1873, a Supreme Court minority had argued that the amendment prevented unreasonable state interference with the property rights of businesses. In *Lochner* v. *New York* (1905), the Court struck down a New York state law limiting the working hours for bakers. The court majority argued that the state law restricted the freedom of "persons"—both the bakers and the businesses they worked for—to make contractual agreements, and hence violated the equal protection of the laws that the Fourteenth Amendment extended to business enterprises. This decision expanded the property rights of corporations and elaborated a legal structure biased in favor of property rights.

Social Reform Strategies

Over the course of U.S. history there have been many visionary social reformers cut from the same cloth as the architects of the European welfare states.[87] Such intellectuals as John R. Commons at the University of Wisconsin and public officials such as Senator Robert Wagner of New York advocated a wide variety of innovative social programs even before 1933. The American Association for Labor Legislation organized social reformers into a nationwide network of activists who battled for labor legislation and for social insurance from 1906 through the 1930s.

These reformers, however, confronted a government structure designed to slow and restrict the pace of social change. Robert Hunter, the nation's leading authority on poverty early in the century, blamed federalism for making "social and industrial legislation more difficult to obtain in America than in any other great industrial country."[88] Some of these reformers, such as Hunter, held that only national government action could alleviate America's social problems. Some adapted to America's policy impasse by making a virtue of necessity, viewing the states as laboratories in which to perfect social policy. Others made a necessity of virtue, insisting on reforms that enhanced state and local power.

Though many reformers viewed the states as social laboratories, the policymaking structure imposed limits on the range of experiments that even the most progressive state could undertake. The most influential Progressive-era social reformers had adjusted to the political realities of the American system by promoting federalism as a valuable and essential feature of the American polity. Many felt ambivalent about national power and sought policies that protected the independent policy choices of the states. They had more successes in the state capitals in Massachusetts, Wisconsin, New York, and other progressive states than in Washington, a fact that reinforced their commitment to state solutions. Widely respected reformers such as Louis Brandeis, whose ideas influenced both Woodrow Wilson and Franklin Roosevelt, argued that new policy departures *should* increase state power. Brandeis believed that vesting power in the states would prevent the national government from exercising excessive central control. Moreover, he welcomed the fact that the states could experiment with different solutions to social problems; if all of the states experimented, the result would be a social laboratory the size of a continent.[89] His views influenced a whole generation of social reformers.

Reformers joined campaigns for uniform state laws in workers' compensation, child labor, and legal and commercial procedures. Rather than seek national social insurance against joblessness or poor health, they wrote model statutes for each state to adopt. The uniform state law strategy was "the Progressive Era's answer to the need for a political device that would take a variety of questions beyond the states but keep them from the national government." The reformers worked hard to prove that uniform laws would leave no state at a commercial disadvantage, but would at the same time improve the "business climate" nationwide.[90] Their arduous state-by-state campaigns to win reforms exhausted their resources and weakened their national impact.

By the time the national government began to implement education, welfare, and health programs in the 1930s, the states already had established social welfare agencies accustomed to state policy control and interested in their own survival and expansion. These agencies resisted federal control even as they accepted federal funds. Federal grants for vocational education and highway construction similarly passed money and policy responsibility through state administrative departments. By using the states to implement federal programs, a system guaranteeing uneven results, complexity, and limited national oversight was established.

THE CONSTITUTIONAL LEGACY

Created by the Constitution's framers to protect the property of the landowners and commercial interests that dominated the late eighteenth-century American economy, the American policymaking structure protected the propertied interests of an industrialized economy a hundred years later. A trader or banker in the 1790s or an industrialist in the 1890s found two levels of government willing to protect property rights. Groups seeking policies to restrict the use of property often found access at both levels limited or closed. The average state seldom adopted policy measures that might have the effect of making it a less desirable business environment in comparison with other states. The national government reflected rather than contradicted this state conservatism. Reformers adapted themselves to the realities of this political structure. By the 1920s the United States had deviated sharply from other capitalist democracies that had begun to adopt policies to mitigate the social consequences of industrialization.

NOTES

1. Samuel Krislov and Robert B. Kvavik, "Constitutional Design and the Channelling of Socio-Political Goals in the Welfare State," *Scandinavian Studies* 59:2 (Spring 1987), 167–83.
2. Joseph L. Davis, *Sectionalism in American Politics, 1774–1787* (Madison: University of Wisconsin Press, 1977); Peter S. Onuf, *The Origins of the Federal Republic: Jurisdictional Controversies in the United States, 1775–1787* (Philadelphia: University of Pennsylvania Press, 1983).
3. On the United States as a developing nation, see Seymour Martin Lipset, *The First New Nation: The United States in Comparative and Historical Perspective* (New York: Basic Books, 1963).

4. Ross M. Robertson and Gary M. Walton, *History of the American Economy* (New York: Harcourt, Brace, Jovanovich, 1979), 125–30; Irwin H. Polishook, *Rhode Island and the Union, 1774–1795* (Evanston, IL: Northwestern University Press, 1969), 103–6.

5. Polishook, *Rhode Island and the Union*, 103–42.

6. Page Smith, *The Constitution: A Documentary and Narrative History* (New York: Morrow, 1978), 71–85; David P. Szatmary, *Shays' Rebellion: The Making of an American Insurrection* (Amherst: University of Massachusetts Press, 1980).

7. Davis, *Sectionalism in American Politics*, 151–2.

8. The position that the framers' self-interest shaped the Constitution is associated with Charles Beard, *An Economic Interpretation of the Constitution* (New York: Free Press, 1965, originally 1913), although the extreme view that finance capital entirely determined the Constitution's provisions is challenged by Forrest McDonald, *We, The People: The Economic Origins of the Constitution* (Chicago: Phoenix Books, 1963). The framers' interest in the protection of property is clearly asserted by a range of constitutional scholars, such as Martin Diamond, "What the Framers Meant By Federalism," in Robert A. Goldwin, ed., *A Nation of States* (Chicago: Rand McNally, 1963), 33, and Calvin C. Jillson and Cecil L. Eubanks, "The Political Structure of Constitution Making: The Federal Convention of 1787," *American Journal of Political Science* 28:3 (August 1984), 435–58.

9. George Washington to Henry Knox, letter, 26 December, 1786, in John C. Fitzpatrick, ed., *The Writings of George Washington* (Washington, DC: 1939), 122.

10. Max Farrand, ed., *The Records of the Federal Convention of 1787* (New Haven, CT: Yale University Press, 1966), 497; John P. Roche, "The Founding Fathers: A Reform Caucus in Action," *American Political Science Review* 55:4 (December 1961), 799–816; Michael P. Zuckert, "Federalism and the Founding: Toward a Reinterpretation of the Constitutional Convention," *Review of Politics* 48:2 (Spring 1986), 166–210.

11. Federalist Paper 45, in the *Federalist Papers*, (New York: Mentor, 1961). For the importance of property at the Constitutional Convention, see, for example, Farrand, *Records*, 512, 533–4.

12. Smith, *The Constitution*, 133–7; Roche, "The Founding Fathers."

13. Alpheus Thomas Mason, ed., *The States Rights Debate: Antifederalism and the Constitution* (New York: Oxford University Press, 1972), 188. On the significance of a state-based system of laws, see Herbert Wechsler, "The Political Safeguards of Federalism: The Role of the States in the Composition and Selection of the National Government," in Arthur W. Macmahon, ed., *Federalism: Mature and Emergent* (New York: Russell and Russell, 1962), 98; Theodore Lowi, "Why Is There No Socialism in the United States? A Federal Analysis," in Robert T. Golembiewski and Aaron Wildavsky, eds., *The Costs of Federalism* (New Brunswick, NJ: Transaction Press, 1984); and Harry N. Scheiber, "The Condition of American Federalism: An Historian's View," in Laurence J. O'Toole, ed., *American Intergovernmental Relations: Foundations, Perspectives, and Issues* (Washington, DC: Congressional Quarterly, 1985), 51–7.

14. E. E. Schattschneider, *The Semisovereign People* (Hinsdale, IL: Dryden, 1960), 1–10.

15. Federalist Paper 10, in *The Federalist Papers*.

16. Federalist Papers 10, 46, in *The Federalist Papers*.

17. Chester J. Antieau, *States' Rights Under Federal Constitutions* (London: Oceana Publications, 1984), 67.

18. Dennis O Grady, "State Economic Development Incentives: Why Do States Compete?" *State and Local Government Review* 19:3 (Fall, 1987), 86–94.

19. This is a point on which leading scholars of state policy outcomes and of business concur; see Jack L. Walker, "Innovation in State Politics," in Herbert Jacob and Kenneth N. Vines, eds., *Politics in the American States* 2d ed. (Boston: Little, Brown, 1971), 366; and Graham K. Wilson, *Business and Politics: A Comparative Introduction* (Chatham, NJ: Chatham House, 1985) 41-2, 134–5.

20. Forrest McDonald, "The Constitution and Hamiltonian Capitalism," in Robert A. Goldwin and William A. Schambra, eds., *How Capitalistic Is the Constitution?* (Washington, DC: American Enterprise Institute, 1982) 49–74; cf. Bernard H. Siegan, "The Constitution and the Protection of Capitalism," in Goldwin and Schambra, 106–26.
21. Stephen David and Paul Kantor, "Urban Policy in the Federal System: A Reconceptualization of Federalism," *Polity* 16:2 (Winter 1983), 284–303.
22. Lipset, *The First New Nation*, 49.
23. Daniel J. Elazar, *The American Partnership: Intergovernmental Cooperation in the Nineteenth-Century United States* (Chicago: University of Chicago Press, 1962), 25-69.
24. George Dangerfield, *The Awakening of American Nationalism* (New York: Harper & Row, 1965), 196–9; Lipset, *The First New Nation*, 49–50; Carter Goodrich, "National Planning of Internal Improvements," *Political Science Quarterly* 63:1 (March 1948), 16–44.
25. Federalist Paper 51, in *The Federalist Papers*; Alvin M. Josephy, Jr., *On the Hill: A History of the American Congress* (New York: Touchstone, 1979), 50–60.
26. Federalist Paper 45, in *The Federalist Papers*; Josephy, *On the Hill*, 35.
27. Federalist Paper 45, in *The Federalist Papers*.
28. Josephy, *On the Hill*, 60.
29. Aage R. Clausen, *How Congressmen Decide: A Policy Focus* (New York: St. Martin's Press, 1973), 182 ff.
30. John A. Ferejohn, *Pork-Barrel Politics* (Stanford, CA: Stanford University Press, 1974), 47–68.
31. Goodrich, "National Planning of Internal Improvements."
32. Josephy, *On the Hill*, 62.
33. John R. Commons and John B. Andrews, *Principles of Labor Legislation* (New York: Harpers, 1916), 94.
34. Wechsler, "The Political Safeguards of Federalism."
35. Dennis R. Judd, *The Politics of American Cities: Private Power and Public Policy*, 3d ed. (Glenview, IL, and Boston: Scott, Foresman/Little, Brown, 1988), 17.
36. Daniel E. Diamond and John D. Guilfoil, *United States Economic History* (Morristown, NJ: General Learning Press, 1973), 64.
37. John A. Garraty, *The New Commonwealth, 1877–1890* (New York: Harper & Row, 1968), 13–30; Samuel P. Hays, *The Response to Industrialism, 1885–1914* (Chicago: University of Chicago Press, 1957), 20-3.
38. Lawrence Goodwyn, *The Populist Movement: A Short History of the Agrarian Revolt in America* (New York: Oxford University Press, 1978), 20–54; Garraty, *The New Commonwealth*, 33–77.
39. Walter B. Stevens, *St. Louis: History of the Fourth City* (Chicago: S.J. Clarke, 1909), 1176.
40. Goodwyn, *The Populist Movement*, 107–11.
41. Alexander Keyssar, *Out of Work: The First Century of Unemployment in Massachusetts* (Cambridge, England: Cambridge University Press, 1986), 52, 58.
42. U.S. Commissioner of Labor, *Report on the Condition of Woman and Child Wage Earners in the United States*, S. Doc. 61-645, vol. VI (Washington, DC: GPO, 1910), 45, 134–5.
43. Ibid., vol. 1, 357-96.
44. Robertson and Walton, *History of the American Economy*, 326.
45. William Graebner, *Coal-Mining Safety in the Progressive Period: The Political Economy of Reform* (Lexington: University Press of Kentucky, 1976), 16-35.
46. J. Joseph Huthmacher, *Robert F. Wagner and the Rise of Urban Liberalism* (New York: Atheneum, 1968), 3–4.
47. Joseph G. Rayback, *A History of American Labor* (New York: Macmillan, 1966), 166–7, 194–207, 258.
48. Robert H. Weibe, *Businessmen and Reform: A Study of the Progressive Movement* (Chicago: Quadrangle, 1962).

49. On the backlash against laissez-faire, see Karl Polanyi, *The Great Transformation* (Boston: Beacon, 1957), and Joseph A. Schumpeter, *Capitalism, Socialism, and Democracy* (New York: Harper & Row, 1950).

50. Peter Wallenstein, *From Slave South to New South: Public Policy in Nineteenth Century Georgia* (Chapel Hill: University of North Carolina Press, 1987). Note that such policy expansion primarily (but not exclusively) benefited whites in the former slave states.

51. Stanley Lebergott, *Manpower in Economic Growth: The American Record Since 1800* (New York: McGraw-Hill, 1964), 517 Table A-8.

52. Based on data collected by Richard I. Hofferbert, available through the Inter-University Consortium for Political and Social Research, "Socio-Economic, Public Policy, and Political Data: The United States, 1890–1960." ICPSR 0015.

53. Stephen Skowronek, *Building a New American State: The Expansion of National Administrative Capacities, 1877–1920* (Cambridge, England: Cambridge University Press, 1982).

54. U.S. Bureau of the Census, *Historical Statistics on Governmental Finances and Employment*, in 1977 Census of Governments, vol. 6, Topical Studies (Washington, DC: GPO, 1979), 43.

55. Woodrow Wilson, *Congressional Government* (Cleveland: World Publishing, 1885).

56. Richard Franklin Bensel, *Sectionalism and American Political Development, 1880–1980* (Madison: University of Wisconsin Press, 1984), 60–72.

57. George E. Mowry, *The Era of Theodore Roosevelt and the Birth of Modern America, 1900–1912* (New York: Harper & Row, 1958), 115–34; Arthur S. Link, *Woodrow Wilson and the Progressive Era, 1910-1917* (New York: Harper & Row, 1954), 71–5; Arthur S. Link, *Wilson: The New Freedom* (Princeton, NJ: Princeton University Press, 1956), 238–40.

58. George F. Break, "Fiscal Federalism in the United States: The First 200 Years, Evolution and Outlook," in Advisory Commission on Intergovernmental Relations, *The Future of Federalism in the 1980s*, Commission Report M-126 (Washington, DC: ACIR, July 1981), 44.

59. Lawrence M. Friedman, *A History of American Law* (New York: Simon and Schuster, 1973), 490.

60. Skowronek, *Building a New American State*, 41.

61. John R. Commons et al., *History of Labor in the United States*, vol. 3 (New York: Macmillan, 1935), 661.

62. Loren P. Beth, *The Development of the American Constitution, 1877–1917* (New York: Harper & Row, 1971), 147–8, 160.

63. James Willard Hurst, *Law and Social Order in the United States* (Ithaca, NY: Cornell University Press, 1977), 98–9.

64. Commons et al., *History of Labor in the United States*, vol. 3 (New York: Macmillan, 1935) 440–2, 694–5.

65. Charles E. Lindblom developed notion that business occupies a "privileged position" in market-oriented democracies in *Politics and Markets: The World's Political-Economic Systems* (New York: Basic Books, 1977), 170–200, and in "The Market As Prison," *Journal of Politics*, 44:2 (May 1982), 324–36.

66. Stephen B. Wood, *Constitutional Politics in the Progressive Era: Child Labor and the Law* (Chicago: University of Chicago Press, 1968), 23–5.

67. Ralph Nader and Mark Green, "Federal Chartering and Corporate Responsibility," in Philip Brenner, Robert Borsage, and Bethany Weidner, eds., *Exploring Contradictions: Political Economy in the Corporate State* (New York: David McKay, 1974), 169–73; Lindsey Gruson, "Tiny Delaware's Corporate Clout," *New York Times*, 1 June 1986, F–6; Stephen Labaton, "Delaware Takeover Curb Near," *New York Times*, 29 January 1988, 27.

68. Josh Barbanel, "Instead of Leaving, Morgan Bank Plans a Tower on Wall Street," *New York Times*, 10 September 1985, 1.

69. Walter I. Trattner, *Crusade for the Children: A History of the National Child Labor Committee and Child Labor Reform in America* (Chicago: Quadrangle, 1970), 78.
70. Richard M. Abrams, *Conservatism in a Progressive Era: Massachusetts Politics, 1900–1912* (Cambridge, MA: Harvard University Press, 1964), 77–9.
71. Mowry, *The Era of Theodore Roosevelt*, 81.
72. Commons et al., *History of Labor in the United States*, vol. III, 571–5; Robert Eyestone, *From Social Issues to Public Policy* (New York: Wiley, 1978), 129-33.
73. U.S. Bureau of Labor Statistics, *Workmen's Compensation Laws of the United States and Canada*, BLS bull. 272 (Washington, DC: GPO, 1921), 9–19.
74. D. M. Schneider and A. Deutsch, *The History of Public Welfare in New York State, 1867–1940* (Montclair, NJ: Patterson Smith, 1969), 190–1. The diverse sources of Mother's Aid laws are discussed in Mark H. Leff, "Consensus for Reform: The Mothers'-Pension Movement in the Progressive Era," *Social Service Review* 47:3 (September 1973), 397–417.
75. U.S. Commissioner of Labor, *Report on the Condition of Woman and Child Wage Earners in the United States*, vol. VI, 141-2.
76. Ibid., 142.
77. Commons and Andrews, *Principles of Labor Legislation*, 104–12.
78. Skowronek, *Building a New American State* 103–7.
79. E. H. Hunt, *British Labour History, 1815–1914* (London: Weidenfeld and Nicholson, 1981).
80. Susan B. Hansen, "Extraction: The Politics of Taxation," in Virginia Gray, Herbert Jacob, and Kenneth N. Vines, eds., *Politics in the American States: A Comparative Analysis*, 4th ed. (Boston: Little, Brown, 1983), 433–7. For state tax increases in the 1980s, see John Shannon, "Federal and State-Local Spenders Go Their Separate Ways," in Robert Jay Dilger, ed., *American Intergovernmental Relations Today: Perspectives and Controversies* (Englewood Cliffs, NJ: Prentice-Hall, 1986), 173–5.
81. Herbert F. Margulies, *The Decline of the Progressive Movement in Wisconsin, 1890–1920* (Madison: State Historical Society of Wisconsin, 1968), 146–7.
82. Gabriel Kolko, *Railroads and Regulation, 1877–1916* (New York: Norton, 1965), 232.
83. Graebner, *Coal-Mining Safety in the Progressive Period*, 16-22.
84. Karen Orren, *Corporate Power and Social Change* (Baltimore: Johns Hopkins University Press, 1973), 28–9.
85. Kenneth J. Meier, *Regulation: Politics, Bureaucracy, and Economics* (New York: St. Martin's Press, 1985), 79; Gabriel Kolko, *The Triumph of Conservatism: A Reinterpretation of American History, 1900–1916* (New York: Free Press, 1963), 101–8; Donna J. Wood, "The Strategic Use of Public Policy: Business Support for the Pure Food and Drug Act," *Business History Review* 59:3 (Autumn 1985), 401–32.
86. Robert G. McCloskey, *The American Supreme Court* (Chicago: University of Chicago Press, 1969), 104–5.
87. For evidence from Europe, see Hugh Heclo, *Modern Social Politics in Britain and Sweden* (New Haven, CT: Yale University Press, 1974).
88. Robert Hunter, *Poverty* (New York: Macmillan, 1904), 333.
89. Barry D. Karl, *The Uneasy State* (Chicago: University of Chicago Press, 1983), 25, 134–5.
90. William Graebner, "Federalism in the Progressive Era: A Structural Interpretation of Reform," *Journal of American History* 64:2 (September 1977), 331–57.

Chapter 3

WHY DID THE UNITED STATES DIVERGE? A COMPARATIVE VIEW

AMERICA'S CONSERVATIVE SOCIAL POLICIES

No one would question the assertion that the American government has grown dramatically more active over the past century. Yet when compared with other advanced Western nations, social policy in the United States has developed more slowly and provides fewer and more uneven benefits than elsewhere.[1] In this respect, the United States clearly began to diverge from other countries after 1900. As an example of this development, Figure 3.1 shows that the United States lagged behind other capitalist democracies in providing for public insurance against old age, sickness, and unemployment.

This conservatism has persisted. Governments in the United States collect and spend less money than is spent in most capitalist democracies. In 1960 government social spending as a percentage of national output (measured as gross domestic product, or GDP) was higher in seven major capitalist democracies than in the United States (only Australia and Japan spent less). Despite a tremendous growth in overall social expenditures during the 1960s and 1970s, the United States remained positioned behind the same seven nations in 1981.[2] The United States also raises less revenue as a proportion of national wealth. In the mid-1980s government tax revenue represented about 31 percent of GDP in the United States, a lower tax burden than in Britain (42 percent), West Germany (45 percent), or Sweden (62 percent).[3] These West European governments impose a heavier tax burden, but the revenue thus generated permits more inclusive and generous public services and benefits.

The United States leaves a larger proportion of wealth and property in the hands of private institutions. The American national government engages in almost no long-range economic planning and exercises little

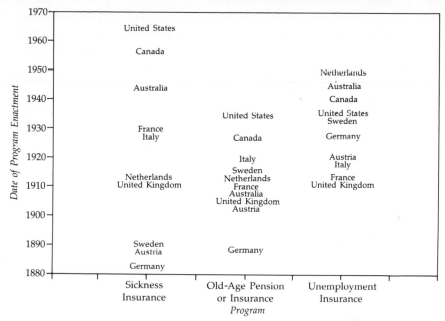

Figure 3.1. *Enactment of national social programs in ten nations*

Sources: Peter Flora and Jens Alber, "Modernization, Democratization, and the Development of Welfare States in Western Europe," in Peter Flora and Arnold Heidenheimer, eds., *The Development of Welfare States in Europe and America* (New Brunswick, NJ: Transaction Press, 1981) 59; Robert T. Kudrle and Theodore Marmor, "The Development of Welfare States in North America," in Ibid., 82–86; T. H. Kewley, *Social Security in Australia* (Sydney: Sydney Univerisity Press, 1965).

control over manufacturing and banking, compared with other Western democracies. When the federal government provides services such as mail, passenger trains, and regional electrical power, it often holds them at arms' length under the control of "government corporations" that resemble private corporations.[4]

In these ways the United States limits its capacity to implement public policy, since the size of the public sector is kept small relative to national wealth, and the government's ability to regulate institutions with significant private wealth also remains weak. In addition to the relatively limited capacity to finance strong policies, the national government's ability to administer consistent and uniform policies is undercut by the incoherence of the policy process in the United States.

Variations in program administration among American states create a situation in which many citizens receive fewer benefits than the national average. All states provide some services and benefits to their residents, and all states tax the property, purchases, or income of their residents to pay for these programs. But tax rates and service levels vary to a remarkable degree. In 1987, state taxes averaged $1,018 per person nationwide, but the tax burden ranged from $2,024 in Alaska, $1,567 in Hawaii, and $1,446 in Massachusetts, to less than $532 per person in New Hampshire and $587 in South Dakota. Beginning with Wisconsin in 1911, most states have taxed incomes in order to finance government programs, but in 1987 six states levied no personal income tax.[5]

State policy spending is closely related to the level of state tax revenues. Table 3.1 shows that state and local spending varies widely from state to state and from policy to policy. It compares two relatively liberal states, New York and Wisconsin, to the traditionally low-spending states of Arkansas and Missouri.[6] The national per capita welfare expenditure average of $318.28, for example, masks the fact that

Table 3.1. *Per capita state and local spending on social policies, U.S. average and selected states, 1985–1986*

	U.S. average	New York	Wisconsin	Missouri	Arkansas
Total expenditure	$2,979.61	$4,324.85	$3,023.40	$2,165.51	$2,085.84
Rank		3	19	49	50
Elementary/secondary education	639.98	842.58	686.19	528.05	590.44
Rank		3	12	45	34
Higher education	234.51	195.38	337.98	176.52	200.87
Rank		41	7	45	39
Public welfare	318.28	637.90	454.69	200.03	213.88
Rank		1	6	37	32
Health	64.50	84.07	111.09	55.76	38.45
Rank		7	3	28	47
Hospital	157.89	278.21	95.98	154.40	120.80
Rank		3	36	18	28
Sewage	55.20	70.67	94.48	48.52	21.70
Rank		8	2	29	48
Parks and recreation	42.16	54.51	42.88	33.75	16.14
Rank		11	17	28	49

Source: U.S. Bureau of the Census, *Government Finances in 1985–86,* Series GF-86, no. 5 (Washington, DC: GPO, 1987), 108–9.

New York spends more than three times the amount that Missouri spends on welfare (and four and a half times the expenditure in Texas, which in 1985–1986 spent $140.55 per capita on welfare). The two high-spending states rank above the national median and the two low-spending states rank below it in every spending category except for higher education (New York) and hospitals (Wisconsin).

In the month of January 1985, the average U.S. family of four receiving benefits through the Aid to Families with Dependent Children program received a maximum grant of $379, but in Mississippi such a family could receive only $120, compared with $660 in California and $636 in Connecticut. The states also differ widely in their spending on education, health, sewage (an indicator of environmental effort), and other services.[7]

"By definition," observes one expert on American social policy, "the poorest states and localities faced the most severe problems while having the least capacity to address them."[8] Beyond these spending differences, some states are far more willing than others to regulate business, protect the environment, and promote land use planning. Thus, not only does the United States exert less policy effort than comparable nations, policies that are implemented generally form a patchwork of vastly differing outcomes from state to state.

WHAT EXPLAINS POLICY VARIATION?

That there are fundamental differences in public policy from nation to nation and from state to state is easy to demonstrate. But it is a daunting task to identify the causes for policy variations. The complexity of the intellectual problem is revealed by the amount of scholarly energy devoted to uncovering the reasons why policies diverge. For example, the literature devoted solely to examining the factors involved in determining state welfare spending levels has become so voluminous that a single listing of all the published research up to 1980 occupies a book.[9]

Currently there are four main intellectual camps represented in the scholarly debate over the question: what explains the relative propensity of governments to finance and administer public policies? The four intellectual traditions can be identified by their underlying propositions:

Proposition #1: Socioeconomic circumstances, which can be measured by the level of wealth, economic development, or demographic characteristics of a polity, determines the willingness and ability of governments to finance social programs or public services. This premise leads to two straightforward predictions: wealthier and more highly developed polities will support more generous levels of policy; and within that constraint, social needs (such as an aging population) will determine the profile of programs that are financed.

Proposition #2: The nature of political parties and the balance of power among interest groups determine the level of public policy effort. When there are well-organized parties that represent constituencies (especially labor) that favor a higher policy effort, more generous policies result. Vigorous party competition also results in greater policy effort because the parties mobilize a larger proportion of the electorate, including voters who want greater policy effort. When interest groups systematically organize labor and economically disadvantaged people, governments will respond by investing in policy reform.

Proposition #3: Cultural values determine the level of public policy that is provided by a polity. Governments implement policies within the context of what is considered right and just. In the United States, a strong belief in individualism and private property keeps government relatively small. Policies that would attempt to redistribute economic or social resources do not find the necessary popular support: a conservative culture supports conservative policies.

Proposition #4: Somewhat independent of their political and cultural environments, governments can powerfully influence policy choices. Government leaders give concrete expression to vague policy demands. Bureaucratic agencies mobilize political support for the programs they administer. Governments often are the most powerful of advocates for the reform of past policies. In addition, government policymaking structures affect policy choices by making some policy options easier to enact and implement than others.

We examine these four intellectual camps, in turn.

Proposition #1: Socioeconomic Circumstances Determine Policy

Over a century ago, as European governments began to develop social insurance programs, the economist Adolf Wagner offered a simple explanation for the new initiatives. Wagner argued that as societies become wealthier, they become more willing and able to provide the benefits of the "welfare state."[10] Using sophisticated statistical methods, many scholars today draw similar conclusions. They believe that neither political institutions nor ideas account for the significant differences in policy between nations because economic circumstances dictate what governments can undertake. However positively inclined its government may be to providing generous social policy, a poor society cannot develop an expensive welfare state. In contrast, affluent societies have designed a complex variety of social programs because they have the capacity to do so. All societies, as they cross a threshold of wealth, embrace new social policies because they can afford them.

In the 1970s Harold Wilensky elaborated this model in his comparison of social security policies in sixty-four nations. He found that social security policies varied widely in their benefit levels and coverage, and he concluded that "over the long pull economic level is the root cause of these differences." Nations that spend relatively more of their national wealth on social security programs started their programs earlier and have experienced economic conditions that permitted the programs to expand over time. In the Soviet Union, Britain, and the United States, for example, the level of social security spending is a function of wealth and need, not politics or ideology: "In any systematic comparison of many countries over many years, alternative explanations collapse under the weight of such heavy, brittle categories as 'socialist' versus 'capitalist' economies, 'collectivistic' versus 'individualistic' ideologies or even 'democratic' versus 'totalitarian' political system." Wilensky concluded that social security policy differs among advanced nations because some have more elderly citizens than others (a social circumstance) and had enough wealth to begin building their welfare states earlier (an economic circumstance).[11]

In the broadest sense, this explanation accounts for major differences in government spending on health across the globe. A study published in the early 1970s showed that the industrial democracies spent an average of 2.6 percent of their national income (measured by gross national product, or GNP) on health care. The communist nations (such as the Soviet Union), which are generally poorer than the industrial democracies, spent 1.6 percent of their GNP on health, and the even poorer Third World nations (such as Zambia and Mexico) spent an average of 1.3 percent. The poorest nations, making up the so-called Fourth World (such as Ethiopia), spent an average of 0.9 percent of GNP for health services. "Clearly," this study concluded, "the level of national income . . . plays a major role in determining how much of its nation's wealth a government can allocate to serve the health needs of its people."[12]

Thomas Dye has asserted that similar factors explain policy differences among the American states. Dye has become the leading advocate of the view that economic development rather than political organizations or culture accounts for variations in state public expenditures. Overall wealth, levels of education, the percentage of workers employed in manufacturing and services, and the percentage of people who live in urban areas all served as indicators, in Dye's research, of the level of economic development in a state. By these measures, such states as California, New York, and Massachusetts are far wealthier than southern states. The better-off states find it easier to raise money because business and citizens can afford to finance government services. Since they find it easier to raise revenues, governments in these states also are relatively more professional and capable of spending money to address social problems. As a consequence, Dye concluded, "[t]he legislatures of urban industrial states introduce and enact more laws than the legislatures of rural farm states."[13] According to him, differences in government structure, leadership, culture, or politics do not significantly influence spending patterns.

Although this interpretation amounts to "policy without policymakers," it is asserted that political groups cannot overcome powerful underlying economic and demographic circumstances.[14] Policy is a captive of the socioeconomic environment. The change from a farming to a manufacturing economy, for example, kindles conflict between farmers and urban workers, which may burst forth in protests and competition between political parties or may simmer in rarely visible campaigns by interest groups. Yet these remain only symptoms of underlying social and economic changes to which government inevitably adapts. Such conflicts no more explain policy variations than different dashboards explain why one automobile accelerates faster than another. The motor in each case lies hidden within.

Proposition #2: Political Parties and Interest Groups Determine Policy

The degree to which socioeconomic circumstances alone determine the level and content of government activity is arguable. Many policy analysts have pointed out that, though very rich and very poor societies differ systematically in policy effort, developed nations with roughly comparable resources have taken significantly different paths. Why, for example, are the social welfare policies in the United States so limited compared with the programs available in Western Europe, despite America's enormous resources? Britain was a prosperous nation when it introduced its social security programs. Sweden and Austria were decidedly "underdeveloped" agricultural societies on the brink of industrial growth when they developed social insurance.[15] Clearly, differences in social policy expenditures among the advanced nations are not explained adequately by measuring economic development or wealth. It therefore seems likely that policies are sensitive to internal political characteristics, such as the balance of power among political parties and interest groups.

Political parties. Among the Western democracies, the United States alone lacks a democratic socialist political party comparable to the British Labour Party, the French Socialist Party, or the West German and Swedish Social Democratic parties. The rise of these parties had the effect of shifting most other parties to the left, making them more inclined to promise increases in social benefits and business regulations in order to win a share of working-class votes.[16] Applying this explanation to health policy, it has been argued that shortly before World War I the British Liberal Party tried to preempt the Labour party's appeal by introducing a health insurance plan. The U.S. Socialist party was not viewed as a similar threat to the Democrats and Republicans, and these parties felt no need to champion similar reforms.

American political parties are not only conservative by European standards, but they are also disorganized and lack ideological coherence. After the Civil War had settled the most divisive national question, "patronage rather than program became the object of politics."[17] The parties of consequence were state parties, which distributed political favors at the state level and controlled the nominations to the House and the Senate. They also selected the delegates to the presidential nominating conventions. Both parties absorbed key progressive leaders, such as Republicans Robert LaFollette (Wisconsin) and Hiram Johnson (California) and Democrats David Walsh (Massachusetts), Robert Wagner (New York), and Alfred Smith (New York). Most West European parties anywhere on the political spectrum have been more disciplined and more capable of articulating coherent policy programs.[18]

Party competition has been used to explain differences in American state policies. V. O. Key argued that in industrialized states such as New York and Illinois, both the Republican and Democratic party organizations have been strong and have competed on even terms to win working-class votes. In these states party candidates tend to compete to offer a more attractive package of policy benefits. In contrast, until the late 1960s, southern states had one-party electoral systems in which a substantial proportion of economically disadvantaged white voters and most blacks were kept from voting. Southern Democrats had no need to promote popular democracy or policy reform in the South. Conservative state policies therefore resulted from the absence of party competition.[19] This conclusion has been supported by research showing that welfare spending per capita tends to be highest in states where one party tends to attract lower-class voters and the other attracts middle- and upper-class voters. When parties organize class conflict in this way and the party representing lower-income voters wins, increased social spending results.[20]

Organized labor. Most studies of political parties suggest that the main determinant of policy positions taken by respective parties is not the strength of left-wing parties *per se* but the working class that stands behind these parties. In the absence of a trade union movement that can make convincing political demands, social policy remains conservative. John Stephens argues that "the growth of the welfare state is a product of the growing strength of labour in civil society."[21] The stronger and more unified the labor movement, the more attention government devotes to social policy. The key labor union organizations in Sweden (the LO, or *Landsorganisationen*) and to a lesser extent in Britain (the TUC, or Trades Union Congress) represent "labor" as America's AFL-CIO cannot, for the AFL-CIO represents a much smaller share of the nation's workers, exercises comparatively little political discipline over its own members, and is only one group among many competing for influence in the Democratic party.[22]

American unions are not as influential in the U.S. policymaking process as are unions in West European nations (especially the smaller nations, such as the Scandinavian countries). American political scientists tend to view unions as participants in a pluralist system in which interest groups slug out their differences in a constantly changing battle for policy influence. In the pluralists' view, trade unions compete with other interest groups, and they seldom win everything they seek or leave the government arena entirely empty-handed.[23]

European scholars have found pluralism to be mostly irrelevant for describing their policy processes. In Europe, large employer organizations and trade unions (especially in the smaller nations) mediate their differences and are officially represented on all important government regulatory agencies and in parliamentary coalitions.[24] This system has been labelled "corporatism": "In essence, corporatist policy making is a process of continuing negotiation among a small number of highly organized and centralized interest groups (especially workers, employers, and professional associations) and an equally well-organized government apparatus that is obliged by law or informal agreement to consider the advice of these groups."[25] At least one scholar has recast the question of why American policy is conservative into the query: "Why is there no corporatism in America?"[26] To answer one question is to answer the other.

Almost by definition corporatist policy processes amplify the voice of organized labor, and social policies reflect this fact. In a study of social spending in eighteen industrial democracies in the 1960s and the 1970s, Francis Castles concluded that social policy effort is maximized where trade unions and democratic socialist parties are the strongest. In the case of health policy, no other factors seem consequential.[27]

Health policy in the United States seems to confirm this observation. The American Medical Association (AMA) has been a powerful lobbying group throughout this century, and its opposition to national health insurance proposals has been more single-minded than doctors' interest groups across the Atlantic. America's unions have been too weak to offset the influence of the AMA. Lacking a labor movement powerful enough to demand the expansion of public health insurance effectively, no American political party seriously pursued the issue at the national level until the 1940s.[28] Only the Democratic landslide in the 1964 elections produced enough political momentum to overcome opposition by doctors and other interest groups to the health insurance programs adopted in 1965.

Policy differences among the American states can be subjected to a similar analysis. The balance of power among interest groups and political parties may either stifle government activity or encourage it. In some American states, notably in the South, business interest groups have been strongest where competition between political parties is weak. Such an organizational balance suggests a reason for the conservative policies of that region. In contrast, where parties are relatively stronger and unions more influential, as in the industrial states, policies are less conservative.[29]

Proposition #3: Political Culture and Ideology Determine Policy

Why is there no democratic socialist party in the United States, and why are trade unions so weak? What caused the organization of conflict in the United States to deviate from other nations after the turn of the century, when trade unions and socialist parties in those nations emerged as powerful political forces? An influential group of policy scholars argue that this is the essential question left unanswered by studies that focus on parties and interest groups. The answer to this question, they maintain, is that American cultural values have been antagonistic to collective endeavors promoted by unions and centralized government. Anthony King has put the case most simply: government "plays a more limited role in America than elsewhere because Americans, more than other people, want it to play a more limited role."[30]

It often has been asserted that Americans resist calling on government to solve social problems because they are especially hostile to collectivism and government action and exceptionally attached to self-reliance, individualism, voluntarism, and localism.[31] It is thought that American business leaders have likewise been more hostile to government regulation than their European counterparts.[32] American labor unions and their leaders (notably Samuel Gompers, president of the American Federation of Labor) allegedly differed from union leaders in other countries in their lack of class consciousness,[33] their commitments to "voluntarism," and their antipathy to protective labor legislation and social insurance.[34] Analysts who identify socioeconomic factors as crucial determinants of policy find the United States a mystery, and these authors fall back on its classical liberal ideology to account for the American anomaly.[35]

If American cultural values encourage people to measure individual worth by reference to personal wealth, they will resent efforts to tax or redistribute the income and wealth they have acquired.[36] If Americans want government to act as a passive "night watchman" that protects property without interfering with people's private dealings, then excessive government threatens freedom, the work ethic, private property, and free markets, and it follows that "that government is best which governs least." Government should guarantee justice (but not results) with fair legal processes that offer "equality before the law" and guarantee "due process." In such a culture, national defense and police services are legitimate public expenditures, as is public assistance for the "truly needy" (the blind, the elderly, and children in needy families) who cannot compete in the job market. But most other programs lack popular support.[37] Samuel Huntington has observed that the "central agony" of American politics is that "because of the antigovernment character of the American Creed, government that is strong is illegitimate, government that is legitimate is weak."[38]

The conservative bent of American health policy can be explained plausibly by referring to Americans' preference for individual self-reliance and their distrust of "big" government. By labelling public health insurance as a tool of authoritarian governments (Imperial Germany during World War I and then the Soviet Union in the late 1940s), opponents made government-provided medical insurance appear to threaten widely shared cultural values. Indeed, these themes have occupied center stage in the American Medical Association's campaigns against "socialist" medicine.[39]

Differences in cultural values can also be used to explain why American state policies vary. In an influential book, Daniel Elazar identifies three distinct political cultures in the United States, each producing its own definition of the proper responsibilities of government. According to Elazar, the most innovative and active states, such as Wisconsin, Minnesota, and Oregon, share a "moralistic" political culture in which citizens value government initiatives to promote the common good. The least active states, such as Mississippi and South Carolina, are "traditionalistic": citizens believe that government's primary role is to maintain the existing social order. The middle range of states mix these two cultures with an "individualistic" political culture in which government is kept to a minimum, business is encouraged, and politics is "business-like."[40] Elazar drew a connection between these cultural differences and the liberalism or conservatism of social policies adopted by individual states. A later study seemed to confirm this theory. It found state populations' political views to be related to policy differences among the states.[41]

Proposition #4: Government Sets Policy Agendas

Governments can shape policy somewhat independently of economic, political, and cultural forces. They can and have enacted policies that violate widely shared cultural norms. They have often defied well-organized political movements and ignored important constituency groups. Governments manipulate public opinion, and when they are unsuccessful at this, they possess a significant capacity to ignore it. Governments are not the mere prisoners of social pressures, or even of economic conditions. They powerfully shape their environment.

As we have argued in Chapters 1 and 2, social conflict also is shaped and directed by the structure of government. In the American context, until the 1930s political conflicts were almost always channeled into political arenas bounded by individual states. Thus pressures for change seldom percolated into national political institutions. In the states, as in national politics, the separation of executive and legislative powers, the division of the legislature into two mutually dependent houses, and powerful court systems ensured that extraordinarily large majorities would be necessary to sustain new policy innovations.

America's mix of government rules and institutions has profoundly influenced its policy agenda. Economic management has been rendered nearly impossible in the United States because of its ponderous national policymaking process. Policy debates have taken place within a perceived reality of what can be accomplished through the policy structure. For example, American policy experts in the Progressive Era, such as John R. Commons and Louis Brandeis, expressed more optimism than their European counterparts about the corporate capacity for benevolence, and they thought that the regulation of business and social reform could be accomplished within the states. In contrast to West European reformers, they were confident that the United States could and should avoid creating a centralized welfare state.[42]

Policy differences among the American states was a logical result. Commons perfected many of his reform proposals in Wisconsin state government, and his students carried his ideas to Minnesota, New York, and other northern states. The American Association for Labor Legislation's "model" health insurance statute attracted reformers in several states, and they proved to be its main champions in the California and New York campaigns.

Thus governmental rules and institutions are not neutral. They powerfully shape or even dictate the political strategies of politicians and political organizations (including the parties). They influence how political demands are put forth and whether these demands are easily blocked or facilitated. This is the case even if government is viewed as an "umpire" among contending interests. But government cannot act simply as an umpire, because the demands that emanate from the political environment have to be given concrete expression by policymakers. Public officials necessarily translate demands into public policy proposals. In his study of the evolution of the Swedish and British welfare states, for example, Hugh Heclo emphasized that government administrators consistently proposed most program alternatives and nearly all program details because they "provided the most constant analysis and review underlying most courses of action."[43] Likewise, in the United States in the 1930s, 1940s, and 1960s, plans for national health legislation emanated primarily from congressional committees, the Social Security Administration, and the Department of Health, Education, and Welfare—and not from independent interest groups or, more vaguely, from the political "culture."

Does "Everything" Cause Policy?

It is beyond dispute that public policies are produced from a multitude of forces. Variations in wealth, political party competition, the balance of power among interest groups, cultural values, the rules of conflict and institutional arrangements—all exert some influence. After writing a book-length account of the enactment of a single U.S. law, one scholar concluded that "(l)egislative policy-making appears to be the result of a confluence of factors streaming from an almost endless number of tributaries."[44] The authors of another book comparing public policies said that debating about the relative merits of any one explanation "is like arguing about which is the most important leg of a three-legged stool." They concluded that "(e)ach explanation in isolation seems inadequate for coping with the complex mesh of forces creating modern social policies."[45]

But it is less than intellectually satisfying to assert that "everything causes policy," and we think there is a way to avoid falling into this trap. Our position on the four schools of thought in policy studies is as follows. First, socioeconomic circumstances, including especially *the level of wealth and economic development, provide a general constraint* within which political battles over policy take place. But nations that are similar in wealth and economic development diverge significantly in both policy effort and the way that policies are implemented. Like most policy analysts, we are interested in exploring these differences.

Second, the organization of political parties and the strength of contending interest groups certainly influence policy outcomes. Our understanding of how parties and interest groups influence policy is that *the political structure provides the access points and organizing features of these organizations*. In the United States, the division of powers among governmental institutions and the federal system structured the development of political parties, trade unions, and other organizations during the transition from an agricultural to an industrial society. Parties and interest groups in the United States reflected this structure: they are decentralized, in the case of the parties, or their strategies reflect the opportunities for institutional access or pressure afforded by the political structure, in the case of the interest groups.

The influence of culture can be understood in this way as well. Cultural values do not express themselves in policy processes. They are expressed by people and organizations with particular political interests.

The connection between an alleged cultural value, such as individualism, and a particular governmental policy, is not usually self-evident— there are various, even contradictory, policies that may be said to represent individualism. Public health care policy, for example, may be (and has been) opposed on the ground that it is socialistic or collectivist; the assertion by opponents is that our society's values contradict such government intervention. But advocates of a national health care system appeal to cultural values as well, often asserting that good health is basic to an individual's ability to realize his or her full potential. It follows that the ideal of equal opportunity requires public intervention. This same observation could be made about nearly every conflict over social policy.

In the United States, advocates of generous social policies that would be administered in a consistent, equitable fashion are inherently disadvantaged by the structure of the policymaking system. Thus, the political structure acts as a filter that is more favorable to cultural values extolling individualism, equal opportunity, and the sanctity of private property in the form of fewer public efforts and fragmented, decentralized policies, than to the expression of these same values in policies that would have the national government actively intervene to ensure that individuals have the personal resources (e.g., education, income, health) necessary to compete on relatively equal terms for success in the society and economy.

As Gary Klass observes, "if American social policy could be described as merely a manifestation of limited government, then a belief in limited government might best account for it." But Klass points out that social policy cannot accurately be described as simply a reflection of limited government. Instead, American programs are fragmented geographically (Medicaid) and by constituency (Medicare for retirees, Medicaid for the poor), so that the overall effect, even when substantial public funds are involved, is one of comparatively limited effort with wide variations within that pattern.[46] Americans seem highly supportive of the most nationalized and expensive programs, such as Social Security and Medicare. It may be that Americans would not resist collective policy solutions so much if most programs were not so decentralized and narrowly focused.

HOW POLICYMAKING STRUCTURE HAS AFFECTED POLICY DEMANDS

The states and the separation of powers are so much a part of everyday political life in the United States that citizens rarely think that there might be alternatives to our policymaking system. Neither do they understand its cumulative effects on their values, the way they organize

their conflicts, or even the way the United States has developed economically. Without the benefit of historical or institutional perspective, one
can easily believe that demands originating from the social and political
environment determine the day-to-day activities of government institutions. Certainly these affect public policy, but each in turn has been
shaped by the way that public decisionmaking is organized.

Federalism, for example, is associated with policy restraint wherever
it exists. Castles, for example, found that federalism has been more
strongly related than the strength of trade unions to differences in public
health expenditures.[47] According to a Canadian federalism scholar,
"[o]ne of the firmest conclusions to emerge from cross-national studies
of expenditure levels is that government expenditure is positively
associated with the degree of centralization in government."[48]

American federalism exerts a much more powerful influence on policy
than is usually recognized, because many of its effects are indirect and
accumulate over many generations of social change and conflict. Before
the United States matured into an urban industrial nation, before conflict in America assumed its modern form of thousands of pressure
groups and two fragmented parties, and before Americans adapted
individualistic beliefs to a manufacturing economy, state governments
held nearly exclusive jurisdiction over social policy. States retained
functional monopoly over domestic policy for a century and a half,
during which cities expanded, regional economies transformed, party
coalitions aligned and then realigned, and organized interest groups
multiplied. All through this period, political parties and interest groups
were forced to adapt to, and thus perpetuate and institutionalize, a
fragmented governmental system.

The state-based policymaking structure largely determined the way
conflicts about industrialization developed in post-Civil War America.
Federalism discouraged centralized national organizations and encouraged parties and interest groups to evolve as loose confederations of
state organizations. Though political parties and interest groups evolved
in some states that were as industrially advanced as the nations of
northern Europe, others developed in the agricultural economies of the
South and West that chiefly exported crops and raw materials to more
developed states and foreign nations. Thus, national political parties
became broad coalitions that encompassed groups of diverse economic
interests and ideological leanings. National interest groups also took on
this character. Trade unions, for example, did not emerge as genuinely
national organizations. Instead they were confederations of smaller
groups that sought special state benefits or political influence.

The Development of Political Parties in the Period of State Activism

States used their control of election laws to maintain the status quo
and weaken "third" (especially radical) parties that challenged domi-

nance by local governing coalitions. Such laws could not themselves eliminate voting for the Populist and Socialist parties between 1892 and 1912, but the laws made it difficult for third parties to establish a stable electoral base. "Winner-take-all" rules, the separation of executive and legislative powers, and malapportioned legislative districts (discussed in Chapter 9) obstructed the success of the left-wing parties that attracted city voters. Their success was limited to a very few cities, including notably Milwaukee, where a Socialist (Frank Zeidler) served as mayor as late as 1960. In contrast, such candidates had little success in statewide elections. Malapportionment in state legislatures through the 1950s grossly underrepresented urban interests in the state legislatures, and this undermined legislative support for laws to mitigate social problems located disproportionately in the cities.[49]

Although a Socialist party overcame the obstacles of state election laws to capture 6 percent of the national vote in the 1912 presidential election, its presidential candidate, Eugene Debs, won no electoral college votes (or policy influence) in exchange for the Socialists' strength. It is fascinating to note that in England at about the same time the Labour party received, in four consecutive elections, less than 6 percent of the total vote twice, and it received a maximum of 7 percent in 1908 (Table 3.2). But as a result of its electoral alliance with the Liberal party in 1903, the Labour party elected several representatives to Parliament in the 1906 national elections. Because the party then had a voice in legislative decisions, it had a base on which to build strength for future elections as well as to influence the executive, a crucial fact of politics that is denied to minor parties in the United States.

In any event, the organizational weakness and ideological catholicism of American parties made it easier for reform-minded American politicians to win office through them than through a third party. Thus progressive politicians such as Robert LaFollette, Hiram Johnson, David Walsh, Alfred Smith, and Robert Wagner could more easily run as Republicans or Democrats than mount an assault on the two-party

Table 3.2. *Comparison of British Labour party and American Socialist party support in national elections, 1906–1912*

	Percentage of Popular Vote in Election of:				
	1906	1908	1910	1910	1912
U.K. Labour party	4.8		7.0	6.4	
U.S. Socialist party		2.8			6.0

Source: Congressional Quarterly's Guide to U.S. Elections, 2d ed. (Washington, DC: Congressional Quarterly, 1985), 347–8; Peter Flora, *State, Economy, and Society in Western Europe 1815–1975* (Frankfurt: Campus Verlag, 1983), 151.

system, as the Populists proved in 1892 and LaFollette confirmed in his ill-fated run for the presidency as a third-party candidate in 1924. Because it was so difficult to organize third parties that would be sufficiently strong in more than one or two states, labor unions devoted their energies to trying to gain influence in one of the two major parties, rather than attempting the impossible task of building an independent labor party.

For a labor party to result in actual representation in Congress, or even the state legislatures, it would have to, in effect, replace one of the two leading parties in many different locations. Winning just a little less than the largest number of voters in several congressional districts or states might show genuine electoral support, but no influence in government would be forthcoming, for no labor candidates would be elected. Unions could gain some concessions from the two parties by eschewing a labor party strategy and exchanging votes for specific concessions. But because the two parties were so decentralized, labor influence was tailored to specific candidates within states or congressional districts, and their demands were limited to issues that did not fundamentally conflict with other groups to which the candidates were beholden.[50]

The contrast with Britain illuminates the effect of structure on parties. British unions only reluctantly came around to the idea of a separate party for labor. At the turn of the century many of the most powerful unions in the British Trades Union Congress (TUC), including the miners and the cotton mill workers, shared the views of their American counterparts that they should lobby the legislature from the outside for special legislation of benefit to their members. Only about 56 percent of the TUC members voting in 1899 supported a resolution to send more unionists directly to Parliament, and after the resolution passed most TUC unions were apathetic about implementing it. After the Taff Vale rule adopted by the House of Lords in 1903 made unions liable for the costs of strikes, even the more conservative skilled unions began to come around to the idea of direct political action in order to enact specific legislation to protect unions.[51] These unionists supported the idea of a "labour party" for the same reasons American unionists supported specific candidates in state elections—to enact laws of special benefit. In Britain this special legislation could not be won without influence in the *national* legislature, and there the logic of special benefits favored a national party. In the United States, crafts unions had access to urban political machines and to parties in a few industrial states that were willing to make some concessions in exchange for union members' votes.

Stretched across the federal framework, political parties developed as confederations of state parties, "founded on the cleavages peculiar to each state."[52] State parties always have differed enormously. Texas

Democrats, for example, have long tended to be more conservative than Connecticut Republicans. National parties have exercised virtually no control over candidate selection by state party organizations, and until very recently they provided few essential campaign resources even to candidates for seats in the U.S. Senate or House of Representatives. Owing little to their national party leaders, local and state candidates frequently ignored or even opposed national party positions. Historically, for example, southern Democrats resisted the expansion of social benefits and civil rights without fear of excommunication from their party, and without running the danger of losing influence in state legislatures and seniority in the U.S. Congress, because national political leaders were in no position to discipline "renegade" party members. When viewed as a set of policymaking rules that have affected party development, federalism is an essential prerequisite for America's disorganized and ideologically incoherent parties.[53]

While reformers in northern states that were as industrialized as parts of Europe began to press for expanded government benefits and legal protections, "reformers" in depressed, rural southern states defended laws that isolated blacks from white society. In the 1890s, the southern states enacted laws that excluded blacks and some poor whites from electoral participation, thus eliminating a large block of potential votes for candidates who favored redistributive social policy. The states became laboratories for reform of the electoral system, each developing innovative ways to restrict voting. The most successful innovations—the "white primary," the literacy requirement, and the poll tax—were adopted by most of the southern states. Such laws reduced turnout, especially among those likely to vote against the white power structure represented by the Democratic party. Table 3.3 (on page 76) shows how dramatically such restrictions cut the protest vote in the South. Turnout had been similar in the South and outside the South in 1876, but by 1904 turnout in the South fell to less than half the turnout in the northern states. While the Republican party became dominant outside the South in the wake of the 1896 election, southern Democrats received about the same proportion of the vote in 1904 as they had in 1876. The percentage of voters casting ballots against Democratic candidates in the South fell by a third in the 1890s and again by a third between 1900 and 1904. With the exception of a few scattered areas, there were no longer serious opponents to Democratic candidates anywhere in the South by the 1910s.[54]

The Development of Interest Groups in the Period of State Activism

The American policymaking structure rewarded important American interest groups that became confederations of state organizations. Self-employed professionals and craftsmen secured state licensing laws that

Table 3.3. *Proportion of men voting for each party and turnout in the South and non-South in selected presidential elections, 1872–1904*

Election	Democrat (%)	Republican (%)	Other (%)	Turnout (%)
South				
1876	38.7	26.7	0	64.9
1884	37.2	25.7	0.3	62.8
1892	33.9	14.6	9.7	58.2
1896	33.3	19.8	3.0	56.2
1900	26.5	15.4	1.2	43.1
1904	19.0	8.3	1.4	28.6
Non-South				
1876	31.9	33.0	0.8	65.7
1884	33.1	35.8	2.4	71.2
1892	30.6	32.9	6.8	70.4
1896	32.7	40.8	2.0	75.4
1900	31.0	39.0	2.0	72.1
1904	22.4	38.7	4.0	65.1

Source: J. Morgan Kousser, *The Shaping of Southern Politics: Suffrage Restriction and the Establishment of the One-Party South, 1880–1910* (New Haven, CT: Yale University Press, 1974), 12.

erected barriers to entry into their occupations (reducing competition) and that protected their professional autonomy. Each American state began to regulate attorneys, accountants, insurance agents, real estate agents, and physicians and surgeons after the Civil War, and each of these professions developed interest groups influential in the states. Potentially mobile interests, notably banking, also won a large measure of autonomy under the auspices of state legislation. Effective national groups were invariably confederations built on the strength of state units.

Interest groups emerged as federations of state associations in large part because control of state policy machinery provided the tangible benefits that bound their members together. Though Massachusetts became as industrialized as Britain, Mississippi remained as backward as many "underdeveloped" countries. Interest groups had little reason to coalesce into national groups because they could win the policy battles of immediate importance to them at the state level. Even relatively focused interest groups, such as the U.S. Farm Bureau Federation and the American Medical Association, have found it difficult to remain cohesive because of dissent among state affiliates.[55] Thus the federal structure stood as the major obstacle to the development of corporatism in the United States.[56]

Trade unions followed the same path. The most successful workers' organizations were the craft unions, more individualistic and skilled than their mass-industry counterparts. Craft unions sought government protection, but in the form of occupational licensing rather than social legislation. They built "workmen's cartels" through state laws licensing their trades and restricting competition.[57] The federal courts permitted little more in the early twentieth century. Craft unions continue to dominate the AFL-CIO today, with policy aspirations that remain more conservative than those of the Swedish *Landsorganisationen* or the British Trades Union Congress.

AN EXAMPLE: THE PROGRESSIVE-ERA CAMPAIGNS FOR HEALTH INSURANCE

The effect of the policymaking structure in channeling political demands is illustrated by the campaigns for health insurance initiated during the Progressive Era. There is no evidence that American health insurance proponents lacked the energy, enthusiasm, or vision of European reformers. Reformers were optimistic about state action on health insurance. In a poll of economists and welfare and corrections experts conducted in the mid-1910s, three out of four respondents endorsed compulsory public social insurance. Ten states established and funded social insurance commissions to examine the issue, and the American Association for Labor Legislation (AALL)'s "model" bill health insurance bill was introduced in fifteen legislatures. Twenty-nine state labor federations endorsed public health insurance despite the opposition of the leadership of the American Federation of Labor.[58]

The failure to enact health insurance in the years before 1920 illustrates the powerful, cumulative, and indirect impediments placed in the way of extended public protections for citizens. The fragmented policymaking structure complicated the reformers' drive for national health insurance in several ways. First, no prominent reformer or group tried to work through the federal government, because few people thought that the courts' interpretation of the Constitution would permit national social insurance. The federal government seemed legally capable of doing no more than collecting statistics, convening meetings of state public health officers, and offering some protections to its own employees (occupational diseases were covered under the federal workers' compensation plan, enacted in 1916).[59]

Second, the isolation of the issue in the states ensured that their responses would diverge and that interstate economic competition would affect state decisions. Four dozen states would have had to enact health insurance legislation before workers all across the nation would be able to benefit from it. Even during the high tide of support for public health insurance in 1917, serious consideration of the proposal was limited to the most industrialized states. In southern states, compulsory health insurance immediately ran into opposition from elites opposed to extending social welfare benefits to blacks. Proponents for the measure exhausted themselves travelling from state to state to promote the plan. The leading AALL speaker, Dr. Isaac Rubinow, delivered a hundred lectures in six states in 1916 alone.[60]

Furthermore, the separation of powers and constitutional limits on state policymaking capacity guaranteed that enacting such a bill anywhere would require extraordinary effort and a high level of public support for a long period. California's generally supportive legislature appointed a commission to study various social insurance measures in 1913, and more funding was provided for another commission in 1915. Though the new commission reported favorably on health insurance in January 1917, it did not recommend legislation because it believed that such a program would be found unconstitutional by the state's courts. Instead, the commission recommended an amendment to the state's constitution that would allow California to enact a health insurance bill. This amendment could not come up for a referendum vote until November 1918, and by that time the war with Germany had altered public attitudes: opponents painted social insurance as a "German" idea. In a parliamentary system acting with greater dispatch, California might have acted positively before the United States entered the war in 1917 or even before war broke out in August 1914.

Third, the isolation of the model legislation in a few state legislatures presented opponents with an important political resource: they could mobilize their resources from all across the nation and focus them on blocking legislative action in a few key states. The medical profession, insurance companies, businesses, and even Christian Scientists formed national coalitions aimed at defeating the insurance bills in New York and California. Prudential Life Insurance Company churned out pamphlets flailing the notion of health benefits for workers, while doctors opposed to the idea travelled a circuit of state capitals to mobilize opposition.

Business had little reason to support health insurance proposals, unlike workers' compensation. Before the advent of workers' compensation laws, individual workers turned to the state courts for financial relief after suffering industrial injuries. Since some state courts sometimes provided high awards to individual workers, *uniform* compensation laws attracted not only reformers but also business leaders interested in a more predictable and less risky compensation system. No similar logic motivated them to move into a new area such as health insurance, where employees could establish no grounds for a suit.[61] Where states imposed greater costs than benefits, business could justify uniform state laws or even national regulation. Otherwise, however, business was not motivated to support reform, but instead opposed any state legislation.

Fourth, doctors were able to win benefits for themselves within the states that made it unnecessary for them to seek public health insurance to bolster their incomes. Medical doctors opposed health insurance (in spite of its endorsement by the American Medical Association in 1916) because through state liability and licensing laws they had already won any benefits that health insurance might offer. The AMA's strength in 1916 derived not from national leaders but from the grassroots. Local and state medical society membership provided doctors with a material benefit by pooling legal liability for malpractice. A member of the medical society could secure far lower rates for malpractice insurance by joining the AMA. Licensing provided a second material benefit, because, though it was nominally controlled by the state government, it was actually delegated to panels of medical society members. Through state licensing requirements, the doctors were able to restrict entry into the medical profession and drive up their incomes. The period from 1916 to 1920, during which the medical profession's attitude on public health insurance evolved from apathy to adamant opposition, coincided with an especially dramatic decline in the number of practicing physicians. The number of doctors who needed health insurance to provide them a steady income also dropped. The doctors' opposition to compulsory health insurance grew intense just as the bill appeared on state legislative agendas. The opposition in New York bubbled up from county medical societies outside of New York City. The national AMA House of Delegates did not officially damn health insurance until after the fate of the proposal in New York was sealed.[62]

Unlike their British counterparts, American doctors did not need insurance to protect their professional independence and their incomes. Had health insurance offered a higher, guaranteed income, the medical profession might never have organized to oppose it. The British Medical Association called a late strike against the law in Britain, but low-paid general practitioners ignored the organization because they could increase their income by 50 percent through the government plan. What the British doctors won through national health insurance, the American doctors had already won through state law.[63]

The Legacy for Health Care Policy

The legacy of the early battles for health care insurance endures. American governments provide citizens with less security against the expenses of illness than is the case in other capitalist democracies, such as Britain, West Germany, and Sweden. In these nations virtually every citizen has access to publicly funded health care, but only a minority of

Table 3.4. *Public health expenditures, 1984, and policy coverage, 1983, selected countries*

	Health Expenditure as a Percentage (%) of GDP in 1984		Percentage (%) of Population Covered by a Public Scheme in 1983 for:	
	Total, Private and Public	Public Only	Hospital Care	Ambulatory Care[a]
Australia	7.8	6.6	100	84
Canada	8.4	6.2	100	100
France	9.1	6.5	100	99
Italy	7.2	6.1	100	100
Japan	6.6	4.8	100	100
Netherlands	8.6	6.8	88	79
Sweden	9.4	8.6	100	100
United Kingdom	5.9	5.3	100	100
United States	10.7	4.4	40	25
West Germany	8.1	6.4	95	92

[a]Physicians' visits, outpatient care, etc.; data for Australia are from 1982.

Source: Organization for Economic Cooperation and Development, *Financing and Delivering Health Care* (Paris: OECD, 1987) 11, and *Measuring Health Care, 1960–1983: Expenditure, Costs, Performance* (Paris: OECD, 1985), 68–9.

Americans are covered by public health care insurance (Table 3.2). Although the national government first enacted health insurance in 1965 (Table 3.1), the Medicare and Medicaid programs enacted in that year covered only 19 percent of the population as late as 1985. Most Americans' security against illness depends on a breadwinner's job security. Thirty-seven million Americans, or 15 percent of the population, had no health insurance in 1987, a significant increase over 1980 expressed in absolute numbers (29.5 million) and percentage (13.5%).[64]

Another striking comparison, revealed in Table 3.4, is that universal access is guaranteed in other nations at individual costs comparable to or less than those in the United States. The United States spends a higher proportion of its national wealth on health care, possibly because American governments pay a smaller share of the cost than governments abroad. Public and private health care together cost about as much as in Sweden and much more than in Britain (where some services are rationed and difficult to obtain).[65]

Moreover, medical coverage within the United States varies enormously from state to state. One reason is that Medicaid permits state governments to decide who is eligible for benefits, what benefits will be provided, and maximum payments levels (Table 3.5). Generally the pattern is that "poor households in the rich industrial states received . . .

Table 3.5. *Variations among selected state Medicaid programs, 1986*

| | Expenditures per Recipient (1985) ($) | Coverage Extended to: | | Limits on: | |
		Medically Needy	AFDC Families with an Unemployed Parent	Inpatient Hospital Days	Physician Office Visits
Five high-benefit states					
New York	3.384	Yes	Yes	No	No
North Dakota	3,155	Yes	No	No	No
New Hampshire	3,104	Yes	No	No	Yes
Minnesota	2,804	Yes	Yes	No	No
South Dakota	2,776	No	No	No	No
Connecticut	2,741	Yes	No	No	No
Seven low-benefit states					
Michigan	1,339	Yes	No	No	No
Kentucky	1,323	Yes	Yes	Yes	No
South Carolina	1,300	Yes	No	No	Yes
California	1,196	Yes	No	No	No
Alabama	1,188	No	No	Yes	Yes
Mississippi	915	No	No	Yes	Yes
West Virginia	821	Yes	No	Yes	No
U.S. average	1.721	35/50	9/50	10/50	11/50

Source: U.S. General Accounting Office, *Medicaid: Interstate Variations in Benefits and Expenditures,* Report HRD-87-67BR (Washington, DC: GPO, 1987), 17, 25, 27.

higher health benefits than poor households in poor states."[66] Prodded by the Reagan administration, Congress in 1981 approved changes in Medicaid that increased the states' power to control costs by tightening eligibility, benefits, and payments. Although the 1982-1983 recession increased the number of poor families across the country, changes in state guidelines induced a fall in the number of people qualifying for Medicaid because of "a substantial cut in services to the poor."[67]

Although some states provide much more generous medical coverage than others, only one state has created a universal medical insurance plan similar to the plans available in capitalist democracies elsewhere. By 1986 eleven states had established programs designed to provide insurance for workers to protect against extraordinarily expensive "catastrophic" health problems.[68] In 1988 Massachusetts, historically one of the most progressive states, adopted a plan to make coverage universal, in effect, by extending coverage to people not covered by other plans. In that year about eleven percent of the state's residents had no health insurance, although the state previously had extended Medicaid coverage to the medically needy and to persons eligible for but not receiving federally assisted income assistance (in some other states more than one-third of all citizens have no insurance).

Remarkable conditions converged briefly to make a consensus on the plan possible: some major employer groups supported the plan, the state unemployment rate was half the national average, the state's budget was in surplus and Governor Michael Dukakis, a candidate for the Democratic presidential nomination, gambled that the plan would become a positive campaign issue. The consensus proved to be extremely fragile, however. Within two months, opposition by the Massachusetts Hospital Association, Associated Industries of Massachusetts, and state legislators had erased early optimism about the bill's chances. The Massachusetts House rejected the proposal and instructed a legislative committee to overhaul it drastically. Nevertheless, in April 1988, the Massachusetts legislature passed a bill providing health insurance to all the state's citizens, just in time for it to become a central component in Dukakis's campaign for the Democratic presidential nomination. In signing the bill, Dukakis said, "As an American, I don't want my country to stand alone with South Africa as the only industrialized nations in the world that do not provide basic health security for their citizens."[69]

The Massachusetts legislation stood in stark contrast to actions by most other states. At the same time, the Congress seriously considered a proposal to require employers to provide health benefits to their employees. This attracted support from such liberals as Senator Edward Kennedy because it would have provided benefits at minimal federal cost. Conservatives strongly objected to the plan on grounds that such a mandate on its face would invade employer prerogatives and reduce employment. But not all business leaders agreed. As the president of American Airlines emphasized,

> I support this legislative approach because I think it is the most efficient and least intrusive way to get a major part of the job done . . . as the world is today, companies like ours pay for health coverage twice—once for our own employees, and then again, by way of taxes and inflated health insurance premiums, for the employees of other companies that do not provide benefits to their own people. Some of those companies, I am sad to say, are our competitors.[70]

Despite such an endorsement, it was certain that without federal incentives a wave of health care coverage was not poised to break over the states.

AMERICAN FEDERALISM IN COMPARATIVE PERSPECTIVE

If the fragmented nature of policymaking affected American policy so profoundly, why is social policy in other federal political systems less limited and more uniform? The answer is that the incoherence of American policymaking is unusually pronounced in comparison with policymaking in Canada, Australia, and West Germany.

First, federalism is constitutionally older and more complex in the United States than elsewhere. Canada's provinces were brought into a national dominion in 1867, and Australia's colonies were united in a national commonwealth in 1901. West Germany's present constitution and its federal system dates only from 1949 (though independent German principalities predated the unification of Germany under Prussian rule in 1870-1871). Federalism in the United States has had a much longer, constant, and more profound effect on political pressures and policy development than in comparable nations.[71] Moreover, the separation of powers at the national and state levels makes coordinated policy infinitely more difficult to achieve in the United States. Canada's national and provincial governments are organized as parliamentary systems. In effect, eleven prime ministers in Canada or seven in Australia can negotiate policy differences. Fifty American governors and the U.S. president do not have a similar authority.[72]

Second, other federal democracies have more willingly established *national* policy standards than has the United States. In these nations, national standards have been more easily applied because there are fewer regional units. There are fifty American states of greatly varying size and fiscal capacity, but there are only ten Canadian provinces, seven Australian states, and eleven West German *Laender*.

The rights and protections offered to organized labor provide an important example of the effect of national standards on politics and economics. As we observed in the Chapter 2, courts in the United States regulated unions until 1935, when the Wagner Act finally provided a national charter protecting the rights of unions. Federal court decisions through the Progressive Era made it a "reasonable fear" that all labor organizations might be defined by the courts as organizations that illegally restricted commerce.[73] Other federal democracies established national protections for organized labor much earlier. Canada's protection was embodied in its 1872 Trade Union Act, which made it impossible to regard unions as organizations in restraint of trade. Australia's protections evolved less formally in national arbitration decisions dating to 1904. Germany proscribed unions before the turn of the century but repealed its Anti-Socialist law in 1890, after which the Social Democratic

Party won increasing shares of votes and the trade unions began to flourish.[74]

Today, American states continue to control many of the terms of union organization, and southern states in particular make unionization difficult through right-to-work laws. In contrast, the western Canadian provinces are very supportive of unions, and there is much less variation in Canadian labor law than in American law. As a result, there is less variation in unionization across Canada. The most unionized Canadian province (Newfoundland, 42.6 percent in 1980) has twice the membership rate of the least unionized province (Alberta, 23.1 percent), but the most unionized American state (New York, 38.8 percent) has five times the membership rate of the least unionized state (South Carolina, 7.8 percent).[75] The obstacles to organizing labor in the United States go far in explaining why labor in Canada, Australia, and West Germany is more unionized than the American labor force[76] and why each of these nations has a socialist party and the United States does not.

Third, the United States does far less to redistribute national wealth among regions than do other federated democracies. These nations redistribute fiscal resources to poorer regions from wealthier regions. Equalizing financial resources, of course, has the effect of reducing disparities in taxes and public services. Policymakers who have pursued this goal in the United States have not had very much success because the national government, particularly Congress, resists such redistribution. The national government takes little responsibility for ensuring that states such as Mississippi have the fiscal capacity to "keep up" with New York, California, or other states that have higher individual income levels. While some American programs calculate grants to the states based on differences in state financial capacity, the complex formulas for distributing most grants include other criteria, such as population, that dilute the equalization of resources. No American program "distributes aid with the exclusive purpose of lessening fiscal disparities . . . unlike [Australia, Canada, and West Germany] the U.S. has no targeted program for equalization aid under which the richer states do not receive any financial assistance."[77]

Canadian federalism most closely resembles American federalism. Tensions among the Canadian provinces often have run high. Residents of Quebec, a French-speaking province, have seriously considered leaving the Canadian union and creating their own nation. Canadian trade unions (while including a large share of the workforce) are, by many accounts, even weaker than those in America. The socialist New Democratic party seldom receives more than 20 percent of Canadians' votes in national elections. Still, Canada's less fragmented national government and its policy of equalizing provincial resources makes it a welfare state that is conservative by international standards but advanced if compared with the United States.[78] In 1988 Massachusetts became the first American state to provide universal health insurance. The Canadian province of Saskatchewan began to implement the first universal hospital insurance program in North America in January 1947.[79]

AMERICA'S EXCEPTIONALISM

The world's industrial democracies differ among themselves in the social policies they offer, and these differences bear significant consequences for citizens in each nation. American government, especially in light of the nation's wealth, has been slower to offer social benefits, more austere in the benefits it offers, less willing to guarantee benefits for its poorest citizens, and extremely resistant to reducing income disparities.

Its policymaking structure explains much of the relative conservatism of America's social policy. Its incoherence has restrained the activism of government at every level. It has drained the energy and limited the vision of social reformers. It has fragmented political parties, dictated the political strategies of the organized interests, and encouraged uneven economic development. As much as it has reflected cultural values it has shaped those values by equating competitive individualism and limited government with business autonomy and fragmented public authority.

These cumulative policy effects surface in periods of intense pressure for social reform. The clamor for public health insurance in the Progressive Era offered one illustration of this effect. As we show in the next chapter, the New Deal offered another example on a much larger scale.

NOTES

1. Anthony King, "Ideas, Institutions, and the Policies of Governments: A Comparative Analysis," *British Journal of Political Science* 3:3–4 (June and October 1973), 291–313, 409–23; Kenneth M. Dolbeare, *American Public Policy: A Citizen's Guide* (New York: McGraw-Hill, 1982).
2. See Table 5.1. Cf. Arnold J. Heidenheimer, Hugh Heclo, and Carolyn Teich Adams, *Comparative Public Policy*, 2d ed. (New York: St. Martin's Press, 1983).
3. Organization for Economic Cooperation and Development, "OECD in Figures," Supplement to *OECD Observer* 152 (June/July 1988), 22–3.
4. Charles F. Andrain, *Politics and Economic Policy in Western Democracies*, (North Sicuate, MA: Duxbury, 1979), 23.
5. Susan B. Hansen, "Extraction: The Politics of State Taxation," in Virginia Gray, Herbert Jacob, and Kenneth N. Vines, eds., *Politics in the American States*, 4th ed. (Boston: Little, Brown, 1983), 426–7; "The Ups and Downs of Taxes Around the

States," *National Journal* (6 April 1985), 767; Council of State Governments, *1988–89 Book of the States* (Lexington, KY: Council of State Governments, 1987), 268–9; U.S. Bureau of the Census, *State Government Tax Collections in 1987* (Washington, DC: GPO, 1988), 35.

6. These states are not extreme opposites in terms of geographic size. New York's population is much more urbanized (85 percent) than that of Arkansas (52 percent), but Wisconsin (64 percent) and Missouri (68 percent) are comparable. This table excludes the two highest spending states, Alaska and Wyoming, which can spread enormous revenues from energy resources across populations of about half a million each. U.S. Bureau of the Census, *Statistical Abstract of the United States 1988* (Washington, DC: GPO, 1988),18–19.

7. See Table 7.5; Council of State Governments, *1988-89 Book of the States*, 244–5, 456.

8. Sar A. Levitan and Clifford M. Johnson, *Beyond the Safety Net: Reviving the Promise of Opportunity in America* (Cambridge, MA: Ballinger, 1984), 82.

9. For one effort, see Robert Savage, *The Literature of Systematic Quantitative Comparison in American State Politics* (Philadelphia: Center for the Study of Federalism, 1980). Cf. Jack Treadway, *Public Policymaking in the American States* (New York: Praeger, 1985). Susan B. Hansen, in "Public Policy Analysis: Some Recent Developments and Current Problems," *Policy Studies Journal* 12:1 (September 1983), 14–42, presents an overview of policy studies through the early 1980s.

10. David R. Cameron, "The Expansion of the Public Economy: A Comparative Analysis," *American Political Science Review* 78:4 (December 1978), 1243–61.

11. Harold Wilensky, *The Welfare State and Equality* (Berkeley: University of California Press, 1975), xi–xiii, 47–8.

12. Howard M. Leichter, *A Comparative Approach to Policy Analysis: Health Care in Four Nations* (Cambridge, England: Cambridge University Press, 1979), 95.

13. Thomas R. Dye, *Politics, Economics, and the Public* (Chicago: Rand McNally, 1966), 291.

14. Neil Mitchell, "Ideology or the Iron Laws of Industrialization: The Case of Pension Policy in Britain and the Soviet Union," *Comparative Politics* 15:2 (January 1983), 177–201.

15. Peter Flora and Jens Alber, "Modernization, Democratization, and the Development of Welfare States in Western Europe," in Peter Flora and Arnold J. Heidenheimer, eds., *The Development of Welfare States in Europe and America* (New Brunswick, NJ: Transaction Press, 1981), 63.

16. Anthony Downs, *An Economic Theory of Democracy* (New York: Harper & Row, 1957), 128.

17. James L. Sundquist, *Dynamics of the Party System: Alignment and Realignment of Political Parties in the United States*, rev. ed. (Washington, DC: Brookings, 1983), 107; cf. Stephen Skowronek, *Building a New American State: The Expansion of National Administrative Capacities, 1877–1920* (Cambridge, England: Cambridge University Press, 1982).

18. See, for example, Kay Lawson, *The Comparative Study of Political Parties* (New York: St. Martin's Press, 1976), esp. 179–86.

19. V. O. Key, Jr., *Southern Politics in State and Nation* (New York: Alfred A. Knopf, 1949), 296–311.

20. Edward T. Jennings, Jr., "Competition, Constituencies, and Welfare Policies in American States," *American Political Science Review* 73:2 (June 1979), 414–29.

21. John D. Stephens, *The Transition from Capitalism to Socialism* (Atlantic Highlands, NJ: Humanities Press, 1980), 89.

22. Andrain, *Politics and Economic Policy in Western Democracies*, 44–5.

23. For a pluralist's presentation along these lines, see David B. Truman, *The Governmental Process* (New York: Alfred A. Knopf, 1953). Theodore Lowi presents a critical view in *The End of Liberalism* (New York: Norton, 1979), esp. 42–63.

24. Peter J. Katzenstein, in *Small States in World Markets: Industrial Policy In Europe* (Ithaca, NY: Cornell University Press, 1985), argues that such small nations as Sweden, Austria, Switzerland, and the Netherlands have well-developed corporatist policymaking systems because their vulnerability to international trade forces employers and unions to cooperate.

25. Heidenheimer et al., *Comparative Public Policy*, 2d ed., 162.

26. Robert Salisbury, "Why No Corporatism in America?" in Phillippe Schmitter and Gerhard Lembruch, eds., *Trends Toward Corporatist Intermediation* (Beverly Hills, CA: Sage, 1979), 218–9.

27. Francis Castles, "The Impact of Parties on Public Expenditure," in Francis Castles, ed., *The Impact of Parties: Politics and Policies in Democratic Capitalist States* (Beverly Hills, CA: Sage, 1982), 46.

28. A. H. Birch, *Federalism, Finance, and Social Legislation* (Oxford: Clarendon Press, 1955), 282–3.

29. L. Harmon Zeigler, "Interest Groups in the States," in Gray et al., *Politics in the American States*, 99.

30. King, "Ideas, Institutions, and the Policies of Governments." Cf. Seymour Martin Lipset, "North American Labor Movements: A Comparative Perspective," in Seymour Martin Lipset, ed., *Unions in Transition: Entering the Second Century* (San Francisco: Institute for Contemporary Studies, 1986), 421–52.

31. King, "Ideas, Institutions, and the Policies of Governments." Louis Hartz, *The Liberal Tradition in America: An Interpretation of American Political Thought Since the Revolution* (New York: Harcourt, Brace, 1955).

32. David Vogel, "Why Businessmen Distrust Their State: The Political Consciousness of American Corporate Executives," *British Journal of Political Science* 8:1 (January 1978), 45–78.

33. Seymour Martin Lipset, *The First New Nation: The United States in Historical and Comparative Perspective* (New York: Basic Books, 1963). Cf. Lipset, "North American Labor Movements: A Comparative Perspective."

34. Michael Rogin, "Voluntarism: The Political Functions of an Antipolitical Doctrine, *Industrial and Labor Relations Review* 15:4 (July 1962), 521–35.

35. Wilensky, *The Welfare State and Equality*, 32–3.

36. Robert A. Dahl, *Dilemmas of Pluralist Democracy: Autonomy vs. Control* (New Haven, CT: Yale University Press, 1982), 175–81.

37. Cf. Hartz, *The Liberal Tradition in America*; Dolbeare, *American Public Policy*, 11–4; Norman Furniss and Timothy Tilton, *The Case for the Welfare State*, (Bloomington,: Indiana University Press, 1977), 53–66.

38. Samuel Huntington, *American Politics: The Promise of Disharmony* (Cambridge, MA: Harvard University Press, 1981), 39. Russell L. Hanson challenges the notion that Americans historically have had a consensus on such key notions as "republican government" in *The Democratic Imagination: Conversations with Our Past* (Princeton, NJ: Princeton University Press, 1985).

39. Paul Starr, *The Social Transformation of American Medicine* (New York: Basic Books, 1982).

40. Daniel J. Elazar, *American Federalism: A View from the States* (New York: Harper & Row, 1984), 114–22, 167–69.

41. Gerald C. Wright, Jr., Robert S. Erikson, and John P. McIver, "Public Opinion and Policy Liberalism in the American States," *American Journal of Political Science* 31:4 (November 1987), pp. 980–1001; Robert S. Erikson, John P. McIver, and Gerald C. Wright, Jr., "State Political Culture and Public Opinion," *American Political Science Review* 81:3 (September 1987), 797–814.

42. David Brian Robertson, "Policy Entrepreneurs and Policy Divergence: John R. Commons and William Beveridge," *Social Service Review* 62:3 (September 1988).

43. Hugh Heclo, *Modern Social Politics in Britain and Sweden: From Relief to Income Maintenance* (New Haven, CT: Yale University Press, 1974), 301–4.

44. Stephen K. Bailey, *Congress Makes a Law: The Story Behind the Employment Act of 1946* (New York: Columbia University Press, 1950), 236.

45. Arnold J. Heidenheimer, Hugh Heclo and Carolyn Teich Adams, *Comparative Public Policy* 1st ed. (New York: St. Martin's Press, 1975), 260.

46. Gary M. Klass, "Explaining America and the Welfare State: An Alternative Theory," *British Journal of Political Science* 15:4 (October 1985), 427–50.

47. Castles, "The Impact of Parties on Public Expenditure," 63.

48. Keith G. Banting, *The Welfare State and Canadian Federalism,* (Kingston, Ontario: McGill-Queens University Press, 1982) 63.

49. E. E. Schattschneider, *Party Government* (New York: Rinehart, 1942); Frank M. Coleman, *Politics, Policy and the Constitution* (New York: McGraw-Hill, 1982), 63–76; Maurice Duverger, "Duverger's Law: Forty Years Later," and William H. Riker, "Duverger's Law Revisited," in Bernard Grofman and Arend Lijphart, eds., *Electoral Laws and Their Political Consequences* (New York: Agathon Press, 1986), 69–84, 19–42. For more detail on malapportionment, see Chapter 9.

50. Martin Shefter, "Trade Unions and Political Machines: The Organization and Disorganization of the American Working Class in the Late Nineteenth Century," in Ira Katznelson and Aristide R. Zolberg, eds., *Working-Class Formation: Nineteenth Century Patterns in Western Europe and the United States* (Princeton, NJ: Princeton University Press, 1986), 197–276.

51. John Lovell, "Trade Unions and the Development of Independent Labour Politics 1889–1906," in Ben Pimlott and Chris Cook, *Trade Unions in British Politics* (London, England: Longmans, 1982), 56.

52. V. O. Key, Jr. *American State Politics: An Introduction* (New York: Alfred A. Knopf, 1955), 51.

53. Theodore J. Lowi, "Why Is There No Socialism in the United States? A Federal Analysis," in Robert T. Golembiewski and Aaron Wildavsky, eds., *The Costs of Federalism* (New Brunswick, NJ: Transaction Press, 1984), 37–53.

54. J. Morgan Kousser, *The Shaping of Southern Politics: Suffrage Restriction and the Establishment of the One-Party South, 1880–1910* (New Haven, CT: Yale University Press, 1977), 12-13.

55. Truman, *The Governmental Process,* 111–29. Cf. Grant McConnell, *Private Power and American Democracy* (New York: Alfred A. Knopf, 1966).

56. Salisbury, "Why No Corporatism in America?", 219.

57. Joseph A. Schumpeter, *Capitalism, Socialism, and Democracy* 3d ed. (New York: Harper & Row, 1950), 331–2.

58. This case is examined in more detail in David Brian Robertson, "The Bias of American Federalism: Political Structure and the Development of America's Exceptional Welfare State in the Progressive Era," *Journal of Policy History* 1 (1989).

59. Hace Sorel Tishler, *Self Reliance and Social Security, 1870–1917* (Port Washington, NY: Kennikat Press, 1971), 181; Starr, *The Social Transformation of American Medicine,* 240; Odin W. Anderson, *The Uneasy Equilibrium: Public and Private Financing of Health Services in the United States, 1875–1965* (New Haven, CT: College and University Press, 1968), 84; John R. Commons et al., *History of Labor in the United States* vol. III, (New York: Macmillan, 1935), 597.

60. Tishler, *Self-Reliance and Social Security,* 169, 173.

61. Ibid., 181–3.

62. Starr, *Social Transformation of American Medicine,* 102-16.

63. Ronald Numbers, *Compulsory Health Insurance: The Continuing American Debate* (Westport, CT: Greenwood Press, 1982); Ronald Numbers, *Almost Persuaded: American Physicians and Compulsory Health Insurance, 1912–1920* (Baltimore: John Hopkins University Press, 1978, *passim;* Starr, *Social Transformation of American Medicine,* 252–7.

64. U.S. Congress, House, Select Committee on Aging, *World Health Systems: Lessons for the United States*, Committee Publication 98-430 (Washington, DC: GPO, 1984); U.S. Congress, Senate, Committee on Governmental Affairs, Subcommittee on Intergovernmental Relations, *Access to Health Insurance and Health Care* (Washington, DC: GPO, 1986), 385; U.S. Congress, Senate, Committee on Labor and Human Resources, *Minimum Health Benefits for All Workers Act of 1987* (Washington, DC: GPO, 1987), 2.

65. Henry J. Aaron and William B. Schwartz, *The Painful Prescription: Rationing Hospital Care* (Washington, DC: Brookings, 1984).

66. Malcolm Goggin, "Reagan's Revival: Turning Back the Clock in the Health Care Debate," in Anthony Champagne and Edward J. Harpham eds., *The Attack on the Welfare State* (Prospect Heights, IL: Waveland Press, 1984), 72–3.

67. John L. Palmer and Isabel V. Sawhill, eds., *The Reagan Record* (Cambridge, MA: Ballinger, 1984), 369–71.

68. U.S. Congress, Senate Committee on Labor and Human Resources, *Minimum Benefits for All Workers Act of 1987*, (Washington, DC: GPO, 1988) 179.

69. Matthew L. Wald, "Massachusetts Considers Proposals to Assure Health Insurance for All," *New York Times*, 21 August 1987, 7; "Delay in Massachusetts on Low-Cost Insurance," *New York Times*, 11 October 1987, 29; Robin Toner, "Health Insurance and Political Hoopla," *New York Times*, 22 April 1988, 8.

70. Robert L. Crandall in U.S. Congress, Senate Committee on Labor and Human Resources, *Minimum Benefits for All Workers Act of 1987*, 17.

71. Advisory Commission on Intergovernmental Relations, *Studies in Comparative Federalism: Australia, Canada, the United States, and West Germany* (Washington: DC: ACIR, 1981), 3–24.

72. Christopher Leman, "Patterns of Policy Development: Social Security in the United States and Canada," *Public Policy* 25:2 (1977), 261–91.

73. John R. Commons and John B. Andrews, *Principles of Labor Legislation* (New York: Harper and Brothers, 1916), 96.

74. Advisory Commission Intergovernmental Relations, *Studies in Comparative Federalism*; Birch, *Federalism, Finance, and Social Legislation*, 178; D.W. Rawson, *Unions and Unionists in Australia* (Sydney: George, Allen & Unwin, 1978), 47; Leichter, *A Comparative Approach to Policy Analysis*, 115; Helga Grebing, *The History of the German Labour Movement: A Survey*, English ed., abridged (Warwickshire, England: Berg Publishers, 1985), 60–2, 67–73.

75. Noah M. Meltz, "Labor Movements in Canada and the United States," in Thomas A. Kochan, ed., *Challenges and Choices Facing American Labor* (Cambridge, MA: MIT Press, 1985), pp. 315–34; Joseph B. Rose and Gary N. Chaison, "The State of the Unions: The United States and Canada," *Journal of Labor Research* 6:1 (Winter 1985), 97–112.

76. Advisory Commission on Intergovernmental Relations, *Studies in Comparative Federalism*, 6, 11; Andrain, *Politics and Economic Policy*, 45–9.

77. Advisory Commission on Intergovernmental Relations, *Studies in Comparative Federalism*, 3, 97–8.

78. Ibid., 7–12; Andrain, *Politics and Economic Policy*, 47–8.

79. Malcolm G. Taylor, *Health Insurance and Canadian Public Policy* (Montreal: McGill-Queen's University Press, 1978), 69–103.

Chapter 4

THE FRAGMENTATION OF NATIONAL ACTIVISM: THE NEW DEAL LEGACY

THE END OF PASSIVE GOVERNMENT

The fragmented policymaking system designed in 1787 endured through civil war, financial panics, bloody labor strife, and world war before the Great Depression threatened to overwhelm it. Through the 1920s, state governments designed the rules that affected everyday life, and most of the states governed as if the nation remained the rural, agricultural society it had been a century before. State legislatures mostly ignored the problems of the rapidly growing cities. Most states did little more than promote business and build highways. The national government levied tariffs, and federal courts discouraged labor union growth and continued to guard business against aggressive regulation by state governments. More than citizens in most industrial democracies, Americans in the 1920s seemed tolerant of limited, incoherent, even amateurish government.

The depression swept away the popular acceptance of the national government's incapacity to enact active economic and social policy. It so badly damaged the economy and left so many Americans destitute that private charities, cities, and state governments found themselves swamped by need. Murmurs of riot, revolution, and dictatorship grew louder as government failed to act. These circumstances set the stage for unprecedented federal action, and Franklin Roosevelt vowed to energize the national government when he took the presidential oath in March 1933.

In this chapter we make three points about Roosevelt's response. First, his social and economic policies, collectively labelled the New Deal, permanently changed the national government from a passive

90

protector of property rights and capitalism to the senior partner, in cooperation with business and powerful interest groups, in maintaining the nation's economic health. Against the background of the constitutional settlement of 1787 that granted restricted power to the national government, the new constitutional settlement of the 1930s gave Washington a central role in promoting economic stability. The New Deal also placed public policy issues—education, housing, employment, and destitution—firmly on the national government's agenda. Many of the New Deal's policies, such as Social Security, laid the foundations for policy departures of the 1960s, 1970s, and 1980s.

Second, by reinforcing and institutionalizing the policymaking incoherence established during the period of state activism, the New Deal ensured that social and economic policy would continue to develop according to a uniquely American pattern. At no other time in American history had the national government held so much authority to create new public institutions and to establish national standards of citizenship, income, and individual security. For the most part the Roosevelt administration helped business and designed decentralized social policy. The New Deal failed to temper business power, to create nationally run programs, and to establish uniform standards in most of the new social policies it created. Instead, the Roosevelt administration surrendered effective control over most (but not all) important public policy decisions to business and to the states. Thus, the New Deal created an *active* national government that served relatively *conservative* purposes.

Third, the New Deal changed the politics of public policy in the United States by creating an intergovernmental battleground, with liberals and conservatives struggling over the respective powers of the state and national governments. On the one hand, by expanding national government capacity, the New Deal handed to reformers the resources necessary to move conflict over public policy to the national political arena. On the other hand, by reinforcing federalism, the proponents of coherent national policies were forced into protracted battles to prevent business and the states from diluting national policy once it was enacted.

The Great Depression

The Great Depression constituted an economic tidal wave that washed away much of the nation's wealth. It created social havoc and left personal calamity everywhere. Stocks lost almost half their value within four years of the stock market crash of October 24, 1929. The banking system collapsed, with a wave of bank failures in late 1930, another in late 1931, and the worst of all in the winter of 1932–1933. More than five thousand banks failed, and with them nine million savings accounts disappeared. The economic calamity destroyed business after business and crippled most of those that survived. Steel mills and automobile plants operated at less than half their capacity. Farm prices, which had fallen steadily in the 1920s, plummeted further. When the prices of wheat, cotton, and other agricultural products dropped, farmers found it harder and harder to repay their debts. Banks foreclosed on family farms, and sheriffs auctioned the farms to pay the debts. In the 1930s, a drought from Texas to the Dakotas compounded the farmers' misery. Swept up by huge dust storms, the topsoil of the nation's agricultural heartland drifted over the East, darkening the skies over Cleveland, falling with the snow in New England, dusting ships in the Atlantic and the carpets in the White House.[1]

Unemployment rose sharply, from a million and a half in 1929 to at least thirteen million in 1932, embracing about a quarter of the workforce.[2] The depression hit hard in the nation's cities, where factory gates closed by the hundreds. Unemployment in Cleveland, Chicago, Akron, and Toledo reached 50, 60, even 80 percent.[3] An historian of the era captured the growing personal despair of millions of people who had lost their jobs:

> And then the search for a new job—at first, vigorous and hopeful; then sober; then desperate; the long lines before the employment offices, the eyes straining for words of hope on the chalked boards, the unending walk from one plant to the next, the all-night wait to be first for possible work in the morning. And the inexorable news, brusque impersonality concealing fear: "No help wanted here . . ." [I]n the meantime savings were trickling away [and] terror began to infect the family . . .[4]

Of those people fortunate enough to retain their jobs, many suffered cuts in pay or in work hours, or both. "Fully one-half the nation's breadwinners were either out of work or in seriously reduced circumstances" by the spring of 1933. The nation's income dropped by nearly half in the period. Families were evicted from their homes, unable to pay mortgages or rents. By 1933, a thousand homes were being foreclosed each week. Relatives crowded together into cramped quarters. Clothing wore threadbare. Some children starved.[5]

The nation's mood grew ugly. In rural areas, mobs of farmers menaced sheriffs and buyers at foreclosure auctions. Public leaders whipped up popular passions against bankers, businessmen, Jews, blacks, or any other group they held responsible for the disaster. Tens of millions of radio listeners in the 1930s heard Father Charles Coughlin, an eloquent speaker with an immense following, develop and defend a political philosophy nearly identical to that of Italy's fascist dictator, Benito Mussolini.[6]

Leading citizens and government officials considered armed revolt a genuine possibility. In the summer of 1932, thousands of World War I veterans travelled to Washington demanding the early payment of a bonus they were scheduled to receive in thirteen years. President Herbert Hoover sent the U.S. army to scatter the "bonus marchers." General Douglas MacArthur's troops routed the unarmed veterans and their families with tear gas and fixed bayonets. This show of brutal force in the face of need deeply wounded trust in government. Ed McGrady, speaking for the AFL-CIO, told a Senate committee that if the Hoover administration refused "to allow Congress to provide food for . . . people until they do secure work . . . I would do nothing to close the doors of revolt if it starts."[7] Even the middle class began to lose faith in government. A landlord warned Senator Robert Wagner that, "[i]f conditions keep on the way they are, we will all become reds."[8]

The Limited Government Ideal in the 1920s

Few people in the 1920s could have imagined that the decade would end with a shattered economy. In the generation before 1929, average hourly wages more than doubled, as did the value of residential land and total national wealth.[9] The ranks of the middle classes swelled with junior executives, doctors, lawyers, real estate brokers, insurance salesmen, clerks, store owners, and teachers. Driven by their demands for goods and services, money flowed rapidly through the economy. Much of this money fueled the growth of the automobile industry, and as auto factories thrived, so did tire plants, oil refineries, service stations, and the firms that constructed new suburbs and the highways linking them to the central cities.[10]

Business leaders enthusiastically took credit for prosperity, denying that government should take any active role in the economy. Their gospel revolved around the principle that prosperity depended on their freedom to amass private wealth. The business catechism held that "free enterprise" drove a market-based economic system that was self-motivating and self-regulating. Government could harm but not help the economy by interfering with business activity. Political leaders, college professors, clergy, and reporters all echoed the same orthodoxy. President Calvin Coolidge, for example, wrote that "The man who builds a factory, builds a temple . . . The man who works there, worships there." In Coolidge's words, "the chief business of the American people is business," and government should promote it ("the law that builds up the people is the law that builds up industry").[11] The French term *laissez-faire* ("to leave alone") summed up this philosophy; government should do as little as possible, leaving markets to judge success and failure and to stabilize themselves. Government should not aid the poor and jobless, but rather let their need motivate them to work harder and find some way to earn a living.

American political institutions and *laissez-faire* philosophy were mutually reinforcing. As it had from the beginning, the policymaking structure blocked national solutions to most social problems but permitted the national government, notably the Supreme Court, to protect business from state government interference. From the 1870s through the early 1930s, the Supreme Court (with the acquiescence of Congress) erected powerful legal obstacles to business regulation and social policy. Using its power to judge whether or not laws conform to the Constitution, the Court struck down many federal and state statutes that interfered with business.

The Court freely utilized the Constitution's "commerce clause" as a weapon for controlling the scope of conflict on behalf of business. According to Robert McCloskey, the Supreme Court read the Constitution not merely as a document creating a governmental system, but also as institutionalizing a belief in unfettered capitalism, with government the servant of private entrepreneurs. In effect, the court held that

> Congress . . . may "foster, protect, and control" commerce to its heart's content; that is, it may do things that are "good" for commerce, but not (so the implication runs) things that are "bad" for it . . . [thus] the Constitution forbids those departures from *laissez-faire* that the court disapproves, and permits those departures that the court thinks reasonable and proper.[12]

The commerce clause proved to be a marvelously flexible tool for controlling the scope of social conflict. By distinguishing between interstate commerce, which was subject only to federal control, and intrastate commerce, controlled by the states the Court assigned conflict to whichever battlefield best served business interests.

The Court's rulings on labor law and on railroad regulation illustrate how it used the American federal structure to manipulate social conflict to help business. By the 1910s, only a few states tried seriously to regulate child labor, for they understood that permitting children to work would attract business while strict regulation of child labor put them at a disadvantage in competing for industry. Recognizing the obstacles to state laws, reformers called for national child labor standards. In the Keating-Owen Act of 1916, Congress made it illegal to move goods produced by child labor across state lines.[13] But the Supreme Court soon struck down the law, arguing that the federal commerce power could not be used to regulate manufacturing since factories were, in the Court's view, manifestly local (*Hammer* v. *Dagenhart*, 1918). By preventing a national resolution of the child labor problem, the Court ensured that businesses would have the freedom to employ children in most areas of the United States.[14]

For the Supreme Court, "national sovereignty was one thing where labor was concerned, and entirely a different thing for capital."[15] Originally opposed to national railroad regulation, for example, the Court changed its view as it became clear that the railroad industry itself sought government regulation. When Congress created the first national regulatory agency in 1887, the Interstate Commerce Commission (ICC), the Court permitted the ICC to function but retained the right to overturn individual ICC rulings that it believed interfered with the railroads' business. By the 1910s the railroad industry began to decline and the ICC gradually assumed the role of its protector. Now the Court permitted the agency more freedom to regulate the railroads "for their own good." Though the Court seemed to change its mind, in fact the interests of corporate business remained its consistent concern. When the federal government seemed too willing to interfere with the railroads, the Court had blocked federal intervention. When federal regulation seemed in business' best interest in the 1920s, the Court stepped back and permitted government to assist the industry.[16]

The cultivation of a *laissez-faire* philosophy did not stop Congress from providing direct assistance to business. Congress approved high tariffs on a broad range of goods, including especially those manufactured in European factories. By doing so, Congress raised revenues and earned the gratitude of industries protected from foreign competition. In the era before the federal income tax amendment of 1913, tariffs constituted most of the federal government's revenues. In the 1870s, the New York customs house alone provided well over 50 percent of all federal revenues.[17] Tariffs became increasingly protectionist in the 1920s. As the nation plunged into the depression, Congress passed the Smoot-Hawley Tariff Bill of 1930 in an attempt to protect American industry. This legislation expanded tariffs to cover twenty thousand different imported products and increased the duty levied on goods that had already been included.[18] The immediate result was higher prices for consumers and a sudden, drastic curtailment in international trade.

Meanwhile, Congress assiduously avoided extending benefits to larger publics, with one notable exception. Beginning in the 1870s, Congress expanded and enhanced benefits for Civil War veterans, who were well organized, politically active, and influential in every congressional district in the nation. "By the turn of the century about one out of every two native-born white men in the North was receiving a[n] . . . old-age pension under the guise of federal aid to Civil War veterans, and over a quarter of the federal government budget was devoted to this purpose."[19] Government in the 1920s expanded the "veterans welfare system," extending pensions to veterans of the world war and creating a system of veterans hospitals and the Veterans Administration.[20]

No matter how needy, nonveterans enjoyed no similar federal largesse; instead, *laissez-faire* principles determined their fate. Before the 1930s the federal government made no general provision for old-age pensions, welfare, aid to the disabled, unemployment insurance, medical insurance, or public employment offices. Such programs had been established in Britain and other European nations by the 1910s, but the American states varied enormously in the degree to which they provided such programs. When the depression made state protections more necessary than ever, state legislatures, which were controlled by rural representatives, turned a blind eye.

Local and State Government in Trouble: 1929–1933

By the end of 1930 it had become manifest that private charity could not keep pace with the needs created by the depression. Charitable organizations and local relief committees spent their budgets faster than they could raise funds. Many of their wealthy supporters became victims of the economy. Just when the need for charity was greatest, the resources of private charity organizations fell. In the year ending in December 1932, the Salvation Army's budget declined 14 percent, Catholic relief spending fell 29 percent, and voluntary local relief agencies lost 69 percent of their income. Private sources provided less than 10 percent of the relief funds in Los Angeles, Chicago, Boston, New Orleans, Louisville, and other major cities. One of the nation's leading social workers told a Senate committee that the "general feeling" in 1929 and 1930 that private charity could cope with the problem of relief "had to be abandoned" as the situation grew worse.[21]

Some city governments tried hard to help the needy. Many cities still maintained understaffed and disorganized relief systems, which the depression overwhelmed. The director of one of its settlement houses described Philadelphia's municipal welfare system as "not only wickedly inadequate but . . . archaic in its methods . . . [The city] faced the collapsed households of the unemployed with practically no money to spend and a firm tradition of no public responsibility."[22]

When the deteriorating economy reduced city revenues, cities reacted by cutting spending. Two-thirds of city revenues were derived from taxes on property. Unemployed homeowners fell behind in property tax payments, and the value of the property that still produced taxes precipitously declined all across the country. As a result, municipal income dropped 40 percent between 1929 and 1933. Nor could cities borrow money to make up for the lost tax revenues. State-imposed debt limits prevented the cities from borrowing to meet their immediate needs (though Ohio set aside these limits in 1931). By 1932, cities could scarcely borrow money even when legally permitted to do so, because investors viewed city bonds as dangerously risky investments. Such cities as Buffalo, Philadelphia, Cleveland, and Toledo could market no new bond issues in 1932 and 1933.[23] According to one federal official, nearly one out of every five communities in New Jersey had become technically bankrupt by 1933.[24]

City officials turned to state capitals for help. The governments of New York, New Jersey, Pennsylvania, and other relatively urbanized states tried to rescue their cities.[25] But state help was generally slow in coming. Only eight of the forty-eight states provided any money for relief at the beginning of the New Deal, and state legislatures, all dominated by rural interests, were not keen to raise taxes to help urban constituencies.[26]

The states entered the depression financially strapped. They had borrowed heavily in the 1920s to build roads, schools, airports, colleges, and public construction projects. Since the states had assumed that gasoline taxes would provide a never-ending source of revenues for meeting debt obligations, they had been willing to incur large debts. But gasoline tax revenues fell rapidly as highway tourism and commerce ground to a halt. As revenues dropped, the states cut spending.[27] States slashed budgets for public works and construction programs. They spent $1.35 billion for public works projects in 1928, $630 million in 1932, and $290 million in the first eight months of 1933.[28] With private construction nearly at a standstill, cuts in public construction swelled the ranks of the jobless, making the economic situation even worse. Beginning as early as 1931, some states began to reverse policy. Between 1931 and 1935, forty-three states enacted legislation to fund emergency unemployment relief, but the level of appropriations varied enormously.[29]

States refused to help the cities for political as well as financial reasons. The states faced a twentieth-century crisis with nineteenth-century governments. State constitutions had been written for a rural, agricultural society that required minimal governance. Most state legislatures met for brief sessions every other year. Legislators were paid, at best, a few hundred dollars, and they worked with no professional assistance. State constitutions normally required balanced budgets, forcing the states to reduce spending precisely when the need for work and relief was greatest. State legislatures represented districts more equal in physical size than in population. Sparsely populated rural counties consistently outnumbered and outvoted city interests in the state legislatures. Traffic congestion, slums, inadequate park space, and smoke pollution excited little interest among rural and small-town legislators, and the same attitudes prevailed about unemployment in the cities.[30]

The depression presented each governor the with the political opportunity to try to bring state policy into the twentieth century, but relatively few of them seized the opportunity. Like their legislatures, most governors remained philosophically conservative, more attuned to rural than to urban constituencies. Many governors chose to do nothing, even extolling as a positive accomplishment their state's reluctance or inability to respond to the crisis. Indiana's governor celebrated the "sound constitutional provision which prevents the state from assuming bonded indebtedness in order to meet the financial demands of modern government." California's governor told his legislature to make its own decisions about relief in 1931, and North Dakota's governor "had to be dragged on a guided tour of poverty before he called for assistance."[31]

A handful of governors, all from states with a long record of progressive social policy, tried a more positive approach. New York, Pennsylvania, Wisconsin, and Minnesota extended relief to the unemployed as well as protections for labor. New York's governor Franklin D. Roosevelt pushed for state programs that later became models for New Deal legislation. In some of these states, however, policymaking fragmentation killed reform. A majority of states remained too intimidated by the interstate competition for industry to try to raise taxes or to protect the eroding rights of labor.[32]

In light of these political and economic realities, it is not surprising that a federal inventory of state relief programs in the mid-1930s showed that America's impoverished citizens received few benefits from a chaotic collection of antiquated state social welfare agencies. The elderly poor were one of the groups victimized by these systems. Until the 1920s most states sent elderly poor people to county-run poorhouses. As late as 1931, only eighteen states had enacted old-age "relief" laws, with the most generous state providing up to $30 a month (roughly, this would amount to a little more than $250 in 1988 dollars). Pennsylvania's highest court invalidated its pension for the elderly in 1924 because it violated a state constitutional provision prohibiting appropriations for "charitable, benevolent, or educational purposes."[33]

Other needy Americans fared little better in most of the states. Only Wisconsin had created an unemployment insurance program by the mid-1930s. Most states had programs to aid the blind on the books, though such programs existed mainly because they cost the states virtually nothing. Most states with widow's pension programs permitted county governments to choose whether or not to provide relief. In 1931, state laws authorized 2,723 counties in the nation to provide such aid, but only 1,490 participated in these programs. Under budget pressures, 171 counties discontinued their programs by 1934.[34]

With charitable and municipal resources overwhelmed by the depression, combined with the fact that most state governments were unable or unwilling to help the jobless, the federal government confronted a building pressure to take an active role in responding to the social crisis. President Herbert Hoover resisted these pressures, trying instead to preserve the old constitutional order.

The Defense of Passive Government

The national government had adjusted itself much better to the twentieth century than had most of the states. Its administrators were more professional and its budgeting system more modern. For a brief time during World War I, Washington actively managed the national economy.[35] The national government could raise money more easily than the state governments and through grant-in-aid programs it had already established a mechanism that could be used to funnel money through the states for national relief programs. Battling to save *laissez-faire* capitalism, for four years President Herbert Hoover frustrated efforts to bring the national government into the fight against economic breakdown and destitution. Federalism and volunteerism offered Hoover a convenient excuse and practical strategy for deflecting the demands for national government intervention.

The depression dominated most of Hoover's term as president, for he had taken the oath of office in March of 1929, only a few months before the stock market crash. At first, he assumed that the economy remained basically sound and that the downturn would be temporary. In 1929 and 1930, he used the White House as a pulpit, preaching the doctrines of self-help, localism, and the soundness of American business. He told the American Federation of Labor in the fall of 1930 that working people should be inspired by the devotion of "our great manufacturers, our railways, utilities, business houses, and public officials." In June of 1930, he had told a delegation of leading citizens that "[t]he depression is over."[36]

Even after 1930, when his own optimism faltered, Hoover held to the belief that the federal role should be limited, and national expenditures restrained, and that help for the jobless should be voluntary and local. As income taxes fell, he grew obsessed with the federal budget deficit. Believing that the "primary duty of Government" was "to hold expenditures within our income," he resisted congressional proposals to infuse federal funds into the economy. He convinced himself that state and local organizations could satisfy the nation's relief needs.[37]

As the situation deteriorated Hoover compromised, though his actions remained modest and mainly symbolic. He appointed prominent businessmen to head an Emergency Committee for Employment in 1930, and it promptly recommended that relief be viewed as a state and local responsibility. "The Committee is agreed upon the principle of State responsibility in the present emergency . . ." proclaimed one of its reports. Another report asserted that "unemployment relief is a local responsibility and . . . the normal welfare work of American communities must be maintained."[38]

The only federal relief program acceptable to Hoover reinforced the unevenness and maintained the inadequacy of American welfare policy. Hoover created the Reconstruction Finance Corporation (RFC) in January 1932, a national agency designed to provide relief not to the unemployed but to banks, savings and loans, railroads, and insurance companies in financial trouble. Concerned about the impending November elections, Congress forced Hoover to accept a bill that permitted the RFC to provide relief to the unemployed and for public works. Hoover, however, insisted that these funds be made available as loans to the states, and his reasons soon became clear. Though the law permitted the RFC to loan as much as $300 million to the states for relief, the president announced that the loans "are to be based upon absolute need and evidence of financial exhaustion." Red tape and delay made it difficult for states to obtain the loans. By the end of 1932, during the depression's worst winter, the states had been able to borrow only $30 million for relief and less for public works. Progressive states, such as Pennsylvania, found the RFC uncooperative. At the same time, six states declined even to apply for RFC assistance.[39]

Few who listened to Franklin Roosevelt's presidential campaign speeches in 1932 would have imagined that his administration would transform the federal government into an active participant in social policy. Roosevelt labelled the Hoover government the "greatest spending Administration in peace times in all our history," and blasted the budget deficits of the early 1930s.[40] But the voters wanted a change in leadership. Roosevelt won 57 percent of the vote in the 1932 election, while Hoover failed to win as much as 40 percent—the worst showing ever for a Republican in a two-party race. The Democrats achieved their largest majority since 1890 in the House of Representatives and elected more senators than in any election since the Civil War.

THE ROOSEVELT ADMINISTRATION

Once inaugurated on March 4, 1933, Franklin Roosevelt drove government at a torrid pace. Within a day and a half, Roosevelt closed the nation's banks and announced a "bank holiday," called a special session of Congress, and asked policy experts (and top bankers) to prepare emergency banking legislation. Congress approved the president's plan to stabilize banking (the Emergency Banking Act) by the end of its first day in session. Over the next three months, Congress approved a program to provide work, food, and shelter for the destitute unemployed (the Civilian Conservation Corps, March 31); a plan to stabilize agricultural supplies and prices (the Agricultural Adjustment Act, May 12); a program of grants to states and cities to assist the jobless and poor (the Federal Emergency Relief Act, or FERA, May 12); a plan for the economic development in sections of the impoverished mid-South (the Tennessee Valley Authority, May 18); regulation of securities markets (the federal Truth in Securities Act, May 27); a national system of state-run public employment offices (the Wagner-Peyser Act, June 6); protection for people holding home mortgages (the Home Owners' Loan Act, June 13); and a major effort to stabilize business (the National Industrial Recovery Act, June 16).

Roosevelt's energy galvanized the nation. The columnist Walter Lippman wrote that before Roosevelt took office, "we were . . . disorderly and panic-stricken mobs and factions. In the hundred days from March to June we became again an organized nation confident of our power to provide for our own security and to control our own destiny."[41] Roosevelt had assured Americans that the national government would actively respond to the economic crisis, and it added to the legislation of 1933 many more laws, including a second series of programs in 1935 that created the Social Security Act, the Wagner Act protecting unions, and additional measures affecting banks, oil, coal, and other vital industries. The New Deal precedent has endured. Since the New Deal, every president, whether a conservative or a liberal, has had to give the appearance of being an activist, particularly during times of financial or social crisis.[42]

A comparison of Table 4.1 (page 102) with Table 2.2 (page 40) shows that policymaking capacity accelerated at all levels of government after Roosevelt's inauguration. Federal direct expenditures doubled by 1936, and after dipping early in the decade state and local expenditures recovered by the late 1930s. Federal civilian employment paralleled this expansion, growing from 581,000 employees in 1933 to just over 1 million by mid-1940.[43] Compared to its negligible role in education, highway, and welfare spending in 1932, by 1940 the federal government directly funded about 9 percent of all public education, health, and welfare expenditures and 17 percent of all highway expenditures. Governments at all levels developed more diverse sources of revenue. For the federal government, income taxes and borrowing made up for stagnant customs collections in the wake of the Smoot-Hawley tariff. For state and local governments, sales taxes and income taxes made up for taxes on property of diminished value.

But "activism" did not mean that the federal government centralized policy, set national standards, or eclipsed the power of private institutions. Most of the new programs reinforced existing business institutions and strengthened state and local governments. That reform went in this direction reflected Roosevelt's instincts, and those of many

Table 4.1. *Per capita government revenues and expenditures, 1934–1940*

	1934		1936		1940	
	Federal	State and Local	Federal	State and Local	Federal	State and Local
Taxes	$23.26	$46.74	$30.29	$52.28	$36.92	$59.11
Individual income	3.20	.63	5.20	1.19	7.26	1.70
Corporation income	3.05	.39	5.81	.88	8.50	1.18
Sales, customs	14.84	7.97	14.86	11.58	16.10	15.00
Property	—	32.23	—	31.93	—	33.53
Direct expenditures	38.78	56.77	63.90	59.63	67.33	69.85
Education	1.38	14.48	1.47	16.98	1.43	19.97
Highways	2.53	11.93	4.06	11.12	4.57	11.91
Welfare	.71	7.03	1.33	6.45	1.20	8.75
Hospitals	.85	2.44	.86	2.74	.66	3.41
Health	.08	.86	.12	.90	.27	1.20
Police	.12	2.30	.13	2.45	.16	2.76
Fire	—	1.49	—	1.60	—	1.78
Sanitation	—	1.40	—	1.59	—	1.57

Source: U.S. Bureau of the Census, Census of Governments, 1967, vol. 6: Topical Studies, no. 5, *Historical Statistics on Government Finances and Employment* (Washington, DC: GPO, 1969), Table 1, 30–1.

of the policy experts who advised him, as well as the political obstacles inherent in the federal system. A closer look at several New Deal measures—the Emergency Banking Act, the Employment Service, the Federal Emergency Relief Act and work relief, and the Social Security Act—reveals the pivotal role of private institutions and the states in implementing these new policy initiatives.

Active Policy, Decentralized Government

In accepting the Democratic party's presidential nomination in 1932, Governor Roosevelt promised "to break foolish traditions" and to begin a "new deal for the American people." His confident campaign speeches offered no clear strategies for economic recovery. His ideas seemed to change from place to place, day to day. In Topeka, Kansas, he pledged an ambitious new federal farm program that would not "cost the Government any money." His inaugural address contained much to inspire ("the only thing we have to fear is fear itself") but little to clarify. Money should be "adequate but sound," he claimed. He would ask Congress for "broad Executive power to wage war against the emergency."[44]

Roosevelt, in fact, entered office without a comprehensive plan for responding to the depression. His instincts and experiences, honed by years of government service and political battles, made him inclined to use government actively for humanitarian ends. Above all he was a pragmatist, open to expert advice on the best solutions to public problems. He was hardly a radical. He sought to strengthen capitalism and he valued decentralized government. Such attitudes informed the New Deal's approach to social reform, increasing national government activism while reinforcing the fragmentation and conservatism of the U.S. policymaking system.

Roosevelt believed that government should actively promote economic health and protect individual well-being. He told an audience during the election campaign that every person had "a right to make a comfortable living" and a right to some measure of security if work was impossible because of "old age, sickness, childhood." He believed that government could legitimately ensure a more equitable distribution of income and provide opportunities for useful employment, such as reforesting depleted lands, when joblessness reached crisis proportions.[45]

Roosevelt sought out a variety of ideas, drawing on the best minds in universities, state government, and social welfare organizations. In turn, these policy experts drew on their writings and experiences, applying the lessons of the settlement house movement, wartime economic management, and state legislative reform. Some of his advisors, such as Rexford Tugwell, emphasized the necessity for national economic planning and national, rather than state, programs; many of them wanted to place more restrictions on business. Others, echoing the view of Supreme Court Justice Louis Brandeis, argued that the national government should encourage the states to assume an active policy role. The president wanted his advisors to argue their views and to disagree with one another, and they did, often engaging in bitter and well-publicized feuds.[46] With so many conflicting ideas, Roosevelt could pick and choose from a number of remedies for each of the economic maladies brought on by the depression.

Roosevelt generally favored the views of his advisors who sought to restrict capitalism as little as possible. Though he criticized business leaders and especially financiers, he was no socialist. But he opposed the stupidity and greed of capitalists when those flaws contributed to economic calamity. In a capitalist economy dominated by large corporations and banks, government planning and regulation could make the economy more stable. Government should force private industry, the utilities, and Wall Street to "play fair" through aggressive regulation of deceitful and cutthroat business practices. As it had during World War I, government and business could join in creating a stable economy that would replace the wasteful, unstable system of *laissez-faire* capitalism. With stability guaranteed, large corporations could rehire workers, raise wages, and even tolerate the unionization of their employees.[47] In Roosevelt's view, government should guarantee a measure of social justice and act as a catalyst for a coordinated capitalism suited to the twentieth century.

Roosevelt also favored the advice of those of his experts who recommended that states should become partners with the federal government in implementing social programs. In this view the national government would establish some policy standards but the states would determine eligibility, benefit levels, and other rules and would provide the day-to-day administration and share program costs. Though he valued national standards, he hoped that some states would use their autonomy to go beyond minimum national requirements, as he had done as governor of New York. In a radio speech delivered to a meeting of governors in 1930, he had explicitly advocated the "state's rights" doctrine: "[in] a great number of . . . vital problems of government, such as the conduct of public utilities, of banks, of insurance, of business, of agriculture, of education, of social welfare and a dozen other[s] . . . Washington must not be encouraged to interfere."[48]

By the end of 1934, policy experts who preferred uniform national policies felt that Roosevelt had abandoned them. Rexford Tugwell thought that the president grew more cautious after his first frenetic year and a half in office and more receptive to Brandeis's view that the states should retain maximum policy discretion because they were potential laboratories for social experimentation and because they were closer to citizens. Tugwell pointed to several New Deal measures introduced in 1935, notably the Social Security Act, as examples of the administration's (he thought mistaken) willingness to turn responsibility over to the states.[49]

Roosevelt guaranteed that important New Deal proposals would be administered more by the states than by the federal government by appointing experts who were sympathetic to the states to draft legislation. Handed the opportunity, these experts recommended policies in which the states retained significant policy control. Reformers who had designed and administered Wisconsin's unemployment insurance law in the 1930s, for example, wrote much of the Social Security Act. Not unexpectedly, they recommended a federal–state unemployment insurance system that would preserve the hard-won Wisconsin program, rather than replace it with a nationally administered system.[50]

A strategy of policy decentralization was adopted not only as a matter of preference but also in response to political necessity imposed by courts that remained reluctant to permit the expansion of government scope. The Roosevelt administration was aware that national standards would meet with institutional resistance from Congress, which was necessarily sensitive to the states, and from the Supreme Court. Four of the Court's nine justices were *laissez-faire* conservatives, ready to use the Court to prevent the national government from interfering with private business. Even the Court's liberals, led by Justice Brandeis, refused to permit the New Deal to go too far toward centralizing government. In the mid-1930s, the Supreme Court struck down the Railroad Retirement Act and the Agricultural Adjustment Act. It ruled unanimously in 1935 that the National Industrial Recovery Act was unconstitutional (*Schecter* v. *U.S.*). By late 1935 emboldened lower court judges had issued sixteen hundred orders to prevent federal officials from carrying out acts of Congress.[51] After the 1936 presidential election the court grew more tolerant of New Deal programs, but by then much of the New Deal legislation had institutionalized the administrative autonomy of state governments, partially in an effort to satisfy the Court.

Congress recognized the need for national action, but many members opposed uniform national programs or effective federal oversight of program operations. Southern congressmen worried that the Social Security Act would improve conditions for blacks in the South by raising wages, thus upsetting the racial relationships in that region. Southern senators bitterly attacked the old age pension proposed by Roosevelt, "it being very evident," as one policy expert reported, "that at least some . . . feared that this measure might serve as an entering wedge for federal interference with the handling of the Negro question." Ultimately, Congress produced a compromise that removed some of the minimal federal requirements proposed by the administration, enhancing the states' authority to fix the level of unemployment insurance and welfare benefits.[52]

Influence by policy reformers who were sympathetic to state political power, together with the political obstacles to genuinely national programs, meant that the path of least resistance for the New Deal led to the administration of policy through the states.

The Banking Crisis: National Action Without National Standards

The substantial collapse of the financial system presented the Roosevelt administration with an imposing challenge. Having lost confidence in the banks, people waited for hours in long lines to withdraw their money, considering mattresses and attics to be safer places to keep their savings. State governments stopped runs on the banks by ordering the banks to close. By Roosevelt's inauguration, thirty-eight states had declared bank "holidays," and on that day the governors of New York and Illinois closed the nation's largest banks.[53]

The bank holiday declared by the president translated what most states had already done into national policy, and it bought Roosevelt some time to craft emergency legislation. He and his advisors could have asked for any number of powers, for the crisis made Congress willing to endorse almost any proposal the administration sent forward. When the bill arrived on Capitol Hill on March 9, only one copy existed for the House. The Speaker recited its provisions for the assembled members. Although most House members had not seen the Emergency Banking Act, they approved it unanimously by four o'clock P.M.. The Senate approved the bill two and a half hours later by a vote of 73-7. The legislation arrived on the president's desk for his signature by eight o'clock P.M.. From introduction to signature, the whole process took about eight hours.[54]

Several of his advisors urged Roosevelt to seize the opportunity to assert federal control over the nation's financial system. Rexford Tugwell pleaded for central planning, hoping to "go all the way in creating a consolidated, national banking system." Tugwell and those who shared his views were disappointed by the conservatism of the New Deal's bank reforms. A generation later he still believed that the president could have taken the initiative, pointing to the "readiness of a paralyzed people to accept drastic solutions offered by a trusted leader."[55]

Roosevelt did not seek such far-reaching legislation. His reforms of 1933 instead helped stabilize and insulate the private banks, a solution that pleased the bankers. Officials from Herbert Hoover's administration met with several prominent bankers to draft the Emergency Banking Act; it "represented Roosevelt's stamp of approval for decisions made by Hoover's fiscal advisers."[56] Among other provisions, the bill offered government financial assistance to help banks reopen. Later in June, Congress approved the Federal Deposit Insurance Corporation (FDIC), which provided a government guarantee of small deposits placed in private banks. Rather than giving the federal government more capacity to manage the economy, these reforms created a policy structure in which the national government and the states shared responsibility for regulating banks. They continued to operate under state charters and regulations, except for some new rules imposed as a condition of the FDIC program. Banks retained nearly complete independence in managing accounts and lending money. The federal government became an "insurance company" for the banks, guaranteeing that banks and their depositors would not suffer the worst consequences of their decisions. The national government also created some regulations that helped insulate the banks from competition.[57] Within these limits, state governments retained most of their historical control over banking and credit.

The consequences of the New Deal's cautious approach to banking continue to surface in the 1980s. In 1984, when faced with the collapse of the nation's eighth largest bank, Continental Illinois Bank of Chicago, the FDIC took bold action: it invested four and a half billion dollars to save the bank—in effect, nationalizing the bank to save its shareholders. Ironically, during an administration ideologically committed to un-fettered enterprise, the FDIC's bank bailout was the largest corporate rescue in American history. The subsequent failure of scores of banks began to drain the agency's assets even more. The FDIC expected to pay as much as four billion dollars to correct bank insolvency in Texas alone in 1988.[58] According to many analysts, banks were encouraged to make bad investments by the knowledge that they would ultimately be res-cued by federal bailouts.

Many of the New Deal banking regulations originally written by bankers during the 1930s were removed during the Reagan administra-tion. Deregulation of the banks has forced states into a predictable "bidding war" to draw banks into their states. South Dakota has gone further than most states in loosening its banking laws. Citicorp re-warded the state by moving all of its credit card operations from New York City to Sioux Falls in 1981, and other banks soon followed.[59]

Employment Offices: National Action Without a National System

Like most new government agencies created during the New Deal's first hundred days, the U.S. Employment Service was forced to run its programs through an impossibly complex and fragmented administra-tive system.[60] In many nations, these offices connect job seekers with employers, helping both while reducing needlessly long spells of unem-ployment. They also administer other labor market services, such as job training, unemployment insurance, and public jobs programs. Such offices are building blocks for economic planning as well as important components of social welfare policy. Most of the European countries had established permanent systems of public employment offices before the end of the first world war, and their administrative networks were quickly expanded in response to the depression of the 1930s.

In contrast, America had no national system of public employment offices in place when the depression struck (Congress had abandoned the wartime employment office system after 1919). On the eve of the nation's worst employment crisis, the few federal offices that remained were little more than mail-order job-finding services. States and cities had established some public employment offices of their own. Slightly over half of the states had created such offices by the mid-1920s. New York, Wisconsin, and a few other progressive states created systems that were later used as models. But limited funds and divisive urban-versus-rural politics kept most of these local offices tiny, staffed by personnel who often, in the words of economist Paul Douglas, "owe their appointment and retention to political influence . . . and many . . . appear only irregularly for work."[61]

Private charities such as the YMCA maintained offices in the cities, but these organizations never had funds sufficient for the task. Some employment offices then as now were run for profit, and many of them took advantage of job seekers by charging exorbitant fees or referring clients to distant, fictitious employers. States could not regulate these private offices, for the Supreme Court had struck down regulation efforts in cases such as *Adams* v. *Tanner* (1917). Even local chambers of commerce provided job-matching services, often providing lists of potential employees who would not agitate for unions or who could be used to break strikes. These services rarely cooperated with one other. An unemployed worker could continue to hunt desperately for work, oblivious to a suitable job opening that an employer wanted to fill.[62]

The Roosevelt administration endorsed a proposal to create a national system of public employment offices and Congress approved the bill in June 1933. The New Deal wanted the offices both to find jobs for the unemployed and to recruit workers for federal work relief projects. By the end of 1933, public employment offices had opened in every county in the nation. Over three thousand federal offices found work for the jobless.

But Washington had not intended to operate the offices directly, and it turned over these operations to the states as soon as agreements could be worked out. By meeting some standards set by the U.S. Department of Labor, the states received federal grants to open and maintain the employment offices. The national government closed its own offices as states built their own employment office systems. States accelerated their efforts to do so after 1935, when the Social Security Act gave them responsibility for managing unemployment insurance. The number of nationally run offices fell below 1,900 in 1934, to below 200 in 1938, and disappeared completely by 1939. While the states operated only 158 offices in 1933, they had opened over 1,200 offices by 1938.[63]

This state-managed employment office arrangement has contributed significantly to the failure of America's contemporary employment policy. One significant problem is a complete lack of coordination across state lines. As a consequence, even though New York and New Jersey share responsibility for the enormous New York City labor market, their employment offices communicate poorly with each other, and this was true even in the 1930s. To this day, the system results in few interstate job placements.

Another problem is that these offices operate in an atmosphere of competition among the states for jobs and economic growth, which strengthens each states' resolve to serve employers more than job seekers. The American system of unemployment insurance, which is funded by taxes on employers and administered through the employment service, intensifies the competition and puts pressure on states to minimize employer taxes. During World War II, unemployment virtually vanished. State trust funds established to pay unemployment benefits swelled. Rather than increase the level and duration of benefits, most states cut tax rates (the average state unemployment insurance tax rate fell from 2.7 percent in 1938 to 1.0 percent by 1948). The system's fragmentation is kept intact by the self-interest of the more conservative state administrators, who participate in an interest group representing state employment insurance offices. For fifty years this organization has successfully lobbied against more federal government oversight over employment offices and unemployment insurance.[64]

In the case of public employment offices, the New Deal committed national resources to the creation of a set of new government agencies to aid the jobless. Since the system was fragmented across the states, the outcome has been conservative. While other countries have outlawed or severely restricted private employment offices, such offices remain important and relatively independent in the United States. When federal jobs programs expanded in the 1960s and 1970s, the depression-era employment offices often proved unwilling to cooperate with these efforts, especially those that were designed to help the poor. Anticipating that employment offices would resist jobs programs created in the 1960s, policy designers in the Kennedy, Johnson, and Nixon administrations created arrangements so awkward and so open to abuse that they helped discredit all jobs programs in the United States, a story we tell in the next chapter.

Public Works and Relief: The Constraints of Federalism and Privatism

The New Deal's public works and relief programs helped millions of jobless, destitute citizens. These programs made the difference between hunger and having food, between idleness and work, between pennilessness and income. But the programs also were designed explicitly to avoid competing with private enterprise in any way, and they delegated to the states the responsibility for helping the indigent who could not work.

Roosevelt signed into law the Federal Emergency Relief Act (FERA) on May 12, 1933. Like the employment service, FERA offered grants to the states to carry out national policy. For each federal dollar, state and local governments were required to provide an additional $3. The Roosevelt administration felt that relief funds could be allocated more quickly through states and cities than through new agencies set up by the federal government. By the end of June, the Federal Emergency Relief Administration had distributed $51 million to most of the states; by year's end, states had received $324 million. In the winter of 1934, twenty million Americans received FERA funds. When the program ended in 1936, it had provided more than $3 billion for relief.[65]

The FERA's structure closely resembled the New Deal grant programs still in effect today. The states received money based on a formula that incorporated measures of state economic and business conditions.[66] In addition to matching federal grants on a three-dollar-to-one-dollar basis, states were required to provide an "adequate administrative structure," usually defined as a state agency staffed with professionals. The availability of FERA funds prompted many states to create a central statewide relief agency to receive and administer federal funds.

The states differed enormously in their willingness and ability to match federal relief grants and to manage federal programs. Figure 4.1 shows that benefits shifted upward in all states, but there was a large variation in average benefits. This fact motivated the FERA administrator, Harry Hopkins, to use considerable discretion in allocating funds. From his viewpoint, it was reasonable that some states should receive

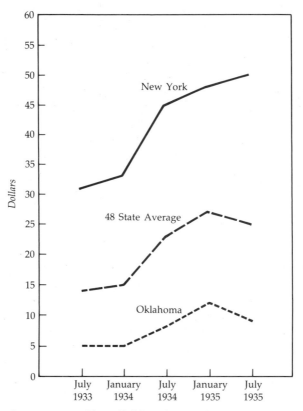

Figure 4.1. *Average monthly relief benefit per family case, by states, in the general relief program of the Federal Emergency Relief Administration, 1933–1935*

> Source: Anne B. Geddes, *Trends in Relief Expenditures, 1910–1935*, Works Progress Administration Research Monograph X (Washington, DC: GPO, 1937), 89.

more assistance than others, because their needs were greater. More-over, Hopkins' integrity made him reluctant to aid local political machines with federal relief money, although some state officials hoped that the FERA and other federal programs would fund patronage jobs for loyal political supporters. Some governors made little effort to match the federal grants, reasoning that the situation was so grave that the federal government would have to provide the money anyway. Often they were right, and those governors reaped political benefits.

The FERA administrators grew so frustrated with local politicians in six states that they nationalized the programs that operated there.[67] From the state politicians' point of view, however, Hopkins unfairly favored particular states. In May 1934, FERA grants to Kentucky aver-aged only $6.78 per family, compared to $45.12 in New York. In general, southern and New England states received much less aid per capita than states in other parts of the country. Predictably, some state political leaders charged that cozy relationships between federal and state offi-cials counted more than economic need in determining allocations.

In fact there is little evidence "that Hopkins deliberately discriminated or that he conceived of FERA as a means of redistributing national income."[68] The FERA did not seek to establish an income floor or even a permanent income maintenance program. The FERA's matching requirement did nothing to reduce and in fact reinforced the economic differences among the states, with better-off states usually qualifying for much more federal money than poorer states. The FERA set no mini-mum level of state aid. Some states raised money to match FERA grants by cutting education or other programs. Other states elected not to request FERA money with its matching requirements, preferring to keep taxes low as a weapon in the ongoing interstate battle to lure business.[69] The fact that a program with such modest intentions provoked so much conflict illustrates the degree to which federalism determines the logic of the policy debate in the United States.

As in the case of banking legislation, there were policy reformers who called for a national administrative solution to relief. Edith Abbott, an experienced social worker, demanded a genuinely national program. "The New Deal," she wrote in 1933, "has been persuaded to keep alive a thoroughly antiquated pauper-relief system that belongs to the days of the oxcart and the stagecoach."[70] Though the New Deal modernized welfare even in the South, it maintained and underwrote state and regional differences in welfare policy.

In contrast to the FERA, work relief remained under the national government's administrative control. Created in March 1933, the Civil-ian Conservation Corps (CCC) employed two and a half million boys and young men in planting trees, building dams, fighting fires, and improving forests. Ultimately, the CCC planted half of all the forests planted in the United States up to 1960.[71] The Civil Works Administration (CWA) was created in late 1933 and lasted less than a year, but it employed over four million people in January of 1934. The Public Works Administration (PWA) (September 1933 to June 1942) contracted, usually with private builders, for major construction projects. Half a million people worked for the PWA in mid-1934. Finally, the Works Progress Administration (August 1935 to June 1943) took responsibility for light construction projects, picking up where the CWA left off. The most expensive New Deal jobs effort, the WPA employed three and a third million people at its peak in 1938, and it spent $13 billion before its termination during World War II.[72]

Public works administrators scrupulously avoided competing with private business. Business leaders warmly endorsed the CCC because its activities never competed with theirs. The WPA limited most of its projects to highways, public buildings, water works, recreational facilities, and other public works. Business and labor groups had lobbied hard for these restrictions. Harry Hopkins complained that business opposed work relief because "all work projects—even ditch digging—were deemed competitive with private industry." According to one analyst,

> Slum clearance and rat extermination projects were frequently closed after opposition from building wreckers and commercial exterminators. Theatre projects were banned after 1939, following outcries from competing private productions and attacks on "subversive" affiliations of some workers. Even WPA book rebinding services to school boards and public libraries aroused private opposition.[73]

For WPA employees, the sensitivity to business pressure meant that one might be laid off, or an entire project abruptly terminated, if administrators believed that private demand for labor could absorb the workers. For the states, it meant that projects would be specific and short term and that money for building and other materials had to be set aside in advance. "If work relief were billed as long-term or indefinite, it was feared, business confidence would be shaken and recovery hindered."[74]

These relief and public employment efforts provided genuine (if temporary) help to people who were able and willing to work, relegating those incapable of joining the workforce—the elderly, the blind, children, and the disabled—to the variable generosity of the states. Efforts to guarantee public jobs for the unemployed have consistently failed ever since. Even at its peak, in 1978, the public employment programs created by the Comprehensive Employment and Training Act (CETA) provided jobs for less than one-tenth of the jobless. The CETA program proved no more permanent than the WPA when, in 1981, the Reagan administration eliminated funds for public service employment.

Social Security: Cornerstone of a Fragmented Welfare System

Though the New Deal policymakers conceived of relief and public works as temporary responses to the depression, they sought to create several permanent welfare programs through the 1935 Social Security Act. By constructing a plan to assist the elderly, the unemployed, the blind, and the indigent, the Social Security Act established a charter for an "enduring and expandable" national welfare system.[75] The law embodied all the often contradictory impulses of the Roosevelt administration: humanitarian concerns, reliance on experts, political caution, a central role for business, and an emphasis on the states as policy partners. No legislation of the period more clearly demonstrates how the New Deal combined policy activism with policy fragmentation.

As far as Roosevelt's advisors were concerned, the Social Security Act's most important section was the one establishing an unemployment insurance program. In sometimes heated debates, experts argued about the virtues of national administration as opposed to a cooperative federal–state system. Ultimately, a committee of experts heavily influenced by Wisconsin reformers recommended that the states receive federal grants and tax rebates to manage unemployment insurance. States were to retain the power to define eligibility and benefit levels and to make other choices about administering the program. The state experts believed that the program should set national minimum standards to which (their) progressive states could add more generous payments to the jobless. They feared that southerners in Congress would scuttle a purely national program. Indeed, the Senate subsequently amended the proposal, making it harder in the future to create a national unemployment compensation system. By July 1937, all of the states had passed laws creating unemployment insurance systems, qualifying every state to receive federal grants.[76]

Today, America's unemployment compensation system remains uneven. Writing in the early 1970s, one policy scholar noted that "[g]reat diversity prevails among the states in practically every significant aspect of the program," adding that "unemployment insurance was designed to be the principal income support program for workers who lose their jobs, and it does indeed play this role.It does not, however, provide for all unemployed persons, nor does it provide adequately for most of its recipients. . . ."[77] In the 1982–1983 recession, for example, less than half of all unemployed people qualified for unemployment compensation. The level of benefits varied widely. Weekly benefits in Michigan averaged twice the benefit level paid in Mississippi. The difference in benefits from state to state was closely linked to interstate competition for business. When Congress created a joint federal–state structure, it "opened up very great possibilities for inter-state [fragmentation], with

Table 4.2. *Average monthly benefit levels under various Social Security grant-in-aid programs in California and Mississippi, 1942*

		Mississippi	California
Title I:	Old Age Assistance (per case)	$ 9.05	$36.91
Title IV:	Aid to Dependent Children (per case)	7.89	23.43
	Aid to Dependent Children (per family)	20.17	57.48
Title X:	Aid to the Blind (per case)	10.63	46.95

Source: Lewis Meriam, *Relief and Social Security* (Washington, DC: Brookings, 1946), 39, 63, 70.

employers in 'less enlightened' states enjoying lower costs for unemployment insurance" than employers in progressive states. In 1982, Pennsylvania taxed employers at seven and a half times the rate in Texas.[78]

The same points can be made about the welfare provisions in the Social Security Act. Title I created a program for the poor elderly, Title IV established a relief program for dependent children, Title V provided maternal and child health services, and Title X legislated a program for the blind.[79] The states rapidly adopted legislation to accept grants for these activities. In each case, the states were permitted to define "needy" and to set benefit levels, with the predictable result that state definitions of need and benefit levels varied widely as soon as the law took effect. California provided relatively generous benefits, while Mississippi's payments were extraordinarily low (Table 4.2). Today large variations in these programs still exist, despite many efforts to bring about some coherence (see Chapter 7).

Coherent Policies: Old-Age Insurance, Labor Standards, and Trade Union Protections

Some New Deal policies that created coherent national policy survived the legislative and judicial gauntlet after 1935. Three of these programs, Title II of the Social Security Act, the Wagner Act, and the Fair Labor Standards Act, have had a large impact on domestic politics and policy since their inception. Their enactment illustrates the circumstances under which powerful surges in public support or strong support from a section of the business community can result in policy designs uncharacteristically coherent for the American policymaking structure.

Title II of the Social Security Act established the Old Age and Survivors Trust Fund as a genuinely national social insurance plan, with uniform eligibility standards and benefits. This is the program most Americans now associate with the term "social security." As we detail in

Chapter 7, an unusually powerful mass movement of retirees coalesced around a public pension scheme called the Townsend Plan in 1934 and 1935. The irresistible force of this movement's demands made some national program virtually inevitable. The entitlements to Social Security created by this section of the act, as enhanced by liberalizing provisions after 1939, are now among the most uniform and generous social benefits offered by the federal government.

The architects of the trust fund argued that the Old Age and Survivors program was a pension program and that it therefore was not "charity" in any sense. They said that its beneficiaries contributed to their retirement during a lifetime of work, as they would in any insurance program. Then, as now, the great majority of recipients were not poor; age was the only criterion for eligibility. In contrast, Title I, which created Old Age Assistance (OAA) for elderly people who were in poverty, was called "welfare." In principle it was based on the public's generosity and not on an individual's earlier contributions. So important was this distinction between the Trust Fund and OAA that Social Security officials in Washington "used discretionary administrative decisions to prevent liberal states (like California) from making old age pensions [under Old Age Assistance] too automatic, too generous financially, or too dignified in their local administration." In protecting their favored program, the trust fund, these administrators "deliberately left many needy older Americans inadequately protected"[80] and isolated a large part of the middle class from any need for making common cause with other recipients of government benefits.

The National Labor Relations (Wagner) Act of 1935 outlawed several unfair labor practices and established the National Labor Relations Board, charged with protecting collective bargaining nationwide. The congressional elections of 1934 seemed to comprise a mandate for liberal policies, for they gave the Democrats a nearly three-to-one advantage in the House and Senate. Roosevelt remained neutral on the law until the Senate enacted it, but Senator Robert Wagner's energetic leadership mobilized Democrats on its behalf. When the Jones and Laughlin Steel Company challenged its constitutionality, the U.S. Supreme Court managed a historic reversal of previous court rulings and upheld the law. Though the conservative coalition could not stop the momentum in favor of federal protection of unions in the mid-1930s, it later tempered its provisions with the Taft-Hartley Act of 1947, which among other things permitted the states to enact right-to-work laws prohibiting the closed shop.[81]

The Fair Labor Standards Act of 1938 unequivocally imposed national wage and hour standards on business. It pitted the industrial North against the low-wage southern states. Most of the participants understood that a national minimum wage and other universal labor regulations would limit business autonomy and reduce the labor cost advantages of the South. On this issue, then, some northern industries were willing to ally themselves with trade unions, sacrificing some control over wages for an improved position vis-à-vis industries located in the South. The law's narrow victory followed dramatic tactical maneuvers in Congress between southern and northern members and close, divisive votes. Today the minimum wage law covers most American workers, in contrast to Britain and other countries where minimum wages cover only a fraction of the workforce in traditionally "sweated" industries.[82]

The New Deal and American Politics

Roosevelt's administration changed American politics. The New Deal realigned American political parties, bringing millions of blue-collar workers and ethnic minorities into the Democratic party. Between 1901 and 1933, the Democrats controlled both houses of Congress only three times, but in twenty-three congressional elections between Roosevelt's election in 1933 and Ronald Reagan's election in 1980, the Democrats failed to control both the House and the Senate only twice.[83]

The New Deal also changed politics by opening a new arena of policymaking, thus expanding the scope of most political conflicts beyond the state capitals. In many areas of social and economic conflict, the national government now could come to the aid of citizens that many of the states had ignored. Groups lacking sufficient resources to win policy victories at the state level could try to place issues on the national agenda and, by enlisting political help from allies outside of their own states, could sometimes win policy battles at the national level that they could not win in their own states.

Under Roosevelt, the federal government encouraged urban and labor interests to fight policy battles in the national political arena. Formed just before Roosevelt took office, the United States Conference of Mayors (USCM) proved to be an invaluable source of information and administrative skill for the New Deal's emergency efforts. Membership in labor unions more than tripled between 1933 and 1939, with the industrial unions in steel, automobiles, and other heavy goods sectors achieving the most significant growth. Labor became an indispensable ally of the Democratic administrations of the 1960s and 1970s. By offering more access and influence to groups representing the interests of cities and workers, the government created a constituency to support national standards and progressive legislation.[84]

The New Deal's emphasis on policy decentralization, though, meant that political victories at the national level would not basically alter America's traditionally conservative social and economic policies. By relying on grants-in-aid and by permitting the states to retain control over most of banking, employment, welfare, and other activities, the national government left most of the basic decisions about public policy, and therefore conflict over policy, to the states.

The New Deal simultaneously made the federal *and* state governments more capable of policymaking. Federal grants for emergency programs provided almost a third of the money that state and local governments spent in 1934. The volume of these grants fell sharply after 1934, but federal expenditures on highways, welfare, and other programs increased in the mid-1930s (compare Table 4.1, page 102). Thus, grants still represented almost 8 percent of state and local budgets in 1938, three times the level of 1932.[85] These grants compelled the states to provide more services and benefits to their citizens than before. Between 1932 and 1934, state and local welfare expenditures doubled, from $444 million to $889 million, and increased from 5 percent to more than 11 percent of total state and local spending. Table 4.3 illustrates the range of state and local policy action that the federal grants inspired. This list only suggests the framework of the intergovernmental grant system that grew vastly in size and complexity after the 1960 election.

Though the states became active in social policy during the New Deal, their politics did not necessarily become any less conservative.

> Before the New Deal, states rights remained a vital if negative dogma which enabled [conservative state leaders] to achieve national prominence . . . But in showing what positive government could do, the New Deal forced politicians to recognize that states' rights without state activism must perish. As Governor Olin Johnston of South Carolina warned his colleagues in 1935, "There has been a continuous decrease of state powers because . . . the states have not used them, and the people wanted government. If a government did not measure up to its responsibility by the exercise of its powers . . . the powers will not be there . . . they will be exercised by the mobs, by the rabble, or something . . . It is God's and nature's law."[86]

Harry Hopkins, writing in 1937, asserted that the states' control over New Deal programs increased just as the nation grew "bored with the poor, the unemployed, and the insecure."[87] Public officials in progressive states such as California, Pennsylvania, Wisconsin, and New York used their discretion to provide generous benefits and eligibility. Public officials in conservative states used their new government capacity for conservative ends, within the loose limits imposed by Washington. Policy leaders in southern states had no intention of surrendering to demands that they grant full citizenship rights to blacks or administer adequate welfare and employment programs. Because the federal government did not require states to do much in exchange for federal grants, southern states actually used federally assisted programs to strengthen their systems of legalized racism.

Table 4.3. *Federal grant-in-aid expenditures, 1925–1939 (thousands of dollars)*

Program	1925	1929	1931	1933	1935	1937	1939
Highways	$ 95,970	$ 82,097	$135,593	$101,266	$12,657	$ 86,692	$161,084
Agricultural extension stations	1,440	3,840	4,340	4,359	4,384	5,611	6,538
Agricultural extension work	5,879	7,151	8,650	8,607	8,580	16,343	17,822
Agricultural and mechanical colleges	2,550	2,550	2,550	2,550	2,550	4,030	5,030
Forestry aids	399	1,393	1,779	1,817	1,547	1,737	1,833
Vocational education	5,615	6,879	7,879	7,726	9,997	9,695	19,553
Vocational rehabilitation	520	665	993	993	1,029	1,585	1,799
Public health	611	650	887	421	264	7,765	10,346
Maternal and child health	933	777	—	—	—	3,002	3,739
Crippled children	—	—	—	—	—	1,991	3,029
Old-age assistance	—	—	—	—	—	124,585	210,160
Aid to dependent children	—	—	—	—	—	14,789	31,467
Aid to the blind	—	—	—	—	—	4,560	5,272
Employment security	—	—	—	—	1,927	12,243	62,338
Total	$114,478	$106,642	$163,188	$128,686	$43,604	$296,258	$542,650

Source: Morton Grodzins, *The American System* (Chicago: Rand McNally, 1966), 49–50.

By giving states both the funds and the freedom to pursue active policies, the New Deal made it possible for seemingly progressive national policies to be translated into strategies to frustrate national standards. The new government activism *expanded* the scope of the policy process and also *elongated* it. The definition of policy objectives might have seemed to be settled when a law was enacted, but this was only the beginning of an interminable process. Some of the most meaningful policy decisions were made when states negotiated federal grants and subcontracted with local agencies or businesses. The new grants system created thousands of new "veto" points in the policy process, where national purposes could be bent to state and local ends. Grants programs opened a new arena to the powerless. But the grants-in-aid system also added sources of delay, frustration, and obstruction, and it institutionalized incoherent policy.

Although Roosevelt's administration gave new voice to the cities and labor, it also strengthened the ability of business to control the content of policy and preserved business's ability to influence the level of government that would make policy. The National Industrial Recovery Act (NIRA) encouraged business trade associations to govern themselves, guaranteeing at the same time minimum labor standards and the rights of labor unions. Trade associations flourished under NIRA. When the Supreme Court struck down the NIRA in 1935, the federal government enacted laws governing individual industries. One of these laws, the Connolly Hot Oil Act, permitted state governments to control the supply of oil produced within their boundaries. In the hands of the state of Texas this power made one of its regulatory agencies, the Texas Railroad Commission, one of the most powerful public agencies in the United States. The Texas Railroad Commission restricted the supply of oil produced within the state, thus keeping oil prices all across the nation artificially high. The Organization of Petroleum Exporting Countries (OPEC) later modeled itself on this agency.[88]

Probably the most important opportunity presented to the New Deal for permanently changing national politics related to organized labor. Despite new federal laws granting unions the right to organize and bargain with companies, the New Deal removed state control over much of labor policy only partially and temporarily. States retained the authority to pass laws restricting union activities, and many states weakened labor unions by passing "right to work" laws after World War II. Even at its strongest point in the 1950s and 1960s, labor in the United States was disorganized throughout the South and West. And the ever-present interstate competition to attract business exerted pressure even on the progressive states to side with business in labor disputes.

After the New Deal, the scope of social and economic conflict—between labor and capital, the poor and the rich, between industries, and between regions—could not be settled by authoritative, active policies implemented by the national government. Voters would henceforth reward or penalize national politicians for their skill at tackling widely recognized public problems. But federalism permitted the national government to avoid taking full responsibility for implementing the solutions agreed upon. They could return administrative detail and political controversy to the states, thus prolonging, complicating, or making impossible their resolution.

THE LEGACY OF POLICY FRUSTRATION

The New Deal years constitute a landmark period in American public policy, a point of revolutionary change from passive to active government. Our survey describes only a portion of the New Deal's activities. It expanded the range of issues that the federal government could legitimately address. It also made government more capable of implementing social policy in the future. Before the 1930s, the federal government had been passive, offering a few benefits to business and veterans but leaving most of the nation's governance to the states. Since the 1930s, the federal government has taken a much more active role in promoting economic development and providing governmental services. The New Deal enlisted the states as partners in this new government activism.

Nevertheless, the Roosevelt administration's activism was conservative, in the sense that it insulated American business from popular pressures for regulation or nationalization and preserved the policy discretion of the states. Flattened by the depression, many businesses had little to lose and much to gain from government assistance. Industry after industry initially embraced federal regulation, because the businesses and industries invariably helped write the rules.

At the same time, the federal government rewarded America's middle class with white-collar jobs. In addition to the 260,000 white-collar jobs created through the WPA in 1938, many of the 500,000 jobs added to the national government were also white-collar positions.[89] Home loans and farm loan programs, government-insured bank deposits, as well as the nationally administered Social Security Trust Fund, proved to be enduring programs benefitting the middle class long after the depression had passed.

It is important to note that programs designed principally for poor people and marginal workers tended to be implemented through the states, while programs for the middle class were often nationally administered. For those who could not work, welfare would remain fragmented, modest, and administratively difficult to obtain. Not only do American welfare programs only remotely comprise a welfare "system," but "still less do they represent a policy commitment to a minimum standard." The New Deal refused to institutionalize help for the able-bodied poor, and no permanent "safety net" for this group has ever been created.[90] By leaving important social policy decisions in state hands, the federal government guaranteed that those who received the least help would be the poor living in the nation's poorest states.

Its reliance on the states remains the least understood of the New Deal's legacies. In 1933, national policymakers literally began to reconstitute American government. By choosing to transform "passive" federalism into "active" federalism, they ensured that social policy would continue to be restrained by interstate economic rivalry and competition. Because this became the policy structure, subsequent efforts to achieve uniform policy across the nation usually would be frustrated.

NOTES

1. Arthur M. Schlesinger, Jr., *The Age of Roosevelt, vol. I: The Crisis of the Old Order* (Boston: Houghton Mifflin, 1956), 174–5; William E. Leuchtenburg, *Franklin D. Roosevelt and the New Deal, 1932–1940* (New York: Harper & Row, 1963), 172.
2. Leuchtenburg, *Franklin D. Roosevelt and the New Deal*, 18.
3. Samuel Eliot Morison, Henry Steele Commager, and William E. Leuchtenburg, *A Concise History of the American Republic* (New York: Oxford University Press, 1977), 598.
4. Schlesinger, *The Crisis of the Old Order*, 100–3, 276–7.
5. Ross M. Robertson and Gary M. Walton, *History of the American Economy* (New York: Harcourt, Brace, Jovanovich, 1979), 405–13; Leuchtenburg, *Franklin D. Roosevelt and the New Deal*, 18.
6. Schlesinger, *The Crisis of the Old Order*, 167–8.
7. Ibid., 167–76.
8. J. Joseph Huthmacher, *Senator Robert F. Wagner and the Rise of Urban Liberalism* (New York: Atheneum, 1968), 119.
9. National Industrial Conference Board, *The Economic Almanac 1956: A Handbook of Useful Facts About Business, Labor and Government in the United States and Other Areas* (New York: Thomas Y. Crowell for the Conference Board, 1956).
10. See Gary A. Tobin, "Suburbanization and the Development of Motor Transportation: Transportation Technology and the Suburbanization Process," in Barry Schwartz, ed., *The Changing Face of the Suburbs* (Chicago: University of Chicago Press, 1976), 102–4.
11. Schlesinger, *The Crisis of the Old Order*, 57.
12. Robert G. McCloskey, *The American Supreme Court* (Chicago: Rand McNally, 1960), 148.
13. Morton Grodzins, *The American System* (Chicago: Rand McNally, 1966), 30.
14. James T. Patterson, *The New Deal and the States: Federalism in Transition* (Princeton, NJ: Princeton University Press, 1969), 11.
15. Ibid., 160.
16. Stephen Skowronek, *Building a New American State* (Cambridge, England: Cambridge University Press, 1982), 121–62, 248–84.
17. Ibid., 61.
18. Robert Pastor, "The Cry and High Syndrome: Congress and Trade Policy," in Allen Schick, ed., *Making Economic Policy in Congress* (Washington, DC: American Enterprise Institute, 1983), 162.

19. Theda Skocpol and John Ikenberry, "The Political Formation of the American Welfare State in Historical and Comparative Perspective," *Comparative Social Research* 6 (1983), 95–7.

20. *Social Security and Retirement* (Washington, DC: Congressional Quarterly, 1983), 175–8.

21. Grace Abbott, *From Relief to Social Security* (Chicago: University of Chicago Press, 1941), 125–38.

22. Helen Hall, *Unfinished Business* (New York: Macmillan, 1971), 10.

23. See James A. Maxwell, *Federal Grants and the Business Cycle* (New York: National Bureau of Economic Research, 1952), 23, Table 7.

24. Patterson, *The New Deal and the States*, 31; Joanna C. Colcord, William C. Koplovitz, and Russell H. Kurtz, *Emergency Work Relief As Carried Out in Twenty-Six American Communities, 1930–1931, With Suggestions for Setting Up a Program* (New York: Russell Sage, 1932).

25. Josephine Chapin Brown, *Public Relief, 1929–1939* (New York: Henry Holt, 1940), 72-96.

26. Ibid.

27. Patterson, *The New Deal and the States*, 39.

28. Ibid., 40.

29. Anne B. Geddes, *Trends in Relief Expenditures, 1910–1935,* Works Progress Administration Research Monograph (Washington, DC: GPO, 1937), 91–2.

30. Patterson, *The New Deal and the States*, 20–1.

31. Ibid., 33–44.

32. Ibid.

33. These data are from reports of the Committee on Economic Security, which framed the Social Security Act. See Robert B. Stevens, ed., *Statutory History of the United States: Income Security* (New York: Chelsea House, 1970), 65–70.

34. Ibid.

35. Skowronek's pathbreaking study, *Building a New American State,* analyzes the modernization of the federal government up to the 1920s.

36. Schlesinger, *The Crisis of the Old Order*, 169, 231.

37. Ibid., 172, 231–2.

38. Patterson, *The New Deal and the States*, 27–8.

39. Schlesinger, *The Crisis of the Old Order*, 240–1; Patterson, *The New Deal and the States*, 31–3.

40. Leuchtenburg, *Franklin D. Roosevelt and the New Deal*, 8–10, 41–2.

41. Quoted in Arthur M. Schlesinger, Jr., "The 'Hundred Days' of F.D.R.," *New York Times*, 10 April 1983, sec. 3, 1.

42. "The modern presidency is said to have begun in the Franklin Roosevelt era. It is characterized by presidential activism in a variety of roles." George C. Edwards III and Stephen J. Wayne, *Presidential Leadership* (New York: St. Martin's Press, 1985), 8.

43. U.S. Bureau of the Census, *Statistical Abstract of the United States, 1948* (Washington, DC: GPO, 1948), 209.

44. Leuchtenburg, *Franklin D. Roosevelt and the New Deal*, 33–4, 63–4.

45. Roosevelt, quoted in Norman Furniss and Timothy A. Tilton, *The Case for the Welfare State* (Bloomington: Indiana University Press, 1977), 158.

46. Ibid., 11–2, 57–8, 162–3; Howard Zinn, ed., *New Deal Thought* (Indianapolis: Bobbs-Merrill, 1966), 51–2; James MacGregor Burns, *Roosevelt: The Lion and the Fox* (New York: Harcourt, Brace and World, 1956), 234–41.

47. Bernard Sternsher, *Rexford Tugwell and the New Deal* (New Brunswick, NJ: Rutgers University Press, 1964), 49, 109–41.

48. Franklin D. Roosevelt, "Radio Address on States' Rights," March 20, 1930, in Franklin D. Roosevelt, *The Public Papers and Addresses of Franklin D. Roosevelt*, vol. 1 (New York: Random House, 1938), 569–75.

49. Sternsher, *Rexford Tugwell and the New Deal*, 128–31.
50. Edwin E. Witte, *The Development of the Social Security Act* (Madison: University of Wisconsin Press, 1963), 111–28.
51. Paul L. Murphy, *The Constitution in Crisis Times, 1918–1969* (New York: Harper & Row, 1969), 133–41.
52. G. John Ikenberry and Theda Skocpol, "Expanding Social Benefits: The Role of Social Security," *Political Science Quarterly* 102:3 (Fall 1987), 407–11.
53. Leuchtenburg, *Franklin D. Roosevelt and the New Deal*, 39.
54. Schlesinger, *The Crisis of the Old Order*, 4–5, 8.
55. Sternsher, *Rexford Tugwell and the New Deal*, 123–5.
56. Leuchtenburg, *Franklin D. Roosevelt and the New Deal*, 43.
57. Ibid., 60; Theodore Lowi, *The End of Liberalism* (New York: Norton, 1979), 281–7.
58. Ronald Brownstein, "After Continental," *National Journal*, 4 August 1984, p. 1484, and "Congress Hesitant About Moving to End Industry Turmoil," *National Journal*, 2 July 1983, pp. 1372–8; Nathaniel C. Nash, "F.D.I.C.'s Texas-Size Asset Drain," *New York Times*, 17 March 1988, 27.
59. Kenneth J. Meier, *Regulation: Politics, Bureaucracy, Economics* (New York: St. Martin's Press, 1985), 74.
60. This section draws heavily on David Brian Robertson, *Politics and Labor Markets* (Springfield, VA: National Technical Information Service, 1981), 104–86.
61. Paul H. Douglas and Aaron Director, *The Problem of Unemployment* (New York: Macmillan, 1931), 342.
62. Raymond C. Atkinson, Louise C. Odencrantz, and Ben Deming, *Public Employment Service in the United States* (Chicago: Public Administration Service, 1938), 29.
63. Patterson, *The New Deal and the States*, 105.
64. Edward J. Harpham, "Federalism, Keynesianism, and the Transformation of the Unemployment Insurance System in the United States," in Douglas E. Ashford and E. W. Kelley, eds., *Nationalizing Social Security in Europe and America* (Greenwich, CT: JAI Press, 1986), 155–80. Cf. David G. Williams, *Cooperative Federalism in Employment Security: The Interstate Conference* (Ann Arbor, MI: Institute of Labor and Industrial Relations, 1974).
65 Patterson, *The New Deal and the States*, 105.
66. Advisory Commission on Intergovernmental Relations, *Categorical Grants: Their Role and Design*, Commission Report A-52 (Washington, DC: ACIR, 1978), 18.
67. Patterson, *The New Deal and the States*, 50–73.
68. Ibid., 54–7.
69. Ibid., 70–2.
70. Ibid., 72.
71. Leuchtenburg, *Franklin D. Roosevelt and the New Deal*, 174.
72. Jonathan R. Kesselman, "Work Relief Programs in the Great Depression," in John L. Palmer, ed., *Creating Jobs* (Washington, DC: Brookings, 1978), 158.
73. Ibid., 212.
74. Ibid., 199–213.
75. Skocpol and Ikenberry, "The Political Formation of the American Welfare State," 133.
76. Witte, *The Development of the Social Security Act*, 111–45; Ikenberry and Skocpol, "Expanding Social Benefits."
77. Merrill G. Murray, *Income for the Unemployed: The Variety and Fragmentation of Programs* (Kalamazoo, MI: Upjohn Institute, 1971), 11, 51.
78. Ikenberry and Skocpol, "Expanding Social Benefits," 409; Donald C. Baumer and Carl E. Van Horn, *The Politics of Unemployment* (Washington, DC: Congressional Quarterly, 1985), 14; Council of State Governments, *1984–85 Book of the States* (Lexington, KY: Council of State Governments, 1984), 504.
79. June Axinn and Herman Levin, *Social Welfare* (New York: Dodd, Mead, 1974), 206–19.

80. Ikenberry and Skocpol, "Expanding Social Benefits," 414.

81. Huthmacher, *Senator Robert F. Wagner*, 190–8; James A. Gross, *The Making of the National Labor Relations Board: A Study in Economics, Politics, and the Law*, vol. I (Albany: State University of New York Press, 1974).

82. U.S. Congress, Senate, Committee on Education and Labor, *Fair Labor Standards Act*, S. Rep. 75-884, (Washington, DC: GPO, 1937); Richard Franklin Bensel, *Sectionalism and American Political Development, 1880–1980* (Madison: University of Wisconsin Press, 1984), 160–3; James T. Patterson, *Congressional Conservatism and the New Deal: The Growth of the Conservative Coalition in Congress, 1933-1939* (Lexington: University of Kentucky Press, 1967), 149–54, 182–3, 193–8.

83. On realignment, see James L. Sundquist, *Dynamics of the Party System: Alignment and Realignment of Political Parties in the United States*, rev. ed. (Washington, DC: Brookings, 1983).

84. Donald H. Haider, *When Governments Come to Washington* (New York: Free Press, 1974), 2–4: Robertson and Walton, *History of the American Economy*, 490–6.

85. Federal grants amounted to 2.5% of state and local expenditures in 1932, 23% in 1934, 11.9% in 1936, and 7.9% in 1938; computed from U.S. Bureau of the Census, *Historical Statistics of the United States, Colonial Times to 1970* (Washington, DC: GPO, 1975), 1125–7.

86. Patterson, *The New Deal and the States*, 196–7.

87. Quoted in Allen Schick, "The Distributive Congress," in Allen Schick, ed., *Making Economic Policy in Congress* (Washington, DC: American Enterprise Institute, 1983), 262.

88. Edward S. Herman, *Corporate Control, Corporate Power* (Cambridge, England: Cambridge University Press, 1981), 212–3; David Prindle, *Petroleum Politics and the Texas Railroad Commission* (Austin: University of Texas Press, 1984, passim.); Pierre Terzian, OPEC: The Inside Story (London: Zed Books, 1985), 78–9.

89. Elizabeth Sanders, "Business, Bureaucracy and the Bourgeoisie: The New Deal Legacy," in Alan Stone and Edward J. Harpham, eds., *The Political Economy of Public Policy* (Beverly Hills, CA: Sage, 1982), 124–9.

90. Furniss and Tilton, *The Case for the Welfare State*, 179; Skocpol and Ikenberry, "The Political Formation of the American Welfare State," 138.

Chapter 5

ACTIVISM AND RESTRAINT: THE GRANTS STRATEGY, 1940s TO 1989

FRAGMENTATION, POLICY EXPANSION, AND POLICY RETRENCHMENT

As World War II drew to a close, each of the industrialized democracies steeled themselves for a return to depression-era joblessness and sluggish economic growth. The twenty years after 1945 unexpectedly blessed these countries with an explosion of prosperity unparalleled in history. Capitalism, which had appeared a "cataclysmic failure" in the 1930s, seemed by 1965 to be "the great engine of prosperity of the postwar Western world."[1] National governments everywhere, including the United States, used a share of their financial bounty to expand social services and benefits. Though rising inflation and unemployment in the 1970s strained public budgets, by historical standards most of the industrial nations remained economically stable and prosperous.[2] Spending for social programs in each nation leveled off on a relatively high plateau.

Especially during the administrations of John Kennedy (1961–1963), Lyndon Johnson (1963–1969), and Richard Nixon (1969–1974), the U.S. government launched dozens of major initiatives that made it a far more active participant in Americans' education, welfare, health, and employment than it had ever been before. In areas such as civil rights, welfare, and environmental protection it developed standards designed to make policy more consistent all across the nation. Nevertheless, American governments continued to spend less on domestic programs (relative to its domestic product) than governments in other industrial nations. Table 5.1 compares the growth of government social spending between 1960 and 1981 in several capitalist democracies (including spending by

125

Table 5.1. *Growth rate of expenditures for education, health, and pensions in selected OECD nations, 1960–1981*

Expenditures of All Governments as a Percentage of GDP, on:

	Education			Health			Pensions			Total Social Expenditure		
	1960	1981	Change	1960	1981	Change	1960	1981	Change	1960	1981	Change
Australia	2.8%	5.8%	+3.0%	2.4%	4.7%	+2.3%	3.4%	5.6%	+2.2%	10.2%	18.8%	+ 8.6%
Canada	3.0	6.2	3.2	2.4	5.6	3.2	2.8	4.6	1.8	12.1	21.5	9.4
France	a	5.7	a	2.5	6.5	4.0	5.9	11.9	6.0	13.4	29.5	16.1
West Germany	2.4	5.2	2.8	3.1	6.5	3.4	9.8	12.5	2.7	20.5	31.5	11.0
Italy	3.7	6.4	2.7	3.2	6.0	2.8	5.5	13.2	7.7	16.8	29.1	12.3
Japan	4.0	5.0	1.0	1.3	4.7	3.4	1.4	4.8	3.4	8.0	17.5	9.5
Netherlands	4.5	7.1	2.6	1.3	6.7	5.4	5.2	13.0	7.8	16.2	36.1	19.9
Sweden	4.6	6.6	2.0	3.4	8.9	5.5	4.4	11.8	7.4	15.4	33.4	18.0
United Kingdom	3.7	5.8	2.1	3.4	5.4	2.0	4.1	7.4	3.3	13.9	23.7	9.8
United States	3.6	5.5	1.9	1.3	4.2	2.9	4.2	7.4	3.2	10.9	20.8	9.9

aNot available
Source: Organization for Economic Cooperation and Development, *Social Expenditure, 1960–1990: Problems of Growth and Control* (Paris: OECD, 1985), 34–40, 66, 69, 72.

state and local as well as national governments), measured as a share of Gross Domestic Product (GDP).

Table 5.1 places American social expenditures in this period in comparative perspective. Total social expenditures were lower in both 1960 and 1981 in the United States than in seven major industrial nations, leading only Japan and Australia. This is significant in light of two facts: the United States produced twice as much GDP per capita as the second most productive nation in the early 1960s, and military expenditures accounted for a smaller share of total federal spending in 1981 than in 1960.[3] American governments spent a smaller share of GDP on health than any of the leading industrial nations, a smaller share than any country except Japan on education, and a smaller share than any country except Australia, Canada, the United Kingdom, and Japan on pensions.

Moreover, it cannot be said that policy uniformity was achieved in these years. Health care was extended to recipients of Social Security and Aid to Families with Dependent Children, but many citizens continued to lack basic health care coverage. The welfare system still varied widely from state to state, though efforts to consolidate it made limited headway with the enactment of Supplemental Security Income in 1972 and court decisions that increased access to welfare. Civil rights legislation reversed historic patterns of discrimination in voting and public accommodations, but the desegregation of housing, education, and employment moved with glacial speed. Stringent environmental legislation was enacted, but enforcement was slow and uneven.

The volume of spending in the United States was constrained in comparison with other industrial democracies, but an antigovernment backlash was mobilized in the United States that was more intense than in countries where public spending was much higher.[4] The American public's trust in the national government and its policy performance plummeted. Three out of four people surveyed in 1980 believed that the government could rarely if ever be trusted "to do what is right."[5] From 1968 through 1980, presidential candidates of both parties cast government waste, fraud, abuse, and red tape as central themes in their election campaigns. Ronald Reagan built a political career on the antigovernmental backlash and rode it to landslide election victories in 1980 and 1984. In his first inaugural address, Reagan asserted that "in the present crisis, government is not the solution to our problem. Government is the problem."[6]

Table 5.2 suggests that the design of public policies helps to explain both the relatively limited growth in social spending and the antigovernment backlash that emerged in the United States. The various programs that were enacted in the 1960s and 1970s differed remarkably in the strength and intensity of political support mobilized on their behalf. The

Table 5.2. *Federal budget outlays for selected items, 1960, 1981, and 1989*

	1960		1981		1989	
	Outlays ($ Billions)	Percent of GDP[a]	Outlays ($ Billions)	Percent of GDP[a]	Outlays ($ Billions)[b]	Percent of GDP[a]
Defense	52.3	10.3	157.5	5.2	295.0	6.2
Entitlements						
Non-means tested						
Social Security (Old Age/ Survivors)	10.3	2.0	119.4	3.9	206.0	4.3
Medicare	—	—	41.3	1.3	92.3	1.9
Federal Employees Retirement (Civilian/ Military)	15.8	3.1	31.2	1.0	49.5	1.0
Veterans Benefits	2.0	0.4	8.4	0.3	11.0	0.2
Unemployment Compensa- tion	2.8	0.6	18.4	0.6	15.0	0.3
Means-tested						
Medicaid	—	—	15.9	0.5	31.0	0.7
Child nutrition	0.2	d	3.5	0.1	4.7	c
Food stamps	—	—	11.3	0.4	12.5	0.3
Family support	2.1	0.4	7.7	0.3	10.9	0.2
Supplemental Security Income	—	—	6.5	0.2	11.4	0.2
Grants-in-aid to state and local governments[d]	7.0	1.4	94.8	3.1	119.0	2.5

[a]GDP is based on 1987 OECD data; figures for 1989 assume 3 percent growth in 1988 and 1989 to a GDP of $4,759 billion in 1989.

[b]Estimates

[c]Less than one-tenth of 1 percent

[d]Grants-in-aid includes portions of other categories, including family support, child nutrition, and Medicaid.

Source: U.S. Office of Management and Budget, *Historical Tables, Budget of the United States Government, Fiscal Year 1989* (Washington: GPO, 1988), Tables 11.3, 12.1; Organization for Economic Cooperation and Development, *Quarterly National Accounts, Historical Statistics, 1960–1971* (Paris: OECD, 1977), 22; and *Quarterly National Accounts, 1987* 4, 34.

most controversial programs tended to be highly decentralized, and these were often targeted for the poor. These programs expanded more slowly than the centralized and popular Social Security, Medicare, and veterans' benefits programs.[7]

Federal old age and survivor's benefits (basically Title II of the Social Security Act) constituted the largest item of federal domestic spending by the 1980s, having doubled as a share of GDP between 1960 and 1981. Means-tested programs, including Aid to Families with Dependent Children (in the category of family support) more than tripled as a share of GDP (from 0.4 to 1.5 percent); although these programs continued to cost much less than half as much money as Social Security.

Means-tested programs (family support, child nutrition, and Medicaid) tended to be subject to substantial state and local control. For example, county governments originally had the option of refusing to participate in the food stamp program, but in 1974 they were required to participate. Unemployment compensation, for which benefits are not means-tested (but require a demonstration that the applicant is available for employment) was also subject to state policy discretion. Federal spending on family support, food stamps, Medicaid, and child nutrition constituted 1 percent of GDP in 1960 and 1.9 percent in 1981 (a 190 percent increase), but dropped to 1.5 percent by 1989. In contrast, federal spending on fully nationalized programs of old age and survivors insurance, Medicare, and veterans' benefits grew from 2.4 percent of GDP in 1960 to 5.5 percent in 1981 (a 229 percent increase) and further increased to 6.4 percent of GDP by 1989.[8]

Federal grants to state and local governments grew from 1.4 percent of GDP in 1960 to 3.1 percent of GDP in 1981, a rate of increase of 221 percent, or about the same rate as the nationalized entitlement programs. But in the 1980s these programs in general contracted as a share of GDP. Indeed, other grants programs such as the Comprehensive Employment and Training Act became synonymous with policy failure in the late 1970s. These programs suffered the brunt of the attack on domestic spending the 1980s, while the more nationalized pension programs that served the middle class proved nearly immune to significant cutbacks.

Thus, it would be inaccurate to conclude that social spending for all programs lagged behind the rate of expenditure in other advanced capitalist nations. It would be most accurate to assert that in the United States, the constituencies supporting social spending were divided from one another, and that *overall* spending lagged. The most important programs benefitting the middle class were taken out of the complex intergovernmental structure and administered directly from Washington. This was made possible because of the political strength of the constituencies backing these programs. In contrast, programs designed to help the poor were left fragmented, uneven, and difficult to administer. Their complexity and unmanageability made them the best targets for conservatives who wanted to find examples of government waste, fraud, and abuse.

Grants-in-Aid: A Feasible but Vulnerable Strategy for Active Policy

The federal policy structure made grant-in-aid programs the most politically feasible strategy for attacking most of the new social problems of the 1960s and 1970s. Spending on grants increased under both Republican and Democratic presidents until the late 1970s. A bipartisan congressional consensus on a grants strategy underwrote the growth of social welfare programs.

However politically necessary, grant-in-aid programs were poor instruments for achieving effective and equitable policy results. By relying on state and local governments as senior partners in the implementation of policy, national administrators found themselves unable to control or even to monitor all of the independent policy actions for which they were being held responsible. Efforts to exert more control over the cumbersome system of policy by proxy drained vast reservoirs of administrative, legislative, and judicial energy. Efforts to impose national standards in these programs met with limited success and often provoked opposition. Political support eroded when the grant system became so complicated that it turned into an administrative nightmare. Reform always took the form of new bureaucratic arrangements and new rules and formulas for distributing money, often with the result of shifting the grants system toward the constituency of the incumbent president. Programs subject to so many contending pressures were rarely administered effectively, inevitably resulting in enough cases of wasted money and failed promises to stoke citizen resentment and calls for cuts in social spending.

These problems slowed the expansion of national policy and prevented grants from redistributing resources to the neediest individuals and regions. The basic objectives of social policy—to solve pressing social problems—were subverted by policy incoherence, and the public's belief that policies of any kind could be effective was soon undermined. American employment policy after World War II illustrates these points.

POSTWAR EMPLOYMENT POLICY

Fearing a return to the unemployment levels of the depression years after World War II, the leaders of governments in all of the industrial nations promised to make employment security a central aim of economic policy. American reformers hoped to enact a law committing the national government to a full employment policy. The Wagner-Murray-Dingell bill of 1943 included provisions for nationalizing the U.S. Employment Service and the unemployment insurance system, both managed by the states (except for a brief period during the war). Sobered by the popularity of the New Deal and cautious about attacking directly the view that government should take responsibility for employment, conservatives in Congress attacked the proposal chiefly on the ground that it threatened to remove administrative responsibility from the state governments. The Wagner-Murray-Dingell bill died quietly.[9]

Instead, Congress approved a measure that rhetorically but not administratively made the national government responsible for employment policy. The Employment Act of 1946 declared that the national government should act to maintain "maximum" employment. It created special units in the White House (the Council of Economic Advisors) and in Congress (the Joint Economic Committee) to study economic problems and to plan policy responses. It did not authorize funds or new programs to improve job conditions. When joblessness shot up in 1949, liberals in Congress offered a proposal to put teeth into the Employment Act. Their bill would have funnelled hundreds of millions of dollars into job training, public works, and other programs whenever the economy experienced a downturn.[10] But the bill never came to a vote. The low jobless rates made possible by the Korean War removed the employment issue from the national agenda until late in the 1950s.

During the Eisenhower administration, unemployment became a serious issue in several states. Pockets of joblessness persisted in areas that the economy had left behind, such as towns near the Pennsylvania coalfields, the New England textile plants, and the northern Minnesota iron range. State leaders in New England attributed their problems to the migration of textile manufacturing to southern states, where wages remained low and labor laws were relatively unrestrictive.[11] Members of Congress representing the affected states introduced a measure in 1955 to provide grants and loans to communities with chronic unemployment. President Eisenhower vetoed the measure, but John Kennedy signed a similar bill, the Area Redevelopment Act, in 1961.

In its six-year journey through the policy process, the area redevelopment legislation was repeatedly revised to provide political benefits to the states of more and more members of Congress. In 1956, for example, amendments added three hundred counties in southern states to the list of eligible "depressed areas," in an effort to make the bill appealing to southern senators. By the time the Area Redevelopment Administration began to administer the act in 1962, eligibility extended to one-third of the counties in the nation, spreading the limited funds so thin that they could exert scarcely any impact on depressed areas. Congress made the problem worse in 1965 by revising the grant formula so that every state would have at least one area eligible for aid.[12] By then the politics of distribution had thoroughly undermined the possibility of redistribution.

The Manpower Development and Training Act (MDTA) of 1962 authorized the U.S. Department of Labor to distribute grants to all the states for retraining workers. The original version of the bill was drafted in the Washington offices of the American Vocational Association, a professional association representing the interests of state vocational educators. Following the pattern set by earlier grant programs, most of these manpower training grants were initially distributed to state vocational education departments.[13] Skeptical of the state "voc-ed" and employment service officials, the Labor Department sought new partners in employment policy so that it could bypass state agencies.

The Economic Opportunity Act of 1964 gave the Labor Department its chance to bypass the state agencies that had administered older grant programs. The War on Poverty offered training and even short-term, subsidized "work experience" to impoverished people who had never been able to secure employment. Officials in the Department of Labor developed contracts with large employers, such as IBM, Westinghouse, and General Electric, and with not-for-profit organizations such as Goodwill Industries. They cultivated relationships with minority-run, "community-based" organizations, such as Philadelphia's Opportunities Industrialization Program, founded by the black minister Leon Sullivan and dedicated to improving the job prospects of ghetto youth.

By 1968, baffling complexity and ambiguous results plagued employment policy. The Labor Department operated its programs through at least 10,000 separate contracts with private businesses, nonprofit and community-based organizations, and state and local agencies. In the meantime Congress had added several small programs for particular constituencies (one example was a public jobs program for older farmers). By the time President Johnson left office, critics agreed that the employment and training system had grown far too complicated and rigid to operate effectively.[14] Although decentralization and ambiguity also characterized West European employment programs, U.S. Labor Department officials were especially frustrated by their inability to control such agencies as the employment service. They believed that Sweden and Britain provided models that were more effective than their own.[15]

In 1969, President Richard Nixon announced a new strategy for implementing social policy, a "new federalism" built on the promise of decentralizing as much program responsibility as possible to state and local governments. Employment programs ranked high on the White

House's New Federalism agenda, and the administration almost immediately began to battle for manpower reforms. Seeking to protect their relationships with community-based and nonprofit organizations, the Democrats in Congress resisted. Following a lengthy battle with Congress, Nixon signed the Comprehensive Employment and Training Act (CETA) in 1973. The CETA streamlined and decentralized the system. The Labor Department now would channel CETA funds through "block" grants directly to 450 state and local governments, which would themselves contract for employment services. The national government would audit their activities. At Congress's insistence, Nixon accepted a provision that permitted state and local governments to use CETA funds for publicly subsidized employment.[16]

By the end of the decade, rapid program growth and limited federal control made CETA look like a policy disaster. Trying to compensate for the sluggish economy of the 1970s, the administrations of Gerald Ford (1974-1977) and Jimmy Carter (1977-1981) augmented the CETA public jobs budget. In 1978, CETA spent $4.5 billion on public employment alone, funding 725,000 jobs. That year marked a high point for the CETA program, for a rising tide of criticism began to engulf it. Most of its problems could be traced to the effects of its rapid growth and the discretion that state and local governments exercised over the use of CETA grants. Many cities used CETA funds to ease their budgetary crises by cutting their regular payrolls and transferring employees to CETA-funded jobs. In other cities, officials used CETA as a veiled form of patronage, using federal funds to hire political allies. Popular magazines such as *Reader's Digest* ridiculed CETA-funded projects. One House Member illustrated the national government's utter inability to control the program by pointing out that state and local governments subcontracted to an "estimated 30,000 to 50,000 subgrantees." No one could estimate within 10,000 how many organizations were actually receiving CETA money.[17]

Ronald Reagan promised to reduce the federal government's responsibility for social policy, and his administration made quick work of CETA. The 1981 federal budget eliminated its public jobs program. In the face of well-publicized problems in the CETA program, few in Congress objected to the cuts. With unemployment rising in 1982, the Reagan administration reluctantly agreed to continue national funding for job training, but insisted that the money be channeled through the state governments, that private business be given a central role in local training policy, and that no monies be used to maintain the income of trainees. All of these features became part of the Job Training Partnership Act of 1982. Once the new law went into effect, the Labor Department virtually ceased to monitor the states' use of federal job training money.[18]

Patterns familiar to students of postwar American social policy surface in the story of employment programs: the high hopes of liberals at the war's end, the conservatism of the 1950s, the Democrats' bypassing strategy of the 1960s, the resurgence of state and local discretion in the early and mid–1970s, perception of policy failure, and the attack on the welfare state beginning in the late 1970s. Grant programs became vulnerable to a backlash because their complexity and loss of purpose provided rich fodder for critics.

THE POLITICAL ATTRACTIONS OF GRANT-IN-AID ACTIVISM

Grants as the Path of Least Resistance

Many of the decentralist features of the American political system began to break down after World War II as the presidency assumed more power, state and local political party organizations gradually weakened, national party committees grew in strength, and television created a more nationally uniform perception of events and ideas. These changes facilitated unprecedented nationalized protections against racial discrimination in the mid-1960s and against pollution in the early 1970s.[19]

But the nationalization of American politics remained limited by the logic of electoral jurisdictions and the legacy of institutional interests established long before the 1960s. The states continued to be crucially important in national policy design, enactment, and implementation. In this fragmented political system, national activism was more welcome than enforceable national standards.

Congress. Assuming, as congressional scholars argue, that winning reelection is of overwhelming importance to individual legislators, they act rationally in pursuit of reelection when they seek additional benefits for their constituents and when they ensure that their local constituency receives visible material benefits. Tangible benefits in the form of increased transfer payments to important constituency groups (i.e., direct payments to individuals, such as Social Security and veterans' benefits), roads, buildings, job training programs, and new health services, to name a few, are better than intangible benefits.[20] This pattern is hardly unique to the United States. Indeed, some evidence suggests that an increase in such benefits immediately before national elections is a feature of all capitalist democracies.[21]

Two conditions peculiar to the structure of the U.S. government made it likely that most new programs would take the form of grants-in-aid. First, the separation of executive and legislative powers and the weakness of political parties in Congress has meant that district service is not offset by forces that could centralize congressional decisions and make them more coherent. In the British, Canadian, and Australian parliaments, the fact that the prime minister and political party organizations exert substantial influence over members' behavior means that legislators have much less opportunity to deviate from party policy than do members of Congress.[22]

Second, the established constitutional and political status of state and local governments and the variations among them has meant that members of Congress feel pressured to tailor programs to their individual states and districts. National legislators in the United States want to make sure that the geographical area they represent can use program benefits for the most politically salient state and local purposes. But the political interests of states and localities vary enormously because of differences in economic structure, demographics, and cultural traditions. Moreover, the governments in these jurisdictions differ widely in form, scope, and fiscal and administrative capacities.[23] To the extent that state and local constituencies disagree with one another, legislators are unable to agree on the details of "national" policy. Members collectively respond to these circumstances in three ways: they approve programs that tailor benefits to particular constituencies, they approve benefits for all constituencies, or they delegate to recipients the authority to design programs to fit state and local political conditions.

The campaign for employment policy reform during the Nixon administration clearly illustrates this logic. In debates and hearings on employment legislation, individual members of Congress frequently referred to the problems of important constituents. Senate Democrats in 1970 attempted to add specific provisions for constituencies disproportionately concentrated in their states. For example, Senator Ralph Yarborough of Texas sought a special provision for Spanish-speaking persons, and Senators Jennings Randolph (West Virginia) and Harrison Williams (New Jersey) wanted to add language favoring midcareer and elderly workers. An inexperienced White House staff member warned a member of the Senate staff that "You'll be the laughingstock of everyone . . . Why, there is something for everyone in that bill." The White House aide's comment became a joke in the Senate office because "of course that was the very reason for the bill's attractiveness."[24]

Political scientist John Chubb has shown that nearly all the new domestic programs that Congress approved in the 1950s through 1970s involved grants and that these measures almost invariably passed the House and Senate by overwhelming margins, with an average majority of more than two-thirds in each Congress since the early 1950s. The majorities were bipartisan, with Republicans joining Democrats. Moreover, the grants were "widely distributed to encourage universal

support" and were usually "distributed evenly among political jurisdictions," whether or not a state or district was capable of financing
the program in question from its own resources. As a result, grant
formulas reflected voting strength more often than need. According to
R. Douglas Arnold:

> [M]any [grant] programs ignore legitimate differences in demand. The
> program whose purpose is to make railroad crossings safe hands out
> funds under a formula that counts population, area, and postal-route
> mileage but not railroad crossings. Law enforcement grants reflect popula-
> tion, not the incidence of crime. Hunter safety grants ignore the concentra-
> tion of hunters in rural areas.[25]

Chubb argued that individual members of Congress reaped political
benefits from the complexity of the grant programs. The large number of
local governments and nongovernmental organizations that received
grants enabled individual members to claim credit when they helped
constituents in their disputes with the "overgrown" national
bureaucracies responsible for managing grants.[26]

Even as Congress approved fragmented policy, it fragmented itself
internally, further strengthening the local bias in policies that survived
the increasingly complicated policy gauntlet. The number of subcommittees mushroomed in the 1960s and 1970s, as did the number of
committee and subcommittee chairs. Each committee chair could assert
oversight over a small chunk of policy and in the process perform special
services for constituents. Many of the committees that *authorized* legislation held little if any authority to determine the amount of money
budgeted, because separate *appropriations* committees controlled spending. But because so many grant programs were funded through formulas fixed by law rather than through annual appropriations, the authorization committees gained new power. The committees that
approved the CETA program, for example, guaranteed that each governmental recipient of CETA funds was entitled to a grant amount
determined by a formula written into the law. This CETA entitlement
reduced the control by the committees that approved program spending.

All committees and subcommittees, as well as individual members,
received more staff and support services (such as computers), which
they put to work to ensure that legislation benefitted their individual
states and districts. Grants formulas were accordingly hammered out to
build legislative coalitions.[27] The fragmentation within Congress made it
almost impossible for policies to survive that disproportionately benefitted a select number of states and districts with especially needy populations.

Exceptions to this pattern were sometimes important. When the 1960 presidential election focused public attention on the dimensions of poverty in Appalachia, Congress created a regional commission to address the problem. Several ambitious members of Congress, including especially Senate Democrats, focused on problems of national concern such as consumer affairs (Senator Warren Magnuson of Washington), environmental policy (Senator Edmund Muskie of Maine), unemployment (Senator Joseph Clark of Pennsylvania), and malnutrition (Senator George McGovern of South Dakota). These policy entrepreneurs expanded the congressional agenda and experimented with efforts to exert national policy authority. For example, Congress made the food stamp program more uniform in 1974 by requiring county governments to participate, and expanded benefits in 1978 by eliminating the requirement that families purchase food stamps with some of their own funds. Congress also attached new strings to many federal grant programs, including national civil rights and other requirements that cut across grant programs.

The increased effectiveness of state and local lobbying. At the same time, "public" interest groups representing state and local governments became more influential in Washington. As local political parties declined, many of these governments became concerned that members of Congress needed to be educated about state and local needs. These governments energized a number of organizations that adapted to the new climate of policy activism.

During the New Deal, Franklin Roosevelt deliberately reached out to the nation's big-city mayors for political support, and the United States Conference of Mayors (the USCM organized just before FDR's first inauguration) worked closely with Democrats on social policy initiatives after that. In 1969, the USCM merged its substantial lobbying efforts with the National League of Cities, representing the smaller and medium-sized cities, where mayors were as often Republicans as Democrats. The National Governors' Conference (later Association, NGA) dates back to 1908, but through the 1950s this group did little but complain (ineffectually) about the growth of national government power. After the mid-1960s, the NGA expanded its staff and began to assert more influence in the design of public policy. Aggressive leadership beginning in the late 1950s turned the National Association of Counties (often viewed as a voice for suburban and rural interests) into an influential public interest group. These groups grew more powerful and lobbied more intensively as grant-in-aid programs mushroomed in the 1960s and 1970s.[28] The decline of local political parties at the same time weakened the influence of party leaders in Washington.[29]

The public interest groups that represented states and localities asserted great influence in the design of new policies. Congressional committees and presidential staff informally consulted these groups before developing final proposals, and policy designers sometimes anticipated lobbyists' preferences even before consultation with them. Since these groups included both Republican and Democratic officials, they could influence the design and adoption of new national initiatives no matter what party held the presidency. Presidents and members of Congress, because their elections depended on key states and House districts, saw grants as a means of placating these important constituents. Members of Congress made a habit of announcing the award of a new grant in their district or state, often by posing for the cameras in the company of governors and mayors.

The courts and the president accommodate the grants strategy. Though federal courts often had obstructed national activism before the New Deal, they generally upheld the constitutionality of programs that gave money to the states if the states were not obligated to accept it. As early as 1923, the court indicated that such grants did not violate the Tenth Amendment, "since the statute imposes no obligation, but simply extends an option which the state is free to accept or reject" (*Massachusetts v. Mellon*). Using similar logic in several rulings on grants disputes through the 1960s and 1970s, the courts acquiesced in the expansion of decentralized activism.[30] David Walker, assistant director of the Advisory Commission on Intergovernmental Relations, argued that

> The paramount thrust of the Court's decisions has been to reaffirm the supremacy of Congress's power to spend in furtherance of the general welfare, rarely to curb its authority to attach almost any conditions to grants— whether reasonably or unreasonably related to the program's basic purpose—and to leave the protection of reserved powers almost wholly to the political process and to the states' and localities' presumed capacity to refuse or withdraw from participating . . . the Court implicitly has endorsed Congress's all-encompassing and intrusive, but politically astute, approach to and prime control over contemporary intergovernmental relations.[31]

Democratic and Republican presidents acknowledged the inevitable parochialism of Congress and the growing influence of the public interest groups, though politics naturally affected the relative access of the various groups to the White House. Aware of their need for votes in cities, Democrats listened most closely to city leaders and urban lobby groups. The NGA was especially influential during Republican administrations, because of the philosophy of federalism that they articulated and because state and county governments were closer to the Republican suburban constituency than the cities favored by the Democrats.[32]

Social Security: The Exception that Proves the Rule

Like the grant programs, the old-age insurance program of the Social Security Act expanded during the 1960s and 1970s. Medicare was added in 1965. Benefits were increased in 1965 (by 7 percent), 1968 (13 percent), 1969 (15 percent), 1971 (10 percent), 1972 (20 percent), and 1973 (11 percent). Amendments enacted in 1972 provided for automatic increases in benefits to keep pace with inflation.[33]

This centralized program constituted an exception to the grants strategy and provided one of the only vehicles for a fully nationalized expansion of social spending. Until the early 1970s, policymaking for Social Security was routine and expanded gradually under the guidance of the Social Security Administration and Representative Wilbur Mills (D, Ark.), the powerful chair of the House Ways and Means Committee. By linking benefit increases to the rising cost of living in 1972, members scored election campaign points by claiming credit for the most generous income guarantee in the history of American social policy. As the constituency expanded, Social Security became almost untouchable. This began to change, but only marginally, in the 1980s, when the rising cost of the programs funded under Social Security became associated with budget deficits.[34]

PRESIDENTIAL STRATEGIES FOR NATIONAL ACTIVISM

Postwar liberal and conservative views of national power were distinguished in an unusually sharp manner in the 1964 election campaign. The Republican nominee, Barry Goldwater, stood for states' rights. The Republican party platform warned that "individual freedom retreats under the mounting assault of expanding centralized power." President Lyndon B. Johnson, a self-styled New Deal Democrat, called for a Great Society constructed from federal action on civil rights, the cities, health care, welfare, education, and employment. He dismissed the "phantom fears . . . that the Federal Government has become a major menace to individual liberties."[35]

Although the parties switched control of the presidency five times after 1952, the actual differences in policy strategy among the Democratic and Republican presidents were not as distinct as the 1964 debate implied, for Republicans found their options limited by the popular support for government activism and Democrats faced the reality of institutional obstacles to centrally controlled policy. Whether Republican or Democrat, each president since 1945 has been expected to energize federal policy and to attack a host of social problems once ignored by Washington. However reluctantly, even conservatives came to understand that citizens expected the president to use his authority to solve such problems as unemployment, inflation, pollution, and segregation. Within that context, liberals—usually but not exclusively Democrats—have pressed for federal government policies dedicated to ensuring a degree of equal economic opportunity and national standards. Conservatives, often Republicans but including many southern Democrats, have advocated limits to government control over policy and the decentralization of the activities that government undertakes.

Reluctant Activism: The Republican Presidents

The Republicans who sought the presidency after World War II hammered home their view that the federal government had grown too big and too powerful during the Democrats' tenure in the White House. As the first Republican postwar president, Dwight Eisenhower set the tone for later presidents of his party. Observing that ". . . the National Government was itself not the parent, but the creature, of the states . . .,"[36] he set out to minimize presidential activism. He established the Commission on Intergovernmental Relations (the Kestenbaum Commission), confident that it would identify an array of federal responsibilities that could be returned to the states. Privately, he hoped that the Supreme Court would not require him to use national police powers to enforce desegregation in the South. "[I]mprovement in race relations . . . will be healthy and sound only if it starts locally . . .," he wrote in his diary in 1953; "I believe that federal law imposed upon the states in such a way as to bring about a conflict of the police power of the states and of the nation, would set back the cause of progress in race relations."[37]

Eisenhower soon found that the nation no longer wanted a passive chief executive. Despite Republican control of the U.S. House and Senate, congressional Republicans as well as Democrats criticized him for not presenting a set of new policy initiatives during his first year in office, while the Kestenbaum Commission, though controlled by conservative Republicans, managed to identify very little federal activity that could reasonably be assumed by the states.[38] Highway construction offered Eisenhower an opportunity to seize the initiative while at the same time enhancing policy responsibility by the states. He expressed the view that the need for new roads exceeded the state highway departments' "collective capacity,"[39] and in August of 1954 Vice-President Richard Nixon told a state governors' meeting of a plan for an interstate highway system to be built through federal grants. By the end of Eisenhower's first term, Congress had enacted the National Defense Highway Act, authorizing $31 billion for grants to the states over a thirteen-year period.[40]

Eisenhower also justified federal involvement in education as necessary to improve national defense. Reacting to the launch of the Russian spacecraft Sputnik, he approved the National Defense Education Act of 1958. Overall, between 1952 and 1960 federal grants-in-aid for education doubled. Though he remained reluctant to use federal powers to enforce desegregation orders issued by federal courts, in 1957 he felt compelled to use U.S. paratroopers to protect black schoolchildren who were attending Central High School in Little Rock, Arkansas.[41]

As the party out of power during the Kennedy-Johnson years, the Republicans more often criticized the administration rather than the purposes of grants. In responding to the housing bill of 1965, for example, Republicans refrained from attacking the principle of nationally assisted housing, preferring to savage the proposal for "new and enlarged urban programs bulging with money and power, designed to step up the pace of creeping federalism . . ." The Republicans offered an alternative that would make "housing programs directly responsible to either state or local governments."[42]

Republican presidential candidates in the 1960s and 1970s renewed their attack on federal executive and administrative authority. Richard Nixon, who defeated the liberal Democrat Hubert Humphrey in November 1968, argued a few months later that "a third of a century of centralizing power and responsibility in Washington has produced a bureaucratic monstrosity, cumbersome, unresponsive, ineffective." During his administration Nixon proposed revenue sharing and block grants, justifying his reforms with the philosophy that "after a third of a century of power flowing from the people and the States to Washington, it is time for a New Federalism in which power, funds and responsibility will flow from Washington to the States and the people." Gerald Ford ran for president in 1976 on a platform that conceded that concerns of a national character—pollution, transportation, civil liberties—"must, of course, be handled on the national level," but that government action "should be taken first by the government that resides closest" to each citizen.[43]

Contrary to his rhetoric, Nixon surprised conservatives and liberals alike by his willingness to propose the expansion of federal programs and regulation. Nixon was the first president to impose controls on wages and prices in peacetime. Among other initiatives, he approved legislation to regulate occupational safety and health, to protect the environment, and to improve consumer product safety. More than any previous Republican president, Nixon proposed national standards to guide social policy. The best example remains the controversial Family Assistance Plan, a proposal to establish a national minimum income for the poor, to be administered solely by the federal government (see Chapter 7).[44]

Despite these initiatives, President Nixon used his New Federalism proposals to present himself as a social policy activist while increasing state and local government control over American social policy and reducing the power of federal bureaucrats (many of whom had been appointed by preceding Democratic administrations) to allocate funds on a "project" basis. The keystone in this effort was the State and Local Fiscal Assistance Act of 1972, which attempted to divorce federal money from federal influence with unrestricted grants distributed on the basis of a formula. One-third of the funds went directly to state governments, and the rest went to general-purpose local governments, such as counties, cities, and villages. Nixon's proposal for general revenue sharing generated little support when he introduced it as a $1 billion measure in 1969. By 1971, he had raised the proposed "shared revenue" (actually unrestricted grants) to $5 billion, enough to attract support from governors, mayors, and public administrators and the national lobby groups organized to represent them. Their lobbying efforts helped secure its congressional enactment by the end of Nixon's first term.[45]

At the same time, Nixon proposed to reform existing grants with what was originally termed "special revenue sharing," and which soon became known as block grants. Originally, the Nixon administration sought to merge 129 categorical grants into six block grants covering law enforcement, education, transportation, rural community development, urban community development, and manpower training. These grants were designed to consolidate several related categorical grants into a single grant over which state and local officials could exercise broad discretion. Formulas would determine state and local funding. One such block grant consolidated seventeen job-training programs into the Comprehensive Employment Training Act of 1973. Another brought together urban renewal, Model Cities, and five other programs into a "Community Development Block Grant" (CDBG), signed into law by President Ford in 1974.[46]

The Nixon administration failed to achieve the degree of decentralization it sought, largely because Democrats in Congress resisted the complete delegation of policy authority to the executive branch and to state and local governments. First, as Table 5.2 shows, about 80 percent of the federal grant money continued to be distributed through categorical rather than block grants. Of the original six block grants that Nixon proposed, only the Housing and Community Development Act of 1974 (merging seven categorical grants) and CETA (consolidating seventeen of sixty-four employment programs) received congressional approval. Each of the new grant programs included more restrictions than Nixon desired. General revenue sharing and block grants, for example, required state and local governments to adhere to national standards on civil rights, minimum wages, and procedures for planning and accounting.[47]

National grants to state and local governments increased dramatically through the Nixon-Ford years (Table 5.3). Certain kinds of federal regulations also expanded. The National Environmental Policy Act of 1969, the Educational Rights and Privacy Act of 1974, and several laws prohibiting discrimination on the basis of sex, age, and the handicapped each added new crosscutting requirements to all federal grants. The Federal-Aid Highway Amendments of 1974 effectively created a national speed limit by requiring state 55-mph speed limits as a condition of federal highway aid. A National Health Planning and Resources Act in the same year required each state to regulate private health facilities as a condition of assistance. Finally, bipartisan majorities in Congress enacted new laws that preempted the state's role in regulating occupational safety and health as well as air and water quality.[48]

The Nixon administration created an expanded constituency for federal grants. Much of the Nixon-Ford money went to suburban, rural, and Sunbelt states, where the Republicans enjoyed more electoral strength than in the big cities. Gradually, grants shifted to medium-sized cities as well. In 1968, 62 percent of all federal grants for cities went to those with more than half a million residents. By 1975, only 44 percent went to these large cities.[49]

In most programs, Nixon successfully fought for enhanced state and local oversight of policy. These reforms left social policy more disorganized than ever before by creating block grants with broad national purposes over which the national government exercised less and less control. The CETA soon became mired in spectacular controversy. Federal funding for CETA increased rapidly in the 1970s, increasing from $3.7 billion in 1975 to $10.3 billion in 1979. But because the spend-

Table 5.3. *Percentage distribution of grant-in-aid funds by type of grant, 1972–1989*

	Fiscal Year			
	1972	1975	1980	1989[a]
General revenue sharing	1.6%	14.1%	9.4%	1.8%
Broad-based grants	8.3	9.2	11.3	11.2
Other grants	90.1	76.7	79.3	87.1

[a]Estimates

Source: U.S. Office of Management and Budget, "Federal Aid to State and Local Governments," *Special Analysis, Budget of the United States Government, Fiscal Year 1989* (Washington, DC: GPO, 1988), H-23.

ing increased so rapidly and because the money was given by formula to state and local governments, the CETA legacy by 1980 was at best ambiguous and at worst sensationally corrupt. By 1980 federal grant programs and federal regulations were easily attacked as wasteful and ineffective.

Ronald Reagan viewed federalism as a tool for conservative ends, and his version of a "new federalism" was aimed not merely at steering grant programs toward different constituents. He intended to reduce drastically the policy capacity of American government. The problems of decentralized activism provided fodder for Reagan's 1980 campaign (as we discuss later in this chapter).

Eisenhower, Nixon, and Ford all advocated a "new" federalism, new in the sense that their administrations pursued a strategy of working through the state governments as much as possible. For them, the grant-in-aid mechanisms previously put in place under Democratic presidents could be used to change federal budgets and priorities. The Democrats found policymaking fragmentation far less congenial to the accomplishment of their goals.

Confined Activism: The Democratic Presidents

Democratic presidents since World War II have reaffirmed Franklin Roosevelt's commitment to an active, assertive national government. Even their legislative programs—Truman's "Fair Deal," Kennedy's "New Frontier," and Johnson's "Great Society"—evoked the memory of Roosevelt, a confident president steering the complicated federal policy machinery into uncharted waters. However committed to national government activism, no Democratic president opted to use the federal government as the exclusive agent of social change. In each administration, new initiatives depended on organizations—either private institutions or state and local governments—over which the national government could exert limited influence.

Harry Truman's administration illustrates the political process by which liberal presidents were led to rely on state and local governments to achieve national ends. As Roosevelt's immediate successor, Truman promoted the idea that the national government should expand its economic and social responsibilities. Four days after the end of World War II, Truman sent Congress a message calling for full employment legislation that would make government the employer of "last resort." In his 1948 State of the Union address, he called for programs to ensure economic security as well as the civil rights, health, and adequate housing of Americans.[50]

Truman's legislative agenda was frustrated by a coalition of Republicans and southern Democrats who held a majority in Congress. The Housing Act of 1949 offers a telling example of the terms on which

Democratic policy would proceed. Cosponsored by conservative Republicans and southern Democrats as well as northern liberal Democrats, the 1949 act authorized a federal program for public housing and urban renewal. The act worked through grants to local urban renewal and public housing authorities. Though the federal government set standards for construction and tenant eligibility in public housing, it delegated significant choices to local government: maintenance, site selection, selection of contractors, and planning. Moreover, the urban renewal programs relied on private developers. Bypassing state governments, the act served the Democrats' urban constituency by creating a direct financial link between local governments and Washington, but with a significant loss of federal control and program equity.[51]

Presidents John F. Kennedy and Lyndon Johnson presented aggressive agendas for the expansion of the national government, and both used federal police powers and budgets more aggressively than had Eisenhower. Kennedy used federal troops to desegregate universities in Mississippi and Alabama. Kennedy and Johnson sent Congress civil rights bills to outlaw state segregation codes. The 1964 Civil Rights Act created a significant new instrument to achieve national standards in grant programs, making discrimination in the administration of any federal grant program illegal—a so-called *crosscutting* requirement that applied to all federal grants-in-aid.[52] When combined with the "carrot" of federal grants, the requirement was supposed to force state and local governments across the nation to conform to a federal rule.

The Democratic administrations of the 1960s enhanced federal power, but at the same time most programs were implemented through state and local governments as well as voluntary or private sector institutions. Johnson relied on his so-called "creative federalism" to accomplish national goals. The way this term was defined in the War on Poverty was that the program had to be "organized at the State and local level and must be supported and directed by State and local efforts"; it could be won "with an actual reduction in Federal expenditures and Federal employment."[53] Johnson's approach won the warm approval of the business magazine *Fortune*, which in 1966 endorsed the federal government as a "junior partner" distributing money to local interests:

> Creative federalism as it is now developing emphasizes relationships between Washington and many other independent centers of decision in state and local governments, in new public bodies, in universities, in professional organizations, and in business . . ." [C]reative federalism" includes a deliberate policy of encouraging the growth of institutions that will be independent of and, in part, antagonistic to the federal government power. Almost every part of every new program transfers federal funds to some outside agency.[54]

Presidents Kennedy and Johnson had something else in mind, however. They envisioned the national government as very much a senior partner that would utilize state, local, and private institutions to accomplish national purposes. Active governments at all levels could cooperate with each other to enhance individual opportunity and economic well-being.

In the case of civil rights enforcement and political equality, Democrats did not rely on grants to achieve their reforms. In cases before the Supreme Court such as *Baker* v. *Carr* (1964), the Kennedy administration argued that state legislative districts that overrepresented rural areas violated constitutional guarantees of equal protection of the law. The Voting Rights Act of 1965 gave the federal government the right to monitor state elections, a remarkably strong national intrusion into a traditional state responsibility.

With regard to social programs, however, both Democratic presidents relied on grants to achieve national ends. In the Public Welfare Amendments of 1962, the Kennedy administration sought grants to the states to fund social services designed to help welfare recipients become more self-sufficient.[55] Whipped into a legislative fury by the Johnson White House, Congress authorized 219 new grants between 1964 and 1966. Among these were the major social commitments of the 1960s. The Medicaid and Medicare programs of 1965 took different directions. Under Medicare, Social Security recipients were insured directly by the federal government, while the states received Medicaid grants to manage a new system for medical care for those eligible for Aid to Families with Dependent Children and other state-run assistance programs.

Other grant programs funded education (the Elementary and Secondary Education Act of 1965) and police (the Safe Streets and Crime Control Act of 1968). The Economic Opportunity Act of 1964 financed new educational and job-training programs for the poor. Long-established grant programs, such as vocational rehabilitation and vocational education, were expanded to provide services for the mentally and physically handicapped. Food stamps, an experiment tried during the Kennedy years, became permanent in 1966, as did a school lunch program. The 1949 Housing Act funding public housing and urban renewal was expanded, and the Johnson administration brought forward an innovative plan for "model cities."[56]

The administration did not deceive itself about the lack of enthusiasm shown by many state and local government leaders for the new social agenda. The new legislation, therefore, often intentionally bypassed state and local governments. Much of the money went to airport, water and sewer, hospital, and local special districts that performed only one or two public functions. Both the War on Poverty and the Model Cities programs channeled funds to community-based organizations established to increase the participation of lower-income residents and to put these programs beyond the control of local power brokers.[57] The Labor Department's job-training programs reflected this strategy by allocating grants to community-based organizations.

Besides bypassing state and local governments, the Democratic administrations targeted grants to try to force the institutions that received them to spend the money on purposes approved by Washington. Before the 1960s Congress had written the larger grant programs as *formula* grants, which distributed funds to eligible recipients on the basis of criteria written into the law (thus bypassing the appropriations committees). Such formulas entitled recipients (such as state governments) to national funds and made it difficult if not impossible for federal officials to control their use. Conservative state and local governments presented the biggest obstacle to liberal intentions, for under formula funding, governments regularly received federal funds as a matter of law. Administrators found themselves helpless to prevent even flagrant deviations from national purpose, as welfare and antipollution grants illustrate (see Chapters 7 and 10).

Most of the Democratic initiatives of the mid-1960s relied on *project* grants (Medicaid was a notable exception). Such grants specified how the money was to be used but did not allocate it automatically to all eligible recipients. Project grants required potential recipients to propose a project (such as a specific water purification system or the purchase of new buses) to a national agency in charge of administering grants for that purpose. Project grants placed potential recipients in competition with one another, making it easier for federal bureaucrats to dictate the use of the funds.

Though a large number of project grants existed in 1962, they were funded with less money than the formula programs. Table 5.4 shows that of 219 grant programs added between 1962 and the end of 1966, 173 (or 4 out of 5) were project grants, mostly added during the eighty-ninth Congress of 1965–1966. In 1964, project grants accounted for one-quarter of grant spending, but they accounted for one-half by 1969.[58]

The Democratic administrations pioneered new methods in an attempt to impose national standards. The most effective new technique was the crosscutting requirement. Although the U.S. Civil Rights Commission in 1957 had recommended that segregated colleges be denied federal grant money, not until the 1964 Civil Rights Act did a federal law make nondiscrimination a condition for receiving any federal grant funds. This was the first of many such national standards applied to all federal grants. Another method for strengthening the hand of federal administrators was the crossover sanction, which was applied selectively. The first example of a crossover condition was contained in the Highway Beautification Act of 1965, which made the control of bill-

Table 5.4. *Growth in authorized grant-in-aid programs, 1962–1966*

Calendar Year	Total	Formula Grants		Project Grants	
		Number	% of Total	Number	% of Total
Through 1962	160	53	33	107	67
Added in 1963	21	8	38	13	62
Added in 1964	40	10	25	30	75
Added in 1965	109	19	17	90	83
Added in 1966	49	9	18	40	82
Total, January 1967	379	99	26	280	74

Source: Advisory Commission on Intergovernmental Relations, *Categorical Grants: Their Role and Design,* Report A-52 (Washington, DC: ACIR, 1978), 25.

boards a condition for receiving highway grant funds. The number of federal requirements attached as a condition of federal aid increased from 4 in 1960 to 1,034 in 1978.[59] Finally, the federal government preempted the rights of states in certain areas, beginning with the Water Pollution Control Act of 1965, which permitted the Secretary of Health, Education and Welfare to set water pollution standards for a state if existing standards were found to be inadequate.[60]

Through these techniques federal policymakers hoped to establish some effective and enforceable national standards to guide federally assisted public policy. But the Democratic efforts to control grants soon met with a political backlash. First, officials representing states and localities resented the regulations. Second, governors protested the fact that the Great Society programs bypassed the states in favor of the cities. The creation of a cabinet-level Department of Housing and Urban Development in 1966 only rubbed salt into the governors' wounds, for it appeared that cities, not states, were favored by federal policymakers.

Third, the grants were unevenly distributed and were disproportionately awarded to jurisdictions that developed skills in "grantsmanship." Governments or organizations that understood how to use the grant application process to their advantage received the lion's share of federal dollars. Local governments or nonprofit organizations that lacked the capacity to hire professionals with grant-writing skills found it difficult to compete whether they were deserving of federal aid or not. Congress and public interest groups objected to this redistributive effect, and even the advocates of federal standards found it difficult to defend the results. Fourth, the grant system soon became so complicated that elected officials in state houses and city halls felt that they were losing control of their governments.[61]

Probably because of the political backlash against previous Democratic programs, Jimmy Carter was the most cautious of the postwar Democratic presidents. And unlike Truman, Kennedy, and Johnson, Carter had developed his policy views and political skills as a state governor rather than as a federal legislator. As president, he took a decidedly ambivalent view toward federal power. "My own inclination," he told an audience of U.S. Labor Department employees, "is to shift as much responsibility as possible to the States and local governments, but to provide conformity and continuity and direction from the Federal Government."[62]

During the Carter presidency federal expenditures for grant programs peaked and leveled off.[63] Like President Gerald Ford, he cut back revenue sharing and allowed inflation to reduce its value further. In some cases, such as CETA, the Carter administration added new restrictions and regulations to grant programs, "targeting" them more specifically to Democratic constituencies in older cities of the Midwest and Northeast.

THE GROWTH IN GOVERNMENT PROGRAMS

Every presidential administration since the 1930s has placed its own stamp on domestic policy, but all have delegated to state and local governments significant control over most new programs initiated by the national government. This general agreement concerning the form of policy activism made federal grants-in-aid the logical policy tool for *both* Democrats and Republicans. Grants appealed both to advocates of national activism and to conservatives who wanted Washington to exert less direct policy control.

With bipartisan agreement on decentralized activism, national grant spending ballooned until the mid-1970s. Both Republican and Democratic presidential administrations increased the level of spending on grants, created new grant programs devoted to social concerns, and reduced matching requirements to induce recipients to take advantage of the programs. By any measure, the grant battlefield expanded dramatically and steadily through Republican as well as Democratic administrations in the 1950s and 1960s and into the 1970s. Table 5.5 shows the national budget for intergovernmental grants at the beginning of each postwar presidency. The first column lists the fiscal year marking a change of presidential administration and adds the significant fiscal years 1978, 1982, 1985, and 1988.

The second and third columns of Table 5.5 show that funding for federal grants consistently increased during Democratic and Republican

Table 5.5. *Federal grant-in-aid expenditures, selected years, 1949–1989*

	Total Spending ($ billions of dollars) in:		Grant Spending as a Percentage of:		
Fiscal Year	Current Dollars	Constant Dollars (1982-100)	Gross National Product	Total Federal Outlays	State and Local Revenues from Own Sources[a]
1946	$ 0.8	$ 4.9	0.4%	1.5%	[b]
1953	2.8	11.3	0.8	3.7	[b]
1961	7.1	24.8	1.4	7.3	15.8%
1963	8.6	28.7	1.5	7.7	16.5
1969	20.1	54.8	2.2	11.0	21.6
1975	49.8	87.1	3.3	15.0	29.1
1977	68.4	103.6	3.5	16.7	31.0
1978	77.9	109.7	3.6	17.0	26.5
1979	82.9	106.7	3.4	16.5	25.5
1980	91.5	105.9	3.4	15.5	25.8
1981	94.8	100.7	3.2	14.0	30.1
1982	88.2	88.2	2.8	11.8	25.6
1986	112.3	96.7	2.7	11.3	20.6
1989	119.0	92.2	2.4	10.9	[b]

[a]Calculated on the basis of national income and product accounts by the Advisory Commission on Intergovernmental Relations. Figures for 1989 are estimates.

[b]Not available

Source: U.S. Office of Management and Budget, *Historical Tables, Budget of the United States Government, Fiscal Year 1989* (Washington, DC: GPO, 1988), Table 12.1; Advisory Commission on Intergovernmental Relations, *Significant Features of Fiscal Federalism, 1988,* vol. I (Washington, DC: ACIR, 1987), Table 8, p. 15.

administrations, reaching a peak in 1978. The second column indicates the growth in actual spending for grant programs, which doubled during the Eisenhower administration, nearly tripled during the Kennedy-Johnson years, and more than tripled again during the Nixon-Ford administrations. Column three demonstrates that even in constant dollars (that is, taking inflation into account), grant spending increased by more than 5,000 percent between 1946 and 1978. President Carter's effort to stimulate the economy in 1978 raised grant spending to a postwar high, in constant dollars.

Until the Carter years, federal grants took a steadily larger share of the nation's national product, of the federal government's overall budget, and of the money collected by state and local governments. Since the late 1970s, that share has declined, settling at levels reached during the mid-1960s.

The national government channeled a substantial portion of this money into new rather than into existing grants. Two years into the Kennedy administration, there existed 160 separately authorized federal grant programs. By 1970, the Advisory Commission on Inter-governmental Relations counted 530 grant-in-aid programs, 143 of which had been enacted during the first two years of the Nixon adminis-tration. An Urban Institute study indicated that administrations in the 1970s successfully consolidated many grants, reducing their number to 428 by 1980. The Reagan administration further reduced that number to 313, primarily by consolidating, rather than eliminating, many pro-grams.[64]

Even as the number and cost of federal grants rose through the 1970s, their priorities shifted. Dwight Eisenhower's interstate highway pro-gram restored the priorities of previous Republican administrations. By 1960, 41 percent of all federal grants were committed to transportation, primarily highway construction. Not since the 1920s had the federal government earmarked such a large portion of its grants for trans-portation.[65]

The purposes of grants-in-aid changed in the 1960s and 1970s, as Table 5.6 indicates. Newer federal grant programs (such as revenue sharing) grew rapidly compared with the grants created during the New Deal and earlier. Agricultural grants, highway grants, and income main-tenance grants (including AFDC) fell as a share of all grant spending. Social programs to enhance health, economic opportunity (early child-hood education, job training for the unemployed, medical care for

Table 5.6. *Percentage distribution of federal aid by function, 1960–1989*

	Percentage of Total Federal Grants Spending			
	1960	1970	1980	1989[a]
Community and regional development	2%	7%	7%	4%
Natural resources and environment	2	2	6	3
Health	3	16	17	29
General purpose fiscal assistance[b]	2	2	9	2
Education, training, social services, and employment	7	27	24	18
Income security	38	24	20	27
Transportation	43	19	14	15
Agriculture	3	3	1	1
Other	—	1	1	1

[a]Estimates
[b]Includes general revenue sharing
Source: U.S. Office of Management and Budget, *Special Analysis, Budget of the United States Government, Fiscal Year 1989*, (Washington, DC: GPO, 1988) H-18.

AFDC families), and environmental quality (urban and rural) were the fastest-growing grant programs. The similarity of the priorities of 1970 and 1980 suggests that presidential administrations of the 1970s did not reverse the policy emphases of the 1960s. Only revenue sharing and environmental grants distinguish the priorities of the 1970s from the previous decade.

To elicit state and local participation in grant programs, Congress and Republican and Democratic administrations kept requirements for matching funds to a minimum. The Eisenhower administration set the precedent. Typically, New Deal programs had required the states to match federal grants on a fifty-fifty basis. This requirement constituted a major hurdle for poor states. But the interstate highway program of 1956 provided a 90 percent federal share, so that states provided only ten cents of every road construction dollar. This formula potentially resulted in "prompt, closer supervision of grant programs," since the objectives being promoted were increasingly national and the federal stakes in the ventures were greater than the recipients'. By making participation so easy, federal policy designers ensured that the states would participate. At the same time, because they were paying most of the costs, the national government could attach "strings" to these monies, requiring state and local governments to meet nationally imposed conditions. As in the 1930s, many of these conditions were administrative, but soon additional civil rights and other standards were added.[66]

Many of the new grants programs in the Kennedy, Johnson, and Nixon years required little or no match from recipients. The trend away from matching requirements continued through Democratic and Republican years alike. The huge Medicaid program of the Great Society required the traditional fifty-fifty match by most states. In 1972 the Nixon administration won its battle for general revenue sharing, which gave states and localities money for almost any purpose and which required no recipient contribution at all. Revenue sharing, as written into the State and Local Fiscal Assistance Act, authorized $30.2 billion over five years for thirty-eight thousand state and local governments.[67] By 1972, before general revenue sharing went into effect, federal grants totaled $32.2 billion. Of that sum, $4.7 billion, or 15 percent, required no matching money. An additional $25.6 billion, or 80 percent, called for a federal share of more than 50 percent of all costs.

The expansion of the intergovernmental grant system required bipartisan aggreement. Presidents of both parties emphasized grants for social programs in the 1960s and 1970s, and they made it easier for recipients to secure grants because they lowered or eliminated matching requirements. Republican and Democratic administrations differed on two aspects of the grant programs: they disagreed about who should receive the funds and about the requirements that recipients should have to meet. The philosophical disputes about American social policy after World War II often narrowed to a series of skirmishes over the distribution of grants and the conditions attached to them. Each time the parties switched control of the White House, as in 1961, 1969, 1977, and 1981, its president steered the grants system in a new direction. Under Democratic presidents, the national government tried to target grants more to the cities and to the industrial states. Republicans attempted to spread grants more broadly, to benefit rural and suburban areas and Republican-controlled Sunbelt states.

THE CONSEQUENCES OF THE GRANTS STRATEGY: ACTIVISM AND POLICY INCOHERENCE

The expansion of social policy in postwar America was destined to be always difficult. The grant strategy provided a politically feasible way to enhance national activism and establish some national standards. However, the features that made grant programs politically appealing reduced their potential effectiveness. The grants battles of the 1960s and 1970s expanded social policy, but this fact did not constitute a triumph for efficient or equitable policy. The accomplishment of national policy goals in the United States requires gargantuan efforts to achieve small results. Every new policy ends up becoming mired in the complexity of the grant system, with its attendant opportunities for delay, failure, and policy embarrassments that fuel popular resentment.

The Growth of Policy Activism

The bipartisan consensus on decentralized activism channeled the day-to-day task of governing social policy away from Washington and into state capitals, county seats, and cities. State governments grew more rapidly than the national government after 1960, as measured by the two key indicators of policy capacity: revenues and personnel. Of course these states sought to subordinate national priorities to their own whenever they could.

Table 5.7 shows that between 1950 and 1980 per capita direct expenditures by the federal government and by state and local governments increased by about 1,200 percent, much faster than inflation.[68] State and local spending on education, welfare, health, hospitals, police, and sanitation each increased at an even faster rate than overall spending, and direct federal spending on welfare and police (and education, between 1960 and 1980) also increased at a faster rate than the overall average. Note that all of these functions were still funded overwhelmingly by state and local governments, as they had been throughout the century (compare Tables 2.2 and 4.1 [pages 40 and 102]). Note

Table 5.7. *Per capita government revenues and expenditures, 1961 to 1985–1986*

	1950		1960		1970–1971		1980–1981		1985–1986	
	Federal	State and Local	Federal	State and Local	Federal	State and Local	Federal	State and Local	Federal	State and Local
Taxes	$231.96	$104.91	$427.81	$200.66	$665.57	$460.47	$1,790.86	$1,079.31	$1,957.46	$1,547.44
Individual income	103.80	5.19	226.20	13.68	418.07	57.69	1,260.45	204.93	1,447.50	308.69
Corporation income	69.14	3.91	119.42	6.56	129.86	16.60	269.86	62.43	261.92	82.76
Sales, customs	51.70	33.98	70.02	65.83	94.19	161.12	214.35	379.49	195.15	559.86
Property	—	48.45	—	91.14	—	183.51	—	330.92	—	463.38
Direct expenditures	249.95	150.22	426.26	288.21	729.30	730.52	2,757.22	1,798.52	3,302.72	2,516.05
Education	16.28	47.31	3.81	104.00	22.44	288.05	53.98	643.51	131.10	874.49
Highways	.45	25.07	.76	52.38	1.46	87.73	1.35	152.74	61.96	204.78
Welfare	.16	19.38	.32	24.47	10.76	88.36	98.85	238.90	291.75	318.29
Hospitals	4.39	9.12	5.43	17.97	9.96	44.05	25.61	116.22	32.35	157.89
Health	1.96	2.40	2.62	3.11	7.64	10.27	24.17	43.13	49.40	64.50
Police	.58	5.12	.96	10.32	2.32	25.34	8.40	65.98	15.12	94.10
Fire	—	3.22	—	5.53	—	11.16	—	27.97	—	39.77
Sanitation and sewerage	—	5.50	—	9.59	—	19.80	—	65.76	—	79.40

Source: U.S. Census Bureau, Census of Governments, 1977, vol. 6, Topical Studies, no. 4, *Historical Statistics on Governmental Finances and Employment* (Washington, DC: GPO, 1979), Table 2, 31–7; U.S. Census Bureau, *Governmental Finances in 1982–83,* GF-83, no. 5 (Washington, DC: GPO, 1984), Tables 2–3, pp. 2–4; U.S. Census Bureau, *Government Finances in 1985–86,* GF-86, no. 5 (Washington, DC: GPO, 1987), Tables 2–3, pp. 2–3. Compare Tables 2.2 (page 40) and 4.1 (page 102).

also that in most policy areas the federal government increased its share of direct expenditures between 1980–1981 and 1985–1986 (for example, the federal share of education spending grew from 8 percent to 15 percent, the federal share of health expenditures changed from 36 percent to 43 percent, and the federal share of welfare expenditures shot up from 30 percent to 48 percent).

A comparison with revenues suggests that neither the federal nor the state and local governments relied solely on the taxes they collected to fund these expenditures. By 1985–1986, the federal government was sustaining a significant portion of its spending by borrowing money. By 1980–1981, state and local governments were receiving about 18 percent of all their revenues from the federal government (that percentage dropped to 14 percent by 1985–1986).[69]

The Power and the Will to Resist National Priorities

Tables 5.8 and 5.9 demonstrate clearly that local and state governments outpaced the federal government in their capacity to implement new programs. Table 5.8 reveals that all government revenues have increased more than tenfold since 1949. Washington's share of the total has dropped during each presidential term except for Jimmy Carter's, with the steepest declines occurring during Republican administrations. Local revenues have stayed relatively constant with inflation since 1960. State government revenues have increased as a share of all revenues during each presidency and now constitute a quarter of all government receipts.

Table 5.8. *Growth and distribution of U.S. public sector tax revenues, 1949–1985 (millions of dollars)*

Year	Total	Federal Amount	Federal Percent	State Amount	State Percent	Local Amount	Local Percent
1949	$ 50,358	$ 35,568	71	$ 7,376	15	$ 6,556	13
1953	83,704	62,796	75	10,552	13	10,356	12
1961	116,331	77,470	67	19,057	16	19,804	17
1963	130,811	86,797	66	22,117	17	20,993	16
1969	222,708	145,996	66	41,931	19	34,789	16
1975	351,435	189,970	57	80,155	24	61,310	18
1977	419,778	243,842	58	101,085	24	74,852	18
1981	650,228	405,714	62	149,738	23	94,776	15
1982	671,424	405,125	60	162,658	24	103,641	15
1984	735,023	414,829	56	196,745	27	123,399	17
1985[a]	801,000	455,000	57	214,000	27	132,000	17

[a]Estimates.

Source: Advisory Commission on Intergovernmental Relations, *Significant Features of Fiscal Federalism, 1985–86 ed.* (Washington, DC: ACIR, 1986), Tables 29, 32, pp. 40–5.

Table 5.9. *Growth and distribution of U.S. public sector employment, selected years, 1944–1987*

Year	Number Employed (thousands)				Percent Distribution		
	Total Public Sector	Federal	State	Local	Federal	State	Local
1944	6,537	3,365	700	2,472	51.5%	10.7%	37.8%
1949	6,203	2,047	1,037	3,119	33.0	16.7	50.3
1954	7,232	2,373	1,149	3,710	32.8	15.9	51.3
1959	8,487	2,399	1,454	4,634	28.3	17.1	54.6
1964	10,064	2,528	1,873	5,663	25.1	18.6	56.3
1969	12,685	2,969	2,614	7,102	23.4	20.6	56.0
1975	14,986	2,890	3,268	8,828	19.3	21.8	58.9
1977	15,459	2,848	3,481	9,130	18.4	22.5	59.1
1981	15,968	2,865	3,726	9,377	17.9	23.3	58.7
1982	15,918	2,848	3,747	9,324	17.9	23.5	58.6
1984	16,436	2,942	3,898	9,595	17.9	23.7	58.4
1987[a]	17,481	3,030	(14,451)		17.3	(82.7)	

[a]Office of Management and Budget estimates, 1988
Source: Advisory Commission on Intergovernmental Relations, *Significant Features of Fiscal Federalism, 1985–86 ed.*, (Washington, DC: ACIR, 1986), Table 79, p. 132; *Special Analysis, Budget of the United States Government, Fiscal Year 1989*, (Washington, DC: GPO, 1988), I–11.

Similarly, Table 5.9 shows that employment by all levels of government has grown since the final years of World War II. The number of national government employees, though, has not increased dramatically since 1964, just before the explosive growth of the project grants. After 1969, the number of national government employees began to decline, and since 1974 the percentage of civilian government employees working for the national government has been lower than the percentage in 1929, when Herbert Hoover took office.[70] Local and state government employment has increased over the same period, with state governments hiring nearly one-fourth of all public employees by the 1980s.

State governments also became more professional. The grants strategy boosted the policymaking capacities of governors' offices, legislatures, and state agencies. "State service delivery has increased steadily throughout the entire [last] quarter century. The federal role increased from 1913 to 1957, leveled off, and declined somewhat over the last twelve or thirteen years. The relative role of local government declined rapidly between 1913 and 1957 and has remained somewhat stable during the last quarter-century . . . states appear to be increasing their role vis-à-vis the [national government] over much of the thirteen years between 1969 to 1982."[71]

The national government, through the grant system, has served as a sort of social policy "bank," writing checks that state and local governments cash and spend. One study conducted in the late 1970s found that "considerably less than one-tenth of the federal budget is allotted to domestic activities that the federal government performs itself."[72]

The cultural, economic, and political differences idiosyncratic to each state and metropolitan area made state and local governments differ in their willingness to cooperate with the federal government. Pressures to win a comparative advantage relative to other jurisdictions gave each grant recipient a strong motivation to try to bend national policy priorities in its direction. Richard Franklin Bensel analyzed the relatively rare close votes in Congress between 1971 and 1980 and found that most conflictual decisions turned on proposals that would have effectively changed the distribution of federal resources or of business regulations to the detriment of one region of the country. These contested votes included proposals to change the formulas for revenue sharing, CETA, community block grants, highway funds, education funds, and federal aid to New York City during its fiscal crisis of the mid-1970s. In these votes, legislators appeared to be much more strongly influenced by the way these changes would benefit their constituents than by their party affiliation or their ideology.[73]

Rarely did federal programs attack interstate resource disparities by equalizing revenues. Grants did little to reduce the resource disparities that fuel this competition. Only one-seventh of grant formulas explicitly included criteria that emphasized the redistribution of aid to needy areas. Instead, many grant programs distributed federal funds based on population rather than demand or need. In the mid-1970s, the wealthiest states actually received the most grants per capita.[74]

The Frustrations of National Policy Management

Under these conditions national activism became increasingly fragmented, complex, and difficult to manage. The grants strategy multiplied veto points by adding state and local governments and a host of other participants to each stage in the policy process. A small 1970 program to encourage new, planned communities turned into a dismal failure when local governments, private developers, and other necessary partners took little interest in the efforts.[75] In an effort to develop the economy of Oakland, California and expand the number of jobs available to Oakland's minority population, the Economic Development Administration provided millions of dollars in project grants to develop port, airport, and other employment-stimulating facilities. After years of effort, the grants resulted in only a handful of permanent jobs for minorities.[76]

In a study of welfare grants in Massachusetts in the late 1960s, Martha

Derthick concluded that achieving federal objectives was difficult because governments receiving funds differed widely from each other and from the federal government on program priorities. Federal administrators can influence policy through informal negotiations, including threats of withholding funds (though they seldom take this draconian step), and to an extent can mobilize client groups and sympathetic state officials to work on behalf of federal objectives. But as Derthick notes, "the acceptance of grants would not be so prompt and widespread if the conditions accompanying them were very costly and were known to be strictly enforced."[77]

Block grants, though designed to reform the hopelessly complex project grant system, caused their own administrative headaches. Employment and training systems in some places (such as Massachusetts) worked very well, but lack of planning and coordination was pervasive.[78] A Labor Department memorandum in 1975 complained that the CETA program was nearly unmanageable:

> Prime sponsor staff are a wholly unsophisticated group in many locales. Some are totally new to the field of manpower, while others can borrow only from experience with narrowly defined categorical programs. Many are totally unprepared to manage and organize a program and are, further, very uncomfortable in exercising their responsibilities and authority as prime grantees, particularly in their dealings with their subgrantees. Sponsors are making demands on regional staff that far exceed even a modified concept of revenue sharing . . . Federal [officials] seem to be forced to concentrate on providing whatever 'hand-holding' they can.[79]

Of 264 reported prime sponsor violations of the CETA law reported to the Labor Department by mid-1976, 66 involved discrimination by local officials, 47 alleged that prime sponsors had failed to maintain previous efforts (thus substituting federal funds for their own), 15 involved nepotism in hiring, 33 involved political favoritism, and 51 involved "miscellaneous misuse of federal funds."[80]

The U.S. General Accounting Office complained that CETA was administered by a complex maze of uncoordinated agencies that inflated the cost of labor market policy.[81] Given responsibility but little control over block grant programs such as CETA and the Community Development Block Grants program, national administrators imposed strict procedural, as opposed to substantive, standards on grant recipients in order to protect themselves against charges of negligence. Grant recipients, in turn, complained of excessive federal regulation and "red tape." The result was "an overwhelming sense of futility and impotence on the part of all concerned."[82]

The reality of grant administration was a far cry from the portrait of insensitive, single-minded national bureaucrats suppressing the creativity and ignoring the needs of local jurisdictions. Condemned to manage policy activism "by proxy," administrators in the national government found themselves facing an impossible task. As early as 1969, one federalism scholar noted that "the federal agencies have not done all that legally they might have done to demand compliance" in welfare and urban renewal programs because angry state or local officials could mobilize members of Congress in their defense.[83]

The 1970s and 1980s generalized this pattern. According to Thomas Anton, "vaguely defined program goals, increased reliance on block grants rather than categorical grants, and federal reluctance to closely monitor federal fund use have all combined to give state and local governments considerable freedom in determining their uses of federal dollars."[84] In Lester Salamon's words, the tools that the national government developed in the postwar era "continually place Federal officials in the uncomfortable position of being held responsible for programs they do not really control."[85]

Such problems sapped the energy of national policymakers and stripped legitimacy from national programs. Although public expenditure increased, it did not reflect a coherent plan to meet national needs. Many concluded that government had simply become "overloaded."[86]

Rather than acting as forceful advocates of national standards and quality services, federal agencies had to bargain with state grant recipients, much like "a rich merchant haggling on equal terms with a sly, bargain-hunting consumer."[87] Bargaining, in turn, made social policy appear "political" in the worst sense of the word. The inability of U.S. Labor Department staff to control the use of CETA funds created a multitude of opportunities for abuse, and reports of waste and fraud in the CETA program rebounded to Washington. When some federally sponsored community action agencies challenged the power of local elites in the 1960s, the wrath of these elites came down upon the Office of Economic Opportunity, which quickly lost credibility on Capitol Hill. The complexities of the grant-in-aid system created a gap between promise and performance that, without doubt, contributed to a growing cynicism about all government efforts.[88]

In the Netherlands and France, two nations where local government spending exceeded national government spending in the mid-1970s, virtually all funds transferred from the national to the local governments were unrestricted, given with no strings attached. In the United States only 13 percent of such transfers were provided in the form of unrestricted grants.[89] The Dutch and French policies seem reckless and out of keeping with the more centralized tradition on the European continent, unless one takes into account historical and institutional factors that made restricted grants unnecessary. Drawing on a long tradition of national standards and central control, European policymakers, confident that local officials would more or less carry out national intent, could confidently increase funding for these governments. In any case, most social policy programs were administered directly by national governments; most grants funded local public services. In contrast, American policymakers had to design grant programs with "strings" if they were to have any influence at all over the way the independent states chose to use their grants. The many conditions placed on American grants in the 1970s underscored the national government's weakness, not its strength.

THE REAGAN ADMINISTRATION'S ASSAULT ON GOVERNMENTAL CAPACITY

Unlike any president in the postwar era, Ronald Reagan believed that his election gave him a mandate to reduce radically the capacity of all governments, including state and local governments, to implement social policies. In most policy areas, this meant the delegation of policy control to state governments, funding cuts, and the reduction of federal standards as a means to ensure some similarity in state and local performance. In his first inaugural speech, Reagan said, "All of us need to be reminded that the Federal government did not create the states; the states created the federal government." Like Nixon, Reagan promised a New Federalism that would return power to the states; "in a single stroke," he pledged in 1982, "we will be accomplishing a realignment that will end cumbersome administration and spiraling costs at the Federal level . . ."[90]

The administration mounted its strongest assaults on government spending immediately following the elections of 1981 and 1985. The 1981 tax cuts and the establishment of tax brackets indexed to inflation limited federal revenues for all purposes. Beginning with the Omnibus Budget Reconciliation Act of 1981, Reagan won battles that reversed many of the postwar grant-in-aid patterns. A large number of grant programs were eliminated or their cost and coverage was reduced. Federal grant-in-aid expenditures in constant dollars dropped significantly, after rising constantly since 1946 (Table 5.4). In contrast to the "new federalism" of the Nixon years, the Reagan reforms slashed all federal grants by 13 percent—a cut twice as large as the overall national budget reduction of that year. Congress resisted further cuts after 1981, and grant spending in 1982 began to increase again, though at a rate slower than it had grown in the 1960s and 1970s.[91]

In addition, the administration enhanced the conservative features of grants. Reviewing the first Reagan term, one federalism scholar argued that the massive budget changes initiated in 1981 created an intergovernmental grant system that restricted state governments less than the one that Reagan inherited. The president's apparent goal was "to arrest [the] trend toward federal prescription of nationally uniform standards for public services."[92] The federal contribution to most grants (such as wastewater treatment, child nutrition, and urban mass transportation) were reduced, requiring grant recipients to contribute a larger share of the cost. The hope was that a higher matching requirement would alter incentives for local government activism in areas previously stimulated when the national government paid most of the bill. The grant system facilitated a reduction in overall policy effort because federal aid explains most of the growth in state activism and because cuts in federal aid are an effective way to slow not only federal but also state and local government activity.[93]

The budget act (as well as other initiatives in the first term) reduced the number of grants awarded on a project basis, and the amount of money allocated through them fell by more than 30 percent. The 1982 budget consolidated seventy-six separate categorical grants into nine block grants in the areas of health, social services, education, and community development and cut funding for these grants by 20 percent, leaving states with the option of ending these services or paying for them out of state revenues.[94]

Reagan's landslide reelection victory in 1984 strengthened the administration's determination to shift social policy back to the states and at the same time to reduce the capacity of the states to pay for social programs on their own. The federal budget introduced in early 1985 required major cuts in grant programs, including the elimination of the $4.6 billion general revenue sharing program as well as transportation, human services, job training, and other grants.

The White House also introduced a major tax reform proposal that would have eliminated the federal income tax deduction for state and local taxes. According to Richard Nathan, who had helped design revenue sharing and block grant proposals during the Nixon administration, eliminating such deductions would "create pressure (especially in high tax jurisdictions) to cut existing state and local tax rates, or, more likely, undercut the political support for future efforts to increase state and local taxes." One analyst estimated that the tax change would slow the growth of state and local taxes by about 10 percent, although the loss of deductibility seemed to have little impact on sales tax increases passed in Texas, Virginia, and North Dakota in 1986.[95] By reducing the tax capacity of all governments, public spending for social purposes would be reduced. In the end, well-organized opposition by state and local officials encouraged Congress to continue the deductibility of state and local income taxes.

The Varied Responses of the States

Overall, the Reagan presidency had enhanced the states' role in implementing American social policy. In a study of fourteen states conducted in the early 1980s, Nathan found that "the Reagan program has led to a stronger state role in the domestic public sector."[96] For several reasons the states did not cut programs as much as might have been anticipated. First, the states creatively juggled funds to postpone or prevent the 1981 cuts from taking as severe a toll on public programs as the cuts implied. Second, Congress restored some of the cuts in order to mitigate the effects of the recession of 1982–1983. Third, some program constituencies in the states mobilized to protect selected programs. For example, the health care industry and elderly recipients effectively deflected cuts in Medicaid in some states (compared with AFDC for the working poor, a smaller and politically less influential constituency). Similarly, the highway, mass transit, and wastewater treatment proponents were more able to prevent state and local program cutbacks than were proponents of housing assistance programs.

States varied enormously in their propensity to compensate for federal budget cuts. Such states as Massachusetts, New Jersey, and Florida aggressively increased state policy activity. Mississippi, Ohio, and Texas made more modest efforts to compensate for the budget cuts. Arizona, Illinois, Missouri, and South Dakota were among the states that did not make up for federal budget cuts with their own funds.[97] No state continued full funding of politically unpopular efforts, such as the community action agencies established by the Great Society. "Lead-based paint, rat control, and school desegregation programs are other examples of strictly federal programs . . . which were cut back or eliminated by most states except where not permitted by the courts," according to another study of the effects of the federal budget cuts.[98]

THE VULNERABILITY OF THE GRANTS STRATEGY

By the early 1980s economic problems and doubts about the direction of public policy helped bring about the election of conservative governments in Sweden, Britain, the United States and other capitalist nations where government activism had expanded to unprecedented levels in the previous decades. But the United States stands out for the strength of its antigovernment backlash.

We have argued that the American federal policymaking structure produced a kind of social policy activism that was especially vulnerable to the backlash given voice by the Reagan administration. The logic of this assertion can be appreciated only in the context of the evolution of America's policy structure since the 1930s. Programs to alleviate the effects of such serious problems as unemployment were characteristically designed as grant programs. Grants were politically attractive to Congress and the jurisdictions it represented; they also provided a form of activism acceptable to the federal courts and to presidents of both political parties. Republican and Democratic presidents accommodated themselves to grants by steering them toward their constituencies and by varying the conditions attached to these grants. The result was bipartisan support for the expansion of decentralized activism. But the poor performance of programs so designed eroded support for them. Ronald Reagan exploited these flaws in winning the 1980 presidential election, and his administration found that grant programs could be easily altered to promote conservative policy outcomes.

NOTES

1.. Andrew Schonfield, *Modern Capitalism: The Changing Balance of Public and Private Power* (New York: Oxford University Press, 1965), 3.
2.. Arnold Heidenheimer, Hugh Heclo, and Carolyn Teich Adams, *Comparative Public Policy*, 2d ed. (New York: St. Martin's Press, 1983), 122–4.
3. Defense spending constituted 52.2 percent of federal budget outlays in 1960 and 23.2 percent of outlays in 1981; U.S. Office of Management and Budget, *Budget of the United States Government, Fiscal Year 1987: Historical Tables* (Washington, DC: GPO, 1986), Table 3.2.
4. Harold L. Wilensky, *The Welfare State and Equality: Structural and Ideological Roots of Public Expenditures* (Berkeley: University of California Press, 1975), 116.
5. Adam Clymer, "Poll Finds Trust in Government Edging Back Up," *New York Times*, 15 July 1983, 1.
6. "Inaugural Address of President Ronald Reagan," 23 January 1981, in *Weekly Compilation of Presidential Documents* 17:4 (26 January 1981), 1–5.
7. Cf. Russell L. Hanson, "The Expansion and Contraction of the Welfare States," in Robert Goodin and Julian LeGrand, eds., *Not Only the Poor: The Middle Class and the Welfare State* (London: George Allen and Unwin, 1987), 169–202.
8. Supplemental Security Income, established during the Nixon administration, essentially nationalized the old age, blind, and disabled assistance provisions of the Social Security Act. Although it sets national standards, the states are permitted to supplement SSI payments. Because state supplementation is so varied, we judge SSI to be a hybrid program and did not include it in Table 5.2.
9. J. Joseph Huthmacher, *Senator Robert F. Wagner and the Rise of Urban Liberalism* (New York: Atheneum, 1968), 292–4, 318–20; Stephen K. Bailey, *Congress Makes a Law* (New York: Columbia University Press, 1950).
10. *Congressional Record*, 15 July 1949, 9547–52.
11. New England Governors' Textile Committee to the Conference of New England Governors, *New England Textiles and the New England Economy*, Conference of New England Governors, 1959.
12. James L. Sundquist, *Politics and Policy: The Eisenhower, Kennedy, and Johnson Years* (Washington, DC: Brookings, 1968), 57–85; Sar A. Levitan, *Federal Aid to Depressed Areas* (Baltimore: Johns Hopkins University Press, 1964); Randall B. Ripley, *The Politics of Economic and Human Resources Development* (Indianapolis: Bobbs-Merrill, 1972), 21–53, 171–2.

13. Sundquist, *Politics and Policy*, 76–7, 85–91.
14. Roger H. Davidson, *The Politics of Comprehensive Manpower Legislation* (Baltimore: Johns Hopkins University Press, 1972).
15. David Brian Robertson, "Labor Market Surgery, Labor Market Abandonment: The Thatcher and Reagan Unemployment Remedies," in Jerold L. Waltman and Donley T. Studlar, eds., *Political Economy: Public Policies in the United States and Britain* (Jackson: University Press of Mississippi, 1987), 70–4; David Brian Robertson "Governing and Jobs: America's Business-Centered Labor Market Strategy," *Polity* 20:3 (Spring 1988), 426–56.
16. Donald C. Baumer and Carl E. Van Horn, *The Politics of Unemployment* (Washington, DC: Congressional Quarterly, 1985), 59–77; Howard Hallman, *Emergency Employment: A Study In Federalism* (University: University of Alabama Press, 1977), 169–83.
17. Baumer and Van Horn, *The Politics of Unemployment*, 130–54; Ralph Kinney Bennett, "CETA: $11 Billion Boondoggle," *Reader's Digest*, August 1978, pp. 72–6; U.S. Congress, House, Subcommittee on Manpower and Housing of the House Committee on Government Operations, *CETA's Vulnerability to Fraud and Abuse* (Washington, DC: GPO, 1980), 1, 30–3.
18. Baumer and Van Horn, *The Politics of Unemployment*, 157–86; National Council on Employment Policy, "The Job Training Partnership Act: Some Encouraging Signs But Important Questions Still Remain," (Washington, DC: NCEP, July 1985), 9–10.
19. William M. Lunch, *The Nationalization of American Politics* (Berkeley: University of California Press, 1987).
20. David Mayhew, *Congress: The Electoral Connection* (New Haven, CT: Yale University Press, 1974).
21. Edward Tufte, *Political Control of the Economy* (Princeton, NJ: Princeton University Press, 1978).
22. Leon D. Epstein, *Political Parties in the American Mold* (Madison: University of Wisconsin Press, 1986), 43–8.
23. Robert D. Reischauer, "Intergovernmental Diversity: Bane of the Grants Strategy in the United States," in Wallace E. Oates, ed., *The Political Economy of Fiscal Federalism* (Lexington, MA: D.C. Heath, 1977), 115–27.
24. Davidson, *The Politics of Comprehensive Manpower Legislation*, 33–7.
25. R. Douglas Arnold, "The Local Roots of Domestic Policy," in Thomas E. Mann and Norman J. Ornstein, eds., *The New Congress* (Washington, DC: American Enterprise Institute, 1981), 268.
26. John E. Chubb, "Federalism and the Bias for Centralization," in John E. Chubb and Paul E. Peterson, eds., *The New Direction in American Politics* (Washington, DC: Brookings, 1985), 281–6.
27. Allen Schick, "The Distributive Congress," in Allen Schick, ed., *Making Economic Policy in Congress* (Washington, DC: American Enterprise Institute, 1983), 260–68.
28. Donald H. Haider, *When Governments Come to Washington: Governors, Mayors, and Intergovernmental Lobbying* (New York: Free Press, 1974), 1–41.
29. Timothy J. Conlan, "Congress and the Contemporary Intergovernmental System," in Robert Jay Dilger, ed., *American Intergovernmental Relations Today: Perspectives and Controversies* (Englewood Cliffs, NJ: Prentice-Hall, 1986), 104.
30. Cynthia Cates Colella, "The United States Supreme Court and Intergovernmental Relations," in Robert Jay Dilger, ed., *American Intergovernmental Relations Today: Perspective and Controversies* (Englewood Cliffs, NJ: Prentice-Hall, 1986), 47, 61.
31. David B. Walker, *Toward a Functioning Federalism* (Cambridge, MA: Winthrop Publishers, 1981), 149.
32. Ibid., pp. 83–8, 103–9.
33. Martha Derthick, *Policymaking for Social Security* (Washington, DC: Brookings, 1979), 431–2.

34. See Ibid.; Tufte, *Political Control of the Economy*; Arnold, "The Local Roots of Domestic Policy," 281–7; John Ferejohn, "Congress and Redistribution," in Allen Schick, ed., *Making Economic Policy in Congress* (Washington, DC: American Enterprise Institute, 1983), 139–42. For a comparative view, cf. Heidenheimer et al., *Comparative Public Policy*; Douglas E. Ashford and E. W. Kelley, eds., *Nationalizing Social Security in Europe and America* (Greenwich, CT: JAI Press, 1986).

35. *Congress and the Nation, 1945–1964* (Washington, DC: Congressional Quarterly, 1965), 1379.

36. Ibid., 1395.

37. Robert H. Ferrell, ed., *The Eisenhower Diaries* (New York: Norton, 1981), 247, 249; Advisory Commission on Intergovernmental Relations, *The Future of Federalism in the 1980s*, Report M-126 (Washington, DC: ACIR, 1981), 46.

38. Morton Grodzins, "The Federal System," in Laurence J. O'Toole, Jr., ed., *American Intergovernmental Relations: Foundations, Perspectives, and Issues* (Washington, DC: Congressional Quarterly, 1985), 44; George C. Edwards III and Stephen J. Wayne, *Presidential Leadership: Politics and Policy-Making* (New York: St. Martin's Press, 1985), 237.

39. Robert L. Branyan and Lawrence H. Larson, eds., *The Eisenhower Administration, 1953–1961: A Documentary History* (New York: Random House, 1971), 544.

40. Robert J. Donovan, *Eisenhower: The Inside Story* (New York: Harper, 1956), 64; Branyan and Larson, *The Eisenhower Administration*, 539–40.

41. *Congress and the Nation, 1945–1964*, 1385.

42. Ripley, *The Politics of Economic and Human Resources Development*, 130–1.

43. Richard Nixon, "Address to the Nation on Domestic Programs," *Public Papers of . . . President Richard M. Nixon, 1969* (Washington, DC: GPO, 1971), 637–45; 1976 Republican Platform, in Donald Bunce Johnson, ed., *National Platforms*, vol. II (Urbana: University of Illinois Press, 1978), 996. Cf. A. James Reichley, *Conservatives in an Age of Change: The Nixon and Ford Administrations* (Washington, DC: Brookings, 1981).

44. Reichley, *Conservatives in an Age of Change*, 130–73.

45. Lawrence D. Brown, "The Politics of Devolution in Nixon's New Federalism," in Lawrence D. Brown, James W. Fossett, and Kenneth T. Palmer, eds., *The Changing Politics of Federal Grants* (Washington, DC: Brookings, 1984), 73–4. Cf. Samuel Beer, "The Adoption of General Revenue Sharing: A Case Study in Public Sector Politics," *Public Policy* 24:2 (Spring 1976), 132–49.

46. Brown, "The Politics of Devolution in Nixon's New Federalism," 87–92.

47. Advisory Commission on Intergovernmental Relations, *The Future of Federalism in the 1980s*, 49.

48. Advisory Commission on Intergovernmental Relations, *Regulatory Federalism: Policy, Process, Impact and Reform*, Report A-95 (Washington, DC: ACIR, 1984), 74–87.

49. Palmer, "The Evolution of Grant Policies," 36.

50. Bailey, *Congress Makes a Law*, 161; *Public Papers of . . . President Harry S. Truman, 1948* (Washington, DC: GPO, 1964), 3.

51. Dennis R. Judd, *The Politics of American Cities: Private Power and Public Policy*, 3d ed. (Glenview, IL, and Boston: Scott, Foresman/Little, Brown, 1988), 263–8.

52. Advisory Commission of Intergovernmental Relations, *Regulatory Federalism*, 71.

53. Lyndon B. Johnson, 1964 State of the Union Address, in *Public Papers of . . . President Lyndon B. Johnson, 1963–64* (Washington, DC: GPO, 1965), 114.

54. Max Ways, " 'Creative Federalism' and the Great Society," *Fortune* 73:1 (January 1966): 121 ff. Cf. U.S. Congress, Senate, Committee on Government Operations, Subcommittee on Intergovernmental Relations, *Creative Federalism* (Washington, DC: GPO, 1967).

55. Martha Derthick, *Uncontrollable Spending for Social Services Grants* (Washington, DC: Brookings, 1975), 7–14.

56. Kenneth T. Palmer, "The Evolution of Grant Policies," in Lawrence D. Brown, James W. Fossett, and Kenneth T. Palmer, eds., *The Changing Politics of Federal Grants* (Washington, DC: Brookings, 1984), 6–15.

57. Ibid., 15–7.

58. Haider, *When Governments Come to Washington,* 55.

59. Walker, *Toward a Functioning Federalism,* 193–6.

60. Advisory Commission on Intergovernmental Relations, *Regulatory Federalism,* 70–88.

61. Haider, *When Governments Come to Washington,* 57–62.

62. Jimmy Carter, "Remarks and a Question and Answer Session with Department of Labor Employees," February 9, 1977, in *Public Papers of . . . President Jimmy Carter, 1977* (Washington, DC: GPO, 1978), 109.

63. David J. Caputo, "Contemporary American Federalism: Implications for American Cities," in Robert T. Golembiewski and Aaron Wildavsky, eds., *The Costs of Federalism* (New York: Transaction Press, 1984), 191–2.

64. U.S. Congress, Senate, Committee on Governmental Operations, Subcommittee on Intergovernmental Relations, *Intergovernmental Revenue Act of 1971 and Related Legislation* (Washington, DC: GPO, 1971), 379; Michael D. Reagan, *The New Federalism* (New York: Oxford University Press, 1972), 55; George E. Peterson, "Federalism and the States: An Experiment in Decentralization," in John L. Palmer and Isabel V. Sawhill, eds., *The Reagan Record: An Assessment of America's Changing Domestic Priorities* (Cambridge, MA: Ballinger, 1984), 230.

65. *Congress and the Nation, 1945–1964,* 1385. Federal grants for highways constituted two-thirds of federal grant expenditures in the 1920s, dropping to 14 percent during World War II and rising only to 18 percent by 1948.

66. Advisory Commission on Intergovernmental Relations, *The Future of Federalism in the 1980s,* 46.

67. Deil S. Wright, *Understanding Intergovernmental Relations,* 3d ed. (Monterey, CA: Brooks/Cole, 1988), 216–22.

68. Between 1950 and 1980 consumer prices increased by 344 percent, and between 1960 and 1980 consumer prices increased 279 percent; cf. World Bank, World Tables, 2d ed. (Baltimore: Johns Hopkins University Press, 1980), 268–9; and United Nations, *Monthly Bulletin of Statistics* 38:12 (December 1984), 226.

69. See sources for Table 5.7.

70. Advisory Commission on Intergovernmental Relations, *Significant Features of Fiscal Federalism, 1985–86 Edition* (Washington, DC: ACIR, 1986), 132.

71. G. Ross Stephens, "State Centralization Revisited," Paper presented at the 1985 Meetings of the American Political Science Association, New Orleans, September 26–30, 1985.

72. Frederick C. Mosher, "The Changing Responsibilities and Tactics of the Federal Government," *Public Administration Review* 40:6 (November/December 1980), 541–8.

73. Richard Franklin Bensel, *Sectionalism and American Political Development, 1880–1980* (Madison: University of Wisconsin Press, 1984), 257–315.

74. Arnold, "The Local Roots of Domestic Policy," 268.

75. Daniel A. Mazmanian and Paul A. Sabatier, *Implementation and Public Policy* (Glenview, IL: Scott, Foresman, 1983), 49–84, 279.

76. Jeffrey L. Pressman and Aaron Wildavsky, *Implementation* (Berkeley: University of California Press, 1973).

77. Martha Derthick, *The Influence of Federal Grants* (Cambridge, MA: Harvard University Press, 1970), 195–216.

78. U.S. Department of Labor, *The Implementation of CETA in Eastern Massachusetts and Boston* (Washington, DC: GPO, 1978).

79. Memorandum, Esther Friedman to Bill Kolberg, April 25, 1975, in U.S. National Archives, Department of Labor, Assistant Secretary of Labor for Employment and Training William H. Kolberg files, 1973–1976, carton 2, "Comprehensive Employment and Training Act" folder.

80. Memorandum, William J. Harris to William Kolberg, "Report of Formal CETA Allegations," in U.S. National Archives, Department of Labor, Assistant Secretary of Labor for Employment and Training William H. Kolberg files, 1973–1976, carton 2, "Comprehensive Employment and Training Act II" folder.

81. U.S. General Accounting Office, *Federally Assisted Employment and Training: A Myriad of Programs Should be Simplified* (Washington, DC: GPO, 1979).

82. Walter Williams, quoted in Charles T. Goodsell, *The Case for Bureaucracy: A Public Administration Polemic,* 2d ed., (Chatham, NJ: Chatham House, 1985), 71; cf. Ibid., 67–76.

83. Duane Lockard, *The Politics of State and Local Government* (New York: Macmillan, 1969), 38–9.

84. Thomas J. Anton, "Intergovernment Change in the United States: An Assessment of the Literatures," in Trudi Miller, ed., *Public Sector Performance: A Conceptual Turning Point* (Baltimore: Johns Hopkins University Press, 1984), 51.

85. Lester Salamon, "Rethinking Public Management: Third-Party Government and the Changing Forms of Government Action," *Public Policy* 29:3 (Summer 1981), 260.

86. Samuel H. Beer, "Political Overload and Federalism," *Polity* 10 (Fall 1977), 5–17.

87. Helen M. Ingram, "Policy Implementation Through Bargaining: The Case of Federal Grants-In-Aid," *Public Policy* 25:4 (Fall 1977), 499–526.

88. Theodore Lowi, *The End of Liberalism* (New York: Norton, 1979), 169, passim.

89. Douglas Ashford, "Territorial Politics and Equality: Decentralization in the Modern State," *Political Studies* 27:1 (March 1979), 71–83.

90. "Inaugural Address of President Ronald Reagan," January 23, 1981; "State of the Union Address, 1982," *Weekly Compilation of Presidential Documents* 18:4 (1 February, 1982), 79–80.

91. Richard P. Nathan, *The Administrative Presidency* (New York: Wiley, 1983), 59–61; Peterson, "Federalism and the States," 228.

92. Peterson, "Federalism and the States," 259.

93. Susan B. Hansen, "Extraction: The Politics of State Taxation," in Virginia Gray, Herbert Jacob, and Kenneth N. Vines, eds., *Politics in the American States: A Comparative Analysis,* 4th ed. (Boston: Little, Brown, 1983), 440.

94. Peterson, "Federalism and the States," 244–5.

95. Richard P. Nathan, "Reagan and the Cities: How to Meet the Challenge," *Challenge* 28:4 (September/October 1985), 5–6; Robert W. Rafuuse, Jr., "Fiscal Federalism in 1986: The Spotlight Continues to Swing Toward the States and Local Governments," *Publius* 17:3 (Summer 1987), 49.

96. Nathan, "Reagan and the Cities," 7.

97. Richard P. Nathan, Fred C. Doolittle et al., *Reagan and the States* (Princeton, NJ: Princeton University Press, 1987), 67–112.

98. Peterson, "Federalism and the States," 244–5.

Chapter 6

CIVIL RIGHTS AND THE STRUGGLE AGAINST "STATES' RIGHTS"

THE STRUGGLE FOR NATIONAL CITIZENSHIP

Racial segregation and discrimination continues as one of the oldest and most explosive political issues in the United States. Racial antagonism is hardly unique to the United States. But the protracted battle to achieve civil rights is strikingly incongruent with the belief in equality of opportunity that is so often said to be the linchpin value of American culture.

This "American dilemma"—long-denied civil rights in a culture so committed in principle to equal opportunity—owes much to America's fragmented government structure. Traditionally, southern states were permitted to enforce policies that segregated the races and ensured economic and political dominance by whites. For decades, southern political leaders used "states' rights" as the principal line of defense to keep blacks from participating on equal terms in civil society. By the time the national government tried to intervene to guarantee civil rights for blacks, the tradition of states' rights was so entrenched that the campaign for civil rights required extraordinary federal effort and created spectacular federal–state conflicts.

When presidential candidates faced an electoral imperative to seek blacks' votes, blacks finally began to gain allies in their struggle against a segregated second-class citizenship enforced by the laws of many states. Because the economic and political position of blacks had changed since the nineteenth century, the national civil rights standards established in the 1960s could not be swept away by a political reaction as easily as they had been a century earlier, when the rights extended by the Fourteenth Amendment were virtually nullified by the courts and by state action.

168

The Reagan administration tried to reverse many of the gains achieved during the 1960s and 1970s by reducing the federal capacity to enforce civil rights laws and by delegating some enforcement authority to the states, even while opposing the rights of state and local governments to apply stricter standards than those enforced (or articulated) by the federal government. But the electoral strength of blacks, particularly in congressional elections, placed a powerful political obstacle in the way of those trying to weaken civil rights laws.

THE END OF SLAVERY AS A PYRRHIC VICTORY, 1787–1877

Slavery in the Political Economies of the North and South

A century before the American Revolution, slavery had become an established institution in every colony. By the 1660s slaves made up similar proportions of the populations of Massachusetts and Virginia, and slavery was recognized in both states as an institution applying solely to blacks.[1]

When the Revolution unleashed powerful rhetoric about liberty and individual rights, northerners could afford to consider reconciling rhetoric with reality by abolishing slavery. Slavery was inconsequential to the northern economy. The small farms in New England needed little more labor than the owner's immediate family could provide. Blacks made up less than 2 percent of New England's population in 1790, and less than one-fourth of them were slaves.[2] The abolitionist movement was strongest in the states with insignificant black populations. In Massachusetts (1.4 percent black in 1790), the courts refused to enforce the slaveowners' property rights. With five times the percentage of blacks in its population and four out of five blacks enslaved, New York moved much more slowly. In 1799 the state enacted its first antislavery bill, but the law provided only that enslaved children were to be freed by their twenty-eighth birthday. As the value of slaves in New York declined, slaveowners sold off their slaves to southern plantations. The proportion of blacks in New York fell to 3 percent by 1817, when the state enacted a ban on slavery, to take effect in 1827.[3]

In contrast, slaves had been an indispensable feature of the southern economy since about 1700. The South became increasingly dependent upon cash crops—chiefly rice, tobacco, and cotton—exported to Europe. Sprawling plantations emerged in the Deep South, and these relied on the regimented, cheap labor supplied by slaves.[4] By the time of the Revolution, the southern plantation economy had almost completely converted from white free to black slave labor. Slaves were necessary for the southern economy and they constituted a large proportion of the South's wealth. In 1790, 700,000 slaves lived in the United States, most of them located in the South. They constituted approximately one-fifth of the total U.S. population. At an estimated value of $200 each, slaves were worth $140 million dollars to their masters.[5]

Predictably, northern and southern elites held generally opposing views on slavery. Southern elites were determined to protect their substantial investment and they agreed to join the Union only with assurances that slavery would remain unchallenged. Like other property owners at the Constitutional Convention, southern delegates sought a national government strong enough to protect the private use of property. General Cotesworth Pinckney of South Carolina expressed the southern view succinctly: "property in slaves should not be exposed to danger under a government instituted for the protection of property."[6] Southern delegates were especially anxious to preserve the states' slave codes. Adapted from the laws of ancient Rome, the slave codes closely resembled laws for owning and transferring cattle:

> Slaves could be bought, sold, bequeathed, inherited, mortgaged, or seized for debt like any other property. They and their children forever belonged to the master. They had no civil status before the law; they could not own property, or marry, or make contracts, or sue or be sued, or testify in most cases, or serve on juries. They had no political status; they could not vote or hold office or acquire citizenship, nor did they enjoy the protection of the common law. Though the wanton or deliberate killing of a slave was murder, he had no protection against the assaults of his master, and whipping was a recognized and customary form of punishment and training. The master was, indeed, held guiltless even of the death of his slave if it was the unintended consequence of punishment.[7]

Slavery and the Constitution

To secure ratification of the Constitution, the framers agreed to a document that legitimated and strengthened slavery by granting the national government the power to protect slaveowners' property rights but not to abolish slavery (though, for the most part, the document mainly ignores slavery, in spite of the fact that the slave trade deeply disturbed Madison and some other delegates). Unlike other forms of property, slaves were mobile, and they could escape from a state where they were property to a state where they were not (i.e., a northern state that outlawed slavery). Article IV, Section 2 of the Constitution established that slaveowners could claim their property across state lines. In another concession to the South, Article I, Section 9 prohibited Congress from outlawing the importation of slaves until 1808. (The provision did allow for a tariff of ten dollars a head on imported slaves, which made the delay more palatable to those seeking to enlarge the national government's treasury.)

The Constitution provided enduring political protection for slavery by granting extraordinary congressional representation to slaveholding states. Under the Articles of Confederation, the South had held 38 percent of the seats in Congress, and on the basis of their white population alone southern states would have held 41 percent of the seats in the new House of Representatives. But the southern delegates insisted that they deserved even more representation because of the vast number of slaves that resided in their states. Northerners at first refused to permit additional representation, but finally agreed to a compromise. Under the "Three-Fifths" Agreement, representation in the House was based on a census of free whites, plus three-fifths of all slaves. Since most slaves were held in the southern states, this formula allowed the South to elect 44.6 percent of the House of Representatives in 1790, establishing the principle that "a man who lived among slaves had a greater share in the election of [federal] representatives than one who did not."[8]

A petition presented to Congress in 1797 demonstrated the constitutional tilt toward slaveowners. Four blacks who had been set free by their North Carolina owner petitioned the House of Representatives to consider the constitutionality of a North Carolina law that reenslaved blacks if they had been freed for reasons other than "meritorious service." When white authorities put a bounty on them (ten dollars if returned alive, fifty dollars if given proof that they had been killed), the four fled to Pennsylvania and begged Congress for help. Though some northern members of the House reacted with sympathy, southerners demanded that the petition be laid aside. A southern House member asserted that, "This is a kind of property on which the House has no power to legislate." James Madison took the middle ground; maintaining that the case rightfully belonged in the North Carolina courts. This early use of states' rights doctrines to deter restrictions on the rights of freed blacks was effective; on a vote of 33 to 50, the House refused to accept the petition.[9]

At the same time, slaveowners found that national power could be put to their advantage. By an overwhelming House margin of 48 to 7 and without recorded opposition in the Senate, Congress passed a law in 1793 that addressed both "fugitives from justice and persons escaping from the service of their masters." Slaveowners or bounty hunters could cross state lines, seize an escaped slave, and appear before any magistrate to obtain a certificate permitting the transport of the recovered slave back to the owner. The law imposed penalties for interfering with the recovery of a slave.[10]

Federalism, Slavery, and Government Impotence, 1800–1861

The South's slave economy became thoroughly codified in state laws during the first half of the nineteenth century. Antislavery attitudes spread throughout the North, but the Constitution had effectively protected the property rights of slaveowners. Only civil war settled the conflict, setting the stage for a short-lived federal effort to protect the civil rights of blacks.

Cotton plantations thrived in Alabama, Mississippi, Louisiana, South Georgia, and east Texas. Only 23,024 whites and 17,088 slaves lived in the Mississippi–Alabama Territory in 1810, but by 1860 the population had multiplied exponentially and slaves outnumbered whites, 436,631 to 353,901.[11] Overall, four million slaves lived in the South by 1860, their value steadily rising.[12]

Southern state governments helped slaveowners control their holdings by isolating blacks from civil society. Beginning in the 1830s, each state tightened its slave code. Louisiana law stated that a slave owed the master "absolute obedience." Even so little as an insolent look, declared a North Carolina judge, "would destroy that subordination, upon which our social system rests."[13] It was illegal to teach slaves to read and write, slaves could not gather in groups larger than five (except to work), and they could not own animals ("and thereby excite . . . a spirit of insubordination"). The slave codes restricted white civil rights as well. States made it a crime to discuss or write about abolition and made it nearly impossible to free slaves. By the 1850s, most of the southern legislatures began to expel or reenslave the few free blacks who remained in the region.[14]

In the North, slavery withered in an economy based on commerce, small farms, and a growing number of industrial manufacturers. Political movements to abolish slavery gained momentum. Many northerners demanded abolition on moral grounds, and many more were driven by practical reasons to oppose slavery. Political leaders from the northern states feared that their grip on Congress would slip away if more and more of the territories west of the Mississippi River were admitted into the union as slave states. Southern agricultural strength in Congress might be translated into laws that would hurt the northern economy, such as a lowering of tariffs on imported manufactured goods.

The regional rivalry exploded into congressional battles over whether or not to legalize slavery in the new states admitted into the union. In Congress, the conflict over slavery was reduced to a series of political "deals" that delayed a final break between North and South. The deadlock over the admission of Missouri as a slave state, for example, was solved by the simultaneous admission of Missouri and free state Maine in 1820.[15] Another compromise hammered out in 1850 brought California into the union as a free state in exchange for a new fugitive slave law and the admission of slavery into the Utah and New Mexico territories. In 1854 the Democratic-controlled Congress made further compromises impossible by allowing slavery as far north as Nebraska.[16]

Presidents preferred to leave the controversy in the hands of Congress. Since the Democratic party had both northern and southern wings, it ignored the slavery issue whenever possible. By the 1840s and 1850s, leading Democratic presidential contenders all tried to observe existing compromises in order to keep the party intact.[17]

The courts generally upheld property rights over civil rights. In the 1857 *Dred Scott* decision, involving a suit brought by a former slave for his freedom (*Dred Scott* v. *John F. A. Sanford*, 1857), the Supreme Court concluded that blacks "have for more than a century been regarded as beings of an inferior order, unfit associates for the white race . . . and had no rights which white men were bound to respect." The Court majority set two important precedents. First, it established that federal constitutional protections did not apply to state laws. Even if states enacted oppressive laws, and even if these laws applied to free whites, the Court said that the federal government could not intervene. Second, the Court established that property rights protection would be interpreted broadly. Since the Fifth Amendment prohibited federal interference with property rights, the Court concluded that Congress could pass no law prohibiting slavery. This meant that it could not outlaw slavery anywhere in the United States, including the North. The ruling, in effect, voided all congressional compromises over slavery.[18]

Ultimately the sectional strains ripped apart political agreements and coalitions. Deep divisions within the Democratic party created the opening for the election of Republican Abraham Lincoln as president in 1860. Lincoln's election provoked the southern states to leave the Union and form the Confederate States of America. In going to war against the Confederacy, Lincoln aimed to maintain the union of states, not to win freedom for the slaves. With some reluctance, Lincoln proclaimed emancipation in 1863 in a move to strengthen northern resolve and weaken the South.

From Slavery to Peonage: The Failure to Nationalize Civil Rights

In the decade after Appomattox, northern Republicans in Congress attempted to nationalize civil rights protection through several constitutional amendments and federal statutes. But after that exceptional decade, in which one region politically dictated to another, America's policymaking system frustrated the goal of elevating civil rights above property rights. By the late 1870s a new generation of Republicans had lost interest in the cause, and southern leaders had discovered that state laws could be used to suppress blacks even without slavery.

Northern Republicans believed that constitutional guarantees were required to protect the rights of the black population living in the South. Three constitutional amendments were adopted. By banning slavery and involuntary servitude in the United States, the Thirteenth Amendment (ratified December 6, 1865) nationalized the Emancipation Proclamation by incorporating it into the Constitution. The Fourteenth Amendment (ratified July 9, 1868), stated that "no State shall . . . deprive any person of life, liberty, and property, without due process of law, nor deny to any person within its jurisdiction the equal protection of the laws." This amendment sought to equalize the legal status of blacks and whites by nationalizing citizens' rights (as Madison had hoped to do in 1787). The Fifteenth Amendment (ratified February 3, 1870) rectified a major omission in the Fourteenth Amendment by specifying that neither the federal government nor the states could restrict the right to vote "on account of race, color, or previous condition of involuntary servitude."[19]

The Republican Congress reinforced these constitutional changes with federal laws intended to ensure blacks their civil rights in the former Confederate states. The Civil Rights Act of 1866 contained many of the guarantees later written into Fourteenth Amendment. The Military Reconstruction Act of 1867 imposed new governments on the South and protected political participation for blacks (although it did not include suggested provisions for changing the southern economic and social structure, such as the redistribution of land to the new freemen). When the Ku Klux Klan and its white racist allies reacted to Reconstruction by mounting a terrorist campaign against blacks, Congress passed three new laws. The Enforcement Act (1870) gave federal officers the authority to punish violations of the Fourteenth and Fifteenth Amendments. The Force Act (1871) replaced state election processes and placed the election machinery (in Democratic New York City as well as in the South) under federal supervision. The Ku Klux Act of 1871 empowered the president to declare martial law in areas where mobs threatened civil rights, an authority President Grant soon used to quell terrorism in South Carolina. The Civil Rights Act of 1875 constituted the last of the Radical Republican legislation, and it was the last federal civil rights law enacted until 1954. Aimed directly at the "black" codes being adopted by state legislatures, the 1875 act declared discrimination to be illegal in railroads, hotels, restaurants, public schools, juries, and cemeteries.[20]

As southern racists had hoped, the Supreme Court stepped in "as a barrier to the sweeping progress of Northern fanaticism."[21] In its most important decisions (the *Slaughterhouse Cases*, 1873, and the *Civil Rights Cases*, 1881) the Court ruled that even the Fourteenth Amendment did not nationalize the Bill of Rights and so did not protect citizens' rights against laws adopted by state governments. The decision in the *Civil Rights Cases* struck down the 1875 Civil Rights Act on the ground that the federal government could not interfere with the private actions of individuals within the states. In *U.S.* v. *Reese* (1876), the Court ruled that the Fifteenth Amendment did not automatically confer a right to suffrage, in that states could impose literacy tests and other criteria on prospective voters. In *U.S.* v. *Harris* (1883), the Court ruled that the Ku Klux Act could not be applied to the "private activities" of individuals. In effect, these decisions left the southern states free to eliminate black civil rights.

STATE ACTIVISM: NEW TOOLS FOR RESTRICTING CIVIL RIGHTS IN THE SOUTH

By the mid-1870s, the once irresistible force of Radical Republicanism began to give ground to an immovable racism fostered by the little-changed southern economy. The need for a large, cheap, and controllable labor force remained as compelling to southern economic elites after 1865 as before. Though the largest plantations had been broken up into small parcels after the war, most of the parcels were rented to tenant farmers in return for a share of the crop that the tenant raised. The black freemen could not afford to buy their own land. Most of them became sharecroppers, as did many poor whites. In Georgia in 1880, blacks owned only 1.6 percent of the farm land, but tenant farmers tilled 40 percent of the land. In the sharecropping system, white owners determined the crops to be raised and how the crops would be sold.[22] Scarcely freer than slaves, tenant farmers worked and lived at the mercy of white landowners.

When the last federal troops withdrew from the South in 1877, racist majorities once again took control of the state legislatures. For a time, these legislatures did not find it necessary to reinforce the tenant farm economy by imposing new legal controls on blacks. But the rise of agrarian discontent that peaked in the Populist movement (as well as the discussion of a new Force bill in the U.S. Congress) prompted southern whites to strengthen their grip.[23] Soon whites began to devise new state laws to subjugate blacks socially, economically, and politically.

The custom of segregating blacks from whites became widespread in the South immediately following the Civil War, and in the 1880s the southern legislatures began to codify the practice, in the so-called "Jim Crow" laws.[24] Jim Crow segregation began in 1881, when Tennessee required the segregation of all railroad cars. Other southern states followed suit, requiring separate facilities in trains, ships, streetcars, and waiting rooms. The states enacted laws segregating blacks and whites in hotels, restaurants, saloons, factories, restrooms, and courtrooms— anywhere blacks and whites might come together. Segregation in schools, already in effect wherever there were schools at all, became mandatory.[25] Alabama made it illegal for blacks to play checkers with whites. Oklahoma segregated telephone booths. In 1915, South Carolina segregated employment by prohibiting textile factories from permitting whites and blacks to work in the same room or to use the same drinking glasses, toilets, stairways, or doors.[26] Separate facilities facilitated discrimination. In 1915, South Carolina spent almost fourteen dollars per capita a year for the education of white children but one dollar per capita a year for blacks, and the school year for white children lasted twice as long as for blacks.[27]

The South relied on still other laws to subjugate blacks in the economic system. Most blacks eked out an existence as sharecroppers. But many of them slipped into peonage, a system in which landowners refused to allow indebted sharecroppers to leave the land until their accumulated debts were paid. At first this forced labor system depended on custom, but almost all the southern states eventually enacted contract labor laws to enforce the owners' authority. Under a law adopted by Alabama in 1885, if a laborer signed a contract, obtained an advance in money, and then left the job without repaying it, he could be punished "as if he had stolen it." In 1908 the U.S. attorney for the area described the peonage laws as intended "to weave about the ignorant laborer, and especially the blacks, a system of laws intended to keep him absolutely dependent upon the will of the employer and the land owner." Although the Supreme Court voided the Alabama statute in 1911 (*Bailey* v. *Alabama*), peonage in the American South continued until the late 1940s, when the Court voided the contract labor laws of Georgia and Florida.[28]

Laws restricting political participation by blacks effectively prevented challenges to the South's "peculiar institution of enforced segregation." Mississippi took the lead in inventing novel ways to limit participation by blacks in civil society. In 1890, Mississippi's constitutional convention developed a plan to circumvent the Fifteenth Amendment by combining a poll tax with residency and literacy requirements. To ensure the intended result, the state provided that voters were to be tested by proving their knowledge of the state constitution face-to-face to a (white) judge.[29] Even if a potential black voter dared to register, discriminatory administration of such a rule guaranteed exclusion from the voting booth. All the former Confederate states and many of the border states adopted literacy tests within a few years.

Several states adopted other legal strategies to disenfranchise blacks. The Grandfather Clause provided that voters were automatically registered if their grandfathers had been qualified to vote, a provision that, by definition, did not apply to the grandchildren of slaves. The "white primary" closed primary elections to blacks. Since the Democratic party was the only viable political party in southern politics, primary elections were the only meaningful electoral contests. Voting turnout for blacks fell to less than 1 percent in the southern states by the turn of the century, and also fell precipitously for poor whites.

In the case of *Plessy* v. *Ferguson* (1896), the U.S. Supreme Court refused to strike down Jim Crow laws as violations of the Thirteenth and Fourteenth Amendments. The Court ruled that a Louisiana statute requiring the segregation of black and white passengers in railroad cars was constitutional. States legally could require "separate but equal accommodations" for the races. To argue otherwise, the Court majority concluded, is to assume that "social prejudices may be overcome by legislation."[30] In 1898 the Court ruled that Mississippi's restrictive voting laws also were constitutional.[31]

The Political Balance of Power

Ironically, the effectiveness of black disenfranchisement in the South removed any incentive for federal elected officials to change southern law. The South was solidly Democratic, and Republicans could not and did not need to break the monopoly of the Democratic party in southern states. Their presidential candidates regularly won the electoral college vote without the South. Democrats, in contrast, had no chance for national power without the South's electoral votes. Any direct challenge to segregation by a Democratic president would have been suicidal.

From the point of view of Republican president Theodore Roosevelt, who was elected in 1904, the Republican party had a reasonably secure electoral base in the North. Party leaders did not need to risk political capital in a futile attempt to reform the South, particularly since southern congressional votes often were needed on divisive issues. Roosevelt discovered this when he invited Booker T. Washington to dine at the White House and when he appointed black Republicans to federal patronage jobs in the South. As a result of such experiences,

> . . . as his term wore on Roosevelt became increasingly friendly to the repressionist South . . . In 1908, for the first time . . . the Republican platform omitted a call for enforcement of the Reconstruction amendments, and in 1912 Roosevelt sought to break the "solid South" by excluding Southern Negro Delegates from the Progressive convention. If anything, Taft as president was even more enamored by a pro-Southern policy. He reduced the number of [n]egro officeholders and initiated the first moves toward segregation in government agencies.[32]

The civil rights issue would have been a political albatross for the national Republican party; for the Democrats it was anathema. Elected because of the Republican split in 1912, Democratic president (and Virginia native) Woodrow Wilson understood that his political future depended on securing the support of the "solid" Democratic South. He won the 1916 electoral college with a razor-thin electoral vote margin of 277–254, carrying every southern and most border states. The fate of his legislative program rested in the hands of a slim Democratic majority in Congress, with southern members holding the balance of power. Though he made vague appeals for racial justice in his campaign speeches, the president rejected requests to create a National Race Commission. In 1913 the Post Office Department, the Census Bureau, and the Bureau of Engraving and Printing began quietly segregating offices, restaurants, and restrooms. Federal postal and other supervisors in the South were given permission to fire black employees.[33]

During World War I the Army segregated black recruits into units commanded by white officers and assigned them positions such as truck driver, mechanic, and laborer. The Navy accepted blacks only as cooks and servants. The Marine Corps refused to enlist blacks at all. By the time Wilson left office, the nation's capital had become as thoroughly segregated as any city in the South.[34]

NATIONAL ACTIVISM WITHOUT NATIONAL CIVIL RIGHTS STANDARDS

The first hints that the national government would consider once again protecting civil rights began to surface in the 1930s. The depression and the candidacy of Franklin Roosevelt brought more blue-collar voters into the Democratic fold in 1932. Roosevelt's programs also convinced northern blacks to abandon the party of the Great Emancipator. Roosevelt owed his 1936 landslide election as much to the huge majorities he won in the nation's big cities (where black wards gave the New Deal its biggest margins of all) as to the electoral votes of the "solid" South.[35] In Congress, Roosevelt owed his legislative success to a coalition representing both the South and the northern cities.

The New Deal's Civil Rights Dilemma

Northern liberals soon put civil rights onto the national agenda. New York Senator Robert Wagner led a fight for a federal antilynching law and for a federal prohibition of poll taxes. New Dealers such as Harold Ickes (a former president of the Chicago chapter of the National Association for the Advancement of Colored People) tried to make sure that some of the New Deal's public jobs programs employed blacks. Though these programs disproportionately aided whites, they provided jobs to northerners and southerners of both races—though not without significant conflict between federal administrators and southern officials. Over its history, the Civilian Conservation Crops enrolled 350,000 blacks; over 40,000 who had been illiterate when they joined learned to read and write while in the program.[36] In 1939, Roosevelt created a Civil Rights Division in the Justice Department, which for the first time provided a legal structure for enforcing civil rights statutes and constitutional guarantees. William O. Douglas and other Supreme Court appointees placed northern liberals in a position to reverse the narrow interpretations of federal jurisdiction set forth in previous court rulings.

Southerners in Congress used states rights doctrines to block the enforcement of most of the national legislation that might have resulted in social and economic gains for blacks in the South. Southern representatives insisted that Roosevelt's programs leave policy control in the hands of state and local elites. As a result, blacks viewed early New Deal recovery programs such as the Tennessee Valley Authority (TVA), the National Industrial Recovery Act, and the Agricultural Assistance Act as programs to help southern whites at the expense of blacks.[37] The TVA, for example, promised to develop the Tennessee River basin with participation from local citizens. In practice, however, its "grassroots" management style limited benefits to the white power elite that controlled the region's politics. The TVA had the effect of strengthening the system of tenant farms that long had limited black social mobility by preserving the authority of white landlords.[38]

Equally important, the New Deal's labor legislation was not used to challenge white control of the black labor force in the South:

> Southern Congressmen routinely supported the legislative goals of the labor wing of the [Democratic] party as long as their effects were limited to the industrial [North]. For this reason, agriculture and most seasonal activities such as canning and cotton ginning were exempted from minimum wage and union legislation; the two clear conditions for southern participation in the New Deal coalition were northern tolerance of race segregation and the confinement of class competition to the political economy of the industrialized [North and Midwest].[39]

Forced to walk a tightrope between northern liberals and southern segregationists, Roosevelt refused to invest his considerable persuasive skills in the service of new civil rights laws. Explaining his public neutrality on the antilynching bill to an NAACP leader, Roosevelt pointed out that members from southern states were "chairmen or occupy strategic places on most of the Senate and House committees. If I come out for the anti-lynching bill now, they will block every bill I ask Congress to pass to keep America from collapsing. I just can't take that risk."[40]

Possibly as a consequence of the New Deal's cautious approach, many of the champions of the New Deal were southerners who invoked Roosevelt's name in defending its limited application to blacks. Claude

Pepper, Democratic Senator from Florida, was a leading advocate of the 1935 Social Security Act. But during Senate debate on the antilynching bill, Pepper argued that the bill "is out of harmony with the New Deal. It runs counter to progressive democracy as it has been given expression by . . . Franklin D. Roosevelt."[41]

Mounting Pressures for Change, 1940–1960

Developments during World War II began to change the economic and political position of black Americans. The insatiable demand for labor in defense industries drew blacks and whites from the rural South into the northern cities. Between 1941 and 1946, more than a million blacks migrated from the South to such cities as New York, Philadelphia, Chicago, Los Angeles, Cleveland, and Detroit. Another two and one-half million blacks moved to cities outside the South by the 1960 census.

The Great Migration, as it came to be labelled by historians, permanently altered the political calculus for the Democratic party. In the North, no state laws prevented blacks from voting; indeed, political machines in some cities, notably in Chicago, mobilized the black electorate. The swelling ranks of black voters concentrated in precisely the states with the largest blocs of electoral votes. Six of these states—New York, Pennsylvania, Illinois, California, Ohio, and Michigan—together could give a candidate two-thirds of the electoral votes needed to win the presidency in 1948.[42]

Black political organizations began to challenge racial discrimination. The NAACP, the Urban League, and the Brotherhood of Sleeping Car Porters demanded the integration of the armed services. In 1941, A. Philip Randolph, President of the Sleeping Car Porters, threatened to lead a hundred thousand people in a civil rights march on Washington. Roosevelt responded by signing Executive Order 8802, which prohibited racial discrimination by defense contractors and government agencies and established a wartime Fair Employment Practices Commission. At the same time, because of critical labor shortages, some northern employers hired skilled black workers for the first time, which had the effect of creating a small middle class in the black communities of northern cities. During the war, black newspapers like the *Pittsburgh Courier* and *Chicago Defender* demanded a "double victory" against Nazi racism and racism in the United States.[43]

Some northern Democrats pushed for civil rights legislation. In 1940, the Democrats for the first time voted a civil rights plank into the Democratic party's convention platform, promising to "strive for complete legislative safeguards against discrimination in government service and benefits and in the national defense forces." The Civil Rights Division of the Justice Department helped persuade the Supreme Court to declare Texas's "white primary" unconstitutional (*Smith* v. *Alright*, 1944). Roosevelt's Supreme Court appointees supported the expansion of federal citizenship rights; the lone dissenter in overturning the white primary was the only justice appointed before Roosevelt became president.[44]

In spite of early southern optimism about his credentials, Harry Truman went further than Roosevelt in supporting national civil rights enforcement. Upon Truman's nomination as vice-president in 1944, Alabama governor Chauncey Sparks said that "the South has won a substantial victory . . . I find [Truman] safe on states' rights and the right of the state to control qualifications of electors." Mob attacks on blacks in 1946 prompted the Justice Department to recommend a new effort to secure a federal antilynching law. A month after the Democrats suffered heavy losses in the 1946 congressional elections, President Truman signed Executive Order 9008, creating a presidential commission on civil rights.[45] And with his own election campaign rapidly approaching, Truman in February 1948 proposed a federal civil rights law more far-reaching than any considered by Roosevelt. The bill would have established a permanent Civil Rights Commission, made lynching a federal crime with severe penalties, authorized the Justice Department to sue for infringement of voting rights, reestablished the Fair Employment Practices Commission, and prohibited discrimination on buses and trains that crossed state lines.[46]

Truman's actions infuriated southern Democrats, who immediately began to shore up the bulwark of states' rights. In preparation for the 1948 Democratic convention they organized a states' rights conference to devise a coordinated southern strategy. A few weeks later, an impassioned speech to the Democratic convention delegates by Minneapolis mayor Hubert Humphrey helped win a narrow platform victory for the Truman civil rights proposals. Most of the southern delegates walked out in protest. Within two weeks the southern delegates formed the States' Rights party, which promptly nominated former South Carolina governor Strom Thurmond as its presidential candidate. At the opposite end of the ideological spectrum, Roosevelt's former vice-president, Henry Wallace, won the nomination of the new Progressive party, which was firmly committed to a strict federal civil rights program.[47] If these parties stripped enough votes from the left and right wings of the Democratic party, the presidential election would be handed to the Republicans.

Truman held the Democratic coalition together only with deft political maneuvering. He issued executive orders to prohibit discrimination in the federal civil service and segregation in the armed forces. He vigorously attacked the "do-nothing" Republican Congress. As his campaign gained momentum, southern leaders reluctantly began to return to the party. Fearing that a Republican civil rights law would go further than Truman's, Senator Richard Russell of Georgia endorsed Truman a few days before the election.[48] Truman managed a narrow victory, taking California, Illinois, and Ohio by razor-thin margins of 17,000, 33,000, and 7,000 votes and losing four southern states to Thurmond. Black voters in the cities of a few key industrial states were crucial to the Democratic victory.[49]

The 1948 election convinced Republicans that it might be politic to include civil rights language in the party's 1952 convention platform. Dwight Eisenhower, however, preferred to take a passive stance on civil rights issues: he permitted the armed forces to complete their desegregation by 1955 and he strengthened the enforcement of antidiscrimination rules in hiring for federal bureaucracies and government contractors. But he believed that most of America's racial problems required voluntary rather than legal remedies and state rather than federal action. He refused to propose federal legislation to deal with civil rights, thus upholding the states' rights position by default.[50]

Not so the Supreme Court, which struck down legally-mandated segregation in public schools in its historic 1954 decision, *Brown* v. *Board of Education*. The Court specifically reversed the Supreme Court's "separate but equal" doctrine, which had been declared in 1896 in the *Plessy* v. *Ferguson* decision. In doing so it withdrew a principle crucial to preserving segregation in the South. According to the Court:

> . . . education is perhaps the most important function of state and local governments . . . It is required in the performance of our most basic public responsibilities . . . [Education] is a right which must be available to all on equal terms . . . Segregation with the sanction of law, therefore, has a tendency to retard the educational and mental development of negro children and to deprive them of some of the benefits they would receive in a racially integrated school system . . . We conclude that in the field of public education the doctrine of "separate but equal" has no place. Separate educational facilities are inherently unequal.[51]

The decision struck down legally mandated segregation in seventeen states and the District of Columbia and in four additional states that permitted local segregation laws. The Court declined to set a deadline for desegregating the schools. Urging desegregation with "all deliberate speed" (in a separate decision), it left the details of implementation in the hands of the federal district courts. Several border states, including Missouri, Kentucky, West Virginia, Maryland, and Delaware, moved steadily to comply with the *Brown* decision.[52]

Southern segregationists referred to the date of the Court's decision as "black Monday" and vowed to defend state segregation laws. In 1956, ninety-six members of the House and the Senate signed a "Southern Manifesto," in which they promised to use "all lawful means to bring about the reversal of this decision which is contrary to the Constitution." The Texas legislature passed a law withholding state funds from schools that desegregated without approval by a popular referendum. Georgia, Alabama, and Virginia forbade desegregation whether or not ordered by a federal court. When federal courts ordered the integration of schools in Virginia and Arkansas, the legislatures in those states closed the public schools. State and local police could not or would not control racist mobs and acts of terrorism. By the end of 1958, church groups reported 530 incidents of racial violence in four years. Seven churches and four schools had been bombed. White mobs that resisted the desegregation of Little Rock's Central High School in 1956 were so threatening that President Eisenhower overcame his oft-repeated reluctance to invoke federal authority: he sent U.S. troops to Arkansas, where soldiers patrolled school hallways during the rest of the academic year.[53]

Dr. Martin Luther King, Jr. led a boycott of the city bus system in Montgomery, Alabama, protesting a requirement that blacks sit behind all whites on the buses. Prodded by popular reactions to the violence of southern resistance, by his own Justice Department, and by the possibility of northern black electoral support for the Republicans (black votes for Eisenhower increased in his second election), Eisenhower finally endorsed federal legislation in 1956, but the proposal was diluted to satisfy southern demands that states' rights principles be respected. Even so, Senator Russell of Georgia attacked the bill as "cunningly designed to vest in the Attorney General unprecedented power to bring the whole might of the federal government, including the armed forces if necessary, to force a commingling of white and Negro children in the state-supported schools of the south."[54]

The Civil Rights Act enacted in 1957 was modified to mollify southern congressional leaders. It created a Civil Rights Commission charged with investigating violations of civil rights and strengthened the investigative powers of the Civil Rights Division of the Justice Department. But there was no practical way for the federal government to enforce compliance when constitutional guarantees were violated.

Motivated by well-publicized southern defiance of federal law, by large Democratic gains in the 1958 congressional elections, and by the approaching presidential contest, Eisenhower submitted another civil rights bill in 1959. This proposal outlined a grants strategy designed to reward compliance with federal law. The bill would have encouraged desegregation by offering financial and technical assistance to state and local school agencies that initiated desegregation policies. It enhanced the investigatory authority of the FBI and proposed that obstruction of court-ordered desegregation be made a federal crime. Simultaneously, in its first report the new U.S. Commission on Civil Rights exposed shocking instances of intimidation of prospective black voters. Congress redrafted the Eisenhower proposal, dropping the proposed desegregation grants and adding provisions authorizing federal oversight of state and national elections if a court found discriminatory practices.

Southern senators resorted to a filibuster to delay consideration of the legislation. Efforts to stop the filibuster proved futile when a vote for cloture lost by a 53–42 margin. The 42 votes on the losing side were cast by senators representing 60 percent of the U.S. population and 70 percent of the voters in the 1956 election. Though disappointed liberals called the modest 1960 Civil Rights Act a victory for the South, they correctly predicted that stronger federal legislation was inevitable.[55]

By 1960, the battle lines between states' rights and national civil rights were clearly drawn. Black college students defied Jim Crow laws by refusing to leave a Walgreen's "whites only" lunch counter in Greensboro, North Carolina. The "sit-in" movement spread across the South to restaurants, beaches, churches, and other segregated institutions. Hundreds of establishments opened their doors to blacks for the first time.[56] In their televised presidential nominating conventions in the summer of 1960, both the Republican and Democratic parties adopted civil rights planks explicitly endorsing the sit-in movement. Southern congressional leaders and state politicians prepared for a last-ditch defense of segregation.

NATIONAL CIVIL RIGHTS STANDARDS SINCE 1960

President John Kennedy was convinced by the 1960 election results that he needed to move cautiously on civil rights. He had defeated Vice President Nixon by less than 119,000 votes of 65 million cast (49.72 percent to 49.55 percent). Kennedy won 68 percent of the black vote, and black majorities in Chicago helped push Illinois into the Democratic column by a total margin of 8,000 votes. But balanced against that was the fact that six southern states had provided 80 of his 303 electoral votes.

The southern wing of the party also was strengthened because the Democrats lost seats in the House and Senate, making the administration's legislative prospects heavily dependent on preserving a coalition between northern Democratic liberals and southern states' rights conservatives. Because of their long tenure in Congress, southerners also sat at the top of the seniority system, and thus chaired 12 of 18 Senate committees and 12 of 21 House committees. Devoted segregationist Howard Smith (D, Va.) chaired the House Rules Committee, which had become a burial ground for liberal legislation.[57] (Legislation virtually never comes to the House floor without approval by the Rules Committee, which sets the rules for debating bills approved by other House committees.)

Kennedy declined to seek a new civil rights law and confined his civil rights actions to executive orders and activities that did not need congressional approval. During his first two months in office the president appointed forty blacks to important and highly visible posts within the administration. These appointments included national NAACP chairman Robert Weaver, who was selected to head the Housing and Home Finance Agency, the core agency of what would become (in 1966) the Department of Housing and Urban Development. Attorney General Robert Kennedy stepped up federal litigation by filing seventy-five civil rights lawsuits by Thanksgiving 1961. Executive Order 10925 (March 6, 1961) strengthened theenforcement of antidiscrimination rules in the civil service and in the awarding of government contracts. Executive Orders 11063 (November 20, 1962) and 11114 (June 22, 1963) banned discrimination in federal housing and federally funded construction.[58]

National Civil Rights Triumphs over States' Rights, 1961–1965

But lawsuits were too slow and executive orders too limited to satisfy the rising demand for black equality and civil rights. In May 1961, an integrated group boarded Greyhound and Trailways buses in Washington, D.C., bound for New Orleans. The "Freedom Riders" intended to test the desegregation of interstate bus terminals ordered by the Supreme Court the previous year. Mobs in Alabama firebombed the buses and beat the passengers. Robert Kennedy sent federal marshals to guard the travellers on the rest of the route through the South.[59] In September 1962, U.S. marshals and soldiers protected James Meredith as he enrolled at the University of Mississippi; in June 1963, George Wallace barred the doorway when blacks tried to enroll at the University of Alabama.

Repeated incidents of brutality in the South provided dramatic television news footage. The most moving scenes were sent from Birmingham, Alabama, in the spring of 1963. Birmingham had become the focus for nonviolent demonstrations against segregated facilities. The city's police chief, "Bull" Connor, arrested Martin Luther King, Jr., and then released him. King decided to use the moral force of a children's march. Children aged six to sixteen sang hymns as they walked through the city on May 2. Chief Connor ordered the Birmingham police to unleash attack dogs and turn fire hoses on the marchers. One congressman recalled the scene: "[O]ne hundred pounds of water pressure knocked youngsters to the ground, swept them down the streets, and threw them against buildings where they were handcuffed and hauled off to jail."[60] Finally and graphically, the brutal treatment that blacks had experienced through more than a hundred years of "states' rights" was televised into the living rooms of millions of American homes. It mobilized thousands of protesters, white and black alike. During the week of May 25, civil rights demonstrations occurred in thirty-three southern and ten northern cities. Faced with the choice of bloody resistance or accommodation to the inevitable, nearly one hundred fifty southern cities took steps to desegregate. One hundred twenty-seven civil rights bills were introduced in the House by mid-June.[61]

Conceding that "the events in Birmingham and elsewhere have so increased the cries for equality that no city or state or legislative body can prudently choose to ignore them,"[62] Kennedy overruled his political advisors and on June 11 announced that he would seek a new civil rights law. He sent a cautious bill to Congress. It relied heavily on the grants strategy, but unlike the Eisenhower version it threatened to cut off a variety of federal funds where governments practiced discrimination. The bill permitted more federal legal intervention in school desegregation cases, created a new federal conciliation service, and provided for the desegregation of public accommodations. Northern congressmen on the House Judiciary Committee amended the bill to make it much tougher and passed it out of committee over southern members' objections. When Kennedy was assassinated on November 22, the bill had just reached the House Rules Committee.[63]

The powerful unifying emotions evoked by Kennedy's assassination temporarily aligned most of the policymaking structure in favor of national civil rights protection. Lyndon Johnson, the first southern president since Reconstruction, proposed a strengthened Civil Rights Act. Opinion polls documented overwhelming public support. Republicans and northern Democrats on the Rules Committee revolted against Chairman Smith and reported the bill to the full House, which approved it 290–130. Because of the large number of southern senators who could sustain a filibuster, proponents feared that the Senate would be a formidable obstacle to enactment. Clergymen persuaded senators from the Plains and Rocky Mountain states to support the bill despite the few blacks in their states. On June 6, 1964, for only the second time in twenty-nine years, the Senate assembled the necessary two-thirds vote (71–29) required to close off a filibuster. Twenty-one of the twenty-nine cloture opponents were southerners. Arizona's Barry Goldwater, one of the few senators outside the South to join the opposition, objected to the bill on states' rights grounds. He found "no constitutional basis for the exercise of federal regulatory authority" over employment and public accommodations.[64]

The 1964 Civil Rights Act attacked racial discrimination in voting, public accommodations, employment, and federally assisted programs. It expanded the powers of the Civil Rights Commission and made it easier to appeal civil rights cases to the highest levels of the federal court system. It strengthened the enforcement of the Voting Rights Act of 1957 and restricted the use of literacy tests.[65]

Title II struck down Jim Crow laws, making it unlawful to deny access to restaurants, lunch counters, theaters, sports arenas, gasoline stations, motels, hotels, and lodging houses (except for small, owner-occupied units) because of an individual's race, color, religion, or nationality. Title II strengthened the federal government's ability to enforce the *Brown* decision and speed up the desegregation of public schools.[66]

The Civil Rights Act also outlawed discrimination in hiring, firing, training, and promoting workers on the basis of race, color, sex, religion, or nationality. The act established a five-member Equal Employment Opportunity Commission to investigate charges of employment discrimination, to conciliate disputes, and to refer potential legal actions to the Justice Department (the commission was not itself given the power to force an employer to stop a discriminatory action). Another provision established legal grounds for individuals to sue employers for discriminatory practices. By 1971 private parties filed 1,200 lawsuits charging employer discrimination against a class of people. In contrast, the federal government filed only 56 lawsuits in the same period.[67]

Title VII of the Civil Rights Act established the first "crosscutting" requirement in federal grant-in-aid programs by barring discrimination in the use of federal grant funds. Though the federal government could, in theory, rescind grants to a state or local government that continued to practice discrimination, federal officials rarely took such drastic action. In 1965, when the federal Office of Education threatened to cut off funds to Chicago because of its lack of effort in desegregating the city's school system, the political backlash from the city's Democratic establishment was so powerful that President Johnson barred the agency from cutting off Chicago's grants. Despite the political obstacles to enforcing such sanctions, the mere threat of a grant termination made many jurisdictions far more willing to police themselves. Among the fifty-nine crosscutting requirements in existence in 1980 were provisions protecting the civil rights of minorities, women, the handicapped, and the elderly.[68]

The Democratic ticket won the 1964 presidential election with 61 percent of the popular vote and swept 486 electoral college votes to Barry Goldwater's 53. But the landslide concealed an ominous development for the Democratic party. Goldwater had abandoned the Republican civil rights plank during the 1964 campaign to "go hunting where the ducks are": to try to appeal for southern white votes by defending "states' rights." He received 87 percent of the vote in Mississippi, almost 70 percent in Alabama, and substantially more than 50 percent in Louisiana, Georgia, and South Carolina. Goldwater carried a majority of white votes in every former Confederate state except Texas.[69] After 1964, Republican candidates began to win southern state elections for the first time since Reconstruction. And even outside the South, Alabama's governor George Wallace showed surprising strength when he entered the Democratic primary elections of 1964 in Wisconsin, Maryland, and Indiana. Wallace captured 43 percent of the vote in Maryland on a states' rights, anti-civil rights platform.[70]

Johnson proposed new laws that unambiguously subordinated states' rights to civil rights. He sought federal voting rights legislation in 1965. Governor Wallace provided another timely show of racism when he ordered a civil rights march halted in Selma, Alabama. After firing tear gas into the praying civil rights marchers, state troopers routed them with clubs, whips, and wetted ropes, injuring dozens of people. The Voting Rights Act of 1965 passed in only five months as public opinion again rallied to the civil rights cause. The House passed the measure 333–85, and the Senate again voted to end a filibuster after twenty-five days, on a 70–30 vote.

The Voting Rights Act of 1965 gave the federal government the authority to intervene in election procedures. The law suspended literacy tests. It gave the attorney general the power to appoint federal examiners to supervise voter registration (and to watch polls) in areas where it appeared that registration procedures had been used to reduce voter participation. Registrars could be sent to Alabama, Georgia, Louisiana, Mississippi, South Carolina, Virginia, and twenty-eight counties in North Carolina, three in Arizona, and one in Idaho. The legislation also required any changes in election laws in these areas to be cleared by the Justice Department. Although the Justice Department sent federal examiners to only thirty-two southern counties four months after the law was signed, the possibility of federal intervention had a dramatic effect. By the end of 1965 local officials had registered 160,000 new black voters in the five Deep South states and federal registrars had registered nearly 80,000 more. Between 1964 and 1972, more than a million new black voters were registered in the states covered by the Voting Rights Act, and eligible black voters increased from 29 percent to more than 56 percent in these states.[71]

Two days after Johnson signed the bill, federal registrars arrived in Selma, Alabama, to sign up voters, and a year later black voters defeated Sheriff James Clark in the Democratic primary.[72]

The Difficulty of Enforcing National Civil Rights Protections

In the fragmented American policymaking structure, asserting federal government jurisdiction in civil rights became a prolonged, halting, and arduous task. Extraordinary effort and resources were required to enforce the law. Following the passage of the Civil Rights Act of 1964 and the Voting Rights Act of 1965, the civil rights struggle entered a new phase. It began to focus on northern cities, and it also turned on economic and social inequalities in housing, employment, and education arising from discrimination of a less obvious sort than *de jure* laws enforced in southern states.

The second phase of the civil rights struggle largely failed. There are many reasons for this failure, but one key element stands out: no outpouring of public support enabled proponents of national civil rights protections *to overcome obstruction by state and local governments*. Incoherence in the policymaking structure remained intact in the American policymaking structure. The enforcement of fair housing legislation passed in 1968 was not nationalized, except in the sense that federal courts could be asked to intervene on a case-by-case basis. School desegregation plans were left in the hands of local school boards, with federal courts intervening as umpires only as a last resort. Enforcement of protections against employment discrimination likewise was left mostly in the hands of the courts.

The decentralization of civil rights policy meant that the enforcement of laws against housing, employment, and school discrimination depended on lawsuits brought by those individuals affected by private, local, and state practices. Northern states and cities proved to be as obstructionist in this second phase of the civil rights struggle as southern states had been in the first.

Property Rights versus Civil Rights Outside the South, 1966–1981

After the 1965 Voting Rights Act was passed, civil rights leaders began to broaden the movement's scope. In the North, blacks seemed to be losing ground economically. Blacks who had moved to northern cities during and after World War II found industrial employment opportunities dwindling as plants relocated into suburban and rural areas. Joblessness for blacks ran more than twice the unemployment rate for white workers, and employed blacks were twice as likely as white workers to hold unskilled, low-paying, dead-end jobs. Discriminatory hiring and firing practices prevented blacks from gaining promotions, seniority, job security, and higher pay.[73]

Falling employment opportunities left huge islands of poverty in central cities. The ghettos in New York and on the south side of Chicago stretched for miles in every direction. Dilapidated, overcrowded schools, high crime rates, indifferent and hostile police, decaying, rat-infested tenements—these were facts of life for blacks in inner cities.

Until the 1960s state legislatures were often insensitive to metropolitan problems. The reapportionment of legislative districts in the 1960s served to enhance the voting power of the suburbs in state legislatures. States tolerated vast disparities between education opportunities and urban services available in white and black areas. Only seventeen states had fair housing laws on the books in the mid-1960s, and none were enforced. Of the large states, neither Illinois nor Michigan had any statutes at all, and Californians voted to repeal their fair housing law in 1964.[74]

Civil rights leaders demanded that the federal government move against employment discrimination and reduce housing and school segregation in the North as well as in the South. Unlike the assault on southern Jim Crow laws, these new demands threatened the jobs and the property of northern working-class whites, whose neighborhoods, schools, and employers were most likely to bear the burden of de-segregation and affirmative action.[75]

Martin Luther King, Jr. discovered northern working-class racism when he moved his civil rights campaign to Chicago. King led marches through working-class white neighborhoods, where he was greeted by defiant whites lining the streets, waving Confederate flags and Nazi banners, shouting "kill the niggers" and "Wallace for President." In Marquette Park, bricks, bottles, and rocks rained down on police and marchers alike. One brick struck King and knocked him to the ground. "I have never seen such hatred," said King, "not in Mississippi or Alabama."[76]

Blacks and whites clashed in Chicago, Philadelphia, and Cambridge, Maryland in 1963. The following summer, civil rights leaders lost control of residents protesting police brutality, southern lynchings, and ghetto conditions in New York's Harlem and Bedford–Stuyvesant sections. During several days of rioting, crowds tossed bricks and bottles at police. Stores were looted and burned. Rioting followed in dozens of cities. In August 1965, a police incident provoked a riot in the Watts section of Los Angeles. The poorly prepared California National Guard opened fire on the rioters. When the smoke cleared in Watts, thirty-four people lay dead and hundreds injured, and $34 million worth of prop-erty had been destroyed. Forty-three disorders and riots occurred in 1966, including major incidents in Watts, Chicago, and Cleveland. In 1967, the violence flared again. Twenty-three people were killed in rioting in Newark during July. Later that month, Detroit exploded in a five-day riot that left forty-three dead and over $50 million in property damage.[77]

A white backlash soon developed. Public and congressional support for civil rights began to wane. In 1966 Congress rebuffed Lyndon John-son when he sought to extend federal civil rights protections to include housing. Northern Republicans joined southern Democrats in a fili-buster when the bill to ban housing discrimination arrived in the Senate. Sponsors could not muster the two-thirds majority needed to close off debate.

Voters battered the Democrats in the 1966 elections. Republicans gained 47 House seats and defeated Democrats for the first time in Atlanta, Memphis, and other southern and border-state congressional districts. In California, Ronald Reagan, who had campaigned for Goldwater in the 1964 election, ran for governor on the Republican ticket, making opposition to California's fair housing law and to the Civil Rights Act of 1964 the centerpieces of his campaign. Californians elected Reagan by nearly a million-vote margin.[78]

In the week following Dr. King's assassination in April 1968, Congress passed the last civil rights act of the Great Society, the Fair Housing Act of 1968, which prohibited discrimination in the sale or rental of housing. The law was expected to apply to 80 percent of housing by 1970, since it exempted only small owner-occupied units. Later that year, however, the House of Representatives refused to consider a Johnson administration request for money to enforce the law. In June, the U.S. Supreme Court ruled (in *Jones* v. *Mayer*) that housing discrimination violated the Civil Rights Act of 1866, a decision more sweeping than the Fair Housing Act because it even applied to single family homes sold directly by the owner. However, enforcement of these protections was very difficult and complex. Victims of discrimination usually had to rely on the courts, and demonstrating discrimination in court required time-consuming and expensive tactics that discouraged all but the most determined plaintiffs.[79]

The Republicans capitalized on white fear and resentment in 1968 by reviving the law and order issue, Goldwater's favorite theme in the 1964 campaign. House Minority Leader Gerald Ford asked "How long are we going to abdicate law and order . . . in favor of a soft social theory that the man who heaves a brick through your window or tosses a firebomb into your car is simply the misunderstood and underprivileged product of a broken home?"[80] In the 1968 presidential contest, the Democratic nominee Hubert Humphrey carried only one southern state, Texas. Across the South, he carried only 31 percent of the vote, running behind both Republican Richard Nixon (34.5 percent) and segregationist third-party candidate, George Wallace (34.6 percent). In the national vote, working-class whites in semiskilled and unskilled occupations gave Humphrey only 38 percent of their vote, less than two-thirds the 61 percent proportion cast for John Kennedy in 1960. Black voters, on the other hand, abandoned the Republicans. Nixon had won 32 percent of the black vote in 1960, but his share fell to 12 percent in 1968.[81]

Since blacks withdrew from the Republican coalition, the new Republican presidential administration had every reason to brake civil rights enforcement. One of the president's closest advisors, John Erlichman, told federal civil rights administrators that "Blacks are not where the votes are, so why antagonize the people who can be helpful to us politically?"[82] Nixon ruled out withholding grants from jurisdictions practicing segregation.[83] The White House let the burden of enforcing civil rights pass to the courts, and subsequently appointed moderates (such as Chief Justice Warren Burger) and conservatives (notably Justice William Rehnquist) to the Supreme Court and to lower federal courts, assuring that the judicial system would slow the pace of desegregation and limit judicial remedies for housing, school, and employment discrimination.

School segregation constituted an extremely volatile political issue during the Nixon years. Despite the 1954 *Brown* decision, southern school districts remained mostly segregated. In 1969, the Supreme Court unanimously ruled that continued delay in desegregating Mississippi schools was no longer permissible (*Alexander* v. *Holmes County Board of Education*). Districts were forced to agree to negotiated timetables to accomplish desegregation. Nixon officials worked to ease the implementation of the court order, but southern school districts were desegregated with remarkable success (Table 6.1) sixteen years after the *Brown* decision.

By 1970, southern school districts were less segregated than those in the north, almost certainly because the Justice Department focused its energies on lawsuits in southern states and because school districts were much larger in the South, thus encompassing both black and white residential areas (see Chapter 8). No similar effort went into desegregating northern states. In March 1970, the White House announced that *de facto* segregation was "undesirable" but should not "by itself be cause for federal enforcement actions."[84] A year later the Supreme Court ruled that busing could be used to remedy the effects of prior *de jure* segregation (*Swann* v. *Charlotte–Mecklenburg Board of Education*). Later, however, in *Milliken* v. *Bradley* (1974), it held that busing across school district boundaries could not be ordered by the courts, a decision in which Nixon's four court appointees joined the remaining Eisenhower appointee to form a 5–4 majority.[85]

If desegregation could not be enforced across school districts, then it could not proceed very far in most northern metropolitan areas, where central city school districts were largely black and suburban districts mostly white. In American urban areas, municipal and school district boundaries tended to reflect patterns of racial and social class segregation. State laws long had facilitated the proliferation of independent suburbs and school districts. Yet the courts ignored this fact. The federal government would not tamper with the tradition of local control of education: it would not require that students from one school district be sent to another to accomplish racial desegregation. The possibility of desegregating schools in most urban school districts in the North thus was eliminated.

Table 6.1. *Percentage of black students attending school with whites,*
1954–1973, selected southern and border states

	1954–1955	1961–1962	1965–1966	1968–1969	1972–1973
South[a]	0.001%	0.241%	6.1%	32.0%	86.0%
Alabama	0.0	0.0	0.4	14.4	83.6
Georgia	0.0	0.0[d]	2.7	23.6	86.8
Mississippi	0.0	0.0	0.6	11.8	91.5
Virginia	0.0	0.2	11.5	42.0	99.4
Border[b]	[c]	52.5	68.9	74.8	53.5
District of Columbia	[c]	85.6	84.8	72.2	64.3
Kentucky	0.0	51.2	78.4	94.8	92.6
Maryland	5.1	41.5	55.6	68.8	76.0
Missouri	[c]	41.4	75.1	66.6	69.4

[a]Alabama, Arkansas, Florida, Georgia, Louisiana, Mississippi, North Carolina, South Carolina, Tennessee, Texas, Virginia
[b]Delaware, District of Columbia, Kentucky, Maryland, Missouri, Oklahoma, West Virginia
[c]Not available
[d]Less than 0.05%
Source: Charles S. Bullock and Charles S. Lamb, *Implementation of Civil Rights Policy,* (Monterey, CA: Brooks/Cole, 1984), 65.

Jimmy Carter's election in 1976 failed to erase the rising level of racial antagonism within the Democratic party. Despite the fact that Carter won all the electoral college votes of southern states except for Virginia, he found himself in an even more precarious position than his Democratic predecessors. Southern white Protestants returned to vote for Carter after abandoning McGovern in 1972, but Carter owed his slim victories in the South as well as in the North to black voters who could now exercise their voting rights everywhere. Like most Democratic presidential candidates after 1944, Adlai Stevenson (1952 and 1956), John Kennedy (1960), Hubert Humphrey (1968), George McGovern (1972), and Walter Mondale (1984), Carter failed to win a majority of the national white vote.[86]

Carter appointed more blacks to administrative and judicial positions than any previous president. White House rhetoric strongly condemned discrimination. The Equal Employment Opportunity Commission and other agencies more actively negotiated goals for minority hiring in firms and public institutions, and many such organizations established affirmative action programs aimed at increasing the percentage of minority and female employees. But Carter pulled back from confronting racist practices with new legislation. The Secretary of Health, Education and Welfare, Joseph Califano, quoted him as saying that "there will never be any attempt while I am President to weaken the great civil rights acts that have passed in years gone by." Califano added that Carter "meant what he said, and not much more."[87]

Carter refused to apply pressure on the university system in North Carolina to desegregate its campuses. North Carolina was a key state in his reelection strategy. The administration took weak and often ambivalent positions in court cases involving affirmative action in employment, such as *Regents of the University of California* v. *Bakke* (1978) and *United Steelworkers of America* v. *Weber* (1980). The administration endorsed new open-housing legislation in 1980, but did not press for it. Carter vetoed additional restrictions on busing as a remedy for school segregation, but did not actively oppose congressional restrictions on busing enacted in 1977 and 1978.[88]

The Reagan Administration: From Civil Rights Erosion to Stalemate

Writing in the fall of 1980, Republican campaign strategist Richard Wirthlin advised that the "Reagan for President 1980 campaign must convert into Reagan votes the disappointment felt by Southern white Protestants, blue collar workers in the industrial states, urban ethnics, and rural voters . . ."[89] In both 1980 and 1984 Reagan successfully played on the "disappointment" of these groups. Among whites nationally, Reagan's share of the vote increased from 56 percent in 1980 to 67 percent in 1984, when three out of four southern whites voted for him. The campaign wrote off blacks. Reagan carried only one in ten black votes in 1980 and slightly fewer in 1984. For the fourth election in succession, the Republicans carried the majority of votes west of the Mississippi River. In three out of four of those elections, nearly the entire South voted Republican (only Georgia voted for Carter in 1980).[90]

In line with its political support, the Reagan administration reinterpreted civil rights policy. The administration made it immediately clear that it would oppose hiring goals to remedy employment discrimination and busing to remedy school segregation.[91] In contrast to the Nixon administration, which had merely slowed the momentum of civil rights enforcement, the Reagan White House actively worked to undo federal civil rights guarantees.[92] Federalism proved to be a useful cover and the favored excuse for an historic reversal in racial policy.

The Reagan administration reduced the federal government's will and capacity to enforce civil rights laws. The staff and budgets of civil rights agencies were slashed: the staff of the Equal Employment Opportunity Commission was cut by 12 percent, the Civil Rights Division of the Justice Department terminated 13 percent of its employees, and the budget of the Office of Contract Compliance was slashed by 24 percent. Loyalty to conservative principles became the litmus test for appointment to civil rights policymaking jobs. William Bradford Reynolds, a zealous opponent of busing and affirmative action (and, in fact, of nearly all remedies for discrimination), was chosen to head the Civil

Rights Division. Blacks received only 4 percent of executive appointments in the Reagan administration (compared to 12 percent under
Carter). When the U.S. Commission on Civil Rights published a report
criticizing the administration's civil rights effort, the president fired
three members of the commission and attempted to fire two more.[93]
Within a year the commission was dominated by conservatives.

The president ordered the Justice Department to slow prosecution for
housing discrimination, and by 1983 the department had virtually stopped initiating such prosecutions.[94] Similarly, the number of employment discrimination suits filed by the Equal Employment Opportunity
Commission (EEOC) dropped by 60 percent between 1980 and 1983, and
the Civil Rights Division had filed only one school desegregation case by
1983—and this was to oppose a desegregation order. The Justice Department's own internal affirmative action plan was so inadequate that
even the Reagan-appointed Equal Employment Opportunity Commission rejected it.[95] Though the White House proposed to strengthen fair
housing legislation in 1983, its plan would have shifted the emphasis
away from real estate practices to individuals wronged in specific cases.
Thus, the Reagan policy would have drastically reduced the number of
people affected by any positive judgment that might be handed down
by the courts.[96]

When it chose not to abandon civil rights openly, the administration
reinterpreted federal jurisdiction. It delegated some civil rights enforcement to state and local governments. At the same time, in what
appeared to be a contradiction to its avowed ideological commitment to
decentralized federalism, executive agencies tried to preempt and void
many private and local civil rights agreements that relied on hiring
quotas or timetables. The Justice Department in particular became "less
aggressive in identifying discrimination and has tried to narrow the
remedies that can be used to correct discriminatory practices."[97]

A few state courts became much more active in protecting civil rights.
One scholar of the "new judicial activism" in the states found that some
courts were making a serious effort to protect civil rights, although she
cautioned that this activism varied widely from state to state, that it
caused controversy, and that its successes could be overstated.[98]

The "New Federalism" provided the best opportunity to use jurisdiction to reduce federal oversight of civil rights. Traditionally, the Equal
Employment Opportunities Commission and the Department of Housing and Urban Development worked closely with state civil rights commissions and provided funding in return for shared enforcement functions. In a survey of state civil rights officials in 1983, state civil rights
agencies found that the budget cuts at the federal level were undercut-
ting their efforts as well.[99]

Of the major federal agencies administering the new block grants
created in 1981, only the Department of Housing and Urban Develop-

ment wrote any antidiscrimination guidelines into their regulations for the grants. In practice, states tended to relax affirmative action rules and antidiscrimination rules when they took control of social programs.[100] A University of Chicago study of the Job Training Partnership Act of 1982, for example, found that the U.S. Labor Department did not even require states to provide information essential for monitoring discrimination in the use of job training funds. Neither the state of Illinois nor the federal government had issued any guidelines about the enforcement of the antidiscrimination provision by 1985, and the state had hired only one professional staff member to monitor compliance.[101]

But the administration was not willing to follow a policy of decentralization through the federal system where institutions or local governments had put busing or affirmative action programs into effect. In such cases the administration tried to use federal power to override state or local institutions. The Justice Department interceded in several court cases to ask that rulings be issued to *deny* local governments the right to maintain affirmative action programs, even when these programs were voluntary and agreeable to both blacks and whites. William Bradford Reynolds led the battle against court-mandated hiring plans in Detroit, New Orleans, and Boston. He won a partial victory in 1984, when the Supreme Court ruled 6–3 that white firefighters in Memphis had been laid off unjustly in order to preserve the jobs of blacks who had been hired under an affirmative action plan. In the decision's wake, Reynolds announced his intention to redouble efforts to persuade the federal courts to strike down local affirmative action plans. The Civil Rights Division subsequently opposed a Seattle voluntary school desegregation plan that included busing and it refused to endorse a St. Louis desegregation plan, even though the plan was supported by the school districts. The Justice Department joined busing opponents who filed suit in Norfolk, Nashville, and Charleston, South Carolina.[102]

Liberals and moderates in Congress prevented the Reagan administration from going further. After trying to stall legislation, Reagan belatedly endorsed the renewal of the Voting Rights Act when Congress debated it in 1982. At first the administration suggested that it might favor weakening the legislation by reducing federal oversight of state and local elections. The Justice Department went further: it flatly opposed renewing the act. But civil rights advocates were able to show lawmakers so many examples of continuing voting rights abuses that Congress strengthened as well as extended the legislation. Moderate Republicans in Congress had to persuade Reagan to sign the bill.[103] Later in 1986, in a perverse interpretation of the bill's objectives, the Justice Department sued black activists for voter fraud, claiming that they had illegally instructed black voters on how to fill out absentee ballots.

The Democrats won a majority of the U.S. Senate seats in the 1986 elections, and black voters had made the difference in the victories of five Democrats in southern states. The importance of these constituents soon became evident when the Senate defeated the Reagan administration on a pair of important civil rights tests. The first was the nomination of Robert Bork to the U.S. Supreme Court. Civil rights groups objected to the appointment of a conservative with a record of decisions they opposed; his nomination galvanized the black community into united and adamant opposition. In an anticlimactic vote in October 1987, the Senate rejected the Bork nomination by a margin of 58–42. Fifteen of the sixteen Democratic senators from the former confederate states voted against the nomination, a demonstration of the policy impact that black constituents could have on national policy. In March 1988, the Senate and House overrode Reagan's veto of a law banning discrimination throughout any institution in which any part received federal aid. All the southern Democrats in the Senate and all but six in the House of Representatives joined to override the veto.[104]

THE UNCERTAIN STATUS OF CIVIL RIGHTS

America's fragmented policymaking structure, especially the institution of states' rights, is a necessary condition for understanding the "American dilemma," the persistence of racial discrimination in a nation that prides itself on providing equality of opportunity. For most of the nation's history, the national government acquiesced in the inferior legal protections afforded to blacks and permitted the states to set the terms of American citizenship. In the southern states, where economics and politics made the denial of black rights advantageous to elites, no national guarantees prevented these elites from legally separating the races and subordinating blacks.

Despite the egalitarian rhetoric of the constitution, this states' rights tradition persisted through the 1950s. When the federal government finally intervened to guarantee civil rights, segregation was deeply entrenched in the laws and the culture of a large part of the nation. Change required extraordinary efforts to modify "the distribution of power between the two levels of government" and to secure a wide range of judicial, legislative, and executive actions.[105] Under these circumstances, national civil rights guarantees were won only at the cost of enormous social upheaval. Efforts to protect civil rights in housing, education, and employment was backed by less political support than the efforts to strike down Jim Crow and voting limitations in the South, and so the policymaking structure yielded far more uneven and weaker protections.

The Reagan administration skillfully used the policymaking structure to return the enforcement of some civil rights protections to the states, the level of government historically less willing and able to guarantee those rights. And in an apparent contradiction, the administration intervened to prevent state and local choice when it resulted in improving civil rights efforts. The fact that some of the state and local governments that resisted relaxed civil rights enforcement are in the South is a tribute to the success of the Voting Rights Act, which made blacks a key constituency for many white-elected officials in southern states. By the late 1980s the national battle over civil rights had become a war of attrition. Civil rights advocates and black voters were generally successful in keeping civil rights statutes on the books, but the Reagan administration was able to undermine enforcement.

NOTES

1. Donald L. Robinson, *Slavery in the Structure of American Politics, 1765–1820* (New York: Harcourt, Brace, Jovanovich, 1971), 40.
2. Ibid., 23.
3. Ibid., 32–6.
4. Dan Lacy, *The White Use of Blacks in America* (New York: McGraw-Hill, 1972), 18.
5. Robinson, *Slavery in the Structure of American Politics*, 220.
6. Ibid., 200.
7. Lacy, *The White Use of Blacks in America*, 20.
8. Robinson, *Slavery in the Structure of American Politics*, 180, 192, 201.
9. Ibid., 288–90.
10. Don E. Fehrenbacher, *Slavery, Law, and Politics: The Dred Scott Case in Historical Perspective* (New York: Oxford University Press, 1981).
11. Charles Sackett Syndor, *Slavery in Mississippi* (Gloucester, MA: Peter Smith, 1965, originally 1933), 186.
12. Kenneth M. Stampp, *The Peculiar Institution: Slavery in the Ante-Bellum South* (New York: Vintage, 1956), 31.
13. Ibid., 206–8.
14. Ibid., 208–16.
15. Robinson, *Slavery in the Structure of American Politics*, 392–421.
16. Alvin M. Josephy, Jr., *On the Hill: A History of the American Congress* (New York: Touchstone, 1980), 195–203.
17. Fehrenbacher, *Slavery, Law, and Politics*, 41–71; William J. Cooper, *The South and the Politics of Slavery, 1828–1856* (Baton Rouge: Louisiana State University Press, 1978), 253–5.
18. Walter Ehrlich, *They Have No Rights: Dred Scott's Struggle for Freedom* (Westport, CT: Greenwood Press, 1979), 137–49.
19. Bernard Schwartz, ed., *Statutory History of the United States: Civil Rights*, vol. I (New York: Chelsea House, 1970), 19–98, 181–334, 367–442.
20. Ibid., 99–158, 443–802. Cf. Robert J. Kaczorowski, "To Begin the Nation Anew: Congress, Citizenship, and Civil Rights After the Civil War," *American Historical Review* 92:1 (February 1987), 45–68.
21. Joseph B. James, *The Ratification of the Fourteenth Amendment* (Macon, GA: Mercer University Press, 1984), 204.

22. Roger L. Ransom and Richard Sutch, *One Kind of Freedom: The Economic Consequences of Emancipation* (Cambridge, England: Cambridge University Press, 1977), 80–8, 179–81.
23. Lacy, *The White Use of Blacks in America*, 104–5.
24. C. Vann Woodward, *The Strange Career of Jim Crow*, 2d rev. ed., (New York: Oxford University Press, 1966), 22–4.
25. Lacy, *The White Use of Blacks in America*, 116.
26. John Hope Franklin, "History of Racial Segregation in the United States," in *Annals of the American Academy of Political and Social Science* 304:6 (March 1956), 1–9; Woodward, *The Strange Career of Jim Crow*, 97–102.
27. Lacy, *The White Use of Blacks in America*, 120.
28. Pete Daniel, *The Shadow of Slavery: Peonage in the South, 1901–1969* (Urbana: University of Illinois Press, 1972), 24–5, 66, 78–81.
29. Lacy, *The White Use of Blacks in America*, 108.
30. *Plessy* v. *Ferguson*, 163 U.S. 537 (1896).
31. *Williams* v. *Mississippi* 170 U.S. 213 (1898).
32. Stephen Skowronek, *Building a New American State: The Expansion of National Administrative Capacities, 1877–1920* (Cambridge, England: Cambridge University Press, 1982), 165–9, 171–3.
33. Hugh C. Bailey, *Liberalism in the New South: Southern Social Reformers and the Progressive Movement* (Coral Gables, FL: University of Miami Press, 1969), 84–5.
34. Arthur S. Link, *Woodrow Wilson and the Progressive Era, 1910–1917* (New York: Harper & Row, 1954), 64–6.
35. James L. Sundquist, *Dynamics of the Party System: Alignment and Realignment of Political Parties in the United States*, rev. ed. (Washington, DC: Brookings, 1983), 208–24.
36. Harvard Sitkoff, "The Impact of the New Deal on Black Southerners," in James C. Cobb and Michael V. Namorato, eds., *The New Deal and the South* (Jackson: University Press of Mississippi, 1984), 124.
37. Ibid., 120–1.
38. Philip Selznick, *TVA and the Grass Roots: A Study in the Sociology of Formal Organization* (Berkeley: University of California Press, 1949).
39. Richard Franklin Bensel, *Sectionalism and American Political Development, 1880–1980* (Madison: University of Wisconsin Press, 1984), 233.
40. John Frederick Martin, *Civil Rights and the Crisis of Liberalism: The Democratic Party, 1945–1976* (Boulder, CO: Westview Press, 1979), 61, quoted by Bensel, *Sectionalism and American Political Development*, 231–2.
41. Bensel, *Sectionalism and American Political Development*, 231.
42. U.S. Bureau of the Census, *Historical Statistics of the United States, Colonial Times to 1970*, vol. 2 (Washington, DC: GPO, 1975), 1075.
43. Lacy, *The White Use of Blacks in America*, 177–8; William C. Berman, *The Politics of Civil Rights in the Truman Administration* (Columbus: Ohio State University Press, 1970), 42.
44. Berman, *The Politics of Civil Rights in the Truman Administration*, 5–6; Sitkoff, "The Impact of the New Deal on Black Southerners," 130–2.
45. Berman, *The Politics of Civil Rights in the Truman Administration*, 21, 54–5.
46. "President Truman's Message to Congress, February 2, 1948," in Albert P. Blaustein and Robert L. Zangrando, eds., *Civil Rights and the American Negro: A Documentary History* (New York: Trident Press, 1968), 380–4.
47. Berman, *The Politics of Civil Rights in the Truman Administration*, 114–6.
48. Ibid., 116–8, 125.
49. Oscar Glantz, "The Negro Vote in Northern Industrial Cities," *Western Political Quarterly* 13:4 (December 1960), 999–1010.
50. Ruth P. Morgan, *The President and Civil Rights: Policy-Making by Executive Order* (New York: St. Martin's Press, 1970), 24, 43–57; James L. Sundquist, *Politics and Policy: The Eisenhower, Kennedy, and Johnson Years* (Washington, DC: Brookings, 1969), 244.

51. *Brown* v. *Board of Education* 347 U.S. 483 (1954); *Brown* v. *Board of Education*, 349 U.S. 294 (1955).
52. Harrell R. Rodgers, Jr. and Charles S. Bullock, *Law and Social Change: Civil Rights Laws and Their Consequences* (New York: McGraw-Hill, 1972), 70–1.
53. Ibid., 70–1; Anthony Lewis, *Portrait of a Decade: The Second American Revolution* (New York: Random House, 1964), 27; Sundquist, *Politics and Policy*, 238–9.
54. Sundquist, *Politics and Policy*, 234.
55. Ibid., 242, 249–50.
56. Rodgers and Bullock, *Law and Social Change*, 60.
57. Charles and Barbara Whalen, *The Longest Debate: A Legislative History of the 1964 Civil Rights Act* (New York: Mentor, 1985), xvii–xviii; Sundquist, *Politics and Policy* 254–8.
58. Victor Navasky, *Kennedy Justice* (New York: Atheneum, 1971), 96; Sundquist, *Politics and Policy*, 257–8; Morgan, *The President and Civil Rights*, 46–8, 88.
59. Thomas R. Brooks, *The Walls Come Tumbling Down: A History of the Civil Rights Movement, 1940–1970* (New York: Praeger, 1978), 161–3; Carl M. Brauer, *John F. Kennedy and the Second Reconstruction* (New York: Columbia University Press, 1977), 11; Navasky, *Kennedy Justice*, 20–2.
60. Whalen, *The Longest Debate*, xix–xx.
61. Sundquist, *Politics and Policy*, 260–1.
62. Whalen, *The Longest Debate*, xxi.
63. Sundquist, *Politics and Policy*, 263–5.
64. Ibid., 266–70.
65. *Congressional Quarterly Almanac, 1964*, (Washington, DC: Congressional Quarterly, 1965), 338–42.
66. Ibid.
67. Ibid.; Herbert Hill, "The Equal Employment Opportunity Acts of 1964 and 1972: A Critical Analysis of the Legislative History and Administration of the Law," *Industrial Relations Law Journal* 2:1 (Spring 1977), 1–32.
68. *Congressional Quarterly Almanac, 1964*, 338–42; Advisory Commission on Intergovernmental Relations, *Regulatory Federalism: Policy, Process, Impact, and Reform* (Washington, DC: ACIR, 1984), 8, 74, 142–6.
69. Numan V. Bartley and Hugh D. Graham, *Southern Politics and the Second Reconstruction* (Baltimore: Johns Hopkins University Press, 1975), 107.
70. Sundquist, *Dynamics of the Party System*, 290–1, 358–62, 388.
71. *Congressional Quarterly Almanac, 1965*, (Washington, DC: Congressional Quarterly, 1966), 533–6; Richard Scher and James Button, "Voting Rights Act: Implementation and Impact," in Charles S. Bullock and Charles M. Lamb, eds., *Implementation of Civil Rights Policy* (Monterey, CA: Brooks/Cole, 1984), 40–2.
72. Sundquist, *Politics and Policy*, 271–5.
73. *Report of the National Advisory Commission on Civil Disorders* (New York: Bantam, 1968), 251–2.
74. *Report of the National Advisory Commission on Civil Disorders*, 392; Sundquist, *Politics and Policy*, 278–9.
75. Gary Orfield, *Must We Bus? Segregated Schools and National Policy* (Washington, DC: Brookings, 1978), 99.
76. Stephen B. Oates, *Let the Trumpet Sound: The Life of Martin Luther King, Jr.* (New York: Harper & Row, 1982), 379, 412.
77. *Report of the National Advisory Commission on Civil Disorders*, 35–108.
78. Lou Cannon, *Reagan* (New York: G.P. Putnam's Sons, 1982), 106–11.
79. *Congressional Quarterly Almanac, 1968*, (Washington, DC: Congressional Quarterly, 1969) 133, 153–64, 465–71; Dennis R. Judd, *The Politics of American Cities, Private Power and Public Policy*, 3d ed. (Glenview, IL, and Boston: Scott, Foresman/Little, Brown, 1988), 286–8.
80. Sundquist, *Politics and Policy*, 285.
81. Bartley and Graham, *Southern Politics and the Second Reconstruction*, 126–7; Everett Carl

Ladd, Jr., "The Shifting Party Coalitions—1932–1976," in Seymour Martin Lipset, ed., *Emerging Coalitions in American Politics* (San Francisco: Institute for Contemporary Studies, 1978), 98; A. James Reichley, *Conservatives in an Age of Change: The Nixon and Ford Administrations* (Washington, DC: Brookings, 1981), 145.

82. Reichley, *Conservatives in an Age of Change,* 186.
83. Augustus J. Jones, Jr., *Law, Bureaucracy, and Politics: The Implementation of Title VI of the Civil Rights Act of 1964* (Washington, DC: University Press of America, 1982), 22.
84. Reichley, *Conservatives in an Age of Change,* 191.
85. Ibid., 202.
86. Gary R. Orren, "Candidate Style and Voter Alignment in 1976," in Lipset, ed., *Emerging Coalitions in American Politics,* 160.
87. Joseph A. Califano, Jr. *Governing America: An Insider's Report from the White House and Cabinet* (New York: Touchstone, 1981), 243.
88. Ibid., 176–7; Jones, *Law, Bureaucracy, and Politics,* 30–4.
89. Theodore H. White, *America in Search of Itself: The Making of the President, 1956–1980,* (New York: Harper & Row, 1982), 381.
90. Rochelle Stanfield, "Reagan May be Courting Women, Minorities, But It May Be Too Late to Win Them," *National Journal* 28 May 1983, 1118–23; *National Journal* 10 November 1984, 2130–2; Paul R. Abramson, John W. Aldrich and David W. Rohde, *Change and Continuity in the 1984 Elections* (Washington, DC: Congressional Quarterly, 1986), 133–58.
91. Jones, *Law, Bureaucracy, and Politics,* 36–7.
92. D. Lee Bawden and John L. Palmer, "Social Policy: Challenging the Welfare State," in John L. Palmer and Isabel V. Sawhill, eds., *The Reagan Record* (Cambridge, MA: Ballinger, 1984), 200.
93. Ibid., 204–8.
94. Charles S. Lamb, "Equal Housing Opportunity," in Charles S. Bullock III and Charles S. Lamb, eds., *Implementation of Civil Rights Policy* (Monterey, CA: Brooks/Cole, 1984), 171–3; William Celis III, "Justice, HUD Oppose Housing Segregation, But Enforcement Lags," *Wall Street Journal,* 28 October 1985, 1.
95. Bawden and Palmer, "Social Policy," 205–6, 208.
96. Lamb, "Equal Housing Opportunity," 172–3.
97. Anthony Neely, "Government Role in Rooting Out, Remedying Discrimination Is Shifting," *National Journal* 22 September 1984, 1772–5.
98. Susan P. Fino, "Judicial Federalism and Equality Guarantees in State Supreme Courts," *Publius* 17:1 (Winter 1987), 51–67.
99. William E. Nelson, Jr. and Michael S. Bailey, "The Weakening of State Participation in Civil Rights Enforcement," in Dennis R. Judd, ed., *Public Policy Across States and Communities* (Greenwich, CT: JAI Press, 1985), 155–68.
100. U.S. General Accounting Office, *Federal Agencies' Block Grant Civil Rights Enforcement Efforts: A Status Report* GAO Report HRD-84-82 (Washington, DC: GPO, 1984); U.S. General Accounting Office, *Education Block Grant Alters State Role and Provides Greater Local Discretion,* GAO Report HRD-85-18 (Washington, DC: GPO, 1984).
101. U.S. Congress, House, Committee on Education and Labor, Subcommittee on Employment Opportunities, "Civil Rights, the New Federalism, and the Job Training Partnership Act," Illinois Unemployment and Job Training Research Project Report Number 2 (Unpublished Mimeo, June 26, 1985).
102. Neely, "Government Role"; Stanfield, "Reagan May be Courting"; Joe Davidson, "School Desegregation Isn't Faring Very Well in Washington Today," *Wall Street Journal,* 22 October 1985, 1.
103. Cannon, *Reagan,* 379; Scher and Button, "Voting Rights Act," 28–9.
104. *Congressional Quarterly Weekly Report,* 3 October 1987, 2369, 24 October 1987, 2601, and 26 March 1988, 774–5.
105. Milton D. Morris, *The Politics of Black America,* (New York: Harper & Row, 1975), 244.

Chapter 7

AMERICAN WELFARE POLICY: FRAGMENTED PROGRAMS, DIVIDED CONSTITUENCIES

THE IRONY OF AMERICAN WELFARE POLICY

Although the United States has been among the world's wealthiest nations for almost a century, poverty has been a persistent, serious, and widespread problem in America. More than thirty-two million citizens lived below the government's official poverty level in 1986.

Many people view the persistence of want in the midst of wealth as a consequence of a culture that places a premium on the work ethic and self-reliance. A stigma therefore is attached to government "handouts." But this portrait is too simplistic. As we demonstrated in Chapter 5 welfare programs for the middle class, notably Social Security, are popular and have grown a great deal since 1960. What really distinguishes the American welfare state is the lateness of national government effort, the fragmentation of American programs, the gaps in its coverage, and the relative paucity of benefits for the poor as opposed to the middle class. As Russell Hanson argues,

> the American welfare state . . . is characterized by the assignment of most social insurance functions to the national government, and the joint provision of public assistance by national, state, and local governments. Indeed, the strongly bifurcated organization of the American welfare state may be its most distinguishing feature . . . Insurance programmes are not means tested; they are broadly-based entitlement programmes that benefit all classes, though not equally. Assistance programmes . . . are means tested, and as such they are targeted on those whose ability to support themselves has been impaired. As such, assistance programmes benefit the lower classes . . . Thus social insurance and public assistance serve

distinctly different constituencies, and in quite different ways . . . National insurance programmes are held in high esteem, and are politically sacrosanct . . . On the other hand, public assistance programmes have long been viewed with suspicion by the general public.[1]

The irony of American welfare policy is that the most broadly supported income maintenance program is the most expensive and most centralized, but Aid to Families with Dependent Children (AFDC), which most people equate with the disdained term "welfare," remains as fragmented and geographically uneven as any American social program, and its cost (in constant dollars) rose relatively slowly after the early 1970s, and fell in the 1980s.

The fragmentation of American welfare policy demonstrates the effect of policymaking structure on the development of American welfare programs. Aid to the poor was fixed firmly as a local task during the period when policy responsibility was divided among governments between the 1780s and Reconstruction. State governments began to take a more active role in relief policy after the mid-nineteenth century, when industrialization, immigration, and business downturns swelled the numbers of poor in the cities. State policies constituted a patchwork of very limited assistance in a few states and no aid at all in others.

When the national government's policymaking capacity expanded and finally entered the field of social insurance and public assistance in the 1930s, new social welfare programs were created. New initiatives in the 1960s and 1970s, such as the War on Poverty, food stamps, Medicaid, Medicare, and Supplemental Security Income, all expanded federal effort. Some of the legislation, together with important federal court rulings, imposed unprecedented national standards on public assistance programs. But the multiplication of new programs made income maintenance policy less rather than more coherent. Programs that delegated significant policy discretion to the states remained almost as variable and inefficient as the state programs had been, although they were funded at a higher level.

Welfare (that is, public assistance) reform in the 1960s and 1970s was motivated by dissatisfaction with the inevitable problems arising from this state-based approach. Efforts to nationalize AFDC failed in the Nixon and Carter administrations in part because state and local political concerns made it politically impossible to reach a national consensus on a replacement for AFDC. In the 1980s, the Reagan administration demonstrated how the policymaking structure facilitated cutbacks in welfare policy for the poor rather than the middle class, accentuating the differences between income maintenance programs.

DIVIDING POLICY RESPONSIBILITY: THE POOR LAW

When the states ratified the Constitution, local governments and private charities bore the entire burden for helping the needy in America. The Constitution granted no authority to the federal government to provide relief to the poor. State legislatures, in turn, routinely made local officials responsible for implementing "poor laws." By copying the British poor law of 1601, the typical state managed to avoid any financial burden for assisting the poor by mandating that "each towne shall provide carefully for the relief of the poor, to maintain the impotent, and to employ the able, and shall appoint an overseer for the same purpose." Local property taxes were expected to support the needy, without state financial involvement.[2]

Americans demonstrated little tolerance for poverty or for poor people. The Puritan tradition held that poverty was a sin, evidence of slothfulness and un-Christian habits. Americans borrowed heavily on this tradition. Poverty was traced to individual weakness, never to social conditions. In the words of the New York Society for the Prevention of Pauperism in 1818, "No man who is temperate, frugal, and willing to work need suffer or become a pauper for want of employment."[3]

The immigrant floodtide of the nineteenth century inflamed Americans' prejudices against the poor. Americans tended to blame poverty on the habits and customs of the immigrant groups, especially the Irish (in the mid-nineteenth century) or Slavs, Italians, and Greeks (in the late nineteenth and early twentieth century). Believing that these groups were naturally inferior, and blaming their plight on their alleged laziness or intemperance, American social and political elites persuaded themselves that the poor deserved little public compassion or assistance.[4]

Campaigns for poor law "reform" were motivated by a desire to minimize cost, above all by ensuring that people who were poor because of their alleged moral deficiencies would not receive assistance. The poor were especially visible in port cities, where the day-to-day uncertainty of work and the flow of incoming immigrants concentrated thousands of destitute families. With local property tax levies for poor relief rising, local officials complained that aid to the poor was too generous. The poor law overseers in Beverly, Massachusetts complained that "the idle will beg in preference to working; relief is extended to them without suitable discrimination. They are not left to feel the just consequences of their idleness."[5] The overseers felt that those without money in the winter had simply been too wasteful to save for hard times.

But problems of rising costs and dependency finally thrust the problem of the poor onto the states' policy agendas. In a 1824 report to the state legislature, New York's secretary of state, J. V. N. Yates, criticized the common practice of child apprenticeship and auctioning the services of the poor in return for their maintenance as careless and counterproductive. At the same time, he attacked "outdoor relief," the practice by which local poor law officials provided aid to the poor while permitting them to live at home. Poor relief costs had increased from $245,000 in 1815 to $471,000 in 1822, a proportionate increase far outpacing population growth. Yates preferred "indoor relief," provided in a public institution where the inmates could be required to work. Only the "truly needy" would be likely to turn to the taxpayers for help if they were forced to live in a "poorhouse" to receive it. Yates estimated that this change would reduce annual per-capita welfare costs from $65 to $35.

A decade before Britain adopted similar measures in its poor law reforms of 1834, the New York state legislature enacted the County Poorhouse Act, which required each county to erect one or more poorhouses. Unless too ill to be removed from their homes, the needy were required to enter the poorhouse if they wanted relief. New York's innovation spread rapidly: Massachusetts, with 83 poorhouses in 1824, had constructed 180 by 1839 and 219 by 1860. Because poorhouses promised fiscal relief especially in cities, city officials were inclined to finance their construction. Since supervision of this requirement was notably lax (because states did not want to spend money to hire administrators), many rural governments continued to rely on outdoor relief.[6]

Conditions in the poorhouses could not conceivably be viewed as excessively humane. In the mid-1850s, the Erie County (New York) Medical Society reported on the atrocious conditions in the poorhouse that served the port city of Buffalo. One out of every six residents of this poorhouse died in 1848, and though conditions improved over the next several years, the mortality rate remained higher in the poorhouse than in major urban hospitals. Ventilation was nonexistent and the diet less than minimal, as the doctors described it:

> Breakfast—a piece of bread about 5 inches square by 3/4 of an inch thick, a little salt port with coffee, made from barley, and sweetened with the cheapest of molasses. Dinner—same as breakfast, minus the coffee. Supper—bread and tea.
>
> Once a week mutton soup.
>
> As to quality, the nurse in charge of the children said that the bread was never sufficiently baked, and was frequently so sour as to curdle milk.[7]

In 1856, the county built a new poorhouse without bathing facilities, which consisted of thirty-four rooms meant to accommodate thirty paupers each. The insane were provided a separate building. Children were kept until the age of sixteen, at which time the superintendent bound them over to an employer.[8]

State and local governments also built institutions for people who could not be expected to "reform" (go off the dole) unless isolated in a specialized environment. Criminals obviously needed to be segregated from others in the poorhouse. New York state erected the first state penitentiaries at Auburn and Ossining (or "Sing-Sing") in the 1820s. Other states copied this reform: Connecticut, Maryland, and Massachusetts in the 1820s, Michigan and Ohio in the 1830s, and Indiana, Wisconsin, and Minnesota in the 1840s. New York and Massachusetts developed separate asylums for the insane in the 1830s, and by 1860, twenty-eight of the thirty-three states supported state schools and hospitals for the insane. Municipal governments began to segregate juvenile delinquents in "houses of refuge" (reformatories). Public orphanages followed in the 1830s.[9] State funds often helped support these local institutions. Though local governments continued to carry most of the relief responsibilities, states increasingly assumed responsibility for prisons and homes for the mentally disabled. By the mid-nineteenth century, state prisons and insane asylums constituted the leading expenditures of state governments.[10]

When the states finally asked the federal government for assistance in supporting the indigent insane, they ran up against the view that this would violate the Constitution's separation of responsibilities between the national government and the states. In 1854 President Franklin Pierce vetoed congressional legislation that would have provided land grants to the states for the purpose of establishing institutions for the mentally ill. Viewing the measure as one conveying to the federal government "the charge of all the poor in the States," Pierce held that the Constitution granted no authority to permit the federal government to become "the great almoner of charity in the United States." Pierce's veto discouraged reformers who sought federal intervention on behalf of the poor. The National Conference of Charities, for example, showed no further interest in winning federal support after 1854.[11] Questions about the national government's role did not arise again until the Progressive Era.

STATE ACTIVISM: TINKERING WITH THE POOR LAW

State responsibility for the poor during the late nineteenth century ensured that antipoverty policy would remain uneven. Concerns about the cost, effectiveness, and quality of the poorhouses grew after the Civil War. Industrialization increased the risk of falling into utter destitution. Many workers left familiar rural communities to live among strangers in the cities. For families wholly dependent on wages, a breadwinner's death, injury, or prolonged layoff could send the whole family to the poorhouse. The ranks of the desperately needy swelled during the panics and depressions that periodically racked the economy. Unemployment and poverty translated into escalating pressures on state and local governments. The states with the most pressing problems took the first steps toward an active role in helping the poor. These reforms reflected two opposing forces: the need to provide assistance to poor people, pitted against state officials' concern about keeping taxes and benefits low in comparison with other states.

State Regulation of the Poor Law

The nation's most industrialized state, Massachusetts, reacted to these pressures by creating the first State Board of Charities, in 1863. New York and Ohio followed in 1867, and nineteen states had established such boards by 1894. Established to exercise more state control over the costs and quality of state-subsidized welfare efforts, state boards had such responsibilities as removing "foreign" paupers from the state and investigating and reporting on the condition of public and private charitable facilities. The boards helped save money in state institutions and set policies for county, municipal, and even private agencies tied to public funds.[12] Many state boards made available "designs of the best and most economical forms of construction to be used in caring for the various classes of dependents."[13] The main object of these designs was to keep relief from being too generous. New York and New Jersey made the State Charities Aid Association, affiliated with the Charity Organization Society, a semiofficial state inspection agency.[14]

State and local governments redoubled their efforts to remove the "worthy poor," especially children, from the overcrowded poorhouses. Massachusetts provided state funds for foster parents in the 1880s. New York's reformers warned of "what these children must grow up to, what they must become, if they are not soon removed from this atmosphere of vice." New York's 1875 Children's Law banned children between the ages of two and sixteen from poorhouses, and this apparently had an immediate impact on poorhouse populations. In the Erie County poorhouse, for example, the proportion of inmates under 14 years of age fell from 30 percent in the late 1860s to 3 percent a decade later.[15] Other "worthy" poor included veterans. New Jersey enacted legislation setting up veterans' pensions in 1857 and 1874, years in which economic recessions cast many industrial workers out of jobs.[16]

States attempted to discourage poor people from moving within their borders, and they tried to turn a profit on those they already supported. Massachusetts passed a law in 1880 to protect "the commonwealth against tramps." The statute required a prison sentence of six months to two years for adult men convicted of vagrancy. An 1896 law amended it to include women. Because the law was not uniformly enforced, paupers did not know what to expect in any town.[17] Other state innovations turned poor relief expenditures over to private institutions. For example, the New Jersey reformatory in Jonesburg leased the labor of juvenile inmates to local shirt-making firms. Missouri passed a law in 1879 providing for the bodies of deceased poor persons to be used in scientific research.[18]

Despite their willingness to enact laws regulating the poor, the states absorbed little of the actual financial burden of relief. A study of county poorhouses in New York in 1880 revealed that only 0.1 percent of the paupers in them were supported by state funds.[19]

The Role of Private Charity

In the large cities, where need obviously outpaced the limited public efforts, private organizations stepped in to fill the gap. The New York Association for the Improvement of the Condition of the Poor was organized in 1845 to "discountenance indiscriminate alms-giving, and to put an end to street-begging and vagrancy." Like similar associations subsequently organized in other cities, it asserted that current charity efforts failed adequately to investigate cases and to ". . . encourage industrious and virtuous habit, and foster among [the poor] a spirit of self-dependence." The association said that the poor should be allowed to receive aid only if they received visitors from the association who were charged with inculcating in them ". . . habits of frugality, temperance, industry, and self-dependence."[20] Instead of cash, the association recommended that aid be given in the form of food, clothing, and stoves for warmth. It was thought that cash assistance would encourage idleness and continued moral degeneracy. In this view, "self-indulgence" and other personal deficiencies produced urban poverty, turning the tenement house into a "sickening caricature of 'home' " and making the "moral atmosphere" of the slums "as pestilential as they are physical."[21]

Charity Organization Societies (COS) "modernized" these ideas in the 1870s. Organized in every major city in the United States, COS branches tried to make charity a wholly private function. The movement's intellectual underpinning was informed by Social Darwinism, which had adopted Charles Darwin's theories about natural selection and applied them to society: individuals endowed with intelligence, good morals, and proper habits would prosper, and those without them would degenerate. The poor had only themselves to blame for their plight. "Sentimental" assistance given without attempts to improve the poor would only cultivate laziness and the expectation of continued charity. Josephine Shaw Lowell, a leading spokesperson for the COS view, opposed public relief unless "starvation is imminent." The COS strongly opposed "outdoor" relief provided by private charities *or* public agencies and succeeded in abolishing it in ten of the nation's forty largest cities between 1873 and 1900 (and it reduced outdoor relief in many others).[22]

Nevertheless, by 1900 local governments still bore most of the responsibility for relief of the poor. In 1900 in New York State, private sources provided outdoor relief for 30,560 people, while poorhouses provided outdoor relief for 209,092 and indoor relief for 73,117 indigents.[23] By the turn of the century, poverty was on the rise and was an increasingly expensive problem for local officials.

The Limits of Progressive Reform

By the turn of the century events began to undermine the traditional assumptions that poverty originated mostly from defects in character or morals. Widely read studies, such as Robert Hunter's 1904 book *Poverty*, asserted that most of the poor were helpless victims of the industrial system. Hunter estimated that in 1900, 6.4 million workers (22 percent of the labor force) were unemployed at some time during the year and that 10 percent of Americans lived in poverty.

Many of the nation's prominent social scientists converged on Pittsburgh in 1907–1908 to begin a detailed survey of social problems. The survey found appalling overwork, underpay, and dependence. The Pittsburgh survey's widely circulated findings severely damaged the arguments put forth by the privately run Charity Organization Societies and boosted demands for simpler and more comprehensive systems for supporting the poor.[24]

The plight of widowed mothers struck many Americans as especially pathetic. In a society that offered no alternative to wages for daily survival, widows often had little choice but the poorhouse. Separating widows from their children seemed both senseless and brutal. Yet local officials, such as juvenile court judges, found that their only option for dealing with impoverished families was to place children in foster homes or reformatories while the mother entered the poorhouse. In 1913, for example, nearly four thousand children were placed in institutions because their parents could not support them.[25] Since institutionalization was more expensive than a subsidy to the mother, the idea of mother's aid appealed to cost-conscious reformers.

Juvenile court authorities recognized that forced separations increased the likelihood of juvenile delinquency and threatened to swamp reformatories as well as poorhouses. Local juvenile courts and poor law officials lobbied for an alternative that would keep families intact. The result was "mother's aid" or "widow's pension" programs. Juvenile court judges in Chicago and Kansas City, Missouri put the first mother's aid programs into effect in 1907 and 1908. Twenty states had enacted mother's aid laws by 1913 and thirty-nine states (as well as Alaska and Hawaii) passed laws by 1920.[26] State legislatures approved the programs by large margins, despite opposition from organized private charities, which resented government competition in their sphere.[27]

What explains the favorable attitude of states toward widow's pensions when none of them were willing to finance unemployment or medical insurance schemes? First, these programs amounted to little more than "outdoor relief" for a narrowly defined group of recipients. Typically, the state laws required that the mother be "truly needy," that is, utterly destitute and "a proper person, physically, mentally and morally fit to bring up her children."[28]

Second, and possibly more important, the law held forth the promise of controlling welfare costs. The Illinois statute, for example, did not grant payments to all widows with children but merely permitted courts to order such payments when warranted. After the law took effect, the Chicago juvenile court was swamped with applications. To contain costs, relief workers rejected two-thirds of them, and Cook County appropriated a tiny amount ($6.33 per child per month) for the few applicants who were accepted.[29] New York's governor specifically instructed the state's juvenile courts to provide allowances to mothers only when institutionalization was the sole alternative.[30] Much like workers compensation laws, "mother's aid laws spread rapidly because they created more certainty and economy in an important social policy area."[31]

Through the 1920s, most states expanded eligibility and raised benefits for mother's aid. But eligibility standards remained very strict. In 1931, 81 percent of the recipients were widows, since even destitute women with dependent children usually could not qualify unless their husband had died. With the depression deepening in 1931, only 93,260 of 3.8 million female-headed families in the United States received mother's aid. The average family grant ranged from $69.31 per month in Massachusetts to $4.33 in Arkansas.[32]

Aid to the aged and the blind was less pressing, politically, than aid to the mothers of dependent children, and therefore fewer states passed relief laws for these groups. Only Arizona (1914) and the territory of Alaska (1915) enacted old-age pensions before 1920, but the Arizona program was struck down by state courts as unconstitutional. Several states passed old-age assistance laws in the 1920s: Nevada and Montana in 1923, Wisconsin in 1925, and Maryland and Colorado in 1927. In five other states, governors vetoed old-age pension laws or the state supreme courts declared them unconstitutional. Each of the programs in operation in 1929 was optional and locally financed; Montana, Alaska, and a few Wisconsin counties accounted for all of the twelve hundred aged Americans who received a total of $222,000 in pensions.

Similarly, Ohio established the first aid-to-the-blind program in 1898, but as late as 1934, one year before Congress passed the Social Security Act, only eleven of the twenty-four states that had programs for the blind on the books allocated any state financial assistance. In most of the states, the legislatures had done nothing more than empower counties or local governments to provide categorical aid to the blind, if they wished, with no state funds. In four of the twenty-four states with this kind of legislation, no money at all was spent even by local governments.[33]

Because the federal government did not participate and because states were reluctant to spend much money even if they had the fiscal capacity, the total cost of welfare and pension programs in the United States remained incredibly low. In 1913, total federal, state, and local spending on public welfare amounted to $57 million, or 1 percent of government expenditures (and 0.1 percent of gross domestic product).[34]

Progressive states were reluctant to implement programs on their own. In 1913, for example, the Massachusetts legislature considered and rejected old-age pensions and unemployment insurance along British lines. Political leaders stated that such programs would place the state's industries at a competitive disadvantage and would tempt them to relocate elsewhere.[35] Economist Paul Douglas argued in the mid-1930s that interstate competition "restrained the more progressive states from pioneering as they would have liked and kept the country as a whole closer to the legal conditions in the less progressive states."[36]

Robert Hunter's call for a nationally administered welfare system fell on deaf ears.[37] The federal government did nothing more than urge states to "modernize" their outmoded relief systems. When Theodore Roosevelt called a White House Conference on Dependent Children in January 1909, he brought together 200 prominent social workers and other reformers who exchanged ideas and laid plans for local and state action. Yet such publicity marked the limit of what was considered legitimate federal action. The conference could do no more than encourage states to adopt mother's aid programs. In 1912, Congress approved the creation of the Children's Bureau. The bureau conducted studies of children's problems and shared its findings with state and local officials, hoping to persuade them to adopt efficient and humane practices.[38]

On the eve of the depression, American provision for the poor was financed and regulated by local governments. State governments managed some institutions (asylums) and regulated the local poor relief systems. Even this level of assistance dismayed private charity workers, who were stunned by a 1928 report that showed that 72 percent of all relief in fifteen large cities originated from public funds.[39] The fact that the governmental role had increased to this extent illustrated the fact that private charities had never responded adequately to the social problems connected to poverty. It is not surprising, therefore, that private charities were quickly overwhelmed by the depression.

In the early years of the depression, state and local governments evinced more interest in controlling costs than in providing relief. Counties, towns, cities, and states competed to avoid responsibility for poor people, who in most places were required to live within a jurisdiction for at least a year before they were entitled to assistance. One study of Missouri welfare law found that "[w]hile a good deal of money has been spent in transporting people out of the county, none appears to have been allowed for transporting county residents back when they were found without funds in some other county or state." Litigation over relief in New York State cost $192,000, compared with $215,000 "that could have been spent to maintain those poor during the time of the litigation."[40]

NATIONAL ACTIVISM: DIVIDING INSURANCE AND PUBLIC ASSISTANCE IN THE SOCIAL SECURITY ACT

As millions of destitute Americans swamped the antiquated and decentralized poor law system in the early years of the Great Depression, the states reacted with new pension and even social insurance legislation. Between 1929 and 1934, twenty-two more states enacted old-age pension laws. But for the most part, these laws passed responsibility for the poor onto local governments without supplying them with additional money. Most states, in fact, slashed welfare budgets. The numbers of needy dependent children all across the nation increased dramatically, and the costs of public assistance for dependent children and the elderly were kept in control only by ignoring most of the needy. Some officials, such as the head of New Jersey's welfare department, seized on the economic situation as an opportunity to economize. Thus, New Jersey enacted an old-age pension law in 1931. But to receive a pension, the applicant had to be seventy years old and a fifteen-year resident of the state, had to be destitute, and even then could qualify only if there were no legal relatives who could provide support. The program had been projected to serve 12,250 persons at an average of $25 a month. It was so economically managed that in 1934 it served only 7,688 persons who received an average of $15.16 a month.[41]

With millions of Americans out of work, Franklin Roosevelt mobilized the national government to provide temporary relief through grants to the states (see Chapter 4). The Democratic party platform in 1932 had promised protection against poverty in the form of "unemployment and old-age insurance under state laws." Independent of the Roosevelt administration, bills to provide federal assistance to the states for unemployment insurance (the Wagner-Lewis Bill) and old-age pensions (the Dill-Connery Bill) gathered momentum on Capitol Hill early in 1934. On June 8, 1934, Roosevelt announced, "I am looking for a sound means which I can recommend to provide at once security against several of the great disturbing factors of life—especially those that relate to unemployment and old age." The president directed a special Committee on Economic Security to study American welfare programs and recommended legislation establishing for the first time a federal role in ensuring citizens' income security.[42]

In September the committee reported that the federal government should work through state welfare agencies rather than use centralized welfare programs. The existing policymaking structure was decisive on this point. Although "the entire program outlined should be considered and developed as a unified national program for economic security," the committee thought that "[u]nder the governmental system that exists in this country . . . such a program will require the cooperation of national, state, and local governments" and "the actual administration of the several social insurance mechanisms proposed . . . will have to be vested in the states (except that it may be possible, if a contributory old age insurance is launched, to have this administered directly by the federal government)."

Still, the plan was ambitious. Emphasizing the importance of guaranteed employment, it proposed a permanent government jobs program in times of high unemployment. Unemployment insurance would be the first line of defense against poverty among breadwinners. The federal government "should subsidize state old age pension laws," although the authors agreed that the federal government should also establish a contributory pension system in which benefits depended on a person's work history. The federal government would also provide health insurance for low-income people and subsidize "mother's pensions" to assist families without a breadwinner.[43]

The Politics of Centralized Social Insurance for the Elderly

One of the most compelling political movements in American history made a national system of social security for retired workers virtually irresistible. A retired California physician named Dr. Francis Townsend proposed a plan for old-age assistance in a letter to a Long Beach newspaper in late 1933. The Townsend plan appeared simple and appealing: the federal government could levy a national sales tax and distribute $200 a month to every American over sixty. If the recipients were required to spend their allocations within the month, the federal government could recoup the $20 billion needed to finance the scheme (through sales taxes on their purchases) and the plan would in effect be self-supporting.

Though few experts thought the plan would work (believing it would merely transfer purchasing power from workers to the elderly), there was a phenomenal public response. As the Committee on Economic Security issued its report, Townsend was receiving two thousand letters a day supporting his idea. In San Diego, with thirty-five thousand residents aged sixty or older, the Townsend movement signed up thirty thousand dues-paying members by early 1935 (one-sixth of the city's entire population). Nationwide, seven thousand "Townsend clubs" enrolled one and half million members only two years after the first club had been founded in August 1934. Rumors placed membership figures as high as four million.[44]

In late 1934, Roosevelt told his top policymakers that "Congress can't stand the pressure of the Townsend plan unless we have a real old-age insurance system . . ."[45] When the House and Senate approved the Social Security Act by large margins (371 to 33 and 77 to 6), the government initiated a fundamental shift from a passive to an active national role in welfare policy. But the new programs were fragmented and administratively complex, and signaled no fundamental philosophical redirection of American welfare policy. The legislation delegated significant control over most income maintenance programs to the states, except for the old-age insurance program (Table 7.1). The Social Security Act segregated welfare recipients into two categories: those who would receive social insurance based on the philosophy that they had earned benefits and those who would receive public assistance based on a demonstration of need.

If many of the titles of the Social Security Act established federal underwriting of state welfare provisions, why did the government create a purely national old-age insurance system? The answer is that the federal officials believed that nationally administered compulsory insurance promised to be less expensive than state-based old-age pensions, especially in light of the growth in the population of the elderly expected in future decades. Treasury Secretary Morgenthau told the House Ways and Means Committee that "we know . . . that, even in the absence of well-considered legislation, we cannot avoid important financial outlays for the care of the aged" because the aged population was expected to double by 1970.[46] Though the bill provided a federal matching grant to the states for existing old-age pensions, the House committee argued that:

> To keep the cost of Federal-State pensions under Title I from becoming extremely burdensome in future years, and to assure support for the aged as a right rather than as public charity, and in amounts which will insure not merely subsistence but some of the comforts of life, Title II of the bill establishes a system of old-age benefits . . . administered directly by the

Table 7.1. *Programs under the Social Security Act of 1935*

I. Contributory (insurance) system
    A. Old-Age and Survivors—Title II. National system financed by taxes on employer and employee, plus subsidy from general revenue.
    B. Unemployment—Title III. State systems, National Trust Fund with state accounts. Financed by tax on employers of eight or more under an approved state program (Secs. 903 and 902, Title IX).
II. Noncontributory system (public assistance)
    A. Old-Age Assistance—Title I. Grants to states for one-half of all payments of up to $30 per month to individuals of 65 or over, if state program approved by Social Security board.[a]
    B. Aid to Dependent Children—Title IV. Grants to states for one-third of payments of up to $18 per month for first child and $12 for each additional child.[b]
    C. Aid to the Blind—Title X. Grants to states for one-half of payments of up to $30 per month, subject to approval by Social Security board.
    D. Maternal and Child Welfare—Title V. Nonmonetary welfare. Payments based on number of births and financial need to states providing hospital, nursing, and public health services under plans. By secretary of labor and children's bureau, up to one-half of cost of services.
    E. Vocational Rehabilitation—Title V. Extension of act of 1920. Nonmonetary welfare.
    E. Public Health—Title VI. Nonmonetary welfare. Grants to states for improved services, personnel, or sanitation.

---

[a]Federal grants were made up quarterly and could be stopped at any time violations of federal standards were discovered. The ceiling and the rates have changed many times since 1935, but the basic structure remains the same. As of 1977, the federal share of old-age assistance is 31/37 (about 84 percent) up to the first $38. The total federal share can be no less 50 percent and no more than 65 percent. *Source: 42 U.S. Code Annotated* s. 303(a), 1301(a).

[b]In 1977 the federal share of AFDC was determined by a two-part formula. The first part awards ⅚ of the first $18 of the average payment per recipient made by the state multiplied by the number of recipients. The second part provides from 50 to 60 percent of the next $14 of the average payment multipied by the number of recipients.

Source: U.S. Department of Health, Education and Welfare, *Social Security Bulletin* (October 1977), 19.

> Federal Government . . . The establishment of the Federal old-age benefit system will materially reduce the cost of Federal-aided State pensions under Title I in future years . . . If the measures we propose will reduce dependency, as we expect, the burden upon employers and consumers may well be smaller than it is at present.[47]

Claims of cost control were necessary to make the old-age insurance program politically palatable to Congress. Humanitarian expressions of concern about the aged played a prominent but secondary role in asserting a "right" to old-age security. This was a peculiar right, however. A person earned that right not as a citizen but as a wage earner in the private sector (civil servants and some employees such as domestics and agricultural workers were not covered by the plan). The "right" carried no universal minimum for elderly citizens, as did most European social insurance plans (although many of the European programs established very low minimum pensions indeed). Instead, a retired worker's benefits reflected lifetime earnings, and the poorest and least frequently employed workers, when they retired, had to resort to the "poor law," as modified by state old-age pension laws and institutionalized by federal grants. In upholding the constitutionality of Title II, the Supreme Court stated that the need for a national system was plain and the risk of a system in which some but not all states had pensions was clear: "The existence of such a system is a bait to the needy and dependent elsewhere, encouraging them to migrate and seek a haven of repose."[48]

Business adamantly opposed the idea of a national wage-related old-age pension. The National Association of Manufacturers and other employers groups lobbied heavily against it. According to a key architect of the legislation, had "this question . . . come to a vote earlier [in the Senate Finance Committee] than it did, I feel quite sure that Title II would have gone out of the bill." Even so, the Senate at one point voted 51–39 to amend the bill to permit employers to opt out of the program voluntarily.[49] While that provision was dropped in the final version, the Senate vote illustrates the political problems that surrounded the enactment of any genuinely national program in the Social Security Act.

The Politics of Fragmented Public Assistance

The political consequences of dividing income protection into an "earned" pension (social security) and unearned public charity ("welfare") were significant if little understood. The elderly, who had gravitated to the Townsend plan, would create a powerful constituency for Title II and programs later attached to it, such as Medicare. Mothers with dependent children would become politically isolated from the non-poor elderly, who would no longer have any motivation to join a broad coalition for more nationalized or generous benefits.

Federal grants to support state-administered mother's pensions generated much less debate than the discussion of unemployment and old-age insurance, because most policymakers thought that these programs would remain insignificant. Under the bill, the federal government would provide only one-third of the support for state mother's pensions (rather than one-half, as under Title I for state old-age pensions). Congress amended even this low matching formula by placing a ceiling of fifteen dollars a month per recipient on the federal contribution. The act's designers felt relieved that Congress retained the grant at all and did not object to any restrictions that would facilitate its approval. No one seriously anticipated that spending for Aid to Dependent Children would begin to expand dramatically a generation later.[50]

Only the opponents of any federal influence over state welfare objected to the mother's aid program. Southern House members and senators demanded minimal federal regulation, mostly because they feared that federal guidelines might be used to challenge the inferior status of blacks in the South. They especially objected to the fact that the grants were to be administered by the Federal Emergency Recovery Administration (FERA), which was run by Harry Hopkins, who opposed segregation. Congressman Howard Smith of Virginia argued before the Ways and Means Committee that the states "should be allowed to differentiate among persons." He asserted that even a minimum payment of thirty dollars a month to rural families headed by a single mother, or to unemployed workers, "is not only going to take care of him, but a great many of his dependents, relatives, and so on, who could much better be employed working on a farm."[51]

Ultimately, those not covered by contributory old-age or unemployment insurance depended on the generosity of the state governments. Federal assistance for relief to intact families, employable men, and single persons was prohibited on the assumption that most poor people in these categories would have jobs when the economy recovered. Even for those who qualified for aid, the goal was to reduce "dependency."

In the new era of the national government's grant-in-aid activism, many principles of the poor law became national policy. The Social Security provisions institutionalized the states' variations in welfare policy, reinforcing the fragmentation and unevenness of public assistance across the country. Though the act required states to establish some standard administrative practices, the states continued to set residency requirements, benefit levels, and eligibility criteria.

The Social Security Act left too many gaps to lay the basis for a comprehensive "welfare state." Its social insurance titles excluded major segments of the workforce, such as farm workers and domestics. It provided no security against illness. It provided neither a national minimum income as a right of citizenship nor, alternatively, a guarantee of public jobs as a fallback for able-bodied people who could not get private employment. Congress refused to approve a job guarantee bill to compliment the Social Security Act, and it rejected an effective "full employment" (guaranteed public employment) bill after World War II. During the high employment period of the war, the public jobs programs created during the depression were phased out, and efforts to revive them failed in 1946 and 1949 (see Chapter 5).

Advocates for a more comprehensive welfare state expanded the Social Security Act's provisions through amendments adopted over several decades. For example, in 1939 "survivor's benefits" were added as part of the insurance package for workers. Proponents believed that this "earned" benefit would support most widows and their minor children, causing the federally subsidized "mother's aid" (Aid to Dependent Children) and "old-age pension" (Aid to the Aged) programs to wither away.[52] But by the early 1960s, it was obvious that this forecast amounted to wishful thinking. The 1939 amendments also marked a step away from strict insurance principles by providing benefits to some retirees who had not contributed enough to cover the cost of their pension.

THE STRUGGLE FOR NATIONAL STANDARDS

From Social Security to War on Poverty

The divided social insurance and public assistance programs stirred little controversy until the 1960s. Indeed, without much opposition Social Security officials and their allies gradually strengthened and liberalized the "entitlement" sections of the act. The term "social security" became a synonym for the old-age insurance program. Because "social security" in this form was viewed as a benefit workers had earned, Americans ceased to think of it as "welfare" at all. Title II served more people than any other title by 1950 (Table 7.2), when it covered 80 percent of workers (it covered 88 percent a decade later). Conservative presidents like Eisenhower did not challenge the program's existence but instead expanded the number of wage earners eligible for old-age insurance. In 1956, Eisenhower approved a new disability insurance title. In 1965 Congress created Medicare coverage for retirees.[53]

For those without the opportunity to secure steady employment to make them eligible for benefits upon retirement, Title I (old-age assistance) remained the only option. And "welfare" became the label for Title IV, Aid to Dependent Children (renamed Aid to Families with Dependent Children, or AFDC, in 1962). The perceived "welfare problem" grew in step with rising costs. As Table 7.2 shows, the number of Title IV recipients approximately doubled between 1955 and 1965 and doubled again by 1970.

The Attack on Public Assistance

By the early 1960s, policymakers recognized that economic growth would not automatically lift all nonaged families out of poverty. Title IV disqualified families with an unemployed father in the house, a provision meant to make it hard for unemployed men to receive any benefits, even indirectly. Costs for categorical aid for the elderly poor, old-age assistance, behaved somewhat more predictably. The number of Amer-

Table 7.2. *Growth in beneficiaries of Titles I, II, and IV of the Social Security Act (in thousands)*

	Number of Benefits Paid under Title II and Related Titles (Old-Age, Survivors, Disability, and Health Insurance)[a]	Title I (Old-Age Assistance)	Title IV Aid to Families with Dependent Children
1936	—	1,108	546
1940	222	2,070	1,222
1945	1,288	2,056	943
1950	3,477	2,786	2,233
1955	7,961	2,538	2,192
1960	14,845	2,305	3,073
1965	20,867	2,087	4,396
1970	26,229	2,082	9,659
1975	32,086	2,325	11,404
1980	35,585	1,827	11,101
1986	37,708	1,490	11,065

[a]These figures are slightly larger than the number of individuals receiving benefits; data contain some duplication due to dual entitlement.

[b]1975–1986 figures reflect aged recipients of Supplemental Security Income and Old-Age Assistance.

Source: U.S. Bureau of the Census, *Historical Statistics, Colonial Times to 1970* (Washington, DC: GPO, 1975), 356; *Statistical Abstract of the United States 1988* (Washington, DC: GPO, 1988), 342, 354.

icans receiving old-age assistance stabilized at about two million at the end of World War II, increased after the 1949 recession, and gradually fell over the next twenty-five years.

As AFDC became synonymous with "welfare," it became the object of a litany of complaints about alleged waste, fraud, and abuse. Resurrecting nineteenth century attitudes toward the poor, critics accused AFDC recipients of immoral life styles and laziness. It was alleged that welfare encouraged unmarried women to have babies in order to get on welfare or increase their welfare allotment. Though AFDC regulations disqualified families with a father living in the house, it was commonly assumed that unemployed men were taking advantage of the program through the back door. Undercurrents of racism fed these suspicions, for black families comprised a disproportionate share of the AFDC population.[54]

Though they became politically important, popular stereotypes of the welfare population had little basis in fact. Simple demographics explained much of the growth of the poverty population after World War II: between 1940 and 1960 the nation's population increased by 33 percent. After 1950, the number of single-parent, female-headed households among all social classes grew explosively. Liberalized eligibility standards in the 1960s and 1970s also contributed to the program's expansion, as did advocacy groups that encouraged eligible poor people to claim benefits.[55]

The politically inspired stereotypes of welfare recipients proved to be misleading in other ways, as well. According to 1967 statistics, more than half the adults receiving benefits were white (51.3 percent), and an overwhelming majority were nonworking mothers (91.5 percent) who were the heads of households (75 percent) containing children under fourteen years of age (74 percent). Sixty-five percent of these families had fewer than three children.[56] In the mid-1970s, 25 percent to 30 percent of the mothers enrolled in AFDC worked at some time during the year. A 1973 study found that 25 percent of all AFDC families remained on relief for six months or less, half the recipients received benefits for two years or less, and three-fifths were enrolled less than three years.[57]

Most recipients used the program as the poor had used the poorhouse a hundred years earlier—as a temporary refuge from utter destitution. Because minorities disproportionately lived in poverty, they were over-represented on AFDC rolls. Since the expansion of AFDC accelerated in the 1960s and 1970s at the same time that the migration of blacks to the North was slowing down, it cannot be concluded that blacks and other minorities were lured to northern cities by the prospect of a life on the dole.[58]

In the 1950s some state and local governments resorted to stern measures to control rising welfare costs. Some enforced residency requirements more strictly in order to disqualify migrants (particularly blacks migrating to the North). Several states enacted "suitable home" and "man-in-the-house" requirements that defined the presence of an unrelated man in the household as evidence that the people in the home needed no financial assistance. In the summer of 1960, Louisiana used such rules to terminate aid to 6,281 cases (involving 23,549 children).

The city manager of Newburgh, New York, received national media attention when he ordered thirteen changes in city welfare policy in order to reduce welfare costs. He stipulated that all able-bodied men who refused to do city work would forfeit benefits, that unwed mothers would lose benefits if they had an additional child, and that all recipients, except the aged and disabled, were entitled to only three months of aid per calendar year. Senator Barry Goldwater applauded. "I don't like to see my taxes paid for children out of wedlock," he said. "I'm tired of professional chiselers walking up and down the streets who don't work and have no intention of working. I would like to see every city in the country adopt the plan."[59]

Other state and local governments adopted less draconian measures to reduce the fiscal burden of relief. Cook County (Chicago), Illinois, for example, established job training and employment placement services specifically to reduce the welfare load. Los Angeles, New York, Philadelphia, and the state of Colorado also tried to use such services to place the poor in jobs.[60] Officials believed that these services would help welfare recipients gain new job skills, learn how to purchase nutritional food, take advantage of education opportunities, and become less dependent on welfare. None of these programs, however, significantly reduced welfare dependency or costs.

Reducing Dependency: Welfare Reform in the Kennedy Administration

As the senior partner in the welfare system, the federal government also felt the pressure of increasing costs. In 1960 Washington funded over half of the public aid spending in the United States (a figure that increased to two-thirds by 1975). During the first year of the Kennedy administration alone, the number of AFDC recipients rose by 502,000, increasing total AFDC spending by $200 million.[61]

Because the New Deal had strengthened the state-based public assistance system, the Kennedy administration decided to prod the states to solve the welfare problem by reducing "welfare dependency." New federal programs would encourage state and local governments to help the poor join the workforce. When he was governor of Connecticut, Kennedy's Secretary of Health, Education, and Welfare, Abraham Ribicoff, had complained that few problems were as "frustrating and as bothersome as the whole problem of welfare costs." State services supported through federal grants represented "the key to our efforts to help people become self-sufficient so that they no longer need assistance."[62] By 1962, policymakers from both parties agreed with Ribicoff that decentralized activism was the right strategy for curbing welfare costs.

Kennedy proposed and Congress passed the Public Welfare Amendments of 1962, which encouraged states to expand services to the poor and increased federal welfare grants. The federal government would now pay up to 75 percent of the costs of "rehabilitation" services provided through the states (previously it had paid only 50 percent of these costs). Such services, it was hoped, would help AFDC recipients to manage their budgets and find and keep a job.[63] The program echoed the nineteenth-century strategy of home visits designed to influence the hearts and minds of the poor.

The amendments departed significantly from previous welfare laws by permitting states to provide AFDC to families with an unemployed father at home (AFDC-UP). The administration of the Public Welfare amendments of 1962 foreshadowed the difficulties later encountered by "creative federalism" of the 1960s and 1970s (see Chapter 5). Few state officials warmed to the notion of AFDC-UP, viewing it as a potentially expensive subsidy for lazy fathers. Only twenty-five states provided for AFDC-UP by 1980. As of February 1969, only 5 percent of all AFDC cases included unemployed fathers (by 1980, the figure had increased to 7 percent).[64]

Nor did state welfare departments rush to take advantage of social services grants, although they eventually learned to exploit the open-ended offer of federal funds dangled before them. In the budget year that began in July 1962, the Department of Health, Education and Welfare released $194 million in social services grants to the states, a figure that rose to only $282 million in 1967. California and, later, Illinois officials discovered that these grants could be used to "purchase" services from other state agencies, in effect transferring the federal subsidy to ongoing state expenditures. Illinois, for example, claimed that prison inmates were potential AFDC recipients and that federal grants should be available to fund services in the state penitentiaries. By 1972, state claims had expanded to $1.7 billion.[65]

At the same time, the federal match for AFDC inhibited the use of AFDC for its primary purpose, to maintain incomes. The federal formula for allocating grants paid a large share of the first few dollars of a monthly AFDC payment; in 1968, the federal government reimbursed a state for fifteen dollars of the first eighteen dollars, and then half of any additional funds up to a maximum of thirty-two dollars. States that wanted to minimize their own welfare spending could do so by providing smaller AFDC payments to many recipients. Ironically, the states that did so, such as Mississippi, Alabama, and other southern states, were already the home of many of the nation's poorest citizens. The formula thus meant an "absolute loss to the poorest people in America."[66]

The War on Poverty

The Economic Opportunity Act of 1964 tried a new strategy characteristic of the Johnson administration: it attempted to bypass the established state-local welfare structure, to link federal programs directly to the "hard-core" poor, and to increase the political participation of the poor. The "War on Poverty" initially authorized $315 million for "community action programs" to coordinate a range of services (day care, reading programs, job training, counseling) in the poorest areas and promised "maximum feasible participation" for the poor in determining how this money would be spent. The concept of the poor shaping poverty policy marked a significant break with the past, but in practice the War on Poverty had a limited impact on American welfare policy for two reasons.

Although it is often portrayed as a radical, massive, expensive, centralized program,[67] the War on Poverty was far more limited in reality. First, even the most "radical" aspects of the Economic Opportunity Act's design were motivated by expectations about cost control. At first glance, it seems unusual that the Bureau of the Budget became the most influential voice for community action organizations before the Johnson administration unveiled its War on Poverty. Why would an agency committed to controlling expenditures champion the poor? The answer is that the strategy of bypassing existing state agencies promised to reduce the cost of services and to concentrate spending in "truly needy" communities. The potential for thereby enhancing the "effectiveness" of federal spending explains why the Budget Bureau and President Johnson supported community action agencies while refusing to support a much more expensive public jobs program.[68]

Second, the Economic Opportunity Act never threatened to supplant or to rationalize the American welfare system. Though Congress authorized $800 million for the War on Poverty in fiscal year 1965, in that year the federal grants to the states for public assistance under the Social Security Act totalled nearly $2.7 billion and the pension funds under the Social Security Act paid out over $15.6 billion.[69] The community action agencies could control only a fraction of the money allocated to the War on Poverty. Of the $760 million actually obligated to the Economic Opportunity Act in 1965, the community action organizations received only $94 million to spend at their discretion; most of the appropriations were earmarked for the Head Start preschool program for poor children ($103 million), work experience programs ($112 million), the Neighborhood Youth Corps ($132 million), and the Job Corps ($175 million). Though the War on Poverty budget increased to $1.773 billion by 1968, the community organizations' discretionary share fell from 12.5 percent to 10.5 percent.[70]

Nor did federal War on Poverty officials have a free hand in distributing the money. Congress ensured that the funds would be distributed on a state-based formula and gave governors the right to veto antipoverty projects in their states. More important, influential mayors, such as Chicago's Richard J. Daley, refused to surrender control over local jobs and policymaking. By the mid-1960s, Office of Economic Opportunity Director R. Sargent Shriver had backed away from the more radical implications of "community action" that had initially required participation by the poor.[71]

In-Kind Benefits: Food Stamps and Medical Services

Programs initiated during the 1960s to address the problems of hunger and illness quickly grew much larger than the War on Poverty. These programs provided benefits "in kind" rather than in cash: they could be used only for a specific purpose. The notion of selling food stamps to the poor originated in a pilot project ordered by President Kennedy in 1961. For $6, a poor family could purchase government stamps that could be redeemed for about $10 worth of groceries. The Kennedy administration viewed the program as one that would benefit not only the poor but also farmers, and even conservative members of Congress from farm states outside the South joined with urban legislators to support the program. Congress expanded the program in 1964 to households where a low income was "a substantial limiting factor in the attainment of a nutritionally adequate diet." Even though states paid none of the costs of the stamps and only a portion of the administrative costs, nine states still were not participating in the program. In 1970 the food stamp program was expanded significantly when the stamps were made free to households with income under $30 a month. In 1974 all counties were required to offer food stamps, and in 1978 the stamps were made available free to all eligible recipients. By 1980 federal expenditures for food stamps ($9 billion) exceeded federal AFDC expenditures ($8 billion), and the gap widened in the 1980s. In 1972 over 17 million persons received food stamps each month. In 1983, a recession year, 22 million persons received food stamps despite tightened eligibility requirements imposed in 1981.[72]

In 1965 Congress approved the first federal health insurance program in the form of Medicare and Medicaid, added as Title XVIII and XIX of the Social Security Act, respectively. Medicare covered all retired persons (except those covered by federal civil service or similar benefits) regardless of their means. Medicare actually consisted of two parts: a basic plan that funded hospital services (with a deductible), posthospital care, outpatient diagnostic services, and home health care (Part A); and a supplementary plan that required participants to pay a small premium for additional coverage (Part B). Medicare was created as a social insurance entitlement program and combined with "Social Security" to create Old Age Security, Disability and Health Insurance (OASDHI), funded through a nationally uniform payroll tax schedule and administered by the federal government.[73]

In contrast, Medicaid was designed as an extension of public assistance for the poor. Like the means-tested Social Security Act programs AFDC, Old Age Assistance, and Aid the Blind, Medicaid was established as a federally assisted state program. Federal grants for Medicaid were designed to help the poorest states, with the formula providing for 50 to 80 percent federal funding, depending on a state's per capita income. Like AFDC, Medicaid coverage and benefits soon varied substantially across the states (see Table 3.3, page 76). By 1981 the federal government spent $14 billion on Medicaid, a sum dwarfed by the $31 billion spent on Medicare.[74]

The Failure to Reduce "Dependency"

At the same time, the social services strategy initiated during the Kennedy administration soon was regarded as a costly failure. The number of AFDC recipients was skyrocketing. A report issued by the Department of Health, Education and Welfare (HEW) in 1968 showed that only 20,000 AFDC recipients had been removed from the rolls through social services, out of a total recipient population of 1.5 million.[75] While this result could have been predicted based on any understanding about the number of "employable" poor and the inherent defects of the services approach (much of the money was siphoned off to pay the administrative expenses of social workers and state agencies), policymakers blamed the poor. An April 1970 report indicated that thirty-nine states had failed to comply with HEW requirements.[76]

In 1967 President Johnson recommended to Congress the Work Incentive Program (or WIN) to require employable welfare recipients to enroll in job training programs. Local caseworkers were instructed to help welfare recipients identify work training programs and conduct job searches. Recipients could lose their eligibility if they refused to take suitable jobs or to enroll in training programs. As a further incentive to find work, welfare mothers were allowed to keep thirty dollars plus one-third of their additional earnings before incurring any loss in aid (note that this still amounted to a marginal tax rate of 66 percent on earnings for welfare recipients). WIN bluntly sought to restrict AFDC and reduce spending. It accompanied a freeze on the amount of federal funds available to states if additional costs were incurred because of an increase in the proportion of children in the program.[77]

The Dilemma of Establishing National Standards for Public Assistance in the 1970s

An unusual alignment between the White House, some members of Congress, and some states in favor of nationalizing the state-run welfare programs emerged in the 1970s. Both the Nixon and Carter administrations advanced proposals to nationalize the system. But state and local interests, amplified in Congress, frustrated these efforts. By the end of the decade "welfare reform" had been reduced to a plan that would subsidize welfare budgets in the most generous states.

Federal courts, federal agencies, and welfare rights organizations battled for liberalized and more coherent public assistance, with significant success. Supreme Court decisions struck down state laws limiting welfare eligibility, such as the man-in-the-house rule (*King* v. *Smith*, 1968), lengthy residency requirements (*Shapiro* v. *Thompson*, 1969), and regulations that denied a hearing to public assistance recipients prior to the termination of their benefits (*Goldberg* v. *Kelley*, 1970).[78] Federal officials and welfare rights organizations pressured state and local agencies to make benefits more widely known and available.

This liberalization of public assistance began to push the most generous jurisdictions to the fiscal breaking point. By 1968, nearly 30 percent of all the nation's AFDC recipients lived in New York or California. In December 1970, Mayor John V. Lindsay of New York rejected a fiscal year 1971 budget request for $2.1 billion for public assistance. Lindsay declared that the "City of New York and taxpayers can no longer meet the rising costs of welfare" and instructed the city's lawyers "to determine the city's legal ability, in light of Federal and state laws, to refuse to pay for increased welfare costs or accept additional welfare cases because of its financial condition." In early 1971, the New York state legislature staged a "budget revolt," requiring a 10 percent cut in welfare payments to dependent families. A few weeks earlier, New York governor Nelson Rockefeller announced a "drastic revision in the state's welfare philosophy," arguing that the existing system "will ultimately overload and break down our society" and that it promoted "permanent dependence on the government."[79]

Despite the actions by federal courts to ease access to welfare, the American welfare system remained very limited and uneven. Of the estimated thirty million citizens living in poverty, only ten million received some form of public assistance. For every $1,000 of personal income in the state, New York spent $16.25 on public assistance while Virginia spent $1.25, South Carolina spent $1.35, Florida spent $1.60, and Arizona spent $1.85.[80] According to the 1969 report of the President's Commission on Income Maintenance Programs:

> . . . there are, in effect, fifty different cash assistance programs each of Old Age Assistance, AFDC, and Aid to the Blind, twenty-five programs of AFDC-UP, and forty-nine programs of Aid to the Permanently and Totally Disabled . . . over 300 separate programs of cash Public Assistance receiving Federal funds, covering different categories of the population under widely varying standards . . . Complete and accurate knowledge of the actual operations of state and local programs is not available at the Federal level. New administrative guidelines may be issued by the Federal government with comparatively little information on how they will be interpreted and instituted below this level. Changes can be implemented locally without the knowledge of Federal policymakers. The multiplicity of governments involved has made effective policy coordinating nearly impossible.[81]

Immediately following the 1968 presidential election, state leaders pressured President-elect Nixon for welfare reform and fiscal relief. Republican governors in New York, Michigan, Pennsylvania, and Illinois were especially adamant, for they managed some of the nation's most rapidly rising AFDC budgets. Convinced that their states' higher payments were luring poor people from the South, the governors pleaded for uniform welfare standards to level benefits nationwide.[82]

Several influential members of Nixon's staff supported a national welfare reform proposal. If it came from a Republican, they reasoned, it might escape conservative criticism and at the same time seize the initiative from the Democratic Congress. These officials included Robert Finch, the Secretary of Health, Education and Welfare, and Daniel Patrick Moynihan, Nixon's domestic affairs advisor, a Democrat who had served in the Kennedy administration. They settled on a plan for a "negative income tax" to guarantee both AFDC recipients and the working poor a low, nationally uniform subsistence income. Nixon's staff astonished conservatives by agreeing to include the Finch-Moynihan "family security system" in the President's first package of legislative proposals in 1969.[83]

In a nationally televised address delivered on August 8, 1969, Nixon laid out his ambitious proposals. The president called for a national "Family Assistance Plan" to replace AFDC. He claimed that a nationalized welfare program would actually strengthen state and local governments by finally putting the brakes on welfare costs:

> Our states and cities find themselves sinking in a Federal quagmire, as caseloads increase, as costs escalate, and as the welfare system stagnates enterprise and perpetuates dependency . . . The tragedy is not only that it is bringing States and cities to the brink of financial disaster, but also that it is failing to meet the elementary . . . needs of the poor. It breaks up homes. It often penalizes work. It robs recipients of dignity. And it grows. Benefit levels are grossly unequal . . . no child is "worth" more in one state than in another . . . tonight I, therefore, propose that we abolish the present welfare system and that we adopt in its place a new family assistance system. Initially, this system will cost more than welfare. But unlike welfare, it is designed to correct the condition it deals with and, thus, to lessen the long-range burden and cost.[84]

The Family Assistance Plan (FAP) constituted a radical departure from previous public assistance plans in that it proposed geographic equity as a principle for income maintenance and provided income support for the working poor. Welfare recipients would receive uniform amounts of aid regardless of where they lived, up to $1,600 annually for a family of four. Recipients would lose $.50 for each $1 in earnings, so that they would still have an incentive to work. Even so, policymakers claimed that it was not a departure from the legacy of previous policies directed against dependency, for a unified income guarantee could improve the identification of the "truly" needy and pare the undeserving poor from the welfare rolls.[85]

Although the administration emphasized that the program ultimately would save money, disagreement on these features probably doomed the proposal from the start. The Department of Health, Education and Welfare projected that the FAP would cost the federal government an additional $1.8 billion in 1972 but argued that the costs of the FAP and AFDC would be about the same by 1976, and that the additional federal money would provide half a billion dollars in immediate fiscal relief to the states.[86]

The House of Representatives approved the proposal in April 1970, but the political difficulties of enacting an income floor became clear when the Senate took up the measure. Senate Finance Committee Chairman Russell Long (Democrat of Louisiana) represented the state that had most aggressively used "man-in-the-house" and other legal restrictions to limit welfare costs in the early 1960s, and he had championed the Work Incentive Program in the late 1960s. In speeches made to the nation's governors in 1971, he emphasized the importance of "man-in-the-house" requirements and urged the governors to retain control of welfare rather than relinquish control to the Department of Health, Education and Welfare. He argued that the government should encourage the poor to accept jobs as servants, instead of providing public jobs or income for the working poor.[87] Indeed, another southern member of Congress worried that if the federal government guaranteed a minimum income to everyone, "Who . . . will iron my shirts and rake the yard?"[88] Surely the notion of giving blacks equal standing with whites as relief claimants aggravated the southern legislators. Outside the South, many moderates and conservatives in both parties objected to the short-term costs and the notion of national standards.

Pressured by conservatives, the administration withdrew its plan. In July 1970, the administration returned with a bill that raised benefits for the working poor to $2,400 for a family of four but reduced other welfare benefits such as food stamps.[89] In response, liberals opposed the benefit floor provided by the administration on the ground that it provided less assistance to the poor than was already available in the most generous states. In November the Senate Finance Committee rejected a one-year trial of the FAP by a vote of ten to six. The coalition of opponents included some of the Senate's most conservative members (Senator Long and Republican Senators John J. Williams of Delaware and Carl T. Curtis of Nebraska) and some of the most liberal Democrats (Eugene J. McCarthy of Minnesota and Fred R. Harris of Oklahoma).[90]

Although Congress refused to enact the Family Assistance Plan, it approved changes in welfare assistance by creating the Supplemental Security Income (SSI) program, which essentially nationalized all the Social Security Act's public assistance programs except AFDC. Old-age assistance and aid to the blind and disabled were now administered directly by the federal government rather than by the states. The nationalization of these programs significantly reduced variations in benefits among the states. It also separated another segment of the poor from the disdained "welfare" system. However, state variation remained significant. According to Martha Derthick, "[p]robably no more striking proof of the persistence of states' individuality exists than the SSI program." The law permitted the states to provide optional supplements to SSI recipients. By 1984, forty-three states were providing such supplements. In January 1985, the legal minimum monthly benefit ranged from the federal minimum of $325 to a high of $586.[91]

Jimmy Carter, the only southern governor to have supported the Family Assistance Plan in 1971, promised comprehensive welfare reform during his presidential campaign.[92] When briefed on the national welfare system, Carter was dismayed by its complexity and inefficiency and insisted that a reform proposal be developed—but at the same time he ordered HEW Secretary Joseph Califano to "give me a comprehensive program at no additional cost." The Departments of HEW and Labor met with state and local officials "who sought to craft a plan acceptable to a sufficient number of states to have a chance of congressional enactment."[93] Daniel Patrick Moynihan, now a Democratic senator from New York and chairman of the new Senate subcommittee on public assistance, independently pressured Carter to submit legislation. Moynihan won Senate Finance Committee approval of a plan to provide a billion dollars in fiscal relief to ease state and local welfare costs.

On August 6, 1977, Carter finally produced a plan entitled the "Program for Better Jobs and Income" (PBJI) that, he said, constituted a "complete and clean break with the past." The Carter reform proposal resembled the Nixon Family Assistance Plan in that it aimed to shift a significant share of welfare finance to the federal government and to reduce projected welfare costs in the long run. By consolidating programs, the administration hoped to standardize administrative rules, application procedures, and eligibility. Centralized federal records would minimize fraud.[94] He proposed to "increase job opportunities for the low-income population and consolidate our major income support programs into one simple and efficient system."[95] Cumulatively, the reform was supposed to reduce the number of people eligible for welfare benefits from forty million to thirty-six million recipients while increasing the number actually receiving benefits from thirty million to thirty-two million.[96] Including the cost savings associated with consolidation of existing programs and elimination of the food stamps program, the administration expected the federal government to spend $31 billion on the program in fiscal year 1981, a projected increase of $2.8 billion over existing programs.[97]

Just as the Carter plan resembled the Nixon welfare reform, so did its political fate. Newspaper editorials praised the proposal, and this time opinion polls immediately after its announcement showed 70 percent of the public in favor.[98] But opposition soon began building. Welfare rights organizations called it "JIP." Senator Long expressed horror that it would expand the welfare rolls and cover single people and childless parents. Unions were concerned that minimum-wage jobs would be used to lower wages. Most devastating of all, neutral analysts questioned the claim that it would save money over the long run. The Congressional Budget Office reported that the program would cost $14 billion, or five times the administration's estimate. Senator Long and other conservatives suggested that costs could reach $60 or even $120 billion. In response, the administration omitted welfare reform as a top priority from Carter's 1978 State of the Union address.[99]

Governors, mayors, and county executives, making up a self-described "New Coalition" demanding fiscal relief, kept the proposal alive through mid-1978. Indeed, the movement for fiscal relief in California (where the tax revolt crested in the passage of Proposition 13, which drastically cut local property taxes) and New York (with New York City still in fiscal trouble) provided the only remaining support for reform. When Senators Long, Moynihan, and Allan Cranston (Democrat of California) presented a new "no frills" welfare package in midsummer, the American Public Welfare Association pointed out that New York and California would receive 40 percent of the benefits in the new proposal, with the remaining 48 states splitting the remaining 60 percent. Like the Carter plan, this proposal died. Congress enacted only marginal reforms: an extension of the income tax credits for the poor and changes in food stamps and job training that better "targeted" these programs (i.e., tightened eligibility).[100]

Ambitious and well-intentioned welfare reform proposals in the 1970s were at once the products and the victims of a state-based relief system. The uncoordinated welfare programs strained the budgets of governments at all levels, and this stimulated a search for a way to reduce welfare "dependency." The "services" strategy and the provision of in-kind benefits only aggravated the problems they were intended to reduce. Comprehensive welfare reform seemed a reasonable alternative. But welfare reform was attacked from both the right and the left, as either inadequate or too costly.

Though comprehensive reform failed in the 1970s, more national government intervention unambiguously made the American welfare system more generous than it had ever been. Despite the controversy surrounding welfare reform, the extension of income tax credits, Supplemental Security Income, food stamps, public employment programs, low-income energy assistance, and other initiatives helped millions of people. In this context, the Reagan administration abruptly broke with the bipartisan goal of devising a welfare system that would be both fair and cost-efficient.

WELFARE AND FEDERALISM IN THE REAGAN ERA

Ronald Reagan did not pretend to balance equity and cost control in the public assistance changes he made as governor of California from 1967 through 1974. In a memo asking his aids to recommend welfare changes, he asserted, "I am determined to reduce these programs to essential services at a cost the taxpayers can afford to pay . . . This is our NUMBER ONE priority." The California Welfare Reform Act tightened eligibility but it made benefits somewhat more generous for those who qualified (the state's basic AFDC payment had not increased since 1957). The program contributed to reversing the growth of AFDC rolls in California, though it failed in its objective of requiring recipients to work.[101] Considering the California program a major success, Reagan promised to apply it nationally when he became president.

President Reagan assured Congress in February 1981 that "those who through no fault of their own must depend on the rest of us . . . can rest assured that the social safety net of programs they depend on are exempt from any cuts." As Office of Management and Budget Director David Stockman and other top administration officials later admitted, the "safety net" concept was merely "a political ploy," a "happenstance list, just a spur-of-the-moment thing that the press office wanted to put out."[102] Included in the "safety net" were such middle-class programs as veterans', old-age, and survivors' benefits and Medicare insurance under the Social Security Act. Each one was an income maintenance program that had never been considered "welfare," probably because a large majority of recipients were nonpoor. Domestic policy advisor Martin Anderson recalled that these programs "would not be closely examined [by the Reagan administration] on the first round of budget changes because of the fierce political pressures that made it impossible" to avoid a "torrent" of criticism if they were discussed. When the administration proposed some eligibility changes in the Social Security program in 1981, the political furor that ensued discouraged any further proposals to restructure the pension system.[103]

Later that year, Congress approved many of the budget cuts and eligibility restrictions that Reagan sought in public assistance programs (see Table 7.3). Funding for food stamps and child nutrition was reduced by $2.8 billion. Medicare benefits were cut by increasing patient contributions and by placing a ceiling on physician charges. Raising eligibility standards and imposing fixed rates for services limited Medicaid costs. Since in most states Medicaid was available only to welfare

Table 7.3. *Effects of the Budget Reconciliation Act of 1981 on income maintenance recipients and programs*

Program Change	Number of Individual Families Affected	Average Dollar Loss (full-year basis)
AFDC		
Tightening of Earnings disregards	260,000 families with reduced benefits (6.9% of caseload) 300,000 families with benefits eliminated (8% of caseload)	$1,400 plus loss of Medicaid for the families eliminated
Counting of stepparents' income	100,000 families (2.7% of caseload)	$1,950 plus Medicaid
Social Security		
Elimination of minimum benefit	1,300,000 individuals	$1,000
Reduced insurance benefits for post-secondary education	250,000 individuals with benefits eliminated beginning 6/82	$3,000
	400,000 individuals with benefits reduced beginning 9/82	$1,970
Termination of parent's benefit when child attains age 16	By August 1983, 200,000 individuals will have benefits eliminated	$2,500
Restriction on lump sum death benefit	785,000 payments	$ 255
Unemployment compensation		
Elimination of national trigger	640,000 individuals	$1,080
Redefinition of state trigger calculation	850,000 individuals	$1,160

Source: U.S. Congress, House, Committee on Ways and Means, *Hearings on National Impact of Budget Reductions* (Washington, DC: GPO, 1982).

recipients, new restrictions in eligibility standards automatically reduced Medicaid expenditures. The Omnibus Budget Reconciliation Act of 1981 had the effect of eliminating three hundred thousand AFDC families and reducing benefits for two hundred seventy thousand more, with the objective of saving $1 billion a year. Public service employment under the Comprehensive Employment and Training Act was eliminated.[104]

As intended, these changes disproportionately hurt the "working poor." For a generation, federal officials had tried to encourage the poor to work by permitting them to receive AFDC, food stamps, and other benefits to supplement their incomes without a complete loss of eligibility. The Reagan administration reversed that policy. Such changes reduced AFDC enrollment by as many as half a million recipients, with those who worked bearing a disproportionate share of the cuts. As many as a million people lost food stamps. Those remaining on welfare had less incentive to take low-wage jobs because every penny of earnings was now applied against benefits, as opposed to a fifty cent reduction for every dollar earned before the Reagan administration. The changes also restricted other income programs for allegedly "able-bodied" individuals. The administration ordered sharp cuts in Social Security Disability enrollment, whose caseload had doubled in the previous ten years (a fact viewed as evidence of malingering by the White House). Tightened unemployment insurance eligibility affected the jobless; 76 percent of the jobless drew some benefits in the 1975 recession, but only 45 percent drew benefits at any time during the more serious recession of 1982–1983.[105]

The administration's strategy for controlling welfare costs differed significantly from the Nixon and Carter strategies in its abandonment of equity as a goal of welfare policy and in its shrewd use of the policymaking structure. Instead of trying to nationalize costs, as administrations in the 1970s had done, the Reagan administration tightened regulations to force the more generous states to become more punitive. Before 1981, for example, working AFDC recipients could deduct the cost of transportation to their job and child care from the earnings they reported to welfare offices, thus qualifying for additional benefits. The 1981 changes limited the costs of deductible work expenses to $75 and child care to $160 per month. Other provisions reduced the value of the possessions an AFDC recipient could own from $2,000 to $1,000 and required recipients to report their income monthly (states had been allowed to collect this information quarterly). At the same time, the administration relaxed other rules that permitted the least generous states to "get tough" with welfare recipients. By cutting matching funds for the states during a recession, the administration's policymakers understood that no state could withstand the pressures to limit welfare costs.[106] States that permitted Medicaid expenses to grow by more than 9 percent annually would be penalized for doing so, and the states were given more discretion to negotiate for lower-cost medical care.

In early 1982, President Reagan introduced an ambitious plan that would have forced the states to cut all forms of social welfare spending.

In his State of the Union Address, he proposed a "New Federalism" program that would have returned all welfare programs except Medicaid to the states, completely eliminating federal participation in funding and administration. The decision to propose the complete centralization of Medicaid—the single most expensive social welfare program states participate in—was offered as a "carrot" to induce political support from state officials. In exchange for federal assumption of Medicaid, the states were to assume the entire responsibility for AFDC, food stamps, and about forty federally assisted social welfare programs. Altogether, these programs cost the national government about $47 billion annually. To help the states finance all these programs, Reagan proposed a Federalism Trust Fund of about $28 billion. The federal government would also eliminate several excise taxes, so that states could increase their taxes on alcohol, tobacco, long-distance telephone calls, and gasoline.[107]

Congress virtually ignored the proposal.[108] It already had approved seven new block grants in 1981 and refused to add more. The New Federalism proposals stalled after 1982. Nevertheless, the administration could justifiably claim to have changed welfare. The 1984 Republican platform proclaimed that "We have begun to clean up the welfare mess . . ."[109] A critic of the Reagan welfare strategy wrote that "Mr. Reagan has forgotten the lesson of the 1930s—that the federal government got into the business of welfare relief because the states could not or would not take responsibility for the poor."[110] The criticism missed an essential point: for conservatives like Reagan, state variability is a virtue rather than a vice. Slightly more than half (27) of the states took steps to maintain their current level of welfare benefits despite the new federal rules enacted in 1981. Nearly half the states did nothing at all to counteract the administration cuts. Many other states compensated for the cuts mainly to "keep working recipients on the rolls so that they would not quit their jobs and reapply for aid at a higher grant level."[111]

Tables 7.4 and 7.5 show the cumulative effects of the welfare limitations imposed by the Reagan administration. Table 7.4 demonstrates that in the 1960s, average benefits increased at a rate faster than inflation, raising the average AFDC benefit for a family with two children from 63 percent of the government's "poverty line" to 71 percent. After 1970, AFDC benefits fell behind the rate of inflation and so dropped back to 57 percent of the poverty line. Even though the inflation rate moderated in the 1980s, the average AFDC benefit lost as much ground five years into the 1980s as it had lost in the previous decade, falling to 43 percent of the poverty line. When cuts in food stamps benefits are considered along with AFDC reductions, the Reagan administration's changes resulted in a drop from 85 percent of the poverty line in 1980 to only 65 percent of the poverty line in 1985.[112]

Table 7.4. *AFDC benefits as a percentage of the poverty threshold, 1960–*
1985

	Sept 1960	Jan 1965	July 1970	July 1975	July 1980	July 1985
Median state's maximum AFDC benefit for a four person family	$155	$163	$221	$264	$350	$379
Percentage of poverty threshold (previous year)	63	62	71	63	57	43

Source: U.S. Congress, House, Committee on Ways and Means, *Children in Poverty,*
WMCP 99-8 (Washington, DC: GPO, 1985), 204–5.

Table 7.5 shows that the erosion of AFDC benefits since 1970 and
especially since 1980 accentuated the geographical inequities of the
system. The maximum benefit for a four-person family was nearly three
times greater in California than in Mississippi in 1970, more than four
and a half times greater in 1980, and five and a half times greater by
1985. (Alaska's high cost of living makes it difficult to compare its
benefits to other states). Though differences between individual states
have changed over time, the variation among all states has been very
substantial and stable for AFDC since 1940 (the coefficient of variation, a
statistic that measures variation in benefits across all the states, has
remained in the .32–.36 range for forty-five years).[113]

From 1970 to 1985, average AFDC payments increased faster than
inflation in only three states, Maine, California, and Wisconsin. Payments were at about the national average in 1970 in California and
Wisconsin, but these states were among the most generous states by
1985, an effect of other states' actions to reduce benefits. Some of the
least generous states allowed AFDC benefits to erode by not changing
benefit levels frequently, and some, such as Texas, permitted benefits to
fall faster by delaying adjustments indefinitely. In 1984 the Texas Welfare Department still used a family standard budget that had been
established in 1969 to determine eligibility for AFDC, even though the
cost of living had gone up 154 percent in the intervening years. A Texas
welfare worker observed that "Texas has never been kind to people who
have needed help, because officials want the people who cannot work to
go elsewhere. You have to become destitute before you can get anything, and you have to remain destitute to keep it. Otherwise, you must
learn how to lie. The government encourages that."[114]

Significantly, the federal food stamp program has mitigated some of

Table 7.5. *AFDC maximum benefit for a family of four in the five most generous[a] and five least generous states, in January 1985*

	July 1970	July 1980	Jan 1985	Percent Change, 1970–1985	Percent Change, 1970–1985, Constant Dollars
Alaska	375	514	800	113.3	−20.4
California	221	563	660	198.6	+11.5
Connecticut	330	553	636	92.7	−28.1
Wisconsin	217	529	636	193.1	+ 9.4
Vermont	304	552	622	104.6	−23.6
Median state	221	350	379	71.5	−36
South Carolina	103	158	229	122.3	−17.0
Texas	179	140	201	12.3	−58.1
Arkansas	100	188	191	91.0	−28.7
Alabama	81	148	147	81.5	−32.2
Mississippi	80	120	120	71.4	−36.0

[a]Figures for New York State not available; Suffolk County maximum benefit was $676 in 1985 and in New York City was $566.

Source: U.S. Congress, House, Committee on Ways and Means, *Children in Poverty*, WMCP 99-8 (Washington, DC: GPO, 1985), 203.

these reductions and reduced the variability of welfare benefits across the states. A combined measure of AFDC and food stamps benefits across the states shows that interstate benefit differences have narrowed since the beginning of the food stamp program. Food stamps are funded entirely by the federal government. Higher food stamp benefits are given to recipients in states where AFDC benefits are relatively low in an effort to compensate for those low payments. In a sense, states have substituted federal welfare funds for their own, because "[a]s federal contributions in food stamps have increased, cash benefit levels set by states have fallen by a corresponding amount."[115]

By the Reagan administration's second term, the debate over welfare reform had narrowed to a few proposals to reduce "welfare dependency." The White House pressed states to make welfare less attractive through "workfare," a requirement that welfare recipients register for employment or work for no pay in return for benefits. Even the Republican-controlled Senate resisted White House pressure to make this requirement mandatory in 1981. Instead, in the 1981 budget act (and the 1982 tax act), Congress encouraged states to experiment with workfare. By late 1985, thirty-six states had adopted voluntary or mandatory workfare programs. Some of these efforts were judged as modestly successful, "success" usually defined as reducing the welfare rolls.

In other cases, such as the widely discussed Massachusetts Employment and Training Program, the state invested millions of additional dollars for day care and other services that are prerequisites for placing welfare recipients in employment. The administration again revealed its view of federalism and workfare when the National Governors Association endorsed federal workfare legislation in early 1987. Reagan agreed with much of their proposal, but he refused the governors' request for an additional $1 billion to fund the program and refused to accept their goal of a minimum national standard for welfare benefits. Later in 1987 the House of Representatives approved a "workfare" plan more similar to the Massachusetts plan and to proposals suggested by Senator Moynihan.[116] Throughout the debate on workfare, little evidence surfaced that welfare recipients would shun the chance to become more self-sufficient if they were given a genuine opportunity. According to a New York State welfare official, "The first thing they [recipients] say to me when I ask what we can do is 'What, are you crazy? I want a job. Help me get a job.' "[117]

Reagan's abandonment of the goal of equity in welfare policy was consistent with other administration policies that had the effect (or intent) of increasing income inequality. Table 7.6 shows the distribution of family income between 1970 and 1986. The table reveals pronounced inequality that increased over a very brief period. In 1970 the average earnings of the bottom one-fifth of families was about 29 percent of the average earnings of families in the top one-fifth; this percentage fell to 27 percent by 1980 and 24 percent by 1986. Among all families with children, the gap grew even wider, with the earnings of the poorest one-fifth falling from 38 percent of the top group's earnings in 1970 to 31 percent in 1980 and 26 percent in 1986. The figures for all families with children masks a more serious problem for single mothers with children, the target population for AFDC. Not only did 40 percent of this group earn less than the federal poverty income in 1986, but the gap between their income and the poverty line had increased between 1977 and 1986, and income inequality (with the bottom one-fifth's income amounting to 19 percent of the top one-fifth's) was more pronounced within this group in 1986 than within the other groups. The Congressional Budget Office concluded that the recession of the early 1980s, combined with falling real benefit levels and tightened eligibility, strongly influenced the decline of incomes for the poorest single-mother families.[118]

The Tax Reform Act of 1986 offset some of these changes by exempting an additional six million people from the federal income tax, though the maximum tax rate for wealthy individuals was sharply reduced. In *The Reagan Record,* the Urban Institute reported that "so far under this Administration, the poor have continued to get poorer, and their long-run prospects do not appear to be appreciably improved by [its]

Table 7.6. *Family income as a percentage of the federal poverty line, 1970, 1980, 1983, and 1986*

	1970	1980	1983	1986
All Families				
Average income of families in the:				
Bottom one-fifth[a]	127	137	130	139
Median	260	291	290	313
Top one-fifth[b]	444	506	525	571
Single mothers with children				
Average family income of families in the:				
Bottom one-fifth[a]	56	57	48	49
Median	112	128	112	114
Top one-fifth[b]	225	258	243	262

[a]Average income of the one-fifth of families with the lowest family incomes
[b]Average income of the one-fifth of families with the highest family incomes
Source: Congressional Budget Office, *Trends in Family Income: 1970–1986* (Washington, DC: GPO, 1988), 69.

policies."[119] As a consequence, the incidence of poverty increased through 1983 (Table 7.7).

Cuts in programs available to the working poor, together with persistent unemployment and growing income disparities in the labor market, evoked the spirit of Social Darwinism of one hundred years before. Such Reagan supporters as George Gilder explicitly blamed poverty on character flaws and the breakdown of monogamous marriages, indicating that the solution to poverty rested on a return to his conception of nineteenth-century family values.[120]

Table 7.7. *Comparison of poverty rate between 1966 and 1986*

	Poverty Rate					
	1966	1970	1975	1980	1983	1986[a]
Blacks	41.8%	33.5%	31.3%	32.5%	35.7%	31.1%
Female-headed families	39.8	38.1	37.5	36.7	40.2	36.4
Children under 6 years old	18.1	16.6	18.2	20.3	25.0	N.A.[b]
Elderly, 65 and older	28.5	24.5	15.3	15.7	14.1	12.4
All persons	14.7	12.6	12.3	13.0	15.2	13.6

[a]1986 poverty threshold was $11,203 for a family of four.
[b]Not available
Source: "Who's Better off Today than Four Years Ago?" *National Journal,* 8 September 1984, 1650; U.S. Bureau of the Census, *Money Incomes and Poverty Status of Families and Persons in the United States* (Washington, DC: GPO. 1987), 23.

THE INCOHERENT RESPONSE TO POVERTY

Every significant advance in American income maintenance programs has followed intervention by the national government. Before the federal government participated actively in assisting the poor during the 1930s, state innovations were adopted mainly as attempts to punish the poor or to save money. It was a rare American indeed who received benefits from social insurance programs of any kind before the Social Security Act was enacted in 1935. The popularity of "widow's pension" programs evidenced the states' interest in controlling the costs of welfare. A half century later, the pattern of AFDC benefits and the variations in the Supplemental Security Income program demonstrated that state discretion in income security continued to result in highly variable levels of economic protection, depending on the state in which the recipient happened to live.

The United States now has a divided income security system. Part of it, social insurance, establishes nationally uniform benefits based on earnings. Another part, public assistance, is a highly fragmented system that is awkward, inequitable, and for many people illegitimate. Its very design promotes the conception of poverty as a problem of "welfare dependency" rather than inadequate income. The segmentation of welfare has impeded the formation of a political coalition that could effectively support a more coherent and equitable alternative.

This analysis has focused on the structural origins of unequal income protection. Other factors, notably identified by many writers as American (cultural) values of self-reliance, individualism, and distrust of government, obviously contributed to these outcomes. On the other hand, the development of income security policy in the United States suggests that Americans willingly embrace the expensive and nationalized guarantees made available through Social Security and Medicare, which comprise the most expensive programs of the domestic budget. The most decentralized welfare programs are precisely those that are designed exclusively to benefit the nation's poorest citizens. Their continued administration by the states guarantees that they will remain extremely limited and politically vulnerable.

NOTES

1. Russell L. Hanson, "The Expansion and Contraction of the American Welfare State," in Robert Goodin and Julian Le Grand, eds., *Not Only the Poor: The Middle Class and the Welfare State* (London: George Allen and Unwin, 1987), 169–202.
2. June Axinn and Herman Levin, *Social Welfare: A History of the American Response to Need* (New York: Dodd, Mead, 1975), 9.

3. Ibid., 56–62.
4. Walter I. Trattner, *From Poor Law to Welfare State: A History of Social Welfare in America* (New York: Free Press, 1974), 52; Michael B. Katz, *Poverty and Policy in American History* (New York: Academic Press, 1983), 12, 81–2.
5. Michael B. Katz, *In the Shadow of the Poorhouse: A Social History of Welfare in America* (New York: Basic Books, 1986), 17.
6. David M. Schneider, *The History of Public Welfare in New York State, 1609–1866* (Montclair, NJ: Patterson Smith, 1969), 219, 229; Trattner, *From Poor Law to Welfare State*, 54–5; James Leiby, *A History of Social Work and Social Welfare in the United States* (New York: Columbia University Press, 1978), 46.
7. Katz, *Poverty and Policy in American History*, 65–7.
8. Ibid.
9. David Rothman, *The Discovery of the Asylum: Social Order and Disorder in the New Republic* (Boston: Little, Brown, 1971), 79–84, 132, 207–9.
10. Leiby, *A History of Social Work and Social Welfare in the United States*, 99.
11. Ibid., 104.
12. Trattner, *From Poor Law to Welfare State*, 80.
13. Amos G. Warner, *American Charities* (New York: Crowell, 1894), 360–1.
14. James Leiby, *Charity and Correction in New Jersey: A History of State Welfare Institutions* (New Brunswick, NJ: Rutgers University Press, 1967), 73.
15. David M. Schneider and Albert Deutsch, *History of Public Welfare in New York State, 1867–1940* (Montclair, NJ: Patterson Smith, 1969), 60–4; Leiby, *A History of Social Work and Social Welfare in the United States*, 144; Katz, *Poverty and Policy in American History*, 73.
16. Leiby, *Charity and Correction in New Jersey*, 75–6.
17. Alexander Keyssar, *Out of Work: The First Century of Unemployment in Massachusetts* (Cambridge, England: Cambridge University Press, 1986), 135–8.
18. Leiby, *Charity and Correction in New Jersey*, 85; Fern Boan, *A History of Poor Relief Legislation and Administration in Missouri* (Chicago: University of Chicago Press, 1941), 182.
19. Katz, *Poverty and Policy in American History*, 151.
20. New York Association for the Improvement of the Poor, First Annual Report for the Year 1845, in *Poverty U.S.A.: The Historical Record* (New York: Arno Press and *New York Times*, 1971), 16–7. Originally printed by John F. Trow & Co., New York, 1845.
21. Paul Boyer, *Urban Masses and the Morale Order in America, 1820–1920* (Cambridge, MA: Harvard University Press, 1978), 146.
22. Axinn and Levin, *Social Welfare*, 90; Katz, *Poverty and Policy in American History*, 191.
23. Katz, *Poverty and Policy in American History*, 190.
24. James T. Patterson, *America's Struggle Against Poverty, 1900–1980* (Cambridge, MA: Harvard University Press, 1981), 8–9; Robert Bremmer, *From the Depths: The Discovery of Poverty in the United States* (New York: New York University Press, 1956), 154–7; Robert Hunter, *Poverty* (New York: Macmillan, 1904).
25. Trattner, *From Poor Law to Welfare State*, 188.
26. Leiby, *A History of Social Work and Social Welfare in the United States*, 214; Issac M. Rubinow, *Social Insurance* (New York: Holt, 1913), 436; Boan, *A History of Poor Relief Legislation and Administration in Missouri*, 54–5.
27. Mark H. Leff, "Consensus for Reform: The Mothers' Pension Movement in the Progressive Era," in Frank J. Breul and Steven J. Diner, eds., *Compassion and Responsibility: Readings in the History of Social Welfare in the United States* (Chicago: University of Chicago Press, 1980), 247–8; Rubinow, *Social Insurance*, 436.
28. Leff, "Consensus for Reform," 248.
29. Axinn and Levin, *Social Welfare*, 149–50; Leiby, *A History of Social Work and Social Welfare in the United States*, 151.

30. Schneider and Deutsch, *History of Public Welfare in New York State*, 190–1.
31. Grace Abbott, *From Relief to Social Security: The Development of the New Public Welfare Services and Their Administration* (Chicago: University of Chicago Press, 1941), 262.
32. Trattner, *From Poor Law to Welfare State*, 189; Patterson, *America's Struggle Against Poverty, 1900–1980* (Cambridge, MA: Harvard University Press, 1981), 27
33. Leiby, *A History of Social Work and Social Welfare in the United States*, 215, 236; Roy Lubove, *The Struggle for Social Security, 1900–1935* (Cambridge, MA: Harvard University Press, 1968), 133–7; U.S. Bureau of Labor Statistics, "Public Pensions for the Blind in 1934," *Monthly Labor Review* 41:3 (September 1935), 584–601.
34. Axinn and Levin, *Social Welfare*, 135.
35. Leiby, *A History of Social Work and Social Welfare in the United States*, 214–5.
36. Paul H. Douglas, *Social Security in the United States: An Analysis and Appraisal of the Federal Social Security Act* (New York: Whittlesey House, 1936), 5.
37. Hunter, *Poverty*, 333.
38. Walter I. Trattner, *Crusade for the Children: A History of the National Child Labor Committee and Child Labor Reform in America* (Chicago: Quadrangle, 1970), 97–8.
39. Josephine Chapin Brown, *Public Relief: 1929–1939* (New York: Henry Holt & Co., 1940), 54.
40. Boan, *A History of Poor Relief Legislation and Administration in Missouri*, 52; Patterson, *America's Struggle Against Poverty*, 30.
41. Robert B. Stevens, ed., *Statutory History of the United States: Income Security* (New York: McGraw-Hill, 1970), 52; Leiby, *Charity and Correction in New Jersey*, 277.
42. Arthur M. Schlesinger, Jr., *The Coming of the New Deal* (Boston: Houghton Mifflin, 1958), 301; Stevens, *Income Security*, 37, 61–3.
43. Stevens, *Income Security*, 71–4.
44. Abraham Holtzman, *The Townsend Movement: A Political Study* (New York: Bookman Associates, 1963), 47, 88; David H. Bennett, *Demagogues in the Depression: American Radicals and the Union Party, 1932–1936* (New Brunswick, NJ: Rutgers University Press, 1969), 145–84.
45. Holtzman, *The Townsend Movement*, 88.
46. Stevens, *Income Security*, 115, 146.
47. Ibid., 156.
48. *Helvering* v. *Davis*, 301 U.S. 619 (1937).
49. Edwin E. Witte, *The Development of the Social Security Act* (Madison: University of Wisconsin Press, 1962), 103–8.
50. Ibid., 164–5.
51. Stevens, *Income Security*, 124–5.
52. Lester M. Salamon, *Welfare: The Elusive Consensus* (New York: Praeger, 1978), 81.
53. U.S. Bureau of the Census, *Historical Statistics of the United States: Colonial Times to 1970* (Washington: GPO, 1975), 348; *Social Security and Retirement: Private Goals, Public Policy* (Washington, DC: Congressional Quarterly,), 16–21.
54. Patterson, *America's Struggle Against Poverty*, 172–3.
55. Ibid., 178–9.
56. Gilbert Y. Steiner, *The State of Welfare* (Washington, DC: Brookings, 1971), 41–2.
57. Harrell R. Rodgers, Jr., *Poverty Amid Plenty: A Political and Economic Crisis* (Reading, MA: Addison-Wesley, 1979), 100; Harrell R. Rodgers, Jr., and Michael Harrington, *Unfinished Democracy: The American Political System* (Glenview, IL: Scott, Foresman, 1981), 420.
58. Patterson, *America's Struggle Against Poverty*, 173; Francis Fox Piven and Richard A. Cloward, *Regulating the Poor: The Functions of Social Welfare* (New York: Pantheon, 1971).
59. Axinn and Levin, *Social Welfare*, 235–6; Patterson, *America's Struggle Against Poverty*, 108.

60. Ralph Winter, "Cities Step Up Job Training, Seek Relief from Relief Outlays," *Wall Street Journal*, 20 July 1961, 1.

61. U.S. Bureau of the Census, *Statistical Abstract of the United States, 1986* (Washington, DC: GPO, 1986), 354; Axinn and Levin, *Social Welfare*, 235.

62. James L. Sundquist, *Politics and Policy: The Eisenhower, Kennedy, and Johnson Years* (Washington, DC: Brookings, 1968), 126–8; Gilbert Y. Steiner, *Social Insecurity: The Politics of Welfare* (New York: Rand McNally, 1966), 146.

63. Stevens, *Income Security*, 629.

64. Frances F. Piven and Richard Cloward, *Regulating the Poor: The Functions of Public Welfare* (New York: Vintage, 1971), 127; Robert B. Albritton, "Subsidies: Welfare and Transportation," in Virginia Gray, Herbert Jacob, and Kenneth N. Vines, *Politics in the American States: A Comparative Analysis* (Boston: Little, Brown, 1983), 381.

65. Martha Derthick, *Uncontrollable Spending for Social Services Grants* (Washington, DC: Brookings, 1975).

66. Steiner, *The State of Welfare*, 21.

67. Stuart Butler and Anna Kondratas, *Out of the Poverty Trap: A Conservative Strategy for Welfare Reform* (New York: Free Press, 1987), 7–25.

68. Sundquist, *Politics and Policy*, 138–9.

69. *Congress and the Nation, 1945–1964* (Washington, DC: Congressional Quarterly, 1965), 1261, 1278, 1327–9.

70. *Congress and the Nation, 1965–1968* (Washington, DC: Congressional Quarterly, 1969), 746, 749.

71. *Congressional Quarterly Almanac, 1967* (Washington, DC: Congressional Quarterly, 1968), 1072; Patterson, *America's Struggle Against Poverty*, 140–1; Dennis R. Judd, *The Politics of American Cities: Private Power and Public Policy*, 3d ed. (Glenview, IL, and Boston: Scott, Foresman/Little, Brown, 1988), 314–21.

72. *Congressional Quarterly Almanac 1964* (Washington, DC: Congressional Quarterly, 1965), 110–3, *Congressional Quarterly Almanac, 1967*, 435–8, and *Congressional Quarterly Almanac, 1970* (Washington, DC: Congressional Quarterly, 1971), 765–7; U.S. Congress, House, Committee on the Budget, *A Review of President Reagan's Budget Recommendations, 1981–1985*, ser. CP-8 (Washington, DC: GPO, 1984), 263.

73. *Congressional Quarterly Almanac, 1965* (Washington, DC: Congressional Quarterly, 1966), 239–42; Theodore R. Marmor, *The Politics of Medicare* (Chicago: Aldine, 1970); Sheri I. David, *With Dignity: The Search for Medicare and Medicaid* (Westport, CT: Greenwood Press, 1985).

74. *CQ Almanac, 1965*, 239–42; U.S. Congress, House, Committee on the Budget, *A Review of President Reagan's Budget Recommendations, 1981–1985*, 205, 220.

75. Frances Fox Piven and Richard A. Cloward, *Regulating the Poor: The Functions of Public Welfare* (New York: Vintage, 1971), 171.

76. Joel F. Handler, *Reforming the Poor: Welfare Policy, Federalism, and Morality* (New York: Basic Books, 1972), 70-71.

77. Patterson, *America's Struggle Against Poverty*, 174–6.

78. Lucius J. Barker and Twiley W. Barker, Jr., *Civil Liberties and the Constitution: Cases and Commentaries*, 4th ed. (Englewood Cliffs, NJ: Prentice-Hall, 1982), 595–9.

79. Daniel P. Moynihan, *The Politics of a Guaranteed Income: The Nixon Administration and the Family Assistance Plan* (New York: Vintage, 1973), 27, 32–3.

80. Ibid., 183; Council of State Governments, *Book of the States, 1970–1971* (Lexington, KY: CSG, 1970), 372–77.

81. The Report of the President's Commission on Income Maintenance Programs, *Poverty Amid Plenty: The American Paradox* (Washington, DC: GPO, 1969), 115.

82. Undated notes of John Ehrlichman on meetings with Governors John Rhodes (R, Ohio), Francis Sargent (R, Massachusetts), Raymond Schaeffer (R, Pennsylvania), and representatives from California, (c. August 1969), in U.S. National Archives,

Nixon Papers, WHSF, Office Files of John Ehrlichman, Box 39, "[Welfare Book] [Congressional Briefing]" Folder. See also A. James Reichley, *Conservatives in an Age of Change: The Nixon and Ford Administrations* (Washington, DC: Brookings, 1981), 132–3.

83. Reichley, *Conservatives in an Age of Change*, 130–9.

84. Richard M. Nixon, "Address to the Nation on Domestic Programs," in *Public Papers of the Presidents of the United States: Richard M. Nixon, 1969* (Washington, DC: GPO, 1971), 637–45.

85. Reichley, *Conservatives in an Age of Change*, 138.

86. U.S. Congress, Senate Committee on Finance, *Hearings on Family Assistance Act of 1970* (Washington, DC: GPO, 1970), 107–29.

87. Memorandum, "H.R. 1 and the Governor's Conference," in U.S. National Archives, Department of Labor, Office of Legislative Affairs Files, 1970–1972, carton 24, "H.R.1/ FW" file.

88. Michael Harrington, *The New American Poverty* (New York: Holt, Rinehart, and Winston, 1984), 3.

89. Reichley, *Conservatives in an Age of Change*, 148.

90. Ibid.

91. Albritton, "Subsidies: Welfare and Transportation," 385; Martha Derthick, "American Federalism: Madison's Middle Ground in the 1980s," *Public Administration Review* 47:1 (January/February 1987), 66–74.

92. Kenneth M. Dolbeare, *American Public Policy: A Citizen's Guide* (New York: McGraw-Hill, 1982), 255.

93. Joseph A. Califano, Jr., *Governing America* (New York: Touchstone, 1981) 334, 346–7.

94. James R. Storey, Robert Harris, Frank Levy et al., *The Better Jobs and Income Plan: A Guide to President Carter's Welfare Reform Proposal and Major Issues* (Washington, DC: The Urban Institute, 1978), 77.

95. Harvey D. Shapiro, "Welfare Reform Revisited—President Jimmy Carter's Program for Better Jobs and Income," in Salamon, *Welfare*, 195.

96. Ibid., 175.

97. Ibid., 77.

98. Laurence E. Lynn, Jr., and David DeF. Whitman, *The President as Policymaker: Jimmy Carter and Welfare Reform* (Philadelphia: Temple University Press, 1981).

99. Ibid.

100. Ibid., 244–7.

101. Lou Cannon, *Reagan* (New York: G.P. Putnam, 1982), 166, 176–83.

102. Quoted in Levitan and Johnson, *Beyond the Safety Net*, 155.

103. D. Lee Bawden and John L. Palmer, "Social Policy: Challenging the Welfare State," in John L. Palmer and Isabel V. Sawhill, eds., *The Reagan Record: An Assessment of America's Changing Domestic Priorities* (Cambridge, MA: Ballinger, 1984), 189; Paul Blustein, "Reagan's Record: Recent Budget Battles Leave the Basic Tenets of the Welfare State Intact," *Wall Street Journal*, 21 October 1985, 1.

104. *St. Louis Globe Democrat*, 25 December 1981, 13a; *Denver Post*, 5 January 1982, p. 4a; U.S. Congress, House, Committee on Ways and Means, *Hearing on Impact of the Administration's Budget Cuts* (Washington, DC: GPO, 1982); *St. Louis Post-Dispatch*, 10 May 1981 and 26 May 1981.

105. Bawden and Palmer, "Social Policy," 190–2; Tom Joe and Cheryl Rogers, *By the Few, For the Few: The Reagan Welfare Legacy* (Lexington, MA: Lexington Books, 1985), 95–6.

106. Joe and Rogers, *By the Few, For the Few*, 33–8, 129; George E. Peterson, "Federalism and the States," in Palmer and Sawhill, *The Reagan Record*, 235–7.

107. Statement of the President, quoted in Levitan and Johnson, *Beyond the Safety Net*, 81.

108. *Congressional Quarterly Weekly Report*, 29 September 1984, 5.

109. Ibid.

110. Patricia Dunn, "The Reagan Solution for Aiding Families with Dependent Children," in Anthony Champagne and Edward J. Harpham, eds., *The Attack on the Welfare State* (Prospect Heights, IL: Waveland Press, 1984), 107.

111. Joe and Rogers, *By the Few, For the Few*, 66.

112. U.S. Congress, House, Committee on Ways and Means, *Children in Poverty*, WCMP 99-8 (Washington, DC: GPO, 1985), 203. Cf. Leonard Goodwin, *Do the Poor Want to Work? A Social Psychological Study of Work Orientations* (Washington, DC: Brookings, 1972).

113. Paul E. Peterson and Mark C. Rom, "Federalism and Welfare Reform: The Determinants of Interstate Differences in Poverty Rates and Benefit Levels," *Brookings Discussion Papers in Governmental Studies* 14 (September 1987), 20.

114. *State Times*, Baton Rouge, LA, 22 March 1983, 1a, 6a.

115. Peterson and Rom, "Federalism and Welfare Reform," 21.

116. Sam Roberts, "Workfare in New York," *New York Times*, 24 October 1985, 18; John Herbers, "Reagan Partly Backs Governors' on Welfare," *New York Times*, 24 February 1987, 1; John Herbers, "Governors Vote a Plan Linking Welfare to Work," *New York Times*, 25 February 1987, 12; Domestic Policy Council, *Up From Dependency: A New National Assistance Strategy* (Washington, DC: GPO, 1986); Julie Rovner, "Panel OKs Welfare Plan on Party-Line Vote," *Congressional Quarterly Weekly Report* 13 June 1987, 1265–6. Cf. U.S. Congress, House, Committee on Ways and Means, Subcommittee on Public Assistance and Unemployment Compensation, *Hearings on Work, Education, and Training Opportunities for Welfare Recipients* (Washington, DC: GPO, 1986).

117. Doron P. Levin, "Many Welfare Clients Don't Seem to Mind," *Wall Street Journal*, 28 October 1982.

118. Congressional Budget Office, *Trends in Family Income: 1970–1986* (Washington, DC: GPO, 1988), 48–53.

119. Marilyn Moon and Isabel V. Sawhill, "Family Incomes: Gainers and Losers," in Palmer and Sawhill, eds., *The Reagan Record*, 317–54.

120. George Gilder, *Wealth and Poverty* (New York: Bantam, 1981), 83–94.

Chapter 8

PUBLIC EDUCATION: OPPORTUNITY AND ITS LIMITS
by Kenneth Cook

AMERICAN EDUCATION AS A MECHANISM FOR PRESERVING INEQUALITY

The amount of money allocated to education in the United States indicates its importance. Public primary and secondary education consumes 29 percent of all the funds spent by both state and local governments in the United States. The total amount of money allocated by all governments for education in 1985 was more than $200 billion, making it the nation's most expensive publically funded function.[1]

Education is considered so important because it symbolizes America's commitment to equal opportunity and individual progress. This explains why education is unique among America's public policies. The United States lagged behind European nations in developing other policies, but it made free public education available long before Europe did. And once offered, education was not consciously used to segregate classes in America, as it was in Europe.

Traditionally, schools in European nations separated working-class students from upper-class students because European educational systems developed when class differences were sharp and well defined. As European school systems in the twentieth century evolved, most students might go to the same schools for several years, then at about age eleven they were segregated by test scores into academic or technical schools. The use of test scores did not seem designed to differentiate on the basis of social class, but "In practice very few children of working-class families [were] assigned to [selective academic] schools . . ."[2] After World War II, a few European governments began to reform education by beginning the process of forming comprehensive schools right through to college, on the premise that all children should be provided with equal educational opportunity.

Sweden was the first to combine schools of different types into "comprehensive" schools. This was accomplished rather rapidly in the 1950s. Though the 1944 Education Act gave the British government the potential authority to create comprehensive schools, the movement did not gain momentum until the 1950s, when comprehensive schools were created in some rural areas, mainly as a cost-cutting device to reduce the number of schools. As late as 1970, little more than half of Britain's schools had become comprehensive, but by the end of the decade the proportion was about 90 percent. In West Germany, by contrast, there has been substantial resistance to comprehensive school movement, and most schools remain differentiated and selective.[3]

Against this background, the United States' school system stands out as exceptional. From its beginning in the mid-nineteenth century, "common" (public) education was supposed to equalize differences in wealth and circumstance, so that all children would have an equal opportunity to advance according to their abilities. Throughout American history, the schools have been the central institutions invested with the cultural promise of equal opportunity. It is ironic, therefore, that American schools ended up reflecting differences in the wealth of students' parents. For despite the promise of American education, it was organized in such a way that it acted as an overwhelmingly powerful mechanism for preserving and promoting racial and social class segregation. Today its effects are so pervasive that probably no other public policies or government actions are as important in preserving inequality from one generation to the next.

Education in the United States works in this way because public schools are financed mainly through a property tax levied by individual school districts. School financing thus reflects the values of the property that happens to be located within a district's boundaries. Consequently, school districts across the nation vary enormously in their ability to raise money and support educational functions.

Differences among school districts tend to reflect the spatial sorting out of economic activities and socioeconomic and racial groups. This occurs in rural as well as in metropolitan areas, but it is most intense in urban areas, where rich and poor, minority and white citizens tend to live in separate residential areas and in separate school districts. School district boundaries make it possible for affluent whites to "escape" central city school districts located in areas with declining property values to predominantly white, suburban districts. In the process, central city districts are increasingly the domain of minority students whose families are unable or unwilling to leave the city. For example, St. Louis's population fell from 622,236 in 1970 to 453,085 in 1980 as white and middle-class families left the city for the suburbs. Over the same period, the number of students in the St. Louis City public schools dropped from 111,233 to 62,968 and the proportion of black students rose from 66 percent to 77 percent.[4] A similar process occurred in all metropolitan areas across the country.

Public opinion polls have consistently indicated overwhelming support for local control of education and resistance to suggestions that it be altered.[5] School administrators and public officials regard local control as a politically untouchable issue and stay well away from advocacy of its reform.[6] Part of the reason is that independent school districts reflect patterns of racial and socioeconomic segregation. Autonomous school districts have served as the major defense protecting white, middle-class suburban communities from encroachment and have ensured that the population composition of individual suburbs is faithfully reflected in the schools.[7]

Despite the popular attachment to local control of the schools, substantial reforms have been accomplished in the past half-century, and some of these have tampered significantly with school district boundaries. Between 1931 and 1980, consolidation reduced the number of independent school districts in the United States from 127,531 to 15,912.[8] As a result, about one-fourth of the students enrolled in public schools reside in districts with 25,000 or more students (most of these are in big cities). About 25 percent of students go to districts of 2,500 or fewer students—three-fourths of all school districts in the nation.[9]

State and federal governments have demonstrated their ability to produce significant changes in educational policy. All state governments have reduced disparities in wealth between school districts by various forms of financial aid, and the federal government used the 1964 Civil Rights Act and the 1965 Elementary and Secondary Education Act to make progress in reducing segregation in some areas and in narrowing the differences in performance between affluent and poor students.[10] It is clear that movement toward equality does not occur unless it is imposed by state and federal governments. Local school districts do not have the ability or the inclination to promote access to equal education as a policy goal. But the attempts to accomplish this goal by the states and by the federal government have foundered on the ability of better-off school districts to preserve their financial advantages, and to resist extensive racial integration.

THE ORIGINS OF AMERICAN PUBLIC EDUCATION

The Political Struggle for American Public Education

Educational reformers who led the crusades for mass public education in the nineteenth century were not especially comfortable with local control of education. In fact, they distrusted parents and political groups that might try to influence the hiring of teachers and to dictate school curricula. But it was a daunting political task to persuade Americans that they should tax themselves to support public schools that would be attended by children of families who could not pay a property tax. In exchange for tax-supported schools, reformers conceded control of education to local groups. This concession was a political compromise, not the reformers' preferred outcome.

The educational system that evolved from the revolutionary period comprised an assortment of institutions. Some were public schools supported by tuition-paying parents, where a few poor children were allowed to attend free. These were religious and parochial schools run by the Presbyterians, Lutherans, Congregationalists, and other Protestant sects, as well as by Catholic schools and some charitable organizations. Private schools educated the children of the rich. In cities, from 20 percent to 40 percent of children attended elementary schools. Manufacturers and mill operators who relied on child labor opposed any attempts to force children to attend school.

Beginning in the late 1830s, education reformers launched campaigns to create a common (public) school system that would provide education to all children regardless of their circumstances. Within twenty years they had succeeded in persuading state legislatures to allow local governments throughout the Northeast and Midwest to adopt property taxes to finance public schools, with the result that most private schools were eclipsed. The reformers had overcome widespread popular opposition to compulsory property taxes, in a culture that resisted government intrusion into any area of life. America adopted publicly funded education (and compulsory education later in the nineteenth century) long before it was available in other Western nations. How was this vast expansion of public institutions made possible?

The drive to create a uniform system of education was energized by a floodtide of immigration that contributed to the explosive growth of American cities in the 1840s and 1850s. As the cities grew they also changed in character. Immigrants poured into the cities: 0.5 million in the 1830s, 1.4 million in the 1840s, and 2.7 million in the 1850s. Many of the immigrants were destitute, without job skills, unfamiliar with American culture, and unable to speak or read English. And they brought with them foreign customs and, in the case of the Catholics and Jews, "un-American" religions.

The reformers fighting for common schools were imbued with the idea that they were engaged in a historic struggle to save the Republic:

> Let us now be reminded, that unless we educate our immigrants, they will be our ruin.

> It is altogether essential to our national strength and peace, if not even to our national existence, that the foreigners who settle on our soil, should cease to be Europeans and become Americans. . . it is necessary that they become substantially Anglo-Americans.[11]

But the fight for publicly funded common schools was intense, and it took decades for school reformers to win it.

> The fight for free schools was a bitter one, and for twenty-five years the outcome was uncertain. Local elections were fought, won, and lost on the school issue. The tide of educational reform flowed in one state, only to ebb in another. Legislation passed one year was sometimes repealed the next. State laws requiring public schools were ignored by the local communities that were supposed to build them. Time and again the partisans of popular education encountered the bitter disappointments that accompany any effort at fundamental social reform.[12]

For the education reformers, it was not enough that a common education be made available only for the poor and the middle class; the notion of the common school required that the same educational curriculum be used by everyone, even including the children of the rich. If education was to reduce rather than intensify distinctions between citizens, if it was to educate the immigrants into American customs and morals, then it had to be free to all, rich and poor alike.

Much of the controversy about tax-supported schools centered around the insistence that public education be available to everyone without regard to ability to pay. Traditionally, education had been the responsibility of the family; public education, where it existed, was essentially a philanthropic activity to help some poor children learn to read and write. Free education was provided only in some places; in Pennsylvania in 1830, for example, education for the poor was offered only in Philadelphia, Lancaster, and Pittsburgh. It was often meager when available, extending no further than "a tolerable proficiency in reading, writing, and sometimes to a slight acquaintance with geography."[13] Poor people often could not take advantage of it even in the few places where it was offered, both because the school-age children of the poor had to work in factories or in the home to support the family and because there were "thousands of children whose parents are unable to afford for them a good private education, yet whose standing, profession, or connections in society effectively exclude them from taking the benefit of a *poor law*."[14]

It was one thing to argue that taxpayers were to pay for the education of a poor child; it was quite another to argue that they should support a rich child as well. The common school movement rested upon the assertion that education was a public good, that education benefited not only those who were the direct recipients—the students—but also the society as a whole, through its role in creating a united citizenry. And what benefited all of the people should be paid for by all of the people.

If education was to be supported by the taxes of the local community, then both politics and ideology argued for control by the same community. Education reformers soon learned that they could not mobilize the political support they needed for public financing of the schools unless they assured citizens that they would have a say in how the schools were run. Community financing required a promise of community control.

But what community? Schools traditionally had been local institutions, and local religious congregations had governed schools in northern cities. As education was secularized and made public, control was taken from congregations and lodged in local political authorities. Similar forms of local control evolved in the western states as well. It was natural for the reformers to use such local governments as the basic element of the new school system. On the one hand, it meant the continuation of the local schools already in existence in some communities; on the other hand, the struggle over taxation was intense enough without mounting an attack on the local control of the schools.

But local school governance led the reformers into a dilemma. At the same time that control of the schools was given over to local school boards as an expression of local democracy, the school reformers considered the tasks of education to be too important to be left to the whims of amateurs who sat on the school boards. Thus, at the same time that education reformers fought for public education by independent school districts, they sought to "professionalize" it by imposing their own standards on the school curriculum, which they thought should be defined by educational "experts."

Historians have remarked on the paternalism of this enterprise, charging that it reflected the notion that "education was something the better part of the community did to the others to make them orderly, moral, and tractable."[15] And critics have attacked the bureaucratization that soon characterized educational systems.[16] Thus, a conflict between community and professional control was implicit in the notion of the common school from its very beginning.

The education reformers looked to state legislatures to establish standards for public education agreeable to school professionals. Local control of the schools would be allowed—even promoted as a virtue of American education—but it would be exercised within constraints imposed by state governments, where, it happened, educational experts wielded substantial political influence. Legislatures responded by requiring local districts to be run by professional administrators, and curricula, including textbooks in many states, were specified on the basis of advice supplied by education reformers. Thus, despite local school governance, the content of education became remarkably uniform across the nation because of the success of school professionals in influencing teacher education and school policy in the individual states.

State Activism and Public Education

State governments' role in education policy began with the formation of state boards of education and the appointment of state school superintendents. State boards of education began in the New England states in the early nineteenth century, and by 1880 all thirty-eight states had some form of chief state school officer. In the early period, most of these officers relied mainly on rhetoric to spread the public school gospel, since they held little authority to influence local school policies. The leading advocate for common schools, Horace Mann, who became the first secretary of the Massachusetts State Board of Education in 1837, used his position as a pulpit from which he promoted his ideal of the common school.

But state governments soon began to use their financial resources to influence local school policy. The money the states used originated from land grants from the federal government. In the Land Ordinances of 1785 and 1787, land had been given to the states for the support of education. When new states joined the union, the federal government designated land grants for education. The states placed the proceeds from the sale of these lands in permanent school funds and used the interest from these funds to help support schools. By 1850, all states had some form of school fund, generally under the control of the state school authorities.

In the South, the money was used to support schools for paupers, rather than to support public schools open to everyone. Elsewhere, however, these nontax revenues were used as matching funds to stimulate local school expenditures in the early days of the public school struggle, when state laws generally permitted, but did not require, local tax support of schools.

Once a state school presence was established, it gradually changed from stimulating voluntary behavior to establishing and enforcing mandatory standards. Thus, the states made school attendance compulsory; Massachusetts did so in 1862, and Mississippi completed the process in 1918.[17] Gradually, control expanded to cover such matters as teacher certification, the nature and content of curricula, standards for school facilities, lighting, heating, and other details. States varied in the extent to which they sought to control local districts. Southern states, which imposed strict state rules following the Civil War (they were forced to do so by carpetbaggers), generally imposed more controls than states elsewhere. These patterns still exist. Thus, in the mid-1970s with regard to textbooks: in sixteen states, local districts could choose books without state approval; thirty-three states required that books be chosen from an approved list; and eleven states, mostly in the South, specified the books themselves.[18]

Much of the expansion of state authority plausibly can be explained as the work of reformers concerned with spreading public education. But material interests were involved as well. As public education grew, so did the number of educational administrators. These professionals shared a vision of what education should be and assumed a leading role in developing specific education policies.

Thus many state educational standards can be understood as attempts to advance the interests of professional educators. Teacher certification, for example, insulated educators from the often idiosyncratic hiring and retention practices of local school boards. It increased the power of the education colleges and their faculties by matching state standards for teachers to the curricula of those institutions. Similarly, teacher certification requirements for local districts ensured that teachers would find jobs waiting when they completed their training.

An early indication of the education profession's interest in stimulating a state role was the formation of the National Education Association (NEA) in 1870. This group, representing teachers, school administrators, and faculties of education colleges, has been and continues to be a major influence in education policy. Its members include more than half of all public schoolteachers. Teachers associations in each state are generally powerful interest groups at the state level.[19] Today the NEA has 1.9 million members, more than any other labor union in the nation.

The influence of the NEA, and of education professionals generally, rests heavily on its ability to portray itself as above politics:

> Rather than conceiving of teachers as workers and superintendents or boards as bosses, the NEA position is that the educator is a professional person with a special commitment to his function in society—educating the young.[20]

School professionals consistently aim to "take the schools out of politics." This tactic is a means of dealing with the conflict between community and professional control of the schools. Its political importance is evident in the wave of education reform enacted during the Progressive Era.

Taking "Politics" Out of the Schools

The changes accomplished in public education during the Progressive Era seemed to go in two opposite directions. On the one hand, reformers sought to democratize school politics by involving the electorate through referenda elections on matters of school policy and by requiring that measures increasing tax rates be approved by two-thirds of the voters. On the other hand, they tried to increase the power of professionally trained school administrators. Progressive reformers wanted to remove the schools from politics because the schools were, in fact, vulnerable to manipulation by politicians. In 1892 Joseph Mayer Rice,[21] in a series of articles in the muckraking publication *The Forum,* traced the problems of the schools to the immersion of the schools in politics. Political machines often controlled schools, which were organized on a ward-by-ward basis. Patronage jobs and contracts for supporters, the fuel of machine politics, made the schools an integral part of those organizations because schools employed so many people and frequently contracted for supplies, services, and construction.

For Rice, the solution was clear: remove the schools from politics and turn them over to professional educators. In education as elsewhere, the Progressives understood "taking the schools out of politics" to mean taking control from the political bosses and the urban masses they represented, however imperfectly, and lodging it in the hands of "responsible" (i.e., middle-class) citizens. The means of reform are familiar. Reformers created special governments that dealt only with education, governed by school boards composed of part-time, nonprofessional citizens and elected in at-large, nonpartisan elections. In most cities the school board became independent of the city government. Day-to-day administration was to be in the hands of professional school administrators. Voters were to exercise control of finance through referenda on tax rates and bond issues.

Such reforms, of course, do not end politics but only change its character. In the case of schools, the Progressive reformers took control of education from the political bosses and placed it, in effect, in the hands of professional educators. As we noted earlier, professional educators have their own interests, which are often in conflict with the interests of parents and taxpayers in local school districts. The myth that schools are above politics has served the function of masking those conflicts, and much of the activity of professional educators on the state and local levels can be understood as directed toward avoiding issues that will make those conflicts overt.

On the local level, the instruments of democratic control—elected school boards and finance referenda—pose potentially grave problems for the maintenance of professional autonomy. Professional autonomy has been preserved by making a distinction between political decisions, to be made by school boards, and administrative decisions, which have been defined as falling within the domain of school professionals. This distinction permeates contemporary school politics at both local and state levels. One clear effect is that education professionals shy away from issues that look "political." This makes issues of educational equality almost certainly anathema to educators at the local level and increases the reliance upon state and federal governments to produce policies that promote equality of opportunity.

After World War II, when the racial segregation of the schools became a contentious political issue, politics were potentially injected into schools. But the way that schooling had been organized in the nineteenth century, financed by local school districts and nominally controlled by local school boards and administrators, proved to be a formidable obstacle to desegregation. In most cases individual school districts and most school administrators avoided direct involvement in desegregation battles by defending the concept of "local control" of education.

STATE AND FEDERAL GOVERNMENTS AND EDUCATIONAL INEQUALITY

Local Control and School Segregation

In 1954, the Supreme Court ruled in *Brown* v. *Topeka Board of Education* that "separate but equal" schools were inherently unequal, and subsequent decisions in the case ordered the southern and border states to dismantle their dual school systems that segregated schools on the basis of race "with all deliberate speed." In fact, progress was agonizingly slow, and school districts dragged their heels until a series of Supreme Court decisions affirmed the responsibility of the districts to adopt effective measures to reduce segregation (*Green* v. *County Board*, 1968), including, if necessary, busing of students (*Swann* v. *Charlotte-Mecklenburg Board of Education*, 1971).

The implementation of the decisions met intense and often violent opposition, but with the flowering of the civil rights movement in the 1960s a national consensus pushed the federal government to confront racial segregation, in the schools and elsewhere in society. As a result,

By 1970 the northern schools had become more segregated than those of the South—and the difference was growing . . . Statistics on changes in urban school districts between 1970–1971 and the 1974–1975 school years show that segregation is actually becoming worse in the northeastern states while it is stagnant in the Midwest and continues to fall in the South.[22]

The desegregation of schools was more effective in the South than in the North for several reasons. Southern segregation was *de jure,* imposed by law, and unambiguous. Spurred by television coverage of civil rights marches in the South, public opinion pushed Congress to enact legislation to attack any form of segregation mandated by state law. The 1964 Civil Rights Act proved to be a powerful tool for ending *de jure* segregation:

The 1964 Civil Rights Act made the Department of Health, Education and Welfare responsible for either assuring compliance or cutting off federal aid funds, empowered the Justice Department to intervene in school cases, and provided some money for desegregation assistance. The law multiplied enforcement resources, shifted the burden of initiating cases from private groups, and made local officials realize that they were eventually going to have to desegregate.[23]

What made the legislation work was the coordinated efforts of the Department of Health, Education and Welfare (HEW) and the Justice Department, backed by a supportive Congress and an activist president. That coalition began to dissolve when attention shifted from the *de jure* segregation of the South to *de facto* segregation in the North.[24] Such segregation occurred not because of legal requirements but because of segregated housing patterns, which, in turn, produced segregated neighborhood schools. The court addressed the issue in *Keyes* v. *School Board* (1973), which moved school desegregation controversies to the North when it ruled that the racial segregation in Denver schools was unlawful even in the absence of an intent to segregate, if school officials, for whatever reasons, made decisions that had the clearly foreseeable effect of intensifying segregation and rejected policies which would have reduced it.[25]

When the civil rights weapons were turned against northern schools, congressional and administrative enthusiasm for enforcement quickly melted away. Beginning with the Nixon administration in 1968, Republican presidents became hostile to civil rights enforcement. Early in Nixon's first term, large numbers of civil rights attorneys in the Justice Department resigned in protest over nonenforcement. Ten years later, in 1981, the Reagan Justice Department adopted a policy of not pursuing desegregation plans and the Reagan administration backed off enforcement of all civil rights laws.[26]

In addition to the failure of political will, desegregation efforts faced formidable structural barriers. One of the reasons for the success of integration efforts in the South was the fact that the basic unit of school governance has been the county or parish, geographic entities that, because of their size, do not usually divide populations into distinct and homogeneous racial and economic subdistricts. Thus, orders to integrate school districts had the effect of intermixing populations within the administrative units governing the schools, because both black and white residential communities were embraced within those districts.

The situation has been very different in the North, where school districts are relatively small and homogeneous. In many metropolitan areas, predominantly black inner-city school districts are ringed by a large number of predominantly white school districts. Many of the inner-city school districts are under desegregation orders but simply do not have enough white students within them to produce meaningful desegregation of individual schools. At the same time, school district boundaries cut them off from the white students in the surrounding communities.

The obvious solution is to merge city and suburban school districts or to devise plans that move students across district lines. But there has been overwhelming resistance to these remedies on local and state levels, and the Supreme Court has been reluctant to order cross-district movement of students without compelling evidence that the school district boundaries were drawn with the explicit intent of producing segregated schools. In *Bradley* v. *Millikin* (1974), the Supreme Court, by a vote of five to four, refused to uphold a lower-court order that a desegregation plan be prepared that would embrace the city of Detroit and fifty-three of the surrounding suburban school districts. The Court ruled that it was permissible to breach school district lines only when there was clear evidence that district lines had been drawn for explicitly racial purposes. Speaking for the majority, Chief Justice Burger cited the "deeply rooted" attachment to local control of the schools:

> . . . the notion that school district lines may be casually ignored or treated as a mere administrative convenience [is] contrary to the history of public education in our country . . . No single tradition in public education is more deeply rooted than local control over the operation of schools; local autonomy has long been thought essential both to the maintenance of community concern and support for public schools and to the quality of the educational process.[27]

The result of the reluctance to pursue desegregation cases and to abridge district autonomy is predictable. A study using 1984 data from the Department of Education found little overall change in the degree of segregation of black students since 1972. In fact, in many states more black students were segregated in 1984 than before. The most segregated states were Illinois, Michigan, and New York. In Illinois, 69 percent of black students attended schools with 90 percent to 100 percent minority enrollment, and 84 percent of black students were enrolled in predominantly (60 percent or more) minority schools. In Michigan, the figures were 57 percent and 84 percent and in New York, 57 percent and 82 percent. Overall in these states, nearly two-thirds of black public school students were in predominantly minority schools.[28]

The picture is even more dramatic when attention is shifted from states to the metropolitan areas within them:

> When one looks at the schools of these metropolitan societies it is apparent that they are evolving in strikingly different ways, even among metropolitan areas whose overall population is quite similar. We have metropolitan areas where there has been no significant desegregated education for a generation and others where there is simply no sign that the Supreme Court ever ruled against segregation. At one extreme are large metropolitan areas with an almost all black and all low-income central city student body surrounded by virtually all-white segregated suburban school systems . . . The fragmentation of districts, particularly those in the urban Midwest and Northeast, is so great that it is impossible to even know with any precision how segregated the metropolitan areas are and how they are changing.[29]

The highest levels of integration were found in states that had maintained dual school systems by law and that were subjected to court orders requiring extensive busing. The most segregated states were "large, highly urbanized states with fragmented school districts."[30]

Most controversies have focused on black segregation, but Hispanic migration patterns, which have occurred within a political environment hostile to new efforts to reduce segregation, have resulted in intense segregation of Hispanic students. Examining the period between 1968 and 1984, Gary Orfield found that:

> Unlike the record for blacks, the figures show a constant growth in the isolation of Hispanics, with segregation becoming increasingly severe in virtually all parts of the country and in almost every period in the sixteen years that national data has been collected . . . While black segregation has remained about the same under Presidents Ford, Carter and Reagan, Hispanic segregation has been growing steadily since the late 1960s when it was first measured nationally.[31]

The federal government, when it desires, can reduce school segregation, but only by overruling the traditional pattern of local school governance.

Left to their own devices, local school districts do not, or cannot, pursue the goal of racial equality.

Federal Aid and Inequality

There are two important points to be made about federal school aid. First, as Figure 8.1 indicates, federal aid to primary and secondary education constitutes a relatively small percentage of total education spending. It reached its highest levels in 1978–1979 and 1979–1980, when the federal government provided 9.8 percent of the nation's education funding. Under the Reagan administration, the federal contribution declined steadily, dropping to 6.5 percent by 1984–1985. The states provide a far greater proportion of education expenditures than does the federal government.

Second, most federal aid is sent to states rather than directly to school districts (Table 8.1). This pattern reflects the long-standing tradition of state responsibility for the schools. This is not to say that the federal government has not been involved in public education; support of

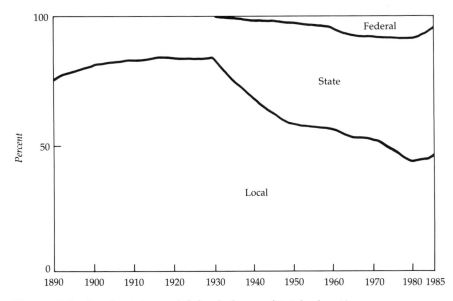

Figure 8.1. *Local, state, and federal shares of total education revenue, 1890–1985*

Source: 1890–1960: W. Norton Grubb and Stephan Michelson, *States and Schools* (Lexington, MA: Lexington Books, 1974), 27; 1970–1985: U.S. Department of Education, Office of Education Research and Improvement, *Digest of Education Statistics, 1987* (Washington, DC: GPO, 1987), 107.

Table 8.1. *Federal aid, direct and through states, to local governments, 1971–1972 and 1976–1977*

Year	Education Aid			Noneducation Aid		
	Billions of Dollars	Direct	Through State	Billions of Dollars	Direct	Through State
1971–1972	$4.0	25%	75%	$ 7.9	46%	54%
1976–1977	$6.4	20%	80%	$22.4	68%	32%

Source: Computed from Advisory Commission on Intergovernmental Relations, *Recent Trends in Federal and State Aid to Local Governments* (Washington, DC: ACIR, 1980)

public education was one of the earliest functions of the federal government. But that involvement has been indirect, generally in the form of nonfinancial aid given to the states in the form of virtually unrestricted grants.

One form of acceptable aid has been one-time, noncash federal land grants. In the Survey Ordinance of 1785 and the Northwest Ordinance of 1787, the Congress of the Confederation decreed that in the territories there "shall be reserved the lot number 16 of every township for the maintenance of public schools in each township," since "Religion, morality and knowledge, being necessary to good government and the happiness of mankind, schools and the means of education shall be forever encouraged."[32]

In 1802, when Ohio was admitted to the Union, Congress established the precedent of setting aside federal land for the support of schools when granting statehood.[33] This practice continued until 1896, when Congress, upon Utah's admission, set aside four sections in every township for the maintenance of schools. In all, eighty million acres in thirty states were dedicated to school support.[34] These land grants were generally used to create permanent state school funds, and they had an important impact upon the development of public education within the states. Nevertheless, the school funds were left entirely under state control.

Impact aid was another acceptable form of federal support. In 1941, Congress passed the Lanham Act, which provided federal aid for districts where tax-exempt military installations imposed burdens on local schools; such money was intended to replace the taxes not paid by the federal government. The legislation, extended in 1950 by the impacted areas program, has proved to be highly popular in Congress. The money is widely distributed, comes with no federal strings attached, and is easy and inexpensive to administer. As a result, the program has survived presidential attempts to cut it back.[35]

Before the late 1950s, efforts to expand federal financing of education or to define a more active federal role were generally unsuccessful. Opponents stood on the constitutional ground that education had been one of the responsibilities left to the states. But the constitutional arguments often masked more practical political concerns, reflecting fears that federal financing would inevitably infringe state and local autonomy. In particular, federal aid was blocked by southern legislators who were concerned that federal involvement would bring pressures for equal funding for black and white schools and ultimately would lead to integration.[36]

The question of aid to religious schools created another barrier to federal involvement. Public school forces, led by the National Education Association, maintained adamantly that federal aid could go only to public schools; public money was not to be used to improve the quality of, and increase the competition posed by, nonpublic institutions. Private school forces, and especially the Catholic Welfare Conference, argued with equal vehemence that their schools should receive federal aid. They maintained that public money should not be used to place parochial schools in a disadvantageous position.[37] Liberal Democrats in Congress who otherwise might have fought for federal aid in any event were reluctant to alienate their Catholic constituents on this issue.

Following World War II, as the costs and complexity of education increased, pressure for federal support mounted and a broad ideological consensus emerged. Conservatives joined liberals in the clamor for federal aid. Senator Robert A. Taft of Ohio, the Republicans' "Mr. Conservative," declared in 1946 that without federal assistance the nation's schools would be unable to provide an adequate education.[38] In his 1952 campaign, Dwight Eisenhower stated that 60 percent of the public school classrooms were overcrowded and that "this year 1,700,000 American boys and girls were without any school facilities." He suggested a solution:

> The American answer is to do in this field what we have been doing for a long time in other fields. We have helped the states build highways and local farm-to-market roads. We have provided federal funds to help the states build hospitals and mental institutions.[39]

But Eisenhower's program foundered upon the same shoals, integration and support for private education, that had wrecked earlier proposals.

The unexpected Soviet success in launching the satellite Sputnik I in October 1957 temporarily broke the stalemate. This dramatic event turned national attention toward the adequacy of the technical preparation provided by the public schools. President Eisenhower responded by proposing the National Defense Education Act (NDEA) of 1958, a

$1.6 billion program designed to improve education in science, mathematics, and foreign languages.

The legislation set an important precedent. For the first time Congress asserted that there was a national interest in the quality of education that justified federal intervention in local educational offerings. The debate over school aid shifted from whether there was to be federal assistance to the form that assistance would take.[40] The NDEA did not provide general support for primary and secondary education. Instead, it mostly funded loans and fellowships for undergraduate college education, though it also included matching grants to assist public schools in the purchase of equipment used in the teaching of mathematics, science, and foreign languages. Significantly, it also included loans but not grants to private schools for the same purposes.

Another breakthrough in federal aid to education came in 1965, when two developments made the expanded federal role possible. First, the religious issue became less contentious. As the costs of education escalated, federal aid became more important to both private and public school interests. Prior experience convinced both groups that without compromise there would be no federal aid for either public or private schools. The tactical solution adopted by the pro-aid forces and embodied in the Elementary and Secondary Education Act of 1965 (ESEA) was to package general school aid as part of President Johnson's antipoverty program, with money distributed to school districts in proportion to the number of families whose incomes fell below the poverty line. The major component of ESEA was Title I, which established a comprehensive program of compensatory education, aimed at meeting the special educational needs of economically disadvantaged children.[41]

This meant that ESEA assistance was directed to students, not to schools. The federal government had earlier directed aid to students by helping pay for school lunches and school buses for both public and private schools. The prospect of federal aid satisfied the private school forces; the focus on students, not schools, quieted the public school interests. The result was a legislative package that drew support from the previously warring factions, including the Catholic Church, the National Council of Churches, the American Jewish Committee, and the National Education Association.[42]

The second development facilitating the breakthrough in federal aid was an emerging governmental focus on social programs, intensified by the assassination of President Kennedy and given electoral impetus by the landslide victories of President Johnson and the congressional Democrats in the 1964 elections. That concern, along with the waning of the religious issue, meant that southern congressmen opposed to school aid because of its civil rights implications could no longer join forces with congressional Republicans to block social legislation. The 1964 Civil Rights Act explicitly linked desegregation to federal education aid. Title IV of that bill authorized the attorney general to bring suits to force school desegregation, and Title V declared that segregated institutions could no longer receive federal money.

The ESEA brought forth a significant commitment of federal money. The total first-year cost of the bill was estimated at $1.4 billion, with $1.1 billion designated to aid poor children under Title I, whose programs were expected to reach 95 percent of the counties in the United States.[43] More important, it marked the beginning of a continuing and, until the 1980s, expanding program of federal assistance.

Its opponents saw the legislation as a direct attack on local control of education. During the congressional debate, Representative Howard Smith of Virginia complained, "We apparently have come to the end of the road so far as local control over our education in public facilities is concerned."[44] But despite the opponents' rhetoric, ESEA did not break with the tradition of local control. Money went not to the school districts but to state school authorities, who in turn distributed it to school districts, in accordance with formulas set forth in the legislation. The predictable result has been that the political struggle over school aid has centered around the level of federal funding and the requirements contained in the federal grants.

Those seeking to achieve equality of educational opportunity through legislation have done so by pursuing expanded funding and categorical grants that limit the discretion of state and local education authorities. Congress has, over time, altered and extended the aid formula of Title I and has added new categorical programs. Thus, Title VII of the ESEA, enacted in 1967, provided federal money to improve the education of children from non-English-speaking families. In fiscal year 1978, an appropriation of $135 million funded 565 demonstration projects, training about 38,000 teachers in sixty-seven different languages and serving 255,000 of the estimated 3.6 million eligible students.[45] Similarly, Title IX of the Education Amendments of 1972 forbade sex discrimination in programs receiving federal assistance and produced changes in admission policies, financial aid, employment, and athletic programs.[46]

Almost from the very beginning, opponents attempted to reduce federal influence by limiting the federal conditions attached to the grants. The first assault came in 1967, when Republican members of Congress proposed amendments that would have transformed the ESEA's categorical programs into a block grant, with states given almost complete discretion over the ways in which the money would be allocated to local school districts. The Republicans supported the "Quie Amendment," introduced by Congressman Albert Quie (R, Minnesota). Though the block grants would be administered within federal guidelines, the amendments constituted an attempt to increase state discretion and reduce federal power in determining how federal aid money was spent. State school officials supported the amendment, but the Johnson administration opposed it, arguing that without specific conditions the legislation would not achieve the goal of providing qualitative improvements in elementary education. The amendment was defeated, largely because of the opposition of private school forces, which feared that state school authorities would not provide money for nonpublic schools without specific legislative direction to do so.[47]

Attempts to transform the ESEA and other education programs into block grants continued. In 1971 and 1973, President Richard Nixon proposed the "Better Schools Act," advanced as a form of revenue sharing for education. In 1976, President Gerald Ford proposed to consolidate twenty-four elementary and secondary aid programs into a block grant. Opponents managed to defeat these proposals, arguing that they represented a reduction in funding and a loss of national direction for education programs.[48]

The next major challenge to national requirements for the distribution of education aid came in 1981, when President Ronald Reagan proposed to combine forty-four education programs into a block grant and cut funding by 25 percent. The alteration was opposed by civil rights leaders, parents of handicapped children, and representatives of the poor, who argued that without the safeguard of categorical programs, poor school districts in greatest need inevitably would be the losers at the state level in battles over shares of declining education dollars. As passed, The Omnibus Budget Reconciliation Act of 1981 consolidated thirty-eight categorical programs into a block grant but left Title I (compensatory education) and aid to handicapped children as separate programs.[49] Congressional supporters of the program also fought off Reagan administration attempts to reduce federal guidelines in 1982 and 1983.[50]

For those programs combined under the block grant in 1981, federal aid was distributed to the states. The states, in turn, were required to pass on at least 80 percent of the money to school governments, which were given wide discretion in the use of the funds. Overall, local school districts used the money to support the same programs they had funded before block grants, except in one important area. According to a report by the Government Accounting Office, "at least 80 percent said they increased or maintained their level of support in all but one program activity—desegregation."[51]

Surprisingly, much of the opposition to the new block grant programs came from education officials on the state and local levels, who pushed for a reimposition of program requirements:

State and local officials complained that the new law and accompanying regulations were too vague. They preferred to keep in place the extra administrative work to which they had grown accustomed rather than risk being audited for noncompliance at some future date.[52]

In response, Congress retreated from the block grants of 1981 and returned to a compensatory education program that was similar to the program which had evolved following the passage of ESEA. Support for the reinstatement of program requirements came from within both political parties.[53]

What Differences Do Federal Programs Make?

Overall federal spending on primary, secondary, and vocational education increased from $482 million in 1962 to $1.6 billion in 1966, $2.9 billion in 1970, and $6.9 billion in 1980 and an estimated $9.4 billion for 1989.[54] Federal aid for compensatory education rose from $1.05 billion in 1968 to $4.2 billion in 1985, and fell to an estimated $3.8 billion in 1989.[55]

The impact of this spending is difficult to measure because of the extremely large number of factors that affect the impact of education and because of the ambiguities of standardized test scores, the most often-used indicators of educational achievement. Studies often show conflicting and inconsistent results, but a recent study of educational achievement commissioned by the Congressional Budget Office did find some clear patterns. The report examined nine studies that compared the performances of minority and nonminority students. "Eight of these nine data sources showed a consistent and unambiguous narrowing of the gap between black and non-minority students, leaving little doubt that this pattern is real and not an artifact of some aspects of the tests or groups tested."[56]

Similarly, the study found improvements in the relative performance of students from disadvantaged urban areas:

> Since 1970, 9- and 13-year-olds in disadvantaged urban communities gained ground relative to the nation as a whole on the NAEP mathematics and reading assessments. In contrast, 17-year-olds in disadvantaged urban communities showed no relative gains in mathematics, and their small relative gains in reading occurred entirely between 1979 and 1983. In two instances—in reading at age 9, and in mathematics at age 13—more than a third of the gap between disadvantaged-urban communities and the nation as a whole was overcome since the early 1970s.[57]

But if the existence of changes in relative performance seemed clear, a subsequent study of the causes of the performance trends offered ambiguous results. The study divided possible causal factors into three categories: modifications of educational policy; changes in the selection of students to be tested; and broad societal and cultural trends. On the basis of available evidence, the study distinguished between factors that could have played a role in producing change and those that could not; Title I, ESEA, and desegregation all are identified as possible causes. With regard to Title I, compensatory education to needy students, the study reported that:

> Gains in test scores of students in the program exceed those of comparable students not in the program by roughly 10 percent to 30 percent, depending on age and subject . . . Title I/Chapter I could have contributed measurably to the relative gains of black and Hispanic students, but probably only in the early grades.[58]

Similarly, with regard to the effects of integration:

> A recent synthesis of research concluded that, in the aggregate, desegregation probably increased the reading scores of black students . . . The contribution of desegregation to the relative gains of black students in the aggregate, however, would have been considerably smaller than the gains of directly affected students, because for many black students the amount of segregation experienced did not change markedly. That is, even though the amount of desegregation between the late 1960s and the present has been substantial, a sizable share of black students remain in segregated environments.[59]

Though evidence of the positive effects of desegregation and compensatory education aid is not overwhelming, it is significant that they are the only factors found to have effects on student performance which are within the control of policymakers. The other factors found to be important reflect the characteristics of the social context within which education is provided. And one major area of educational reform, increased testing and educational requirements for teachers, seemed to have no significant effect on improved student performance.

SCHOOL DISTRICTS AND FINANCIAL INEQUALITY

The ESEA constituted an explicit attempt to increase educational opportunities for disadvantaged students, and the available evidence suggests a modest but genuine impact. But the ability of the federal government to equalize educational finance, and thus school quality, is inevitably limited by the relatively small proportion of education funding the federal government provides (that proportion was indicated in

Figure 8.1). If the political will existed, the states could equalize education spending among school districts.

The combination of local school districts and a school finance system that relies heavily upon local resources has inevitably meant financial inequality among school districts. Over the past several decades, most local governments have been turning away from property taxes, traditionally their major source of revenue. Concern with inequity and difficulties caused by the political sensitivity and declining yield of property taxes have triggered a movement away from such taxes. Many states have adopted a variety of reforms forcing local governments to reduce the most grating inequities of property taxes, chiefly their impact on those with fixed incomes. School districts are the one major exception to this pattern of movement away from property taxes. Table 8.2 contrasts the reliance on property taxes of school districts to local governments of other kinds.

There are a number of reasons why school districts have stayed with the property tax. One is predictability: the yield from property taxes is a product of the tax rate, which by law must gain the approval of local voters, and the assessed valuation of physical property within the district. Tax revenues are thus quite stable over time, since they are not as subject to economic fluctuations as are sales and income taxes. School districts can predict tax revenues accurately, making budgeting simpler and planning more precise than if other taxes were involved.[60]

Table 8.2. *Proportion of locally raised general revenue derived from property taxes, selected years, 1932–1986*

Year	Local Government Total	School Districts	Local Government Less School Districts
1932	85.25%	93.5%	83.0%
1942	80.1	92.3	77.7
1952	70.9	89.7	64.7
1962	69.0	86.2	61.1
1966–1967	66.2	84.2	57.3
1971–1972	63.5	86.0	52.4
1967–1977	59.0	84.6	47.7
1978–1979	53.3	81.2	42.0
1979–1980	50.5	78.6	39.8
1981–1982	48.0	78.4	37.0
1985–1986	46.0	80.7	34.6

Sources: 1932–1971/72: U.S. Bureau of the Census, 1972 Census of Governments, vol. 6, no. 4: *Historical Statistics on Government Finances and Employment* (Washington, DC: GPO, 1974); 1967–77: Advisory Commission on Intergovernmental Relations, *Recent Trends in Federal and State Aid to Local Governments* (Washington, DC: ACIR, 1978), 5; 1978–1986: U.S. Bureau of the Census, Government Finances . . . (Washington, DC: GPO, 1981, 1982, 1984, 1987).

More importantly, however, property taxes appear to be suitable to a system of local control. Property taxes are based on real property, fixed in physical location. School district boundaries can thus enclose an essentially immovable tax base. Immovability of property makes casual avoidance impossible, unlike sales or income taxes, which can be avoided relatively easily by shopping or working in other taxing jurisdictions.[61] In addition, property taxes appear to be effective instruments of democratic control. Property taxes are highly visible. Unlike income taxes, which are paid continuously through tax withholding, or sales taxes, which become habitual, and largely unnoticed, increments in the purchase prices of goods and services, property taxes are imposed as lump sums, and tax bills clearly indicate how the money is being spent. This visibility, coupled with the need for a two-thirds majority to pass tax referenda in most states, makes approval of tax rates far from automatic. Of the 858 school finance elections across the nation in 1976–1977, nearly 45 percent went down to defeat.[62]

Reliance on property taxes means that poor school districts whose assessed property values are relatively low will be able to raise less money—even at the same tax rates—than richer districts. The school districts of St. Louis City and County offer an illustration. Table 8.3 presents data on the fiscal capacity of these school districts. Column 2 indicates that the districts vary widely in their property wealth. Clayton, the richest school district, has more than five times the per-student tax base as the poorest district. That wealth provides Clayton with the largest tax yield per student, despite the fact that Clayton taxes its property at a relatively low rate. Even when districts such as University City or Webster Groves tax at rates considerably higher than Clayton, their per-student tax yield remains less than half that of Clayton.

Fiscal inequality cannot be addressed at the level of the local school board. Any solution requires redistribution of money from richer to poorer communities or some limitation on the freedom of richer districts to spend their money, or both. The state, constitutionally responsible for education, has been the natural level to which reformers turn, and virtually all of the states, sometimes prompted by legal challenges to disparities among school districts, have passed legislation seeking to equalize school district revenues.

One way to achieve fiscal equality is to remove financial discretion from the local school districts. One way to remove that discretion is by going to full state funding of education, with all money for education coming from the state and being distributed in a way that gives each district an equal amount per student. Another way to eliminate local discretion is by mandating a uniform per-pupil expenditure rate or a uniform property tax in each district, and making up differences in local expenditures or revenues by distributing more state funds to poorer districts. Such reforms produce equal expenditures among districts

Table 8.3. 1984–1985 financial data, school districts, St. Louis City and County

| District | Assessed Valuation per Pupil | Tax Rate per $100 | Expenditure per Pupil | | Revenue Sources | | |
			Total	Local Share	% Local	% State	% Federal
Brentwood	$121,261	$2.49	$5,098	$3,019	66%	33%	1%
Clayton	176,895	2.55	6,309	4,511	77	23	0
Ferguson-Florissant	75,003	3.48	3,544	2,610	53	43	4
Hancock Place	29,110	3.51	2,303	1,022	27	69	4
Jennings	48,708	3.76	2,316	1,831	53	43	4
Kirkwood	84,877	2.84	3,467	2,410	69	30	1
Ladue	147,981	2.05	4,860	3,034	75	25	0
Mehlville	62,654	2.47	2,655	1,548	47	53	0
Normandy	32,517	3.23	2,784	1,050	29	65	6
Ritenour	48,469	2.75	3,064	1,333	45	50	5
Riverview Gardens	43,213	2.88	2,639	1,216	39	60	1
University City	44,679	3.49	3,126	1,559	45	50	5
Webster Groves	62,657	3.12	3,384	1,955	62	37	1
Wellston	29,335	3.98	3,145	1,168	48	44	8
St. Louis	41,864	3.16	4,164	1,323	31	62	7

Note: Expenditures are for operating expenses. Revenue sources include all funds.
Source: 1984–1985 Report of the Public Schools (Jefferson City: Missouri State Board of Education)

by removing fiscal control from local school boards and lodging it with the state school authorities or the state legislatures.

A second approach to equalizing fiscal resources leaves intact local control and tries to reduce disparities through state grants. Such grants, in various forms, have long been a major and growing proportion of local district expenditures. They are equalizing insofar as more money is given to poorer than to richer districts.

The development of state aid reflects different conceptions of state responsibility. In the beginning, state aid was predicated on the assumption that states owed their citizens a minimum level of education, regardless of the ability of local school districts to afford such minimums. State aid took the form of flat grants, given on a per-pupil basis to school districts regardless of their wealth. Since equal grants went to each district, the effect was not significantly equalizing. Nor were flat grants intended to equalize; they sought only to ensure that each district could provide at least a minimal education to pupils. Most districts, of course, spent far above the minimum level.

Flat grants evolved into foundation grants, in which the states established minimums for per-pupil expenditures and paid the difference between that amount and the funds that local districts were able to raise at mandated tax rates. As a political matter, foundation formulas typically guaranteed even the wealthiest districts a minimum state grant and preserved the ability of those districts to spend much higher per-pupil amounts at similar or lower tax rates than poorer districts. Foundation plans did provide poor districts more money than rich districts but did little to sever the relation between district wealth and ability to raise education funds.

More recent approaches to educational finance on the state level, variously called percentage equalizing or district power equalizing, have explicitly sought to weaken the relationship between property values and school financing, while preserving local control over tax rates and level of expenditure. In district power equalization, the state equalizes the taxing "power" of each district by distributing funds so that equal tax rates raise equal amounts of money. The states generally guarantee a minimum per-pupil expenditure and a maximum property tax rate. Districts that tax at the maximum rate receive a sum from the state equal to the difference, if any, between the minimum per-pupil expenditure guaranteed and the district's actual tax yield. School districts are free to tax at lower rates, down to a state-determined minimum, with correspondingly lower state contributions.

The 1970s was a period of considerable movement in school finance on the state level. From 1971 through 1981, twenty-eight states enacted some form of school finance reform. The goal in each of these reforms was to improve the equity of school finance, either by reducing the difference between districts in the amount of money actually spent per pupil or by weakening the relationship between the wealth of a district and its level of expenditure.[63] By 1984, ten states had enacted power equalization or similar reforms and fourteen had combined equalizing components with foundation programs specifically directed at fiscal equalization.[64]

Legal challenges to school finance systems have been a major stimulus of reform. From the late 1960s to the early 1980s, suits challenging the constitutionality of school finance systems were brought in twenty-four states. As of 1982, school finance systems had been found unconstitutional in five states and constitutional in eight, and litigation was still underway in eleven.[65]

For a time it appeared that inequity in school finance would attain the same constitutional status as school segregation. In 1971, the California Supreme Court ruled in *Serrano* v. *Priest* that the California system of local school finance violated the equal protection clause of the Fourteenth Amendment to the U.S. Constitution because the quality of a child's education was "a function of the wealth of his parents and neighbors." The facts in the case were striking. John Serrano's son was a student in the Baldwin Park school district near Los Angeles. Baldwin Park, with property values at $3,706 per pupil, taxed itself at a rate of $5.48, raising $577 per student. Nearby Beverly Hills, with per-pupil family property values exceeding $50,000 and a tax rate of only $2.38, raised $1,232 per student. State aid, with Baldwin Park receiving $307 and Beverly Hills $125 per pupil, offset the difference somewhat, but a discrepancy of more than $405 per pupil remained.[66] The California court ruled in favor of Serrano, commenting, "affluent districts can have their cake and eat it too; they can provide a high quality education for their students while paying lower taxes. Poor districts, by contrast, have no cake at all."[67] The court directed the state to enact legislation within five years that would reduce disparities between districts to no more than $100 in expenditures per pupil.

Reformers reacted with joy to the court ruling, anticipating that *Serrano* would have the same effect upon school finance that *Brown* had exerted upon school segregation. But their optimism was short-lived. In 1973, the U.S. Supreme Court overturned a federal district court ruling in a Texas case similar to *Serrano, Rodriguez* v. *San Antonio*. A majority of the Court found that in the absence of a specific constitutional guarantee, education was not a fundamental right under the U.S. Constitution with the same stature as freedom of speech or religion. Thus, variations were allowable if they had a reasonable basis, and the Court found that the state interest in preserving local control was such a basis.[68]

A subsequent rehearing in California of *Serrano* in 1977, referred to as *Serrano II*, found education to be a fundamental right under California's constitution and ruled the state's finance system to be in violation of the state's equal protection clause.[69] Again, the court ordered the state legislature to reform finance arrangements. In response, the California legislature passed Senate Bill 65, which transferred property tax money from richer to poorer districts through power equalization. But the solution was overtaken by events a few months later, when California voters passed Proposition 13, the Jarvis-Gann initiative, which sharply reduced property assessments and limited tax rates, and restricted tax increases. The passage of the initiative eliminated 60 percent of local property tax revenues, in effect wiping out the equalization of Senate Bill 65.[70]

The state then tried a new tack, supplementing local revenues with state funds, which were distributed according to school district wealth. The California Supreme Court approved this strategy in 1983.[71] But the limitation on property tax revenues, coupled with the state's own fiscal problems, meant restrictions on state funds for education and a very limited degree of equalization. In the eyes of some, the quality of public education in California deteriorated as well.[72]

How Equalizing Is School Finance Equalization?

The actual equalizing effect of school finance reform has been very limited, for a number of practical political reasons. In states with power equalization systems, state legislators have been unwilling to impose upper limits on school district expenditures. Rich districts are able to raise funds exceeding the level of state guarantees; few states have passed "recapture" provisions to redistribute such excess funds to poorer districts. In addition, the states have typically failed to fund foundation and other equalization programs fully. Thus, rich districts can still spend more than poor ones, even in states with power equalization.

Reformers have typically sought to broaden support for foundation programs by promising each district, however wealthy, some minimum amount of state money. Subsequent reforms aimed at equalization have included, as a practical necessity for legislative passage, "hold harmless" provisions, guaranteeing that no district will receive less support under the new legislation than under previous legislation. This has meant that equalization reform has involved not the redistribution of existing school funds but the distribution of new funds to poorer districts. Equalization has thus been limited by the extent to which new education money is made available on the state level.[73]

Movement toward equality of school funding has been limited by action at the district level as well. Local school authorities in poorer districts often have used increased state funds as a means of keeping local property tax rates low. In these cases district expenditures have thus remained relatively stable despite the greater availability of money from the state. Equally important, equalization aid typically constitutes less than half of total state school aid. Much of the remainder is in the form of incentive grants. Such grants, through which states stimulate local districts to undertake desired programs by matching local contributions, are more likely to be affordable to rich than to poor districts and thus actually produce more inequality.

The inability of states to equalize effectively is a product of the political character of state legislatures. Effective equalization measures require representatives from districts containing richer school districts to vote against the interests of their own school districts, something they have been unwilling to do without the lures of minimum grants and "hold harmless" provisions.

The actual equalizing effect for one state, Missouri, is indicated in Table 8.3. Columns 4 and 5 compare the amount of money each district in the St. Louis area raises itself and the total amount it spends, on a per-pupil basis. The difference between the two columns primarily reflects the state's contribution. Poorer districts receive more state and federal aid than do richer districts, reducing some of the disparities produced by differing fiscal capacities. But significant variations still remain, with Clayton still spending more than twice as much per student than the poorest districts.

These disparities remain despite significant legislative changes in Missouri in recent years. In 1977, the state revised its foundation program, adding a minimum guaranteed tax base component (state grants would bring a poor district up to a minimum) and an income factor reflecting the wealth of each district (poorer districts would receive proportionately more aid). But subsequent changes reduced the importance of the equalizing formula—in 1983, voters passed Proposition C, which gave each district a flat grant of $500 per pupil, distributed without regard to district need. Meanwhile, districts have increased their reliance on local revenues, raised primarily through the property tax. As a result, aid distributed through the equalization formula accounts for only about 25 percent of average district revenues in the state.[74]

Studies of the impact of the 1977 reforms on finance equalization in Missouri have revealed a decline in the relationship between wealth and spending. Poorer districts received more state aid, but wealthier districts tended to have higher tax rates, so that the difference in spending between the highest-spending districts and the lowest actually increased.[75] A 1987 study of Missouri's school finance system found that,

The variation in revenues/expenditures among Missouri's school districts is moderate. That is, the level is well below similar levels found in other states . . . [But] the link between property wealth and revenues/expenditures is too high. About 30 percent of the variation in spending among districts can be explained by per pupil property wealth alone.[76]

The story is apparently similar elsewhere. A *New York Times* survey showed that school finance reform that swept across the states in the 1970s had not significantly narrowed the gap between the richest and poorest school districts.[77]

THE REAGAN ADMINISTRATION'S RETREAT

In 1983, the National Commission on Excellence in Education issued its report, "A Nation at Risk." The commission, appointed by Secretary of Education Terrell Bell, was responding to national concern about the quality of American public education. The concern had emerged in the wake of steadily falling standardized test scores among American schoolchildren. The report found a "rising tide of mediocrity" in American public schools and called for higher pay for teachers, longer school days, and other reforms.[78]

At a reception for the national commission, President Reagan restated his belief that education should remain in the hands of the states, and he outlined his own agenda for educational reform: school prayer, tuition tax credits, and abolishing the Department of Education.[79] Reagan's desire to leave education to the states was partly an effort to get the government "off the backs" of local governments and was partly motivated by a desire to cut the federal budget. But it was also explicitly an attempt to get the federal government out of the business of addressing issues of educational equality at the local level.

The federal government's retreat from a commitment to school integration most clearly demonstrates that goal. Beginning in 1981, the Justice Department countermanded efforts instituted during the Carter presidency to compel interdistrict busing in Houston and Chicago.[80] In 1982, the department announced that it planned to seek an end to mandatory busing in East Baton Rouge and was considering seeking to end busing in Boston and Denver.[81] The Reagan administration cut funding for public school desegregation plans, leading the U.S. Commission on Civil Rights to charge that the government's actions were detrimental to the futures of poor children. "A right without a remedy simply is illusory," the Commission said.[82]

And the Reagan administration sharply reduced funding for education, with the result that the federal government, which had provided 9.8 percent of the revenue of public elementary and secondary schools in 1979–1980, provided 6.5 percent in the 1984–1985 school year. The deepest cuts were applied to federal aid to disadvantaged students. But though the administration slashed aid to disadvantaged students, it was willing to absorb new costs in the form of tax credits for tuition payments. Such tax benefits would make it easier for middle- and upper-income parents to pay for private school education, which would further segregate education along class lines.

As the federal government reduced its commitment to public education, state governments were responding to pressures to raise educational quality. From 1980 to 1987, forty-five states stiffened minimum requirements for graduation from high school, forty-two states increased their mathematics requirements, and thirty-four states raised science requirements. Thirty-eight states adopted policies designed to reward and encourage good teachers.[83]

The measures produced some signs of progress, including improved Scholastic Aptitude Test scores in some states, an outcome the Reagan administration said reflected the success of its policies. The evidence is that these changes have raised dropout rates and enhanced inequalities between school districts. The results led former Education Secretary Terrell Bell, now a university professor, to comment, "The school reform movement has had no significant impact on the other 30 percent. The 30 percent are the low-income minority students, and we are still not effectively educating them."[84]

A study prepared by the Congressional Budget Office showed that rising scores were more a reflection of broad demographic and cultural changes than the new policies supported by the Reagan administration. The one area in which government policy had, in the past, made a measurable difference was in the improvement in scores among disadvantaged and minority students, which seemed due to compensatory education programs for disadvantaged students and to desegregation efforts.[85]

"THE FOUNDATION OF A DEMOCRATIC SOCIETY"[86]

American public schools always have carried an enormous cultural and political burden. In the 1980s education still is regarded as the panacea for a wide variety of social problems. Schools are expected to prepare people for the job market by teaching them basic skills of reading, writing, and arithmetic, but they are also considered crucial for solving social problems and for socializing citizens. Thus a national educational commission reporting in 1986 commented on job and skill training: the educational system "must be rebuilt to match the drastic change needed in our economy if we are to prepare our children for productive lives in the 21st century." The commission also discussed the social consequences if the schools were to fail: "A growing number of permanently unemployed people strains our social fabric." Finally, the commission commented on the role of the schools in creating cultural consensus: education "must provide access to a shared cultural and intellectual heritage if it is to bind its citizens together in a com-monweal."[87]

The main argument in favor of local control of the schools is that this promotes democracy. When it is structured and financed as in-coherently as in the United States, it also promotes racial and social class inequality. A devotion to a fragmented, extremely decentralized system of education may or may not be "democratic," depending on one's point of view. School board elections, for example, normally bring fewer citizens to the polls than any other elections. But it is manifest that investing education in local school districts creates a system of inequality that is nearly impervious to challenge.

NOTES

1. U.S. Bureau of the Census, *1981 Statistical Abstract of the United States*, (Washington DC: GPO, 1988), 258.
2. Arnold J. Heidenheimer, Hugh Heclo, and Carolyn Teich Adams, *Comparative Public Policy: The Politics of Social Choice in Europe and America*, 2d ed. (New York: St. Martin's Press, 1983), 34.
3. Ibid., 21–51.
4. Gary Orfield, "The St. Louis Desegregation Plan," unpublished report to Judge James H. Meredith, United States District Court, 2 May 1980, 4.
5. Gary Orfield, *Must We Bus? Segregated Schools and National Policy* (Washington, DC: Brookings, 1978).
6. See, for example, the poll results cited in Arnold J. Meltsner et al., *Political Feasibility of Reform in School Financing* (New York: Praeger, 1973), 18, and Allan Odden and John Augenblick, *School Finance Reform in the States: 1981* (Denver: Education Commission of the States, January 1981), 32–6.
7. Ronald F. Campbell, Luvern L. Cunningham, Roderick F. McPhee, and Raphael O. Nystrand, *The Organization and Control of American Schools*, 2d ed. (Columbus, OH: Merrill, 1970), 61–4.
8. National Center for Education Statistics, *Digest of Education Statistics 1983–1984* (Washington, DC: GPO, 1984), 62.
9. Ibid., 62.
10. See, for example, Orfield, *Must We Bus?*, and Paul E. Peterson, Barry G. Rabe, and Kenneth K. Wong, *When Federalism Works* (Washington, DC: Brookings, 1986).
11. *Transaction of the Fifth Annual Meeting of the Western Library Institute and College of Professional Teachers* (1836), excerpted in David B. Tyack, ed., *Turning Points in American Educational History* (Waltham, MA: Blaisdell Publishing, 1967), 149.
12. Lawrence A. Cremin, *The Transformation of the School* (New York: Teachers College, Columbia University, 1951), 13.
13. Lawrence A. Cremin, *The American Common School* (New York: Teachers College, Columbia University, 1951), 35.
14. Ibid.
15. Michael B. Katz, *Class, Bureaucracy and Schools: The Illusion of Educational Change in America*, exp. ed. (New York: Praeger, 1975), 48.
16. See, for example, ibid.; Raymond E. Callahan, *Education and the Cult of Efficiency* (Chicago: University of Chicago Press, 1962); David B. Tyack, *The One Best System: A History of American Urban Education* (Cambridge, MA: Harvard University Press, 1974).

17. Campbell et al., *The Organization and Control of American Schools*, 11.
18. Frederick M. Wirt, "Education Politics and Policies," in Herbert Jacob and Kenneth N. Vines, eds., *Politics in the American States*, 3d ed. (Boston: Little, Brown, 1976), 299. For a table showing variations in state-mandated educational policies, see ibid., 324–5.
19. Frederick M. Wirt and Michael W. Kirst, *The Political Web of American Schools* (Boston: Little, Brown, 1972), 51.
20. Robert H. Salisbury, "State Policies and Education," in Herbert Jacob and Kenneth N. Vines, *Politics in the American States*, 2d ed. (Boston: Little, Brown, 1971), 402.
21. Collected as *The Public School System of the United States* (New York: Century, 1893).
22. Orfield, *Must We Bus?*, 57.
23. Ibid., 279.
24. Ibid.
25. Ibid.
26. See, for example, U. S. Congress, House, Committee on Government Operations, *Report on the Office for Civil Rights of the Department of Health and Human Services* Report 100-56 (Washington: GPO, 1987).
27. Quoted in Orfield, *Must We Bus?*, 33.
28. Gary Orfield, Franklin Monfort, and Rosemary George, *School Segregation in the 1980s: Trends in the States and Metropolitan Areas* (Chicago: National School Desegregation Project, University of Chicago, July 1987), 3 (mimeographed).
29. Ibid., 11–12.
30. Ibid., 3.
31. Ibid., 1.
32. *Education for a Nation* (Washington: Congressional Quarterly, 1972), 59; Mike M. Milstein, *Impact and Response: Federal Aid and State Education Agencies* (New York: Teachers College Press, Columbia University, 1976), 8.
33. Ralph W. Tyler, "The Federal Role in Education," *The Public Interest* 34 (Winter 1974), 164–5.
34. Milstein, *Impact and Response*, 8.
35. Norman C. Thomas, *Education in National Politics* (New York: David McKay, 1975), 22–3.
36. Frank J. Munger and Richard F. Fenno, Jr., *National Politics and Federal Aid to Education* (Syracuse, NY: Syracuse University Press, 1962), 71.
37. Ibid., 54–65.
38. *Education for a Nation*, 45.
39. Quoted in James L. Sundquist, *Politics and Policy: The Eisenhower, Kennedy and Johnson Years* (Washington, DC: Brookings, 1968), 155.
40. Ibid., 179.
41. Ibid., 211–2.
42. Ibid., 212–3.
43. *Education for a Nation*, 69.
44. Quoted in Sundquist, *Politics and Policy*, 215.
45. *Congressional Quarterly Almanac, 1978* (Washington, DC, Congressional Quarterly, 1979), 560. In 1980, the Department of Education issued final regulations requiring schools with non-English-speaking students to provide bilingual education. The measure stimulated considerable congressional opposition, and in February 1981, Reagan's education secretary, Terrel H. Bell, called the regulations "harsh, inflexible, burdensome, unworkable and incredibly costly," and singled them out as the sort of over-regulation the Reagan administration had pledged to end. *Congressional Quarterly Almanac, 1980* (Washington, DC: Congressional Quarterly, 1981), 469–70.
46. *Congressional Quarterly Almanac, 1975,* (Washington, DC: Congressional Quarterly, 1976), 661–5.
47. Thomas, *Education in National Politics*, 74–9.

48. *Congressional Quarterly Almanac, 1975,* 592–4.

49. *Congressional Quarterly Almanac, 1981,* (Washington, DC: Congressional Quarterly, 1982), 499–502.

50. *Congressional Quarterly Almanac, 1982,* (Washington, DC: Congressional Quarterly, 1983), 486–7; *Congressional Quarterly Almanac, 1983,* (Washington, DC: Congressional Quarterly, 1984), 400.

51. U.S. General Accounting Office, *Education Block Grant Alters State Role and Provides Greater Local Discretion,* GAO Report HRD-85-18 (Washington, DC: GPO, 1984), v.

52. Peterson et al., *When Federalism Works,* 146.

53. Ibid.

54. U.S. Office of Management and Budget, *Historical Tables, Budget of the United States Government, Fiscal Year 1989* (Washington, DC: GPO, 1988), Table 3.3.

55. Peterson et al., *When Federalism Works,* 48; U.S. Office of Management and Budget, *Budget of the United States Government, Fiscal Year 1987* (Washington, DC: GPO, 1986), 5–87; U.S. Office of Management and Budget, *Budget of the United States Government, Fiscal Year 1989* (Washington, DC: GPO, 1988), 5–95.

56. U.S. Congressional Budget Office, *Trends in Educational Achievement* (Washington, DC: GPO, 1986), 150.

57. Ibid., 79.

58. U.S. Congressional Budget Office, *Educational Achievement: Explanations and Implications of Recent Trends* (Washington, DC: GPO, 1987), 94–5.

59. Ibid., 96.

60. Joel S. Berke and Michael Kirst, *Federal Aid to Education: Who Benefits? Who Governs?* (Lexington, MA.: Lexington Books, 1972), 22, 385.

61. Charles S. Benson, *The Economics of Public Education* (Boston: Houghton Mifflin, 1961), 171–4.

62. National Center for Education Statistics, *Digest of Education Statistics, 1981* (Washington, DC: National Center for Education Statistics, 1981), 75.

63. Patricia Brown and Richard Elmore, "Analyzing the Impact of School Finance Reform," in Nelda Cambron-McCabe and Allan Odden, eds., *The Changing Politics of School Finance* (Cambridge, MA: Ballinger, 1982), 107–8.

64. Kent McGuire and Van Dougherty, *School Finance at a Glance, 1983–1984* (wall chart) (Denver, CO: Education Finance Center, Education Commission of the States, 1984); John Augenblick, "The Current Status of School Financing Reform," in Van Mueller and Mary McKeown, eds., *The Fiscal, Legal, and Political Aspects of State Reform of Elementary and Secondary Education* (Cambridge, MA: Ballinger, 1986), 12–3; Jonathan Friendly, "Efforts Are Failing to Close Gaps Separating Rich and Poor Schools," *New York Times,* 19 February 1985, 1.

65. Tyll van Geel, "The Courts and School Finance Reform: An Expected Utility Model," in Cambron-McCabe and Odden, eds., *The Changing Politics of School Finance,* 71–4.

66. Walter I. Garns, James W. Guthrie, and Lawrence C. Pierce, *School Finance: The Economics and Politics of Public Education* (Englewood Cliffs, NJ: Prentice-Hall, 1978), 341–5.

67. James W. Guthrie, ed., *School Finance: Policies and Practices* (Cambridge, MA: Ballinger, 1980), 11–2, 37–8.

68. Ibid., 39–40.

69. *School Finance Reform in the States: 1979* (Denver, CO: Education Finance Center, Education Commission of the States, 1979), 15–6.

70. Diane Massell and Michael Kirst, "State Policymaking for Educational Excellence: School Reform in California," in Mueller and McKeown, *The Fiscal, Legal, and Political Aspects of State Reform,* 128.

71. Ibid.

72. Robert Reinhold, "School Reform: 4 Years of Tumult, Mixed Results," *New York Times*, 10 August 1987, 1.

73. Stephen J. Carroll, *The Search for Equity in School Finance: Results from Five States* (Santa Monica, CA: Rand, 1979).

74. John Augenblick, *Assessing the Equity of Missouri's School Finance System: A Report to the Missouri Department of Elementary and Secondary Education and the School Finance Review Committee* (Denver, CO: Augenblick, Van de Water & Assoc., 1987), 2–3.

75. Ibid., 5.

76. Ibid., 58. A study of midwestern states by the Mid Continent Regional Educational Laboratory found generally greater variations in revenues and expenditures between school districts than Augenblick found in Missouri. See *Policy Notes*, Spring 1987 (Aurora, CO: Mid-Continental Regional Educational Laboratory).

77. Friendly, "Efforts Are Failing to Close Gaps Separating Rich and Poor Schools."

78. Edward Fiske, "All at Once Everyone Is Worried About Schools," *New York Times*, 8 May 1983, 8EY.

79. Ibid.

80. Robert Lindsey, "School Desegregation Is Sent to the Back of the Bus," *New York Times*, 30 August 1981.

81. William Freivogel, "Justice Dept. Wants to End Busing for Desegregation," *St. Louis Post-Dispatch*, 26 September 1982, 1.

82. "U.S. Rights Panel Is Critical of Reagan Education Policies," *New York Times*, 8 December 1982.

83. Reinhold, "School Reform."

84. Ibid.

85. Edward Fiske, "Report Warns School Reforms May Fall Short," *New York Times*, 24 August 1987, 1.

86. Quotation from the Carnegie Forum's Task Force on Teaching As a Profession, excerpted in *The Chronicle of Higher Education*, 32:12(1986), 44. The complete quotation is: "From the first days of the Republic, education has been recognized as the foundation of a democratic society for the nation and the individual alike."

87. Ibid.

Chapter 9

NATIONAL URBAN POLICY: UNDERWRITING SEGREGATION AND FRAGMENTATION

THE POLITICS OF SEGREGATION IN URBAN AREAS

The unequal distribution of political and economic resources in American society is imposed in a complicated mosaic on its metropolitan areas. Racial discrimination and social class inequality stands out in the contrast between all-minority and all-white neighborhoods, and between dilapidated rows of houses in central city slums, and new suburbs. The political fragmentation of governments in urban areas underwrites and intensifies racial and social class segregation and operates as a redistribution mechanism that benefits affluent individuals and groups.

Metropolitan fragmentation is the logical outcome of policies that state legislatures enacted beginning in the nineteenth century. Virtually from the constitutional period, state legislatures meticulously circumscribed both the legal powers of cities as political units and the influence of city electorates in state politics. Even after "home rule" charters gave cities more autonomy during the Progressive Era, cities continued to be underrepresented in state capitals and they were confronted by state laws that made suburban incorporation easy but annexation by central cities difficult. Metropolitan fragmentation inevitably resulted.

The incorporation of wealthy and middle-class suburbs beyond the boundaries of the cities permitted their residents to cordon themselves off from the central cities, mainly through the adoption of restrictive zoning laws. Poor people, recent immigrants, and minorities always have been segregated within the old industrial cities, but since World War II their segregation has been reinforced by a complex political system that allows affluent suburbanites to minimize their share of the

279

financial burden of attending to the needs of the less privileged groups in society.

Unlike urban policies in other Western nations, national policy in the United States reflected and underwrote segregation and political fragmentation in urban areas. National policy took on this character because policymakers responded to the multitude of different constituencies representing (or represented by) local governments. Some policies were designed to "save" central cities, but other well-funded policies had the effect of accelerating the movement of people out of the cities to the suburbs and depressing land values in the urban core. Policies promoting governmental fragmentation and decentralization gained political support, in part, because they gave political expression to the idea that government should be close to the people:

> The dogma of local self-government is enshrined in our Constitution and laws; a federal system divides powers among thousands of counties, townships, municipalities, and other local units . . . In order to survive, the modern metropolis is thus forced to create a staggering number of special district governments . . . It is free enterprise in government—with every municipality, every district for itself . . . If there is a political explanation of why we fail to come to grips with the problems of community welfare and metropolitan planning, it is here, in the tyranny of the locality, made possible by federalism.[1]

The multitude of local governments in metropolitan areas stand in the way of policies that might (for example) equalize service delivery, desegregate schools, or equalize tax rates. Any concept of metropolitan-wide planning and policymaking would necessarily confront issues of segregation and inequality. But such a process would conflict with the express purpose and with the effect of political fragmentation.

CITIES AS CREATURES OF THE STATES

In American law, cities have been treated mainly as legal and administrative creations of state governments and are not mentioned in the Constitution. In the nation's early years state legislatures carefully began to limit the governmental power of cities. Anti-city attitudes motivated state legislators. This bias against cities derived from a culture in which the small farm epitomized individual independence and moral rectitude. For most Americans the city symbolized political corruption, vice, and foreign influence. Most citizens would have agreed with the opinion expressed by a delegate to a New York State constitutional convention that "the average citizen in the rural district is superior in intelligence, superior in morality, superior in self-government to the average citizen of the great cities."[2]

State legislatures, composed mostly of representatives from rural areas, were convinced that the people living in cities would soon govern the states if they were not kept in check. To accomplish this, Maine's Constitutional Convention of 1819 established a ceiling on the number of legislators who could represent towns in the state legislature. In 1845, the Louisiana legislature limited New Orleans to 12.5 percent of the state's senators and 10 percent of the state's assemblymen (New Orleans's population then was 20 percent of the state's total).[3] In Georgia, each county was represented equally in the legislature regardless of its population.[4] Louisiana provided that each parish would have at least one representative in the state senate and house, no matter what its population, and Rhode Island applied this standard to each town.[5] No matter how large the cities became, rural legislative districts in every state would continue to hold a controlling legislative majority in the state capitols.

State legislatures also took other measures to assert direct control over the cities. Beginning in the 1850s, state legislative committees or governors controlled the police departments of Detroit, Baltimore, Boston, St. Louis, Kansas City, and New York City. Legislative committees sometimes governed every detail of municipal service and expenditure, from the construction, paving, and naming of streets and the buying of land for parks to the awarding of sewer contracts.

The political control of cities became an even more urgent matter when immigrants flooded into them, setting off a period of frenetic urban growth. Between 1820 and 1920, 33.5 million immigrants arrived on American shores, most of them settling into a few big cities. By 1870, more than half the population of at least twenty American cities were foreign-born or were children of foreign parents,[6] but the biggest flood of immigrants was yet to come. Between 1870 and 1920, 26 million immigrants poured into the industrial and port cities. Often, first-generation immigrants and their children accounted for three-fourths or more of all residents of big cities. In 1910, the fifty largest cities averaged 29 percent first-generation foreign-born.[7] The immigrant floodtide was stemmed only by restrictive national legislation adopted in 1921 and in 1924.

Individual cities grew extraordinarily fast. In 1820 New York City's population was 137,000; it neared 1.2 million by 1860, surpassed 3.4 million at the turn of the century, and exceeded 5.6 million by the 1920 census. Chicago went from a frontier village of 445 people in 1840 to over 112,000 by 1860, and it grew to 2.7 million people by the 1920 census.[8] Other port and industrial cities grew at similar rates.

Such population growth made it necessary for cities constantly to expand urban services. Frequent cholera and yellow fever epidemics forced local governments to supply water and sewage services, since disease could not be isolated to the immigrant wards. Crime rates soared, prompting demands for better police protection. Cities built bridges and streets, created modern fire and police departments, constructed waterworks, and laid sewer pipes. After the 1890s, cities contracted with private companies for gas and electric lights, electric streetcars, and telephones. Clearly, the city governments were indispensable. But state legislatures severely restricted their ability to tax, organize and expand new services, and borrow money.

When cities challenged state control, state and federal courts consistently upheld the authority of the states. In 1819, in the *Dartmouth College* case, the U.S. Supreme Court held that cities were creatures of the states and that states could amend or rescind their powers at will.[9] In 1868, an Iowa magistrate, Judge John F. Dillon, made the doctrine of state control of cities very explicit:

> Municipal corporations owe their origin to, and derive their powers and rights wholly from, the legislature. It breathes into them the breath of life without which they cannot exist. As it creates so it may destroy. If it may destroy, it may abridge and control. Unless there is some constitutional limitation on the right, the legislature might, by a single act, if we can suppose it capable of so great a folly and so great a wrong, sweep from existence all of the municipal corporations of the state, and the corporations could not prevent it. We know of no limitation on the right so far as the corporations themselves are concerned. They are, so to phrase it, the mere tenants at will of the legislature.[10]

This doctrine later became the basic legal fact of life for cities everywhere, and it became enshrined in municipal government textbooks as "Dillon's rule."

States still delegate self-government to cities in increments, even though cities in most states were granted home rule charters in the early years of the twentieth century. Almost all states limit city options for choosing political structure, personnel practices, and financial operations. For example, most western states require nonpartisan elections and council-manager governments for smaller and middle-size cities.

Most states constrain local governments' ability to raise and spend money: forty-six of them impose limits on local government debt, and thirty-nine states limit local tax rates. Cities in most states are required to end the year with a balanced operating budget. Three states still require local governments to submit their budgets for approval by a state oversight body. Local governments in most states are allowed to levy regressive property and sales taxes with restrictions on overall rates and the

amount of increase allowed each year. Only eleven states permit localities to levy income taxes (and 87 percent of the local governments that
levy income taxes are in Pennsylvania).[11]

Cities would have been more successful in obtaining financial assistance from states for the expansion of urban services, and they would
have been freed from many restrictions, if their influence in state legislatures had grown in step with their populations. But without exception,
rural districts were guaranteed control over the legislatures of all the
states, and statewide political parties reflected this imbalance. Rural
elites firmly controlled the party caucuses that nominated governors,
congressmen, or senators. As a result, immigrants and labor unions that
favored the regulation of business or more governmental services had
no effective means of influencing government policies, at either the state
or national levels. Underrepresentation of urban areas resulted in in-
difference to the problems faced by big cities in state legislatures, governors' offices, Congress, and the White House. Traffic congestion,
slums, inadequate park space, sewage problems, smoke pollution, and
other urban problems did not interest rural and small-town legislators or
a Congress or president beholden to state party leaders representing
rural constituents.

In the cities, underrepresentation all through the federal system had
profound consequences, for the social conditions connected to poverty
went untreated. But the political effects flowed the other way as well. It
is certain that states would have been more supportive of social welfare
program innovations and services for urban dwellers if city populations
had been able to influence politics beyond their borders commensurate
with their potential voting strength. National politics would have been
transformed in a similar way. National involvement in the economy and
in the everyday welfare of citizens might have occurred decades earlier
than it did if this single aspect of American federalism—intentional
political impotence for cities—had not existed.

The federal courts finally moved against legislative malapportionment
in the 1960s, more than forty years after the 1920 census showed that a
majority of Americans lived in "urban places" of twenty-five hundred or
more. In the 1962 case of *Baker* v. *Carr,* a group of Knoxville, Tennessee
residents challenged the fact that the Tennessee legislature had not been
reapportioned since 1901.[12] Their lawyers argued that citizens living in
urban areas were being deprived of "equal protection of the law," as
guaranteed by the Fourteenth Amendment to the U.S. Constitution. A
federal district court dismissed the suit, claiming that the federal courts
lacked jurisdiction. But subsequently, the U.S. Supreme Court ruled
that federal courts did indeed have jurisdiction over such cases. The
important subsequent decision came on June 15, 1964, when the Supreme Court, in *Reynolds* v. *Sims,* ruled that state legislative apportion-

ments must follow a "one man-one vote" principle.[13] Within a few years, for the first time in the nation's history, state legislative districts were apportioned on the basis of population.

Ironically, these decisions benefited suburbs more than the big cities. Though the shift in apportionment aided *metropolitan* representation, it came after twenty years of rapid suburban expansion outside the boundaries of the central cities. Thus representatives from suburban jurisdictions became increasingly powerful in state legislatures.[14] The apportionment decisions came twenty years too late to empower city electorates.

The Isolation of the Central Cities in Metropolitan Areas

Through much of the period of their rapid growth, American cities expanded their boundaries outward by annexing new land. But even in the nineteenth century, state legislatures eased the chartering requirements for villages and towns that found themselves in the path of the encroaching cities. Unincorporated communities at the edges of big cities used state statutes to charter themselves and to prevent their own annexation. As early as the 1840s, Boston was ringed by a profusion of independent jurisdictions. Already in the 1850s, there were more than fifty separate settlements around Chicago, and though many of these were subsequently absorbed by the city of Chicago, some of them remained independent.

With the rise of the political party machines and the immigrant influx after the 1870s, upper- and middle-class urban dwellers increasingly fled the cities with the intent of isolating themselves from the noise and crowding of city life. To assure their separation, the new suburban dwellers formed independent towns and villages. When New York City annexed parts of Westchester County in the 1870s and again in the 1890s, for example, subdivisions in the path of the city's expansion quickly incorporated themselves to preserve their political independence.

At the edges of all the big cities, the incorporation of municipalities proceeded rapidly from the 1890s to the Great Depression. In 1890 Cook County, Illinois, whose principal city is Chicago, had 55 governments. By 1920 it had 109 governments. Similarly, the number of general-purpose governments in the New York City area grew from 127 in 1900 to 204 in 1920. There were 91 incorporated municipalities in the Pittsburgh area in 1890 but 107 in 1920.[15]

In most of the urbanized states, the "rules of the game" were biased toward suburbanization. Some states added to the central cities' problems by requiring that they provide services to newly incorporated communities at central city rates.[16] No state tried to control or even to keep track of new incorporations.

In the 1920s the pace of suburban growth quickened. For the first time in the nation's history, the number of people moving to the suburbs exceeded the number moving into the central cities (see Table 9.1). Areas just beyond city boundaries had been growing at a faster rate than cities for a couple of decades, but this did not seem to be a threatening development, since the cities continued to grow so rapidly themselves. Cities always had been teeming with new immigrants.

During the depression years, the cities' fortunes declined precipitously. Many of them even lost population. Though the Great Depression sharply reduced movement to the suburbs, it even more drastically slowed central city population growth. The depression signaled the twilight of the city-building era in the older cities that had benefited from post-Civil War industrial expansion. As shown in Table 9.1, Boston, St. Louis, and Cleveland all lost population in the 1930s. So did Philadelphia, Kansas City, and the New Jersey cities—Elizabeth, Paterson, Jersey City, and Newark. San Francisco, which had grown by 27 percent in the 1920s, was no bigger in 1940 than it was in 1930. A great many small manufacturing cities of New England and the Midwest declined in population—Akron and Youngstown, Ohio; Albany, Schenectady, and Troy, New York; Joplin, Missouri; and New Bedford, Massachusetts.

The Great Depression affected the suburbs as well as the cities. Private industry provided neither the incentive nor the means for a suburban exodus at the 1920s rate. The growth rate of New York's suburbs fell to 18 percent for 1930–1940, compared with 67 percent for 1920–1930; Chicago's suburban expansion slowed from 74 percent to 10 percent; Cleveland's from 126 percent to 13 percent; and Los Angeles' from 158 percent to 30 percent.

It seemed likely that once the economy recovered, residential development beyond the boundaries of the cities would accelerate and the older central cities would grow slowly, if at all. The depression, however, was followed by an imposition of new constraints. During World War II, because construction materials were commandeered for wartime use and soldiers of marriageable age were sent abroad, suburban development nearly halted. After the war ended, suburbanization resumed. While the cities added just over six million people to their populations during the 1940s, their suburbs gained over nine million people. These numbers were but a portent of things to come, for the 1950s and 1960s witnessed an unprecedented suburban boom.

Between 1950 and 1960, central cities averaged an 11 percent increase in their populations (see Table 9.2). In comparison, the suburbs of these cities grew by 49 percent—nineteen million more people lived in the suburbs by the end of the decade, compared with just six million more

Table 9.1. *Population movements in areas of the United States, 1900–1940*

Districts	1900–1910 Central City	1900–1910 Outside Central City	1910–1920 Central City	1910–1920 Outside Central City	1920–1930 Central City	1920–1930 Outside Central City	1930–1940 Central City	1930–1940 Outside Central City
New York City[a]	38.7% (1,329,681)	60.9% (91,636)	17.9% (835,165)	35.2% (98,692)	23.3% (1,310,398)	67.3% (424,785)	7.6% (524,549)	18.2% (193,291)
Chicago	28.7 (486,708)	87.7 (122,226)	23.4 (512,185)	79.1 (210,797)	24.9 (673,292)	73.9 (419,906)	0.6 (20,370)	10.4 (104,214)
Boston	19.6 (109,693)	23.4 (161,273)	9.0 (61,968)	21.2 (179,148)	4.4 (33,128)	21.2 (267,344)	-1.3 (10,372)	3.1 (47,741)
St. Louis	19.4 (111,791)	90.6 (67,357)	12.5 (85,868)	26.4 (37,412)	6.7 (56,643)	71.3 (165,344)	-0.7 (5,912)	15.7 (74,896)
Cleveland	46.0 (176,492)	46.5 (16,698)	40.1 (227,978)	140.0 (75,171)	11.8 (95,007)	125.8 (164,128)	-2.7 (24,135)	13.0 (38,824)
Los Angeles	206.1 (214,932)	553.3 (100,232)	80.7 (257,475)	107.6 (156,692)	114.7 (661,375)	157.9 (661,548)	21.3 (263,918)	30.1 (324,138)
Mean for all metro districts	33.6%	38.2%	25.2% (5,385,116)	32.0% (2,236,795)	20.9% (5,851,909)	46.4% (4,819,770)	4.4% (1,498,186)	13.6% (2,086,607)
Nonmetro population increase	16.4%		9.6%		9.5%		7.2%	
Total U.S. population increase	21.0		14.9		16.1		7.2	

[a]Includes growth of population in New York City proper and in satellite areas of New York State. New Jersey population is excluded.

Note: Increases in population expressed as percent growth and number of people added (in parentheses).

Source: U.S. Department of Commerce, Bureau of the Census, *The Growth of Metropolitan Districts in the United States, 1900–1904,* by Warren S. Thompson (Washington, DC: GPO, 1947), especially Table 2.

Table 9.2. *Population movements in areas of the United States, 1920–1980*

Some Large Districts	1940–1950 Central City	1940–1950 Outside Central City	1950–1960 Central City	1950–1960 Outside Central City	1960–1970 Central City	1960–1970 Outside Central City	1970–1980 Central City	1970–1980 Outside Central City	1980 % Population in Central City
Frostbelt									
New York City	5.9%	23.2%	-1.4%	75.0%	1.5%	26.0%	-10.4%	0.4%[a]	77.1%
Chicago	6.6	31.2	-2.0	71.5	-5.2	35.3	-10.8	13.6	42.1
Boston	4.0	11.5	-13.0	17.7	-8.1	11.3	-12.2	-2.6	20.3
St. Louis	5.0	33.8	-12.5	50.8	-17.0	28.5	-27.2	6.3	19.2
Cleveland	4.2	41.6	-4.2	67.3	-14.3	27.1	-23.6	0.4	30.3
Detroit	13.9	54.8	-9.7	79.3	-9.5	28.5	-20.5	7.8	27.6
Pittsburgh	0.8	8.9	-10.7	17.2	-13.9	4.4	-18.5	-2.2	18.7
Minneapolis	6.0	76.2	-7.5	115.7	-10.0	55.9	-14.6	20.6	17.5
Mean for all SMSAs	14.0	35.9	10.7	48.6	6.4	26.8	0.1	18.2	
Number added	6,021,074	9,199,931	6,251,181	19,081,702	3,849,814	15,974,243		80,054	15,631,197
Nonmetro population increase	6.1%		7.1%		6.8%		15.1		
Total U.S. population increase	14.5		18.5		13.3		11.4		

[a]Nassau and Suffolk counties were deleted from New York City SMSA in 1971 but have been included here for purposes of comparability. The actual "outside central city" figure for the revised New York City SMSA is -1.4.

Note: Increases in population expressed as percent growth and number of people added.

Source: U.S. Department of Commerce, Bureau of the Census, *1950 Census of Population,* vol. 1, *Number of Inhabitants,* pt. 1 (Washington, DC: GPO, 1952), 69, Table 17; *1970 Census of Population,* vol. 1, *Characteristics of the Population,* pt. A, 180, Table 34; and *1980 Census of Population,* Supplementary Reports, *Standard Metropolitan Statistical Areas and Standard Consolidated Statistical Areas,* 2, Table B, 6, Table 1, and 49, Table 3.

people in the cities. Most of the big cities in the Northeast and Midwest lost population because they were locked into their previous boundaries, surrounded by incorporated suburban jurisdictions.

These trends accelerated in the 1960s. Central cities across the nation *on the average* grew by 6 percent, but the average was deceptive. Older industrial cities suffered disasterous population declines: St. Louis lost 17 percent, Cleveland 14 percent, and Minneapolis 20 percent. All across the nation affluent people continued to flee the cities. In this decade the suburbs grew by almost sixteen million people.

The long-term decline of the old industrial cities continued in the 1970s. National economic development and population movement favored suburbs, smaller towns, and cities in areas outside the Northeast and Midwest. Virtually all the big cities in the North experienced huge population losses, St. Louis declining by 27 percent, Pittsburgh by 18.5 percent, and Detroit by 20.5 percent. By 1980 only a small proportion of the metropolitan populations of most northern and midwestern urban areas lived within the central cities—less than 20 percent for St. Louis, Pittsburgh, and Minneapolis (see the right-hand column of Table 9.2).

Throughout the period of population movement to the urban fringe, the older industrial cities found it difficult or impossible to expand their boundaries to encompass new population growth, since they were already substantially surrounded by independently incorporated jurisdictions and state laws made it easy for residential subdivisions beyond the cities' boundaries to incorporate themselves. The result was that hundreds of municipalities and special-purpose districts were created in metropolitan areas. The extent of the fragmentation can be appreciated by examining Table 9.3. For the twenty large metropolitan areas shown in the table, there were an average of 401 local governmental units in 1980 but for the Philadelphia area there were 1,194 governments and in and around Pittsburgh there were 739 governments.

Fragmentation and Racial Segregation

The political fragmentation of metropolitan areas sharpened patterns of social class and racial segregation. Throughout American history, there has been a tendency for affluent people of old-immigrant stock (who called themselves "native Americans") to try to segregate themselves from immigrants. After World War II, the new immigrants, blacks, were walled off in the inner cities by the suburbs. By the 1960s, old central cities held millions of low-income minorities in ghettos of dilapidated housing, riddled with crime, poverty, and other social pathologies. Surrounding the cities were nearly all-white, relatively affluent suburbs willing to use all the means at their disposal to preserve their racial and social class character.

Table 9.3. *Local government and population statistics for the twenty largest U.S. metropolitan areas, 1980*

Metropolitan Area	1980	Number of Local Government Units	Units of Local Government per 100,000 population[a]	Population Served per Unit of Local Government[a]
New York	9,120,346	352	3.9	25,910
Los Angeles	7,477,503	276	3.7	27,092
Chicago	7,103,624	1,194	16.8	5,949
Philadelphia	4,716,818	867	18.4	5,440
Detroit	4,353,413	345	7.9	12,619
San Francisco	3,250,630	331	10.2	9,821
Washington, DC	3,060,922	95	3.1	32,220
Dallas-Fort Worth	2,974,805	392	13.2	7,589
Houston	2,905,353	622	21.4	4,671
Boston	2,763,357	337[b]	9.2[b]	10,869[b]
Nassau-Suffolk, NY	2,605,813	369	14.1	7,062
St. Louis	2,356,460	663	28.1	3,554
Pittsburgh	2,263,894	739	32.7	3,063
Baltimore	2,174,023	49	2.2	44,368
Minneapolis	2,113,533	424	20.1	4,985
Atlanta	2,029,710	175	8.7	11,598
Newark	1,965,969	279	14.2	7,046
Anaheim, Santa Ana & Garden Grove, CA	1,932,709	128	6.6	15.099
Cleveland	1,898,825	217	11.4	8,750
San Diego	1,861,846	169	9.1	11,017
Average		401	12.8	12,936

[a]Figures are calculated.

[b]Boston governmental data are for the consolidated metropolitan area of 3,662,832. Calculations are figured on that population base.

Sources: 1980 U.S. *Census of Population;* 1982 U.S. *Census of Governments.* Compiled by: Richard H. Patton, Center for Metropolitan Studies, University of Missouri-St. Louis, September 1985.

In the thirty years between 1940 and 1970, more than four million southern blacks moved to northern cities, most prompted to move by the prospect of better jobs. From Texas and Louisiana, blacks streamed into cities of the West, especially California; from the middle South, hundreds of thousands moved to St. Louis, Chicago, Detroit, and the cities of the Midwest; and from Mississippi eastward in the Deep South, blacks moved to the cities along the eastern seaboard. In 1940, 77 percent of the nation's blacks still lived in the southern states (compared with 87 percent in 1910). By 1950, only 60 percent of the country's blacks lived in the South, and in the next two decades the South's share declined to 56 percent (1960) and to 53 percent (1970).[17] Nearly all of the northward-bound migrants ended up in the cities. According to the 1970 census, 90 percent of all the blacks who lived outside Standard Metropolitan Statistical Areas were located in the South.

For most of the twelve cities shown in Table 9.4, the strongest surge in black population occurred between 1950 and 1970. Many white families stayed in the cities until the suburban housing boom, following the Korean War. Thus, although the proportion of black residents climbed during the 1940s in all of the cities except St. Louis, the increase understated the extent of the migration. With the movement of white families to the suburbs that occurred later, black proportions of central cities' populations shot up dramatically, to over 72 percent in Washington, D.C., by 1970, to 47 percent in Cleveland, and to over 41 percent in St. Louis. Not until the 1970s did blacks move into the suburbs in increasing numbers.

The suburbs exploded in population—and remained mostly white. The number of blacks in the suburbs increased 1.5 million between 1950 and 1970, but the number of suburban whites increased by 33.5 million. Thus, the proportion of suburbanites who were black changed little, increasing for all metropolitan areas from 4.5 percent to 4.9 percent during the 1960s.[18] Of the twelve metropolitan areas shown in Table 9.4, only the St. Louis and Washington, D.C. suburbs were even slightly less than 90 percent white in 1980.

These statistics understate the degree of racial segregation in metropolitan areas. Within the cities, blacks remained segregated from whites, and this was the case in the suburbs as well. Most suburbs have very few blacks. Within suburban communities that have black populations, the black areas usually comprise distinct enclaves. A study using 1970 data found that in Orange County, California, 70 percent of the black population lived in one town, Santa Ana. Three towns in northern New Jersey held 89 percent of Essex County's suburban black residents. More than 80 percent of the Chicago area's black suburbanites lived in 15 of 237 suburban municipalities.[19] In the Detroit area, blacks constituted over 4 percent of the population in only 7 of 65 suburbs.[20] Such suburbs are not integrated in any meaningful sense.

Many of these communities border on the central cities, in areas where the housing is older and less sound than that of newer, more distant suburbs. Blacks who moved to the suburbs in the 1960s had higher incomes, better education, and higher-status jobs than inner-city blacks.[21] But income is only one barrier that keeps blacks out of suburban communities—and, in fact, income is not nearly as important as racial prejudice. A much higher proportion of poor whites than poor blacks have been able to locate in the suburbs.[22]

Table 9.4. *Percentage of blacks in central cities and suburban rings in twelve selected SMSAs, 1940–1980*

	Central City					Suburban Ring				
	1940	1950	1960	1970	1980	1940	1950	1960	1970	1980
All 12 SMSAs	9.0	13.7	21.4	30.8	32.6	3.9	4.4	4.4	6.0	7.4[a]
New York	6.4	9.8	14.7	23.4	25.2	4.6	4.5	4.8	6.4	6.8[a]
Los Angeles-Long Beach	6.0	9.8	15.3	21.2	16.4	2.3	2.7	4.1	7.4	9.6
Chicago	8.3	14.1	23.6	34.4	39.8	2.2	2.9	3.1	4.1	5.6
Philadelphia	13.1	18.3	26.7	34.4	37.8	6.6	6.6	0.3	7.1	8.1
Detroit	9.3	16.4	29.2	44.0	63.1	2.9	5.0	3.8	4.0	4.2
San Francisco-Oakland	4.9	11.8	21.1	32.7	24.1	3.6	6.8	6.8	9.4	6.5
Boston	3.3	12.3	9.8	18.2	22.4	0.9	0.8	1.0	1.6	1.6
Pittsburgh	9.3	18.0	16.8	27.0	24.0	3.6	3.5	3.4	3.6	4.0
St. Louis	13.4	5.3	28.8	41.3	45.6	6.7	7.3	6.3	7.7	10.6
Washington, D.C.	28.5	35.4	54.8	72.3	76.6	13.7	8.7	6.4	9.1	16.7
Cleveland	9.7	16.3	28.9	39.0	43.8	0.9	0.8	0.8	1.1	7.1
Baltimore	19.4	23.8	35.0	47.0	54.8	11.9	10.2	6.9	6.2	9.1

[a]This figure includes data from the Nassau-Suffolk SMSA, which was deleted from the New York City SMSA in 1971. These data are included to maintain comparability across time periods. The suburban ring figure for the redefined New York SMSA is 7.6%; the figure for all twelve SMSAs is 7.5%.

Source: Adapted from Leo F. Schnore, Carolyn D. André', and Harry Sharp, "Black Suburbanization, 1930–1970," in Barry Schwartz ed., *The Changing Face of the Suburbs,* (Chicago: University of Chicago Press, 1976), 80. Reprinted by permission. These figures were transposed to yield data on black percentages. 1980 data from U.S. Department of Commerce, Buruea of the Census, *1980 Census of Population,* Supplementary Reports, *Standard Metropolitan Statistical Areas and Standard Consolidated Statistical Areas* (Washington, DC: GPO, 1981), 3, Table 1.

291

The blacks in suburban communities either have about the same social status as their white neighbors or are middle-class blacks settled in moderate numbers in upper-income white suburbs.[23] In the Detroit area in 1960, only 11 percent of poor black families lived in the suburbs, but 45 percent of poor white families were suburbanites. A similar pattern existed in all of the ten largest metropolitan areas.[24] Essentially the same relationships still existed at the time of the 1980 census, when more than 60 percent of all poor white families in metropolitan areas lived outside the central cities but only 12 percent of poor black families lived in suburbs. These statistics seem to suggest that racial as opposed to social class discrimination is still important for explaining patterns of segregation. For the most part, white suburbs remain white. Black suburban growth is not (in the main) integration into the suburbs, but central city segregation spilling beyond city boundaries.

ZONING: KEEPING OUT THE "UNDESIRABLES"

Independent general-purpose governments multiplied outside the cities because incorporation of homogeneous suburbs permitted their residents to exclude people of certain social classes, ethnic groups and races.[25] For more than half a century, zoning has been the central strategy for preserving the racial and social composition of the suburbs. Through zoning laws, communities are able to regulate the uses of land within their boundaries, making it difficult or impossible for "undesirables" to find housing in their community. The list of "undesirables" has changed from time to time (though it seems always to have applied to blacks), and sometimes it differs from one jurisdiction to another.

The nation's first zoning law was enacted in New York City on July 25, 1916. By the end of the 1920s, 768 municipalities with 60 percent of the nation's urban population had enacted zoning ordinances.[26] As pointed out by Seymour Toll, "That such a swift spread of law could occur despite the intricate processes of many state legislatures and hundreds of local governments is at least statistically extraordinary."[27] Quick adoption all across the nation, despite the complexity of the federal system, was made possible by the unanimity of real estate interests in advancing the concept that zoning was a useful tool for protecting valuable land against uses that might lower land values. In state after state, real estate groups and politicians lobbied for state laws enabling local governments to zone property within their borders.

New York City's zoning ordinance had been prompted by fears that fashionable sections of Fifth Avenue might be invaded by loft buildings from the Garment District on the West Side. The Garment District, characterized by clusters of tall loft buildings that employed thousands of poorly paid immigrant seamstresses and cart-pushers, threatened to destroy the exclusive shopping district of upper Fifth Avenue. The Fifth Avenue Association, composed of wealthy retail merchants and landowners, lobbied the city to exclude tall loft buildings from their district. At first they sought restrictions only on building height, but they soon proposed carving Manhattan into distinct-zoned areas.

New York's law specified five zones, the distinctions based on the different uses and values of land. In the zoning pecking order, residential uses assumed first place, followed by business districts. Warehouses and industries were allotted last place. Zoning laws subsequently adopted elsewhere followed a similar logic. Following New York City's enactment of its zoning law, New York officials and business spokesmen launched a national campaign to promote similar laws in other cities and to get enabling legislation passed in other states. Most cities virtually copied the New York ordinance. By 1920, ten states had passed enabling legislation. Nine more states were added in 1921.[28] A majority of states had acted by the time a legal challenge to zoning reached the U.S. Supreme Court in 1926.

Encouraged by business' unanimous support, the federal government gave its blessings to this movement. Herbert Hoover, then Secretary of Commerce, established a committee to draft model legislation to guide the states in writing enabling statutes that would delegate state police powers to municipalities.[29] By the time the committee completed its work in 1924 by producing the Standard State Zoning Enabling Act, 218 municipalities representing twenty-two million residents had adopted zoning.[30]

In a landmark 1926 decision, the Supreme Court declared that zoning was a proper use of the police powers of municipalities.[31] The Court's decision was remarkable in light of its typical decisions in the period, when it almost always struck down any expansion of government powers that seemed to interfere in "free market" processes. In one stroke, the court vastly expanded municipal powers.

The delegation of land use regulation by the states to local governments became virtually irreversible and impeded later efforts to bring about more coherent land use policies. In the 1970s, when attempts were made to get the states to implement statewide land use plans, local governments fought hard to retain their "borrowed" police powers. The states' actions doomed most future attempts to achieve comprehensive land use planning.

Zoning became popular at the same time that well-to-do suburbs proliferated around the large cities—Beverly Hills, Glendale, and a host of wealthy communities outside of Los Angeles; Cleveland Heights, Shaker Heights, and Garfield Heights outside Cleveland; and Oak Park,

Elmwood Park, and Park Ridge on the borders of Chicago. At the heart of zoning lay the fear of what urban life might become if movement by the poor were not controlled: the owners of property always threatened by or forced to mingle with people of "inferior" social or racial characteristics.

Zoning worked by raising the costs of housing available within a community. Most ordinances excluded apartments entirely, so that they could be built only if variances were granted. Minimum lot sizes, setback requirements, or minimum floor space requirements restricted the density and size of homes. These restrictions raised the cost of new houses, thus automatically segregating residential areas on the basis of wealth and income.

In some respects, zoning resembled the planned use of urban space. But in fact, it almost never worked as, nor was it designed to be, a planning device. First, comprehensive land use planning for a metropolitan area would obviously be impossible in the face of the various zoning laws adopted by a multitude of different jurisdictions. Second, zoning usually was adopted to protect land uses already arrived at; that is, an existing suburb or subdivision would enact an ordinance to restrict or prohibit new residential or business development that was deemed undesirable.

The constitutional status of zoning was not challenged again until the 1970s. Though zoning ordinances often were the subject of litigation in local and state courts, most suits were initiated by developers who questioned the application, rather than the constitutionality, of zoning ordinances. From 1948 to 1963, for example, 52 percent of all litigation in the local courts of suburban New York City involved zoning and land use cases.[32]

Constitutional challenges to zoning surfaced in the federal courts when civil rights organizations tried to open the suburbs to blacks who wanted to purchase homes. Zoning ordinances were also challenged when suburbs attempted to keep out developments—usually low-income apartments that would provide housing opportunities for poor blacks living in the inner cities. After several successive waves of "white flight" from the central cities, the suburbs had become almost entirely white. Upward mobility for blacks would require that they, too, move to the suburbs. But how could they move if suburban jurisdictions kept housing so expensive that it was beyond the financial reach of most middle-class blacks, and if lower-income blacks could not find housing of any kind?

The Courts

In the 1970s, attempts to forge a link between the racial effects of zoning and the civil rights movement failed. Civil rights organizations found that federal courts were reluctant to intrude on the traditional exercise of power by states and localities. In one of the first important challenges in the federal courts, a suit was brought to challenge a provision of the California constitution that allowed communities to veto low-income public housing projects if the residents voted "no" in a referendum. In San Jose and in San Mateo counties, voters had repeatedly rejected public housing projects. The litigants claimed that such rejection amounted to denial of equal protection of the laws, but the U.S. Supreme Court in 1971 upheld the referenda on the grounds that the California statute had not been specifically designed to stop low-rent public housing projects that might house minorities, for it could be applied to any housing projects, regardless of who the tenants were. Referenda aimed at the poor, and not specifically at racial minorities, could not be held to violate the U.S. Constitution.[33]

Subsequent court cases placed limits on the zoning power of municipalities. In a case from Black Jack, Missouri (a small suburb located north of St. Louis), the municipality's zoning ordinance, which prohibited the construction of a low-income housing project, was found to be unconstitutional. In its decision handed down in September 1974, the Eighth Circuit Court of Appeals rejected the litigants' arguments that the Black Jack zoning ordinance was intentionally discriminatory, but found that it had a discriminatory effect and that therefore the ordinance was unconstitutional. In June 1975, the Supreme Court refused to review the decision.[34]

Since a great many suburban zoning ordinances easily might be shown to have a racially discriminatory effect, the decision seemed to presage a challenge to exclusionary zoning laws. But a Supreme Court decision of January 11, 1977, made it clear that discriminatory zoning, in most cases, would be difficult to challenge successfully. In reviewing the zoning ordinance of Arlington Heights, Illinois, which barred a federally subsidized townhouse project from being built, the court declared that the racial impact of zoning laws could not be used as the only argument against them; rather, they had to be shown to have been enacted specifically because of a racially motivated intent: "Disproportionate impact is not irrelevant, but it is not the sole touchstone of an invidious racial discrimination."[35] In the case of Arlington Heights, the city's zoning ordinance had predated the plans for the proposed townhouse construction. If intent rather than effect had to be proved, then zoning in very few communities could ever be effectively challenged.

A few zoning ordinances have been invalidated by the courts. In 1975, the New Jersey Supreme Court struck down the zoning ordinance of Mount Laurel, a New Jersey municipality that sits close by cities with large black and Puerto Rican populations. Mount Laurel's zoning law was unusually restrictive, prohibiting anything but large single-family houses with at least four bedrooms, on large lots. Following the Court's decision, Mount Laurel amended its ordinance, but in 1983 the New Jersey Supreme Court struck that down too.

These decisions were considered resounding victories by opponents of exclusionary zoning. But standing alone, court decisions such as the Mount Laurel cases cannot change metropolitan patterns of racial and social class segregation. Municipalities can stall in the courts for years, and litigation is expensive. And zoning laws must be quite extreme, as in the case of Mount Laurel's law, for opponents to prevail.

The Executive Branch

The federal government always has been reluctant to get involved in local land use disputes, for these invariably revolve around contentious battles pitting blacks or the poor against defenders of "local democracy." The litigation initiated during the 1970s took place against the background of civil rights pressure on the Nixon administration to take a strong stand on residential integration. Exclusionary zoning had become a national issue, a symbol of suburban racial segregation.

On December 10, 1970, the National Committee Against Discrimination in Housing accused the Nixon administration of supporting the suburbs in integration conflicts. The case subsequently embroiled the administration in a public conflict over its policies regarding the suburbs. But in fact, even if the administration had been inclined to push hard for a greater degree of racial integration in urban areas, its tools would have been limited by the structure of the federal system.

There was much conflict within the Nixon administration over whether to push communities to integrate. George Romney, the Secretary of the Department of Housing and Urban Development (HUD) and his department favored housing programs to open up the suburbs. Not only did HUD seek subsidized housing in suburbs through the "Fair Share" housing program, but Romney urged the Justice Department to challenge discriminatory zoning laws such as Black Jack's.

The president sided with Attorney General John Mitchell's view that the federal government should stay out of "local" controversies. But HUD and the housing branch of the Justice Department urged the federal government to institute a suit against Black Jack for using its zoning power to block low-income housing. The president and his advisors stalled. In January, the American Civil Liberties Union (ACLU) filed suit in the Black Jack case, and the controversy was soon in the national news.

The White Houses's response to these events was not encouraging to open housing proponents. In January 1971, Nixon said, "To force integration in the suburbs, I think, is unrealistic."[36] Later, in March, Nixon said that most suburban segregation was caused by economic inequality rather than by racial discrimination. He also said that the government was not justified in breaking up communities over housing integration.[37]

The conflicts within the administration led to the assertion of stronger federal actions than might have been anticipated by Nixon's comments alone. Only three days after a presidential announcement on suburban housing, in which Nixon indicated that he sympathized with the desires of suburbanites to keep out "the social conditions of urban slum life," Secretary Romney announced that suburbs that used zoning for racial discrimination would not receive federal construction, sewer, or water grants. But on its face, such a threat did not carry much weight, since it was clearly unlikely that HUD would pick any consequential fights with suburban jurisdictions. It soon became apparent that the policy was meant for public consumption more than as a substantial change, when administration officials emphasized that federal intervention in suburban housing would be limited to cases of manifestly overt racial discrimination.[38]

The political cross-currents involved in zoning disputes make strong action by any national administration extremely unlikely. Zoning is assumed to be an exclusively local concern and responsibility. It enjoys almost sacred status as an expression of local democracy, as advocates of national land use policy learned in the early 1970s.

THE ATTEMPTS TO ACHIEVE NATIONAL LAND USE STANDARDS

For a brief time in the early 1970s, some policymakers in the national government expressed interest in overcoming the chaotic system of land use imposed by the restrictive zoning policies administered by the thousands of different jurisdictions across the United States. Civil rights pressure alone did not provide a sufficient push for national action. Concerns about environmental despoliation often involved land use issues, but these also proved insufficient to prod national political leaders to take action.

Agencies in the executive branch and some members of Congress were finally motivated to do something about the crazy quilt of local land use restrictions when corporations and the business organizations representing them complained that their search for new sites were made much more expensive and difficult by the inordinate complexity of local land use regulations. Corporations in search of industrial sites, government agencies looking for airport space, water projects, and parks; utilities wanting to build new power-generating plants; shopping center planners, large housing developers—all were growing frustrated. They would have agreed with a leading land use expert that "Land-use planning is in chaos. . . . I doubt that even the most intransigent disciple of anarchy ever wished for, or intended the litter that prevails in the area of land-use regulation."[39]

On January 29, 1970, Senator Henry Jackson (D-Wash.) introduced into the Senate a proposed National Land Use Policy Act. The bill was designed to encourage the states to supersede the authority of local governments in land use decisions. It would make $100 million in grants available to the states, requiring them to set up statewide land use agencies, which would then initiate a process of comprehensive land use planning. First, these agencies would have to compile data on existing land uses and natural resources and project the land use needs of future economic activity. These studies would provide the information for a second planning stage—a comprehensive, statewide land use plan that would define "the states' industrial, commercial, residential, and recreational land use needs for the next fifty years."[40]

Following a three-year period, the state land use agency would be required to show that its state had given it the authority to implement a comprehensive land use plan. A new federal agency, the Land and Water Resources Planning Council, would oversee the state plans. If implemented, states might end up asserting eminent domain and police powers that would supersede the powers of local governments, even acquiring private property, if necessary. If states failed to make progress in defining their land use objectives, they would be subject to losing not only the federal land use assistance funds made available in the legislation, but airport and highway funds as well.

The hearings on Jackson's bill were more harmonious than might have been expected, probably because witnesses appearing before Jackson's Interior Committee represented state government interests or businesses that felt that local land use control retarded economic development. Two state governors appeared before the committee to support strong legislation. Utility company spokesmen favored it because they had encountered trouble finding sites for new power plants. But some industry representatives—the National Association of Manufacturers, the National Association of Home Builders, the timber industry—expressed concern that the states themselves might not allow development because of sensitivity to environmental groups.[41]

Prompted by a concern that Jackson's proposal might be adopted, the Nixon administration introduced a weaker version of national land use planning. Under the administration's proposal, the states would not be required to engage in comprehensive planning and would not be required to assert statewide control over land use policy. The proposal did not specify any federal standards for state land use guidelines, except to say that the states should put emphasis on "areas of special concern," "key facilities," and "development of regional benefit." Nevertheless, the bill encouraged the states to "exercise their full authority over the planning and regulation of non-federal lands."[42] The states were expected to achieve some coordination of local land use regulations by establishing criteria that federal and state economic development or environmental agencies, or state and federal judges, could use in reviewing local land use decisions. Though the criteria would be left entirely to the individual states, once criteria had been specified, state or federal administrators and the courts might be able to overrule municipal decisions on land use by invoking the standards set forth by state administrators.

Within a few months, Jackson backed away from the idea of requiring the states to devise comprehensive land use plans, and he amended his proposal to require the states only to identify broad land use objectives, as proposed by the Nixon administration. The White House approved this change and withdrew its own proposal. Even so, Jackson's bill contained sanctions that could force states to come up with state land use objectives that could be used by courts in adjudicating land use disputes. The sanctions included the possibility of withdrawing land and water conservation funds (which financed state parkland acquisitions) and airport and highway construction grants.

In the debates over the bill, federal officials denied that they had any of their own land use objectives in mind, aside from giving the states more power to review local decisions and to consider their overall goals for future development. Senator Edmund S. Muskie (D, Maine) objected that the legislation amounted to standardless regulation that "creates an outline for national land use policy with no substance. . . . Legislation of this magnitude with far-reaching impacts on many federal programs . . . must provide some federal government guidance."[43]

But conservative Republicans and local officials vehemently opposed even this much state oversight. The U.S. Conference of Mayors, the National Association of Counties, and the National Service to Regional Councils organization, along with many local officials, insisted that any new legislation must leave municipal land use prerogatives intact. Several amendments to the legislation failed to assuage these opponents.

Jackson claimed that the opposition was overly nervous, insisting that he only wanted the states to identify procedures for mediating important land use conflicts: "This is not a subjective thing where the federal government can intercede and substitute a subjective judgement for the state's judgement. As long as the plan covers the principal areas . . . then the federal government is required to accept it."[44] In a final attempt to mollify the opposition, Jackson accepted an amendment to his bill that dropped any federal sanctions if the states failed to devise standards for making land use decisions. The Senate passed the much-amended national land use legislation by a large margin on September

19, 1972. Conservative Republicans expressed dismay that the bill, even watered down as much as it was, might "alter the traditional system" of land use in the United States[45]

In November 1973, Congressman Morris Udall (D, Arizona) introduced a similar bill into the House of Representatives. Faced with the prospect that Congress might actually enact the legislation, opponents organized an intense lobbying campaign. The U.S. Chamber of Commerce contacted its chapters to ask the question "What would happen if the government . . . says you may continue to own your land, but you may not build anything on it." Congress was deluged with mail opposing the legislation as a "threat to freedom and individual liberty."[46] When Udall's subcommittee on environment met in April 1974 to hold hearings, loggers and cattle ranchers, farmers, oil drillers, executives from construction firms, realtors, and developers all appeared to express their opposition. These groups were convinced that states might constrain development even more than some localities. A chaotic system of local controls was preferable to the uncertainties of a new system, where, for example, environmentalists might have more influence.

Local control over land use remained the most important issue. Udall tried to reassure the opponents by claiming that: "If a community wants to choose sprawl constitutionally and openly after having public hearings involving the citizens and local government, they can damn well choose sprawl under this."[47] He added that like the Senate bill, his bill would only require procedures for making land use decisions, but it would not force local governments to abide by decisions made elsewhere. But all efforts to weaken the legislation were insufficient. By a close six-vote margin, the House refused to vote the bill out of the Rules Committee, and it never came to the floor of the House for open debate.

It is useful to put these battles into a comparative context. The extreme fragmentation of land use policy in the United States is unique among Western nations. Planning on a metropolitanwide basis is common in European countries. Planning decisions impacting metropolitan regions, such as highway building, housing construction, and sewer and water facilities, are made by national or metropolitan authorities. Britain provides an example. Before World War II, problems of traffic congestion and overcrowded housing in London led the government to limit the size of the city. A five-mile wide "Green Belt" was drawn around the city to preserve an area of open space immune from development. Parliament helped finance the building of entirely new communities beyond this belt. As a result of the Green Belt and new town construction, the decentralization of people and jobs from London could take place within the context of a comprehensive regional plan.[48]

In other European nations, central governments likewise exert direct influence over city development and planning.[49] For example, Stockholm owns much of the land in its own city, and in contradiction to the American pattern it is able to bank land throughout its metropolitan region. Dutch municipalities also engage in extensive land banking. This allows public authorities to control patterns of land speculation and housing and business construction much more thoroughly than would be possible in the United States.

When the U.S. government began to implement policies impacting urban growth and development, it underwrote rather than discouraged the political fragmentation of urban areas. It could hardly have done otherwise, since the states controlled the chartering of cities and patterns of land use.

NATIONAL ACTIVISM WITHOUT NATIONAL STANDARDS: FEDERAL HOUSING POLICY, 1933–1960s

With the onset of the Great Depression of the 1930s, the idea that cities would continue to prosper came up against a harsh reality: much of the housing stock was old and outdated, the slums were spreading, and, as the wave of suburbanization of the 1920s so clearly showed, the suburbs, and not the cities, had the brightest future. All of the nation's older cities contained at their core block after block of dilapidated housing. Landlords and owners had little or no money to invest in repairs and renovation. Slums surrounded the central business districts, themselves in need of new investment and construction.

Second only to agriculture as an employer, the housing industry had experienced a devastating retrenchment. Before the stock market crash of October 1929, new housing was being built at the rate of 900,000 units a year. By 1934, only 90,000 units a year were being constructed.[50] Across the nation, 63 percent of workers in the housing industry were unemployed.[51] The housing problem threatened financial institutions and the middle class. Millions of families lost their homes through foreclosures, and the banks held title to devalued property. Banks, homeowners, homebuilders, city officials, and construction workers all looked to the federal government for help.

Private Housing Policy: Underwriting Segregation

The National Housing Act of 1934 embodied the major New Deal response to the housing crisis. Title I provided insurance through the new Federal Housing Administration (FHA) for loans from banks and savings and loans to be used for repairing or renovating existing property. The sponsors of this section saw it as a means of eliminating substandard living conditions in the central cities by offering property owners the opportunity to rehabilitate their properties. City officials hoped Title I would help entice affluent people to stay in the cities, and downtown business leaders wanted Title I to bolster property values in central business districts.

But the other principal section of the legislation served to undercut the objectives of Title I. Section 203 authorized FHA insurance for loans to finance new housing. This section attracted considerable political support from lending institutions, realtors, and developers. Very little money was ever appropriated for Title I, but Section 203 eventually assisted millions of people to move out of the cities to the suburbs. The 1934 Housing Act set a precedent for future urban policy, in that the left hand did not know what the right hand was doing. Money allocated to "save" the cities was vastly outweighed by policies that had the effect, though rarely the intent, of hanging the cities in a suburban noose.

Section 203 of the FHA legislation revolutionized the housing industry by sharply reducing the risk for financial institutions making mortgage loans. Before the FHA program, home loans often required 40 percent down, with the balance to be paid in ten or eleven years. With up to 80 percent of the loan value insured by the federal government, banks participating in the FHA program lowered down payments to 5 percent (in the 1930s), for amortization periods of up to thirty years.[52] Coupled with the Home Mortgage Loan Program offered to veterans through the Servicemen's Readjustment Act enacted in 1944, the credit market for private housing was loosened even more before the end of World War II. The no-down payment policy of the Veteran's Administration (VA) helped increase the federally insured share of the mortgage market from 15 percent in 1945 to 41 percent by 1954.[53]

FHA- and VA-insured mortgages made their mark on the home credit market. Between 1935 and 1974, the FHA insured 11.4 million home mortgages totalling $107 billion dollars. Nearly 9 million of these mortgages—77 percent of the total—went for new housing.[54] About one-third of all homes purchased in the 1950s were financed through FHA or VA loans. In 1930 about 48 percent of families owned their own homes, but by 1960, 62 percent of families were homeowners. Largely because of the loan insurance programs, more than 85 percent of all housing starts in the 1950s were for sale rather than rental units.

The proportion of government-insured loans generally declined after the 1960s, but they had already exerted an overwhelming impact on metropolitan residential patterns. From the 1930s through the mid-1960s, the FHA and VA heavily favored newly constructed homes in the suburbs. More than 90 percent of the new homes insured by these programs were constructed outside the central cities.[55]

From the beginning, the FHA absorbed the values, policy orientations, and goals of the real estate industry.[56] FHA personnel were drawn from the ranks of the housing and banking industries. It was only logical that the philosophy of FHA administrators would reflect the financial conservatism of these industries; thus "FHA's interests went no farther than the safety of the mortgage it secured."[57] Like the real estate industry, FHA administrators preferred racially segregated neighborhoods. In fact, when it issued its Underwriting Manual to banks in 1938, the FHA advised its loan officers that:

> Areas surrounding a location are [to be] investigated to determine whether incompatible racial and social groups are present, for the purpose of making a prediction regarding the probability of the location being invaded by such groups. If a neighborhood is to retain stability, it is necessary that properties shall continue to be occupied by the same social and racial classes. A change in social or racial occupancy generally contributes to instability and a decline in values.[58]

In order to obtain FHA-insured financing, many FHA administrators instructed developers of residential projects to draw up restrictive covenants barring sale of property to nonwhites. Between 1935 and 1950,

> more than 11 million homes were built . . . and this federal policy did more to entrench housing bias in American neighborhoods than any court could undo by a ruling. It established federally sponsored mores for discrimination in suburban communities in which eighty percent of all new housing [was] being built and fixed the social and racial patterns in thousands of new neighborhoods.[59]

Blacks purchased less than 2 percent of all the housing financed with the assistance of federal mortgage insurance between 1946 and 1959.[60] In the Miami area, only one black family received FHA backing for a home loan between 1934 and 1949, and there is "evidence that [the man who secured the loan] was not recognized as black at the time the transaction took place.[61]

In 1948, in *Shelly* v. *Kraemer*, the U.S. Supreme Court ruled that racial covenants could not be enforced in the courts.[62] In response, the FHA rewrote its underwriting manual in 1950 so that it no longer recommended racial segregation or restrictive covenants. Nevertheless, until at least the mid-1960s mortgages continued to be insured mainly in areas where minorities were excluded. Since the Federal Housing Administration and the Veteran's Administration relied on the finance and real estate industries, federally insured loans became a mechanism for underwriting, in effect, the practices of those institutions. Banks commonly engaged in "redlining," a practice derived from the "red line" drawn on maps to designate neighborhoods considered poor investment risks (usually areas where minorities and lower-income people lived). Until the Fair Housing Act of 1968 was passed, no pressure was put on banks and realtors to change these lending practices.

The FHA and VA policies had effect of adding the national authority and financial backing to local patterns of racial and social class segregation. This inevitably would have been the case for any housing program that relied exclusively upon local private lending and real estate institutions, which were themselves part of the pattern of metropolitan political power. By thoroughly localizing national housing policies, federal administrators could distance themselves from the actual effects of their policies. By the time that the federal government undertook efforts to reverse these policies in the 1960s, the effects of past policies were difficult, perhaps impossible, to overcome.

The federal government's housing policies interacted with its transportation policies to accelerate suburban growth. The National Defense Highway Act of 1956 funded the interstate expressway system. The federal subsidy, which covered 90 percent of all construction costs, led to a rush of highway building. Expressways soon connected central city areas with the suburbs, and although "the intention of the various highway acts was not urban redevelopment, their consequences were often more far-reaching in terms of urban land uses and residential construction than urban renewal and housing programs."[63] Combined with the FHA and VA loan programs, the expressways virtually guaranteed the exodus from urban centers, far outweighing the policies that were designed to save city neighborhoods and business districts.

Slum Clearance and Public Housing: Local Control

The National Industrial Recovery Act of 1933 funded the first federal program designed to address the housing crisis in the central cities. This act authorized the "construction, reconstruction, alteration, or repair, under public regulation or control, of low-rent housing and slum clearance projects."[64]

The Housing Division of the Public Works Administration (PWA) tried to implement this program through the "carrot" of low-interest federal loans to private developers. But the private housing industry showed little interest, and only seven projects were approved. To get the program moving, the PWA undertook the direct financing and construction of government-owned housing units. The United States Emergency Housing Corporation was created for this purpose in 1933.

Ruling on cases brought by housing industry representatives in Louisville and Detroit, federal courts in 1935 struck down the federal government's authority to use eminent domain to take slum land for clearance.[65] To save its program, the Emergency Housing Corporation decided to work through local public housing authorities. Because the states chartered these authorities, the courts upheld their power to use eminent domain to assemble slum land for clearance. Subsequently, the PWA provided grants to local housing authorities that resulted in the construction of 22,000 public, low-income housing units in thirty seven cities.[66] Local housing authorities constructed and managed all of these units.

The PWA experience established the model for implementing all future public housing programs funded by the federal government. Local housing authorities became the recipients of federal funds. By the end of the PWA public housing program in 1937, twenty-nine states had passed the enabling legislation allowing local governments to create housing authorities, and forty-six such agencies had come into existence.[67]

Following World War II a variety of interest groups agreed that the economic health and social well-being of the cities were threatened by urban decay, and liberals and conservatives concurred on this general principle. Private business interests, primarily real estate and organized housing trade associations, were deeply concerned over the adverse economic impact and the capital loss in blighted areas. As owners and investors in urban real estate, the business interests of the cities "had a tremendous stake in the maintenance of residential and commercial property value."[68]

Conservative interests representing the housing industry were united in their opposition to low-rent public housing as a solution to the inner-city slum crisis. Their cure for the slum crisis included slum clearance and the private construction of low-income housing. Liberals and the organizations that they represented, including especially the labor unions, traced the social evils of slum living, in part, to urban housing shortages and overcrowded housing.

When proposals for national legislation surfaced after the war, conservatives who wanted to save business investments in the city and liberals who wanted to increase the supply of low-income housing worked out a policy compromise. The political coalition that passed the landmark postwar redevelopment legislation, the Housing Act of 1949, included both Republicans and Democrats, liberals and conservatives.[69] The compromise that made congressional approval possible was a piece of legislation that contained a little bit for everyone, a bill that encapsulated conflicting purposes.

Title I of the act empowered the Housing and Home Finance Agency (HHFA) to assist local efforts of blight and slum removal. This agency offered federal grants-in-aid to encourage states to authorize local public urban renewal agencies that would absorb the cost of the "write-down" on the land that had been cleared of slum buildings. The "write-down" was the difference between the local agency's cost of assembling and clearing a site and the price that private developers were willing to pay.

In addition to the write-down subsidies, the HHFA was authorized to extend loans to local renewal authorities for land assembly and site clearance. The act gave private developers preference in redeveloping the cleared sites.

The renewal programs promised to supply displaced slum residents with "decent, safe and sanitary dwellings." Title III of the legislation authorized the production of 810,000 government-subsidized public housing units over the next six years. This amounted to 10 percent of the estimated national need for new low-income housing. Congress appropriated annual operating subsidies to local public housing authorities and established a temporary loan fund to finance initial construction.

The national objectives of the urban renewal legislation were fundamentally compromised when local agencies implemented the program. Private commercial and industrial developers soon captured the urban renewal program.[70] Local renewal administrators, working closely with politicians and business leaders, selected the developers as well as the sites to be cleared, and thus they decided to what ends the program would work. Because the program was funded through grant-in-aid and loan programs allocated to local urban renewal and local public housing authorities, the federal government could exert little direct control.

Public housing immediately ran into trouble. In the abstract, housing for low-incôme people might seem worthwhile, but a "not in my backyard" syndrome held up construction in city after city. For example, Chicago's politicians in the 1950s wanted federal subsidies for the city, but none of them wanted the projects in their own wards.[71] The National Association of Real Estate Boards (NAREB) prodded their local chapters to organize in their cities. In these campaigns, opponents of subsidized housing claimed that housing projects would force racial integration on communities. Between 1949 and the end of 1952, public housing programs were rejected by referenda (a tactic advocated by the NAREB) in forty communities, including a fèw of the nation's larger cities—Akron, Houston, and Los Angeles. These results made local officials acutely aware that "there could hardly be many votes to be gained in championing the cause, and perhaps a great many lost."[72]

In contrast, many politicians advanced their careers by claiming credit for the economic development of central business districts. By aggressively pursuing federal funds to save central city land values, an enterprising mayor could forge an alliance between local government on the one hand and the business community and construction unions on the other. Such an alliance was built, for example, in New Haven, Connecticut, where the young Democrat Richard Lee hung his mayoral aspirations and his political future on the prospect of a successful urban redevelopment program.[73] He won the 1952 election and several terms thereafter by putting together an unusual alliance that united the most conservative members of the business community with local Democratic party officials who were close to the construction unions.

Similar coalitions sprung up in cities all across the nation. In every older industrial city, business and financial interests concerned about urban decay and its impact on their property investments supported slum clearance. Areas closest to the dowtown business districts were generally the oldest in the cities and were therefore susceptible to blight. It was only logical that businesses would seek to protect their investments through revitalization of their immediate environment. As a result of the nature of the alliance between politicians and downtown businesses, most redevelopment projects were located in downtown business areas and in nearby slums.

The coalition supporting public housing in local communities was far more fragile. Low-income housing received support from the urban renewal alliance so that federal funds could be obtained for slum clearance, but actual construction of public housing lagged far behind the goals set forth by the national legislation. By the end of 1961, urban development and renewal had eliminated 126,000 housing units, 80 percent of which were substandard, but the 28,000 new units that replaced them were in no way sufficient to house the 113,000 families and 36,000 individuals who were displaced. [74] Across the nation, in the big cities, thousands of acres of cleared land grew weeds, waiting for the day when developers could be persuaded to build car dealerships, hotels, and other projects on renewal sites.

Because the oldest and most dilapidated housing generally was located near the central business district, racial minorities frequently were displaced by renewal projects and relocated in slums more distant from downtown. Thus, "black residents of the inner cities [and] black businesses were among the prime victims of federally sponsored urban renewal programs referred to as 'urban black removal' "[75] Over three-fourths of the people displaced by urban redevelopment and renewal in the first eight years of the program were black, and 66 percent of those displaced through 1961 were either Puerto Rican (in New York City) or, more likely, black.[76]

In most cities, public housing was segregated as a matter of policy, and tenants of public housing projects were selected to reflect the racial composition of surrounding areas. The federal government did not question these practices until 1963. By 1961, 46 percent of public housing tenants were black, but in the large inner cities racial segregation among projects was the norm. Even so, most slum residents displaced by renewal could not get into public housing, since the supply lagged far behind need. Less than one-fourth of the housing units town down were replaced, and many of the new units were too expensive for slum residents.[77]

Public housing policy reinforced class and racial segregation in American metropolitan areas. Urban renewal and slum clearance simultaneously reduced housing options for poor and minority residents of central cities. These programs had the effect of increasing the size and density of inner-city racial ghettos. In short, the political and economic setting within individual cities molded the policies financed through the 1949 Housing Act. Racism, class discrimination, residential segregation, land values, and the profit motive motivated the local coalitions that controlled the implementation of urban renewal projects.

THE LIMITS OF NATIONAL STANDARDS: THE ENDURING LEGACY OF INCOHERENT URBAN POLICIES

Integration in Private Housing

In 1968 the national government finally took action to try to break down patterns of segregated housing in metropolitan areas. Provisions of the Civil Rights Act of 1968, known as the Fair Housing Act, proscribed discrimination by lenders through "either denying the loan or fixing the amount, interest rate, duration, or other terms of the loan."[78] The statute also mandated that each of the federal regulating agencies involved in the real estate industry take affirmative steps to enforce both the letter and the spirit of the law.[79]

Developments at the national level drew on efforts in some states and communities and stimulated others to follow suit. In 1957 only fourteen cities had laws prohibiting discrimination in housing. By the end of 1964, sixty cities had laws against discrimination, and by 1970 there were 229 state and local fair housing laws. Such a proliferation of legislation probably would not have been possible without extensive grassroots action. The National Committee against Discrimination in Housing's publication, *Trends in Housing*, enthusiastically described the nature of some the local involvement in the open-housing movement in 1962:

> housing is the latest area in civil rights to be tackled by nonviolent direct action. Sit-ins, sleep-ins, equality vigils, picketing, protest marches, sympathy demonstrations, and "operation windowshop" are being used increasingly to further open occupancy in many sections of the country.[80]

The real estate industry officially ceased its longstanding opposition to open housing legislation after the passage of the Fair Housing Act. The National Association of Real Estate Boards, the most powerful and effective national organization opposing fair housing legislation, called on its eighty-five thousand members to comply with the new laws by writing to local chapters that "those who have oposed open-housing laws should now understand that their position is forever negated."[81]

Nevertheless, the enforcement of fair housing laws was frustrated by the complex institutional web involved:

> After decades of openly advocating housing discrimination and segrega-
> tion, the federal government is now under a clear mandate to promote
> affirmative action for open housing. But the mandate requires reciprocal
> action by housing consumers, private investors, builders and developers,
> as well as by the real estate industry, if open housing is to take a more than
> token reality.[82]

Federal administrators had very limited means to bring about this recip-rocal action. Legal challenges to realtors, owners, or rental managers had to be brought through the courts on a case-by-case basis. Compiling evidence of discriminatory behavior involves a complex set of legal tactics. Many minority families seeking housing "may decide that the cost and delay of going to court are not worth the effort."[83] Thus, the impact of antidiscrimination statutes and court decisions on the real estate industry has been minimal. National policies that underwrote segregation for decades had long-lasting effects that could not be un-done by mere statutory language and piecemeal challenges in protracted court proceedings.

The Social and Economic Plight of the Inner Cities

Before the Kennedy administration, the only major federal aid pro-grams to be targeted specifically to central cities included urban renewal and public housing. The partisan change in the White House in 1961 marked the beginning of a new era. Federal assistance in urban areas rose from $3.9 billion in 1961, the last Republican fiscal year, to $14 billion in President Lyndon Johnson's last budget, eight years later. Most of the new money and programs labelled "urban" went to people and problems in the cites. And in contrast to previous programs tar-geted at blight and housing decay, a new concern emerged about the *social problems* in inner-city areas—juvenile delinquency, crime, poverty, education, racial discrimination, and joblessness.

The shift to a social welfare orientation was accomplished between 1965 and 1967, when Congress enacted 136 new grant authorizations. Fiscal year 1965 marked the beginning of a dramatic upswing in outlays for social programs, particularly in the areas of health, education, and employment training. Grants-in-aid to state and local governments within these fields rose from 14 percent of federal domestic aid in 1960 to one-third of such aid in 1970. Similarly, the proportion of assistance outlays for housing and community development nearly quadrupled during the decade, rising from 3 percent to 11 percent of the domestic budget.[84]

It is important to note that a significant portion of the new federal money did not go directly to local governments but reflected the bypassing strategy (see Chapter 5) in channeling funds to nongovernmental, nonprofit organizations—for example, to legal aid offices, community action agencies, Model Cities agencies, nonprofit housing corporations, and neighborhood associations. The rapid growth of programs and their complex and varying purposes, funding arrangements, and application procedures quickly led to serious problems of intergovernmental program coordination, impediments to federal oversight, and conflicts among agencies and groups at the local level.

Governors, mayors, and other state and local officials expressed frequent irritation about the lack of coordination among programs, the complexities of application and administration, and the lack of available information on programs. A study contracted by the Department of Housing and Urban Development reported in September 1967 that federal agencies had no standardized procedures for conveying information on their grant programs and that there were few standard practices concerning the frequency of updating information. During 1966, four agencies issued four different catalogs with information on programs of both their own agencies and those of others. In July 1967, local administrators reported that they turned to an average of 8.2 sources to obtain information about grant programs.[85] The most frequent source of information came from federal agency publications and federal officials, but newspapers were used nearly as often.

From the point of view of local public officials, the worst problem was not that there were so many programs but that city governments were being bypassed in favor of the new institutions—particularly those associated with the Economic Opportunity Act (the antipoverty program) and the Model Cities program. The antipoverty program, for example, was established to create a direct link between federal executive   agencies and inner-city black neighborhoods. New governmental and quasi-governmental agencies were established that did not have to answer to city hall or other local governmental authorities. Of all the community action funds spent by the Office of Economic Opportunity (OEO) by 1968, only 25 percent were given to public agencies at all, the remainder going to private organizations, including universities, churches, civil rights groups, settlement houses, family services agencies, United Way Funds, or newly established nonprofit groups.[86] Likewise, only 10 percent of HEW program grants operating during the beginning of 1967 were limited to governmental units.[87] Of course such arrangements upset local officials, especially when some of the groups and agencies receiving federal dollars protested city hall policies or contested local elections.

From the point of view of federal officials, these unorthodox grant programs aimed to solve the political problems of the Democratic presidency; that is, their chief purpose was to preserve and strengthen the Democratic party's advantage in the urban, industrial states holding the largest blocs of electoral college votes. Rather than work through local politicians who had repeatedly shown a reluctance to incorporate blacks into party organizations and government bureaucracies, the federal strategy bypassed local Democratic (and Republican) leaders and established direct links between the national government and the inner-city electoral constituency. "The hallmark of the Great Society programs was the direct relationship between the national government and the ghettos, a relationship in which both state and local governments are undercut."[88] Great Society programs accomplished this result by providing services, funds, and patronage directly to ghetto organizations and leaders.

New urban programs co-opted the black leadership into mainstream politics by offering the same inducements that old-style city machines had offered. Perhaps in the short run such programs as the War on Poverty and Model Cities had created discontent, and on a sustained basis they encouraged blacks to demand more from political systems. But the main political purpose was accomplished: black civil rights activitists and organizational leaders were brought into the political system, with at least three results—political discontent was lowered; the political strength and effectiveness of moderate ghetto leaders was enhanced; and these same leaders were co-opted into local and national Democratic party politics.[89]

Soon mayors and congressmen reacted in dismay to these programs. Robert Wagner, mayor of New York City, echoed the mayors' concern before a House subcommittee meeting in 1965, when he argued that "the local governing bodies, through their chief executives or otherwise, should have the ultimate authority . . . for the conduct and operation of the antipoverty program." Through 1965 and 1966 the mayors complained that the federal government was trying to foment revolution through its programs. In 1965 the Johnson administration appointed a deputy director of the OEO who was more sympathetic to these claims. Before long, mayors were given at least an informal veto over antipoverty funds, and by the end of the Johnson administration, all such funds had to receive a sign-off from city hall before they could be released.

A similar fate befell the Model Cities program. Initially, the program was designed to demonstrate (thus its first title, "Demonstration Cities") what could be accomplished if a big effort was made in the slums of a few cities. Initially, the number of cities was supposed to be as low as five.[90] But by the time the interests of powerful congressional leaders were taken into account, the number of cities increased to fifty. By the time the bill was passed in 1966, the number of cities had mushroomed to seventy-five, and a year later another seventy-five cities were added in a "second round" of funding.[91] Like the antipoverty programs, Model Cities at first was supposed to rely on and promote citizen participation. But within a short time, as a result of protests from mayors about the independence of Model Cities agencies, mayors were given veto power over fund allocations.

Beginning with the congressional elections in November 1966, a back-lash against social programs began building. In 1969 the Nixon adminis-tration took advantage of the political climate, first by trying to terminate important programs identified with the Great Society. However, this strategy failed because local officials already had gained control over grant programs by the end of the Johnson administration, and they lobbied their congressional representatives to fight hard to keep the federal dollars flowing into their cities. Next, the Nixon administration sought to change the nature of urban aid from grants-in-aid with specific purposes to revenue sharing or block grants with few strings attached. The components of the "New Federalism" important to the cities in-cluded the State and Local Fiscal Assistance Act of 1972 (general revenue sharing), which passed money to state and local governments with few restrictions, the Concentrated Employment Training Act of 1973, which consolidated a multitude of employment programs into a block grant, and the Housing and Community Development Act of 1974. This block grant consolidated seven programs, including the very important urban renewal and Model Cities programs.

Block grants reduced even the mild targeting features of urban assis-tance. Though the formula that determined the allocation of funds to particular cities favored needy jurisdictions to some degree, revenue sharing funds went to local governments all across the country, includ-ing even wealthy suburbs. Community Development Block Grants (CDBGs) funded through the 1974 legislation gave almost complete discretion to cities to spend federal money as they saw fit. As a result, CDBGs were less targeted to needy jurisdictions than the programs they replaced. Between 1975 and 1979, the number of low- and moderate-income census tracts receiving CDBG funds fell by 30 percent and the number of wealthier tracts receiving funds increased by 50 per-cent.[92] The block grants had this effect primarily because local politi-cians used their new freedom from federal oversight to send funds to areas where the important segments of their electoral constituencies were located.

Block grants also lost their targeting features because of Congress's penchant for distributing money to a large number of congressional districts. For example, Congress amended the CDBG program in 1977 to make sure that older fiscally distressed cities would continue to receive a large share of the CDBG funds (under the 1974 formula for distributing grants, allocations were tied, in part, to a city's population, and thus older industrial cities that were losing population stood to receive less money over time). Congressional members from Sunbelt cities strenuously objected that any new formula might result in fewer dollars in their districts, where the cities were growing in population. To get the legislation through Congress, a compromise was struck to add more money to the programs, so that cities in the Sunbelt would not suffer reduced allocations, and an amendment allowed cities to elect the original 1974 formula instead of the new one, depending on which formula resulted in a higher allocation to the city.

In the last two years of the Carter administration, attention turned away from urban policy toward the "reindustrialization" of the economy. The National Development Bank was the most important new proposal for urban policy placed before Congress by the White House. The bank would have promoted economic development by allocating loans and grants to depressed urban and rural areas. But the legislation did not emerge from Congress, and by 1980 the Carter administration had abandoned any policy designed to turn declined cities or urban areas around. Instead, a commission appointed by Carter recommended that national economic growth should be promoted without regard to where that growth took place:

> It may be in the best interest of the nation to commit itself to the promotion of locationally neutral economic and social policies rather than spatially sensitive urban policies that either explicitly or inadvertently seek to preserve cities in their historical roles.[93]

This recommendation presaged the political agenda of the Reagan administration after it took office in January 1981.

PROMOTING INEQUALITY: URBAN POLICY IN THE 1980s

Abandoning urban policy in the 1980s made political sense for the Republican party. Party leaders have long sought to capitalize on white suburbanites' disaffection from Democratic civil rights and antipoverty policies. Ronald Reagan took advantage of this sentiment in 1980 and 1984. Jimmy Carter and Walter Mondale carried the vote of large cities by substantial margins, while Reagan won slightly more than one-third of the big city vote in each election. But Reagan carried the suburban and small city vote by a margin of 53 percent to 37 percent in 1980 and 57 to

42 percent in 1984. Since only 12 percent of the 1984 vote was cast in large cities, while 55 percent was cast in the suburbs and the small cities, the Republican advantage was overwhelming.[94] In the 1980s, cities were almost as politically isolated in the federal political structure as they had been one hundred years before.

Consistent with its ideology and its political base, the administration sought to withdraw the national government from urban policy and to restore state control over the urban programs that remained. In the administration's view, federal urban programs improperly finance

> . . . activities that logically and traditionally have been the responsibilities of State and local governments . . . Individuals, firms and State and local governments properly unfettered, will make better decisions than the Federal government acting for them . . . it is State governments that are in the best position to encourage metropolitan-wide solutions to problems that spill over political boundaries . . . and to tackle the economic, financial, and social problems that affect the well-being of the State as it competes with others to attract and retain residents and businesses.[95]

The administration intended to devolve the "maximum feasible responsibility for urban matters to the states and through them to their local governments." Cities were instructed to improve their ability to compete with one another by ". . . increasing their attractiveness to potential investors, residents, and visitors."[96] Thus, national urban policy was to be built not on grant programs, but on advice guided by the assumption that free enterprise would provide a bounty of jobs, income, and neighborhood renewal.

Compared to the past, the new aspect of Reagan's policies involved the judgment that individual cities were not valuable cultural, social, or economic spatial units *except to the degree* to which they contributed to a healthy national economy. The logical next step was to eliminate national intervention in the cities entirely. The Reagan administration attempted to move in that direction. Deep cuts were initiated in all urban aid programs.

Table 9.5 shows the reductions scheduled for the major urban programs through 1989. Overall spending dropped from $6.1 billion in fiscal year 1981 to $5.2 billion in fiscal year 1984. The $5.2 billion spent for the fiscal year 1984–1985 amounted to a decline in spending of almost 20 percent, when inflation is taken into account. By the 1989 budget year, money for urban programs was cut to $4.4 billion—a further reduction of about 40 percent, when the effects of inflation are considered. In fiscal year 1986 the general revenue sharing program ended, and for the first time since the early 1960s, a majority of general-purpose governments in the United States received no direct federal assistance.

Table 9.5. *Federal outlays for urban and regional programs to state and local governments in fiscal years 1981–1989 (billions of dollars)*

	FY 1981	FY 1984	FY 1989 (est.)
Community development block grants	$4.0	$3.8	$3.0
Urban development action grants	0.4	0.5	0.4
Economic development administration and Appalachian Regional Commission	0.7	0.5	0.3
Other community and regional development	1.0	0.4	0.7
Total	6.1	5.2	4.4

Source: Office of Management and Budget, *Historical Tables, Budget of the U.S. Government, Fiscal Year 1989* (Washington, DC: GPO, 1988), Table 12.3.

Other budget cuts also affected the cities. Nearly all subsidies for the construction of public housing were ended. Only 10,000 new units a year were to be authorized after 1983, compared with the 111,600 new or rehabilitated units authorized in 1981.[97] Urban mass transit grants were reduced 28 percent from 1981–1983 and were cut another 20 percent by 1986. The programs of the Comprehensive Employment and Training Act (CETA) were eliminated entirely after the 1983 budget. The counter-cyclical urban aid programs initiated under President Carter ended early in the Reagan administration.

Under the new policy of interjurisdictional economic competition for investment, local governments try to replace reduced federal aid with private investments. Their attempts to promote healthy local economies lead them to desperate use of the tools permitted by superior governments to retain and attract business. These tools include tax abatements, tax increment financing, industrial revenue bonds, Urban Development Action Grants (UDAGs), and other inducements to lure business and middle-class residents to the cities. At the same time, many suburban governments offer similar incentives. Businesses and affluent residents of metropolitan areas thus find themselves in a kind of governmental "free-trade zone" in which they can shop around for the best combination of public subsidies.

RISING INEQUALITY

Because older cities are not isolated within larger local and regional economies in most European countries, they are much less subject than American cities to critical fiscal problems resulting from declining economic performance in the urban center. Many urban services are provided by metropolitan-wide authorities. Equally important, most European central governments provide substantial unrestricted revenues to metropolitan authorities and to cities.[98] In Britain, as of 1978, 55 percent of local revenues for municipalities originated from Parliament. In France, the national government provided 47 percent of local budgets and in the Netherlands, 84 percent. Although 27 percent of local revenues came through intergovernmental transfers in the United States in the same year, most of it was in grants-in-aid of various kinds, and although many of these funds originated in relatively unrestricted block grants, such as the Community Development Act of 1974, they were not guided by the same assumptions as those underlying most European intergovernmental transfer programs, which were informed by a philosophy that it is the central government's responsibility to help pay for a large variety of services and functions administered by cities.

In the United States, segregation between central city neighborhoods and between the cities and suburbs will continue. Between 1970 and 1982, the median income of suburban families remained at 115 percent of the national average, but the median income of central city residents fell from 99 percent to 93 percent.[99] The fate of central cities will be decided entirely by their ability to turn around their own economies. In the struggle to lure business, industry, and tourists, generous business incentives are the rule. Biased in this way, the unquestionable objective of revitalization has been to replace less profitable (and less symbolic) smaller businesses with corporate towers, hotels, and shopping malls. In the neighborhoods, revitalization means gentrification—the attempt to replace poor residents with affluent people. Even before Ronald Reagan's election, about 37,000 households were displaced each year by such housing conversions as officially sponsored redevelopment, gentrification, and conversion of apartments into condominiums. Central cities find irresistible any formula for revitalization that appears to enhance "the economic position of the community in its competition with others."[100] And thus, the fate of cities as well as of individual suburbs is to be decided by a Darwinist struggle for survival. This is the ultimate consequence of extreme political fragmentation that puts the stamp of governmental authority on segregation between rich and poor and between racial minority and white.

NOTES

1. Harold L. Wilensky and Charles N. Lebeaux, *Industrial Society and Social Welfare* (New York: Free Press, 1965), xviii–xix.
2. Quoted in Mark I. Gelfand, *A Nation of Cities: The Federal Government and Urban America* (New York: Oxford University Press, 1975), 11.

3. Ibid., 11.
4. Robert G. Dixon, Jr., *Democratic Representation: Reapportionment in Law and Politics* (New York: Oxford University Press, 1968), 174.
5. Ibid., 71–5, 80, 86–7.
6. U.S. Department of the Interior, Superintendent of the Census, *The Ninth Census (June 1, 1870)* (Washington, DC: GPO, 1872).
7. U.S. Bureau of the Census, *Thirteenth Census of the United States in the Year 1910* (Washington, DC: GPO, 1913).
8. Dennis R. Judd, *The Politics of American Cities: Private Power and Public Policy*, 3d ed. (Glenview and Boston: Scott, Foresman/Little, Brown, 1988), 17.
9. *Dartmouth College* v. *Woodward*, 4 Wheat 518 (1819).
10. *City of Clinton* v. *Cedar Rapids and Missouri River Railroad Co.*, 24 Iowa 455, 475 (1868).
11. Joseph F. Zimmerman, *State-Local Relations: A Partnership Approach* (New York: Praeger, 1983), 6, 52–6, 62–4.
12. *Baker* v. *Carr*, 369 U.S. 189 (1962).
13. *Reynolds* v. *Sims*, 377 U.S. 533 (1964).
14. Samual P. Patterson, "Legislators and Legislatures in American States," in Virginia Gray, Herbert Jacob, and Kenneth N. Vines, eds., *Politics in the American States: A Comparative Analysis* (Boston: Little, Brown, 1983), 139–40.
15. Data cited in Robert C. Wood, *Suburbia: Its People and Their Politics* (Boston: Houghton Mifflin, 1958), 69, and in National Municipal League, Committee on Metropolitan Government, *The Government of Metropolitan Areas in the United States* (New York: National Municipal League, 1930), 26.
16. Kenneth T. Jackson, *Crabgrass Frontier: The Suburbanization of the United States* (New York: Oxford University Press, 1985), 153.
17. U.S. Bureau of the Census, *Census of Population 1970: General Social and Economic Characteristics* (Washington, DC: GPO, 1972), 448–9, Table 3.
18. Ibid.
19. Michael N. Danielson, *The Politics of Exclusion* (New York: Columbia University Press, 1976), 8–9.
20. Leo F. Schnore, Carolyn D. André, and Harry Sharp, "Black Suburbanization, 1930–1970," in Barry Schwartz, ed., *The Changing Face of the Suburbs* (Chicago: University of Chicago Press, 1976), 88–90.
21. Harold K. Connolly, "Black Movement into the Suburbs," in James W. Hughes, ed., *Suburbanization Dynamics and the Future of the City* (New Brunswick, NJ: Rutgers University, Center for Urban Policy Research, 1974), 205–8; Frederick M. Wirt, Benjamin Walter, Francine F. Rabinovitz, and Deborah R. Hensler, *On the City's Rim: Politics and Policy in Suburbia* (Lexington, MA: D.C. Heath, 1972), 41.
22. Wirt et al., 43.
23. Connolly, "Black Movement into the Suburbs," 205–22.
24. John H. Kain and Joseph J. Persky, "Alternatives to the Gilded Ghetto," *The Public Interest* 14 (Winter 1969), 76.
25. Michael N. Danielson, *The Politics of Exclusion* (New York: Columbia University Press, 1976).
26. Seymour I. Toll, *Zoned America* (New York: Grossman, 1969), 193.
27. Ibid.
28. Mel Scott, *American City Planning* (Berkeley: University of California Press, 1971), 193.
29. The "police power" refers to the implied powers of government to adopt and enforce laws necessary for preserving and protecting the immediate health and welfare of citizens. The meaning of this is, of course, subject to a wide variety of interpretations.
30. Scott, *American City Planning*, 194.
31. *Village of Euclid* v. *Ambler Realty Co.*, 272 U.S. 365, 47 Sup. Ct. 114, 71 L. Ed. 303 (1926).

32. Kenneth M. Dolbeare, "Who Uses the State Trial Courts?" in James R. Klonoski and Robert I. Mendelsohn, eds., *The Politics of Local Justice* (Boston: Little, Brown, 1970), 69.

33. *James* v. *Valtierra*, 402 U.S. 137 (1971); *City of Eastlake* v. *Forest City Enterprises, Inc.*, 426 U.S. 668 (1976).

34. *Park View Heights Corp.* v. *City of Black Jack*, 467 F. 2d (1972), reversing: 335 F supp. 899 (1971). See account in Judd, *The Politics of American Cities*, 185–9, and sources cited therein.

35. Quoted in *St. Louis Globe-Democrat*, 11 January 1977.

36. *St. Louis Post-Dispatch*, 3 June 1971.

37. Ibid.

38. *St. Louis Post-Dispatch*, 15 June 1971.

39. Richard F. Babcock, *The Zoning Game: Municipal Practices and Policies* (Madison: University of Wisconsin Press, 1966), 12.

40. Sidney Plotkin, *Keep Out: The Struggle for Land Use Control* (Berkeley: University of California Press, 1987), 170.

41. Ibid., 171–2.

42. Ibid., 182.

43. Quoted in ibid., 184.

44. Quoted in ibid., 186.

45. Quoted in ibid., 189.

46. Quoted in ibid., 196.

47. Quoted in ibid., 198.

48. Arnold J. Heidenheimer, Hugh Heclo, and Carolyn Teich Adams, *Comparative Public Policy: The Politics of Social Choice in Europe and America*, 2d ed. (New York: St. Martin's Press, 1983), 241.

49. Ibid., 237–73.

50. Stephen David and Paul E. Peterson, eds., *Urban Politics and Public Policy: The City in Crisis* (New York: Praeger, 1973), 94.

51. Charles Abrams, *The Future of Housing* (New York: Harper, 1946), 213.

52. Henry J. Aaron, *Shelter and Subsidies: Who Benefits from Federal Housing Policies* (Washington, DC: Brookings, 1972), 77.

53. Peter Marcuse, "Determinants of State Housing Policies: West Germany and the United States," in Norman I. Fainstein and Susan S. Fainstein, eds., *Urban Policy Under Capitalism* (Beverly Hills, CA: Sage, 1982), 107.

54. U.S. Department of Housing and Urban Development, *1974 Statistical Yearbook of the Department of Housing and Urban Development* (Washington, DC: GPO, 1976), 116–7.

55. Marcuse, "Determinants of State Housing Policies."

56. Chester W. Hartman, *Housing and Social Policy* (Englewood Cliffs, NJ: Prentice-Hall, 1975).

57. Ibid., 30, citing Michael Stone, "Reconstructing American Housing" (unpublished).

58. Quoted in Brian J. L. Berry, *The Open Housing Question: Race and Housing in Chicago, 1966–1976* (Cambridge, MA: Ballinger, 1979), 9.

59. Quotation of Charles Abrams, in Norman N. Bradburn, Seymour Sudman, and Galen L. Gockel, *Side by Side: Integrated Neighborhoods in America* (Chicago: Quadrangle Books, 1971), 104.

60. Gelfand, *A Nation of Cities*, 221.

61. Nathan Glazer and Davis McEntire, eds., *Housing and Minority Groups* (Berkeley: University of California Press, 1960), 140.

62. *Shelly* v. *Kraemer*, 334 U.S. 1 (1948). The Court had struck down racial zoning some thirty years earlier, in *Buchanan* v. *Warley*, 245 U.S. 60 (1917).

63. Susan S. Fainstein, Norman I. Fainstein, Richard Child Hill, Dennis Judd, and Michael P. Smith, *Restructuring the City: The Political Economy of Urban Redevelopment*, rev. ed. (New York: Longman, 1986), 14.

64. Public Law 73-67 (1933).
65. *United States* v. *Certain Lands in Louisville* 78 F. 2d 684 (1935).
66. Glen H. Boyer, *Housing: A Factual Analysis* (New York: Macmillan, 1958), 247.
67. Nathaniel S. Keith, *Politics and the Housing Crisis Since 1930* (New York: Universe Books, 1973), 29.
68. Gelfand, *A Nation of Cities*, 112.
69. Keith, *Politics and the Housing Crisis*, 71–100.
70. Chester Hartman, et al., *Yerba Buena: Land Grab and Community Resistance in San Francisco* (San Francisco: Glide Publications, 1974); John H. Mollenkopf, *The Contested City* (Princeton, NJ: Princeton University Press, 1983).
71. Martin Meyerson and Edward C. Banfield, *Politics, Planning and the Public Interest* (Glencoe, IL: The Free Press, 1955).
72. Leonard Freedman, *Public Housing: The Politics of Poverty* (New York: Holt, Rinehart and Winston, 1969), 55.
73. Robert A. Dahl, *Who Governs? Democracy and Power in an American City* (New Haven, CT: Yale University Press, 1961).
74. Martin Anderson, *The Federal Bulldozer: A Critical Analysis of Urban Renewal, 1949–1962* (Cambridge, MA: MIT Press, 1964), 65–6.
75. Arthur I. Blaustein and Geoffrey Faux, *The Star Spangled Hustle* (Garden City, NY: Doubleday, Anchor, 1973), 71.
76. Anderson, *The Federal Bulldozer*, 65; Peter H. Rossi and Robert A. Dentler, *The Politics of Urban Renewal—The Chicago Findings* (New York: The Free Press, 1961), 224.
77. John Mollenkopf, "The Post-war Politics of Urban Development," in William Tabb and Larry Sawers, eds., *Marxism and the Metropolis* (New York: Oxford University Press, 1970), 117–52.
78. Public Law 90-284, 90th Cong. (1968), Title VIII ("Fair Housing"), sec. 805.
79. D.C. Public Interest Research Group, Institute for Local Self-Reliance and Institute for Policy Studies, *Redlining: Mortgage Disinvestment in the District of Columbia* (Washington, DC: DCPIRG, Institute of Self-Reliance, and Institute of Policy Studies, 1975), 3.
80. Juliet Saltman, *Open Housing: Dynamics of a Social Movement* (New York: Praeger, 1978), 59.
81. Rose Helper, *Racial Policies and Practices of Real Estate Brokers* (Minneapolis: University of Minnesota Press, 1969), 70.
82. Morris Milgram, *Good Neighborhood: The Challenge of Open Housing* (New York: W. W. Norton, 1977), 200.
83. Donald L. Foley, "Institutional and Contextual Factors Affecting the Housing Choices of Minority Residents," in Amos H. Hawley and Vincent P. Rock, eds., *Segregation in Residential Areas: Papers on Racial and Socioeconomic Factors in Choice of Housing* (Washington, DC: National Academy of Science, 1973), 127.
84. U.S. Office of Management and Budget, *Special Analyses: Budget of the United States Government: Fiscal Year 1975* (Washington, DC: GPO, 1975), 207.
85. U.S. Congress, Senate, Committee on Government Operations, *Creative Federalism*, pt. 1, 138–9. HUD was also participating in forty-one different "interagency agreements, understandings, Executive Orders, and Directives."
86. Frances Fox Piven and Richard A. Cloward, *Regulating the Poor: The Functions of Public Welfare* (New York: Pantheon, 1971), 295.
87. U.S. Advisory Commission on Intergovernmental Relations, *Fiscal Balance in the American Federal System*, vol. 1 (Washington, DC: GPO, 1967), 169.
88. Piven and Cloward, 261.
89. Ibid., 274.
90. R. Douglas Arnold, *Congress and the Bureaucracy: A Theory of Influence* (New Haven, CT: Yale University Press, 1979), 160.
91. Ibid., 168.

92. Jeffrey R. Henig, *Public Policy and Federalism: Issues in State and Local Politics* (New York: St. Martin's, 1985), 184–5.

93. President's Commission for a National Agenda for the Eighties, *A National Agenda for the Eighties* (Washington, DC: GPO, 1980), 66.

94. Gerald Pomper, "The Presidential Election," in Gerald Pomper ed., *The Election of 1984: Reports and Interpretations* (Chatham, NJ: Chatham House, 1985), 68–9.

95. U.S. Department of Housing and Urban Development, *The President's National Urban Policy Report: 1982* (Washington, DC: GPO, 1982), 54–7.

96. Ibid.

97. Henry J. Aaron and Associates, "Nondefense Programs," in Joseph A. Pechman ed., *Setting National Priorities: The 1983 Budget* (Washington, DC: The Brookings, 1982), 119.

98. For these statistics, see Heidenheimer, Heclo, Adams, *Comparative Public Policy,* 284.

99. U.S. Department of Housing and Urban Development, *The President's National Urban Policy Report: 1984* (Washington, DC: GPO, 1984), 39–40.

100. Paul E. Peterson, *City Limits* (Chicago: University of Chicago Press, 1981).

Chapter 10

THE POLITICS OF NATIONAL STANDARDS: ENVIRONMENTAL PROTECTION

THE IRONY OF AMERICAN ENVIRONMENTAL POLICY

Most environmental policy emerged in an era in which the media made pollution a national issue and in which citizens expected national government leadership. In response, the national government enacted strict laws that unarguably aimed to limit business discretion to pollute the water and air. Even more striking, when compared with other "countries American environmental law is in principle the most rigid and rule-oriented to be found in any industrial society . . . [it] makes more extensive use of uniform standards for emissions and environmental quality than does any other nation . . . [and] makes virtually no use of industry self-regulation . . ." Even so, these stringent American statutes appear no more effective than the more informal and conciliatory approach adopted by Britain.[1] Why is this so?

The rule-oriented character of American environmental law partially reflects the frustrations of federal policymakers who, over time (until the Reagan years), pushed for greater government capacity to regulate the environment, only to find that the incoherence of the policymaking structure frustrated their efforts. Their attempts to nationalize policy by fits and starts resulted in a progressively more limited but still important role for the states, institutional cross-pressures in the national government, uneven enforcement of apparently strict statutes, and frequent political conflicts over federal regulation. These conflicts have pitted government officials against one another as much as government against regulated industries, probably accounting for the fact that "in no nation has environmental policy been the focus of so much political conflict as it has in the United States." The conflict has not produced better enforcement; quite the contrary: "American environmental laws

321

. . . have not been uniformly enforced. Enforcement has been relatively strict in some areas, lax in others."[2]

We begin this chapter by discussing the inherent difficulties involved in any effort to reduce environmental pollution. Second, we argue that the American policymaking system severely compounds the difficulties of designing effective environmental laws. Third, we trace the growing involvement and frustration of federal policymakers with state water and air pollution programs from 1948 to 1970, when political conditions favored aggressive federal policy. Fourth, we analyze the ways in which jurisdictional fragmentation frustrated the enforcement of the stringently written statutes of the 1970s. Finally, we analyze the Reagan administration's effort to reduce federal involvement and increase state control over environmental policy.

POLLUTION: FROM PERSONAL IRRITANT TO THE PUBLIC AGENDA

For the first half of this century citizens viewed environmental pollution as an inevitable personal inconvenience rather than as a social problem. Soot-blackened air became a frequent reality in cities as the number of factories, automobiles, and coal-heated homes multiplied. Many people who could afford to escaped to the suburbs and, when it became available, installed air conditioning.

Public concern about air pollution first focused on the city governments with the worst problems. St. Louis adopted an antismoke ordinance in 1940. In the 1940s most big cities passed similar legislation. But air pollution was not contained within single cities. Whole industrial areas produced smog. In October 1948, smog trapped for a week over Donora, Pennsylvania caused hundreds of people to experience nausea, vomiting, headaches, choking, abdominal pain, and other disorders. Twenty people died. "Killer" smogs settled over London, England, in 1952 and 1962.

Studies conducted in St. Louis in the late 1950s and early 1960s found an accumulation of strontium-90 in children's teeth and contributed to the pressures for passage of the nuclear test ban treaty. Scientists like Barry Commoner and Paul Ehrlich produced readable accounts of environmental degradation. One of the most influential books was Rachel Carson's *Silent Spring*, published in 1962. Her highly controversial bestseller took its title from "Fable for Tomorrow," a riveting scenario of the future:

> Some evil spell had settled on the community: mysterious maladies swept the flocks of chickens; the cattle and sheep sickened and died. Everywhere was the shadow of death. The farmers spoke of much illness among their

families. In the town the doctors had become puzzled by new kinds of sickness appearing among their patients. There had been several un-explained deaths, not only among adults but even among children, who would be stricken suddenly while at play and die within a few hours.[3]

Carson's fable read alarmingly like historical accounts of the Black Plague as it swept across Europe in the fourteenth century. But in this account, a future world was poisoned by the toxic effects of insecticides. Her book went on to describe the persistence of chemical pesticides in the environment, the fact that they had become widely dispersed throughout the world, and the fact that they were concentrated in the fatty tissues of all living organisms.

Carson's work gained support as the environmental damage caused by pesticides became better documented. The numbers of ospreys, bald eagles, peregrine falcons, and pelicans declined precipitously. Research-ers found that DDT interfered with the calcium functions of these birds, so that the shells of their eggs were little more than thin membranes. At each higher level in the biological chain, DDT residues increased. It was present in the body fats and milk of all human beings, even including the Eskimos of Greenland.

Prior to 1969, the concern about the environment was limited to a relatively small, better-educated, more affluent segment of the popula-tion. Some of these people were active in environmental groups. Some were editors and reporters.[4] But public opinion surveys conducted in the 1960s showed a rising popular concern about environmental pollu-tion. The percentage of people who believed that water pollution was a "very serious" problem doubled from 13 percent in 1965 to 27 percent in 1968, and the percentage that viewed air pollution as a very serious problem increased from 10 percent to 25 percent.[5] Only 17 percent mentioned pollution as one of the three most important problems requiring government action in 1965, but by 1970, 53 percent mentioned pollution as one of the top three issues.

The symbolic high point of public concern was "Earth Day," April 22, 1970. Hundreds of thousands of people in schools and communities across the country took part in rallies, teach-ins, car burials, and moral-ity plays portraying evil polluters. Unlike the protests against the Viet-nam War, Earth Day drew a wide spectrum of the public as well as politicians of every persuasion. So many congressmen were speaking at Earth Day rallies (usually in their home districts) that Congress closed down. Earth Day received funds and public support from a large num-ber of corporations, even including oil companies, and it made page one news in the *New York Times, Washington Post,* and most other daily newspapers across the country. For a brief time, the environment had attained the status of a "motherhood" issue, a cultural symbol of citizen concern and popular participation.

Energy shortages and economic sluggishness in the 1970s tempered but did not erase the popular support for environmental regulation. Though public support for air and water pollution control did not remain at the peak levels of the early 1970s, large majorities since then have continued to view pollution control measures as important (Table 10.1). After falling below 50 percent in the late 1970s, the proportion of people believing that "we are spending too little on the environment" returned to mid-1970s levels (56 percent) by 1985. In 1982 more people felt that environmental problems had gotten worse over the preceding decade (48 percent) than felt they had improved (34 percent), and worries about toxic wastes were especially pronounced.[6] The environmental groups that expanded in the early 1970s maintained their strength through the decade and grew stronger in the wake of controversies that erupted during the Reagan administration.

Table 10.1. *American attitudes toward environmental regulation, 1965–1981*

"As for their effect on your way of life in the next few years . . . how would you rate the importance of . . . air pollution control measures?" (Trendex)

	1965	1972	1974	1977	1980	May 1981	August 1981
Very	64%	80%	61%	62%	60%	54%	62%
Some	27	15	27	25	30	32	27
Not	6	5	11	13	10	14	11
Other/n.a.[a]	2	—	—	—	—	—	—

"As for their effect on your way of life in the next few years . . . how would you rate the importance of . . . water pollution control measures?" (Trendex)

	1965	1972	1974	1977	1980	August 1981
Very	74%	90%	75%	71%	72%	75%
Some	19	7	19	22	19	20
Not	4	2	6	7	9	6
Other/n.a.[a]	2	1	—	—	—	—

"Are we spending too much, too little, or about the right amount on . . . Improving and protecting the environment?" (National Opinion Research Center General Social Survey)

	1973	1975	1977	1980	1983	1985
Too little	61%	53%	48%	48%	54%	56%
About right	26	31	35	31	31	32
Too much	7	10	11	15	8	8
Other/n.a.[a]	6	6	7	6	4	4

[a]n.a.: not available

Source: John M. Gilroy and Robert Y. Shapiro, "The Polls: Environmental Protection," *Public Opinion Quarterly* 50:2 (Summer 1986), 270–9.

HOW FRAGMENTED POLICYMAKING COMPLICATED ENVIRONMENTAL REGULATION

Jurisdiction and Air Pollution: A Tale of Two Cities

The practice of burning wood, coal, and trash in open incinerators made the air in St. Louis hard to tolerate by 1940. In the winter of 1939–1940, thick smoke hung over the city almost 40 percent of the time. The *St. Louis Post-Dispatch* reported that the McDonnell Aircraft Corporation, which was planning a new factory near the airport, might move to a city with less polluted air. In February 1940, a citizens committee recommended that the city require the use of smokeless fuels in factories or mechanical fuel-burning equipment and a strengthened City Division of Smoke Regulation. Despite protests by coal mining companies located in the neighboring state of Illinois, the city council approved the ordinance by a nearly unanimous vote in April. Although the council at first exempted the railroads, it reversed itself and banned coal-burning railroad engines from the city. The law was the first of its kind in an American city and became a model copied by several cities, including Pittsburgh, Los Angeles, and East Chicago, Indiana.[7]

East Chicago passed its an antipollution ordinance in 1949, but neighboring Gary, Indiana, did not enact a similar law until 1962, even though the two cities shared air far more polluted than the national average. United States Steel's dominance over Gary's economy motivated city officials to delay placing the issue on the political agenda. In contrast to East Chicago, where several smaller steel companies were located, U.S. Steel's Gary works was the second largest steel plant in the world. City officials refused to consider seriously any proposal to restrict or to impose costs on their city's principal employer.

Though the steel firms located in East Chicago cooperated in writing that city's ordinance, U.S. Steel opposed any local action in Gary. Only when the federal and state governments threatened to intervene in 1961 did U.S. Steel become interested in a local ordinance. Political scientist Matthew Crenson believed that this shift followed from the company's concern that "the power of U.S. Steel would be somewhat diluted if the local air pollution issue were to become a state political issue, and it would be diluted still further if the debate were transferred to the national political arena."[8]

The contrasts between St. Louis, East Chicago, and Gary highlight the critical difference that jurisdiction makes in the way that local governments address environmental concerns. With a more diverse economy, key segments of the St. Louis business community, especially downtown retailers, pushed for pollution abatement. The balance of political power in Gary obviously was more hostile to controls. While the complaints by coal mine owners located in another state had little impact on St. Louis officials, the fear of the consequences of regulating U.S. Steel discouraged most officials in Gary from even raising the issue of pollution in public.

Fragmented Jurisdiction and Environmental Policy Development

There are four reasons why the American policymaking structure has complicated the design of coherent and effective environmental policies, despite the increasing capacity of government to police pollution. First, the potential impact on local economic vitality tends to limit most jurisdictions' effort. Second, policy varies across jurisdictions, and the variation does not necessarily reflect differences in environmental pollution. Third, pollution problems that cross political boundaries require jurisdictional cooperation that is difficult to achieve. Finally, fragmented national policymaking institutions often cannot align on behalf of coherent policy implementation; instead Congress, the courts, and the bureaucracies frequently undermine one another.

Unless public concern is strongly expressed and an influential segment of the business community supports environmental regulation, state and local governments tend to resist regulating pollution because of a fear that the affected industries may flee regulation by moving to other jurisdictions. In any case most state and local governments are unable to finance an effective antipollution effort. Enforcement requires the cooperation of state and local agencies that deal with highways, land use, natural resources, and economic development. At best, these agencies are not accustomed to dealing with pollution. At worst, they have viewed pollution control as an invasion of their responsibilities and a threat to their constituencies.[9]

In the absence of compelling national government incentives to mitigate pollution, state governments respond only when a manifest crisis occurs. This was the impetus that drove California to respond to one of the worst air pollution problems in the world, in the Los Angeles basin. After angry citizens of Los Angeles marched on city hall in 1946 demanding steps to reduce smog, city officials requested advice from a principal architect of the St. Louis ordinance. He concluded that the political fragmentation in the Los Angeles area prevented a citywide ordinance from having much of an effect and therefore urged the creation of an areawide pollution abatement district. Soon after, in 1947, the California legislature passed the nation's first state air pollution law. Although the railroad and oil industries objected that the bill would "unlawfully burden interstate commerce," advocates for the bill successfully played on the sense of crisis. The bill allowed the Los Angeles area to create a "pollution abatement" district that could control emissions through a system of permits.[10]

By 1963, thirty-three states and territories had enacted air pollution laws. These excluded several states (including Michigan, Wisconsin, and Missouri) with some of the largest and most polluted urban areas in the country. Only five states had developed water pollution abatement programs. Most others left responsibility (and expenditure) to local governments.[11] Pennsylvania's 1960 air pollution statute typified the cautiousness of the states that enacted smog statutes. Having declared it state policy to ensure "a reasonable degree of purity of . . . air resources," the legislation asserted that "the measures for the accomplishment of this purpose shall not unreasonably obstruct the attraction, development and expansion of business, industry, and commerce within the Commonwealth, but shall be technically feasible and economically reasonable."[12]

Jurisdictional fragmentation complicates pollution abatement in the United States because pollution rarely is confined neatly within one jurisdiction's boundaries. Particularly in the eastern half of the country most states share at least one urban area—and thus a serious pollution problem—with another state. Watersheds also sprawl across state lines, so that pollution in a river in one state often becomes a problem for cities, counties, and states downstream. Thus a city or state with stricter standards may find its efforts overwhelmed by the effluents from a neighboring jurisdiction with lax laws or unenforced regulations. The inability to regulate a pollution source combines with interstate competition to provoke bitter conflicts. For example, in the 1970s, "Pennsylvania has claimed . . . that Ohio's failure to meet air quality standards pollutes Pennsylvania air and gives a cost advantage to Ohio steel mills over Pennsylvanian mills operating under more stringent laws."[13]

Uniform regional or national regulations are hard to devise and enforce. Members of Congress often battle against environmental solutions opposed by their constituents, especially business. The "scrubber" battle in Congress, for example, pitted eastern against western coal-mining states. Faced with installing expensive smokestack "scrubbers" to reduce emissions, utilities suggested that they could comply with the 1970 Clean Air Act simply by using low-sulfur western coal instead of eastern coal. Eastern coal mine companies and the United Mine Workers pressed hard instead for "scrubber" legislation, which was eventually adopted.[14] The increasing number of congressional subcommittees in the 1970s (Chapter 5) compounded the problem by increasing the number of rivalries and battles within Congress.

The Air Quality Act of 1967 prompted a battle between the California congressional delegation, seeking to protect its state's right to enforce strict regulations on automobile emissions, and the delegation from the Detroit area that sought a uniform national standard less stringent than the California code. Likewise, actions by Congressman John Blatnick (D, Minnesota), long the chair of the House Subcommittee on Rivers and

Harbors, revealed the problems often posed by Congress's closeness to local interests. Blatnick was a leading sponsor of increasingly stringent federal water quality legislation in the 1960s. But in 1969 he discouraged the publication of a report by the Interior Department that the Reserve Mining Company, one of the largest employers in his district, was violating water pollution standards by dumping sixty thousand tons of potentially cancer-causing waste daily into Lake Superior.[15]

The dual nature of the federal court system, which is structured to conform to existing jurisdictional lines, created irresistible cross-pressures that garbled federal environmental regulation. The ninety-one U.S. district courts decide most of the cases in the federal judicial system. These courts are divided along state lines, so that no district court has jurisdiction in more than one state. The eleven circuit courts of appeals and the Supreme Court hear challenges to district court decisions. According to R. Shep Melnick, an analyst of court decisions in environmental law, appellate court decisions have tended to interpret national environmental laws very strictly and to require the Environmental Protection Agency (EPA) to deal rigidly with states and businesses (the reasons that the legislation set such strict standards are discussed on pages 335–341). But district courts and appellate courts in areas where strict enforcement could hurt the local economy frequently have frustrated the enforcement of these strict laws.

> It is only a slight exaggeration to say that trial judges [in the district courts] and appellate judges see the entire regulatory world differently. The former not only directly observe the effect of imposing strict regulations, but share responsibility for imposing these burdens on local citizens. The latter, more removed from local concerns, better able to place responsibility for enforcement on others, and more likely to be inspired by statements about broad public goals, value uniformity more than flexibility. To the trial judge justice requires being responsive to the peculiar needs of individual citizens and localities. To the appellate judge it means consistent, unbending application of the laws and the intent of Congress.[16]

The structure of the courts and their independence of the EPA and Congress helped to make environmental policy inconsistent and contradictory in the 1970s. Environmental groups seeking strict enforcement of antipollution laws won major victories in the U.S. circuit courts of appeals, particularly in the District of Columbia. That court, for example, decided that states with air that was already cleaner than national standards had to take steps to prevent a deterioration to the national norm (*Sierra Club* v. *Ruckelshaus*, 1972). This decision forced the EPA into a confrontation with western governors seeking to promote industrial growth in their states. Individual industries concentrated all their legal resources at the district court level (and in a few favorable circuit courts) to frustrate the enforcement of the rules.

Midwestern utility companies in Ohio, Indiana, and Illinois contributed heavily to sulfur dioxide emissions east of the Mississippi, but they persuaded some carefully selected state and federal courts to delay the enforcement of most EPA regulations through the 1970s. In the case of a St. Louis utility, *Union Electric Co.* v. *Environmental Protection Agency,* a district court delayed enforcement of air quality standards rules in 1975, only to be reversed by the circuit court and the Supreme Court. When Union Electric was taken to court again for noncompliance in 1978, the district court again delayed enforcement.[17]

National policymakers often have recognized that America's policy structure makes it extremely difficult to design an effective response to environmental pollution. As a former Bureau of the Budget official noted in the early 1970s,

> The influence of polluting industries tends to be greater at the state and local level than at the national level. Such industries are more important to the economy of the locality or state than to the national economy and thus have more bargaining power. They can threaten to leave the locality . . . Also, the state and local governments must carry on a continuing relationship with the industries involved, and it is the states and localities who must take specific actions directed for or against specific groups . . . The greater vulnerability of the state and local governments to polluters carries over to the national level by way of the local orientation of the Congress. The industries affected adversely by pollution regulation can generally find a more sympathetic ear in the Congress than they can in the Executive Branch.[18]

Abraham Ribicoff, a former state governor and Secretary of Health, Education and Welfare (HEW) put it more bluntly in 1963: "we understand the great pressures against doing anything in our respective States when it comes to air pollution and water pollution. It takes a lot of courage and a lot of guts."[19]

THE FRUSTRATIONS OF INCOHERENT POLICY ACTIVISM: 1948–1969

From Passivity to Limited Activism

The national government showed little interest in environmental pollution until after World War II. The Rivers and Harbors Act of 1899, which outlawed the dumping of debris in navigable waters, was intended to promote commerce rather than reduce pollution.[20] The rising popular concern about pollution led to the national government's first antipollution legislation in 1948. Enacted with the support of Republicans who controlled the House and Senate, the Water Pollution Control Act of 1948 laid to rest any doubt that state and local governments would retain most of the control over pollution policy.

> In connection with the exercise of jurisdiction over the waterways of the Nation and in consequence of the benefits resulting to the public health and welfare by the abatement of stream pollution, it is hereby declared to be the policy of Congress to recognize, preserve, and protect the primary responsibilities and rights of the States in controlling water pollution, to support and aid technical research . . . and to provide Federal technical services to State and interstate agencies and to industries, and financial aid to State and interstate agencies and to municipalities, in the formulation and execution of their stream pollution abatement programs.[21]

The legislation permitted the U.S. Public Health Service to coordinate research, provide technical assistance, and enforce water quality standards in interstate waters *if* requested to do so by an affected state. The federal government would establish a laboratory to research water pollution. The program provided for low-interest loans (not grants-in-aid) to state and local governments for the construction of waste treatment facilities. This approach suited key congressional Republicans, led by Senator Robert A. Taft of Ohio. A candidate for his party's 1948 presidential nomination, Taft wanted to appear to be an activist on this issue, but within the tradition of states' rights. Thus, the water pollution law essentially exhorted states and localities to do more, without significantly expanding the federal government's authority or financial commitment.[22] At the same time, it provided constituent benefits for which legislators could claim credit. The first water research laboratory was built in Taft's home state of Ohio, and eventually laboratories were built in the districts of the chairmen of the relevant House Appropriations subcommittee and the House and Senate Rivers and Harbors Committees, despite protests that dividing the research among several laboratories would impair research.[23]

Disagreement over water pollution legislation became sharp and partisan when Congressman Blatnick proposed to convert the loan program to grants in the mid-1950s. Efforts to defeat the bill in the House failed on party-line votes won by the majority Democrats. The Water Pollution Control Act of 1956 authorized a small grant program ($50 million a year) that President Eisenhower objected to but did not veto. State and local sewage treatment construction increased from $200 million in 1955 to $300 million in 1957 to $400 million in 1958.

Organizations of state public officials at first were skeptical of the grants, but as federal dollars poured in, they lobbied with increasing fervor for them.[24] They objected when President Eisenhower vetoed a bill passed in 1959 that would have doubled the authorization. Eisenhower argued that ". . . pollution and its correction are so closely involved with local industrial processes and with public water supply and sewage treatment, that the problem can be successfully met only if State and local governments and industry assume the major responsibility for cleaning up the nation's rivers and streams."[25]

The Eisenhower administration firmly resisted any national intervention to reduce air pollution. An official of the Department of Health, Education, and Welfare insisted that "instances of troublesome interstate air pollution are few in number . . .," while the Bureau of the Budget asserted that "unlike water pollution, air pollution . . . is essentially a local problem."[26] The Clean Air Act of 1955 did little more than authorize $5 million for federal research. One of the bill's sponsors, Senator Thomas Kuchel (R-California), assured colleagues that "It is not thought that Congress has anything to do with control of air pollution . . . That problem remains where it ought to remain—in the States of the Union, and in the cities and the counties of our country."[27]

The Kennedy Administration: Increasing National Leverage

During the 1960 election campaign Kennedy attacked the Eisenhower administration for vetoing the water pollution bill, and he endorsed a stronger version that would double available federal funds. Republican leaders conceded the value of the program but opposed doubling the grants and demanded that the state governments share the financing of waste treatment. To build support, the Kennedy administration sought to increase state and local activism and at the same time to achieve more uniform results.[28] Perennial gadfly Representative H. R. Gross (R, Iowa) questioned why Mississippi would qualify for grants when it "substantially reduced its taxes on corporations and individuals, and now comes crying to the U.S. government for help . . . Iowa [does] not benefit as much as does the state of Mississippi under the terms of this bill."[29]

Opponents attacked a clause in the bill that extended potential federal jurisdiction to "all navigable waters." Previously limited specifically to *inter*state waters (about four thousand of the twenty-six thousand bodies of water in the United States), the 1961 proposal authorized the federal government to address *intra*state water pollution for the first time. Representative Blatnick countered that the federal government should intervene against intrastate water pollution only if a state or city requested that it do so, and even then the governor or state water agency had to agree to federal intervention. Provisions that could conceivably threaten states' rights had already been removed. When a proposal to create a Federal Water Pollution Control Administration was withdrawn by the Secretary of HEW, the Public Health Service and its allies, the associations of state health officers, sanitary engineers, and legal officials protested the change.[30]

Senator Edmund S. Muskie (D, Maine), the chair of the Subcommittee on Air and Water Pollution (created in 1963), pressed the Kennedy administration to take similar steps to control air pollution. The administration was divided about strengthening national authority, with the Bureau of the Budget opposed to a new permanent grant program and the Public Health Service opposed to national enforcement powers. The Department of HEW and the urban public interest groups supported the stronger legislation that eventually was introduced. Such a bill would, in the words of an urban lobbyist, attract liberals because "it *does* something, and indicates forward movement," while it would attract conservatives because it "does it at relatively little cost."[31]

Again, congressional debates turned mainly on state and local autonomy. Senator Gaylord Nelson (D, Wisconsin) warned that state discretion in air pollution control would result in irresistible industrial pressures and lax enforcement.[32] At the Senate hearings, key business groups, such as the National Association of Manufacturers and the U.S. Chamber of Commerce, objected that a strong federal role violated states' rights. The Manufacturing Chemical Association opposed national enforcement of air quality standards even when pollution in one state affected citizens in another.

Despite this well-organized business opposition, Congress enacted the popular Clean Air Act of 1963. For the first time, the national government was given a role in air pollution enforcement, as opposed to research. As in the case of water pollution, however, the law set up a cumbersome, state-dominated enforcement process. The act authorized federal lawsuits against polluters only at the request of a governor. The law set no federal standards for air quality; instead, state officials (or, in interstate cases, the Department of HEW) would determine when air pollution threatened health. The mayors' organizations successfully added a provision that limited any one state to one-eighth of the $95 million authorized for the three-year program.[33]

The Johnson Administration: The States' "Last" Chance

Unusually large Democratic majorities elected to Congress in 1964 made possible a more direct federal participation in pollution control. President Johnson supported stronger antipollution legislation in general and more rigorous controls on industry in particular. In his autobiography, Johnson recalled asking a speechwriter to draft a "tough" statement to tell the stockholders of the guiltiest industrial polluters "what their companies are doing to our environment."[34] But except for automobile exhausts, the antipollution legislation that emerged between

1964 and 1969 still relied on the states. The failure of this legislation to clean up polluted air set the stage for the unprecedented strictness of the environmental laws of the 1970s.

The Water Quality Act of 1965 authorized the Secretary of HEW to establish standards for the quality of interstate waters, created a new enforcement agency in HEW, and increased water pollution grants from $100 million to $150 million. Once again, the expansion of federal authority implied by nationally established standards generated the most heated opposition. "Standards of water quality are concededly badly needed," argued House Republicans, "but should be established by the state and local agencies which are most familiar with all aspects of the matter in a given locality, including the economic impact of establishing and enforcing stringent standards of water quality."[35]

The Senate defeated an effort to drop the federal standards-setting power by a vote of fifteen to sixty-two and also defeated (by twenty-nine to fifty-four) an amendment to require the secretary to consider the "practicability and economic feasibility" of such standards. As enacted, the law gave the states two years to set standards for interstate waters (and portions of waters within a state). Congressman Blatnick said of this outcome, "Let it not be said that the states have not been given full power to establish for themselves" water quality standards.[36] The Clean Waters Restoration Act of 1966 sharply increased federal financing of sewage treatment by authorizing $3.55 billion for five years, increasing the potential federal share of a project from 30 percent to 50 percent, and removing the dollar ceiling on individual grants.[37]

Problems with this state-based approach soon became obvious. The states moved slowly and inconsistently in response to the opportunity to set water quality standards. Four years after the 1967 deadline for state plans, fewer than thirty states had formulated plans in an attempt to meet federal standards, and many of these plans omitted any means of enforcement. "Most states . . . made little or no effort to write an enforceable scheme of careful emission controls against major pollution sources" and "most states . . . permitted some deterioration of existing clean water bodies when writing quality standards for them."[38]

State opposition to national standards began to undermine federal authority. In February 1968, Secretary of the Interior Stuart Udall announced that future state water quality standards would include a provision that prohibited the deterioration of water quality even if the current quality met the requirements of the legislation. Governors in the more rapidly growing states vehemently attacked such regulation in the belief that it would slow new construction and industrial expansion in their states. Colorado Governor John Love declared that "the control of the use and development of water is tantamount to absolute control of the state. For we Governors to accept such an edict and to grant such power to any agency would be no less than traitorous."[39]

Congress further fragmented water pollution control procedures when it enacted additional grant-in-aid programs. Four new grant programs for sewer and waste treatment construction enacted in 1965 authorized four cabinet departments to distribute funds with virtually no coordination other than a common preliminary application form.[40]

The expansion of the federal role in air pollution took the same path as the development of water pollution policy. In 1964, when the state of California set emissions limits for new cars to be sold in the state beginning in 1967, the federal government set similar standards for its fleet and Congress directed the secretary of HEW to publish national standards for motor vehicle emissions. Because automobiles were manifestly sold in interstate commerce, no one seriously questioned federal authority to regulate automobile emissions. Automobile manufacturers in 1965 indicated that they could meet the standards.[41]

The auto industry supported federal legislation because bills to regulate automobile exhausts already had been introduced in eighteen state legislatures by February 1967. These bills contained a dizzying variety of engineering and design requirements. If enacted, they would have required the auto companies to tailor their models to individual states. The auto companies began to argue that state variation "could create chaos not only within the industry but in the economy and be harmful to the consumer as well."[42]

Conflict over the automobile emissions section of the 1967 Air Quality Act narrowed to a battle over California's right to maintain stricter standards than the federal government. Detroit area Representative John Dingell tried to add a section preempting California's law, but because of the united support of the California delegation, the House voted 152 to 58 to permit California to continue to enforce its rules (however, on a voice vote the House rejected another amendment that would have allowed other states to set stricter standards).[43]

The Air Quality Act of 1967 expanded federal responsibility for regulating air pollution, but unlike the regulation of automobile exhausts, the states retained the authority to monitor stationary sources of pollution. The Air Quality Act gave the states a "last chance" to assume primary responsibility for policing stationary sources of air pollution. The law required states to set criteria for air quality and permitted the national government to do so if a state failed to act. Congress rejected uniform national emission standards sought by the Johnson administration, preferring instead Senator Muskie's approach:

> Muskie wanted to give the states a big responsibility and force them to rise up to it. It was his view that we should not write them off but add to their responsibility and make them realize that. This was a mistaken assumption because the states simply lacked the capability to take on this responsibility.[44]

The federal government would publish criteria for setting standards of air quality, but the states would actually set and enforce the standards. The law delegated enforcement to new administrative agencies staffed by participating states, based on an atmospheric region (or "airshed").

In effect, the Air Quality Act put the federal government in the position of being an adversary against the states without enhancing federal capacity to enforce clean air regulations. Local officials soon concluded that the act was a disaster—"difficult to administer," "terribly ponderous," and "cumbersome." The Department of HEW was slow to provide the criteria for air quality, and the states were slow to respond once standards were forthcoming. By the end of the three-year authorization period, no state had completed all of the required steps for regulating air quality mandated by the law. Local officials, who had the most experience in managing air pollution programs, concluded that the regional air quality offices mandated by the law were even worse than complete state control. They constituted just another layer of bureaucracy that allowed "somewhat better coordination, a confusing set of jurisdictional relationships, and a great deal more paperwork."[45] By 1970, efforts to leverage better voluntary state performance and interstate cooperation had failed.[46]

FROM NATIONAL ACTIVISM TO NATIONAL ENVIRONMENTAL STANDARDS IN THE 1970s

Political conditions in 1969 and 1970 favored the adoption of more stringent federal environmental regulation. The surge in public concern about pollution (Table 10.1) created a climate of environmental "hysteria" in the White House and on Capitol Hill. The overwhelming public consensus led Republicans and Democrats to jockey for the position of vigilant environmental guardian. Edmund Muskie, the Senate's leading environmental policy expert, was at the time emerging as the leading contender for the Democratic presidential nomination for the 1972 election. Muskie's political ambitions prompted President Nixon to become an environmental advocate. Moreover, the White House hoped that an emphasis on environmental issues would reduce the hostility engendered by the administration's conduct of the Vietnam War.[47]

"Frustration was the major impetus that pushed policy along the escalation course," concluded Helen Ingram.[48] The ineffectiveness of state-controlled water and air pollution programs made more centralized and stringent regulation attractive to key political figures.

From Carrot to Stick

In January 1969, the U.S. Justice Department brought a suit against the Automobile Manufacturers Association charging that the auto companies had conspired to delay emissions controls. An out-of-court settlement created the impression that the automakers had placed profit before public health. A massive oil spill off the coast of Santa Barbara, California in 1969 convinced Secretary of the Interior Walter Hickel that private corporations were obstructing environmental protection. When Hickel found widespread rule violations on oil rigs in the Gulf of Mexico, he concluded that "You've got to hit them with a two-by-four to make them believe you."[49] Auto industry leaders failed to convince Nixon that tightened emissions standards for the 1973 and 1975 models were unreasonable, and Commerce Secretary Maurice Stans could not persuade the president to remove injunctive procedures and stiff fines from the air and water quality proposals the administration introduced in 1970.[50]

The National Environmental Protection Act of 1969 (signed by the President on January 1, 1970) established a Council on Environmental Quality (CEQ) in the Executive Office of the President. The CEQ played an intelligence-gathering and monitoring role similar to that of the U.S. Civil Rights Commission. The Act required all federal agencies to file "environmental impact statements" with the CEQ that would specify the effects of new dams, river improvements, or other construction projects on environmental quality.[51] Suddenly it seemed to politicians and policy-makers that effective pollution control required a powerful federal agency.

By 1970, forty-four agencies in nine federal departments divided responsibility for environmental and national resources policy. Bureaucratic and interest group resistance made an overarching Department of Natural Resources politically infeasible, but in July 1970 the administration proposed a limited plan to place air and water pollution agencies in a new Environmental Protection Agency. The legislation sailed through Congress with ease. The first administrator, William D. Ruckelshaus, ordered strict enforcement of environmental laws to "single out violators with the greatest visibility in order to get the message across." During his first months in office Ruckelshaus ordered legal actions against 185 violators, including U.S. Steel, ITT, and the cities of Detroit and Cleveland.[52]

The political competition to claim credit for stringent environmental regulations peaked as Congress renewed the Clean Air Act in 1970. Frustration with the states' lax enforcement of air pollution statutes made strict national standards more acceptable than ever before.[53] In February Nixon committed himself to tougher federal control. The administration proposed national standards for air quality, stronger federal enforcement, and a timetable for the reduction of automobile exhausts (despite the automakers' protests that they could not develop an adequate technology in time to meet mid-decade deadlines).

The Democrats in Congress proposed an even stronger bill by moving up deadlines, mandating fixed emissions standards that the administration could not delay, and by giving citizens the right to take the EPA to court to compel it to enforce the law. In early June, the House Interstate and Foreign Commerce Committee approved a version of the Nixon bill that strengthened six of its eight main provisions. The House voted 374–1 in favor of the bill a week later. With his reputation as an environmental champion questioned by consumer advocates on the left and Nixon on the right, Muskie and his subcommittee further strengthened the bill when it reached the Senate. In September the Senate passed it unanimously.[54]

The Water Pollution Control Act of 1972 set forth an even more ambitious mandate by stating as a goal "that the discharge of pollutants into the navigable waters be eliminated by 1985." As in the case of clean air statutes, "dissatisfaction with what states were accomplishing pushed Congress to take each successive step in establishing a dominant Federal presence."[55] This act combined an expansive grants strategy with federal standards. It authorized $24.7 billion for grants for local waste treatment and required industries to install the best "practicable" technology by 1977 and the best "available" technology by 1983. The law passed the House and Senate by overwhelming majorities, and when president Nixon vetoed the bill in October (against the advice of the EPA), Congress quickly overrode his veto.[56]

These two laws were exceptionally stringent compared with previous federal statutes and to regulations in other industrial nations. Yet a fully nationalized policy still was not set in place. Substantial state discretion in choosing how to make a specific polluter comply with the law was preserved.[57] The Clean Air Act required states to adopt state implementation plans (SIPs) that spelled out the politically difficult decisions about what specific requirements were to be imposed on each stationary pollution source within their borders. The congressional debate made it clear that Congress intended to establish a clean air standard that would simultaneously preserve state discretion and at the same time achieve uniform policy:

> Rep. Harley Staggers (D, West Virginia): . . . no one is preventing any State from having stronger standards . . . We are not holding them back, but we say that all of the States must comply with the nationwide standards. . . . if any State does not come up with a State plan to the satisfaction of the federal Government then the federal Government will step in and establish a plan for such a state . . .

> Rep. John Jarman (D, Oklahoma): The promulgation of federal emissions standards for new sources in the aforementioned categories will preclude efforts on the part of states to compete with each other in trying to attract new plants and facilities without assuring adequate control of extra-hazardous or large-scale emissions therefrom.

Concerns expressed by Representatives Robert Eckhardt (D, Texas) and George Mahon (D, Texas) about the effect of the law on the competitive position of steel mills and cotton gins in their respective districts underscored the point.[58]

The Environmental Protection Agency Walks a Political Tightrope

Few of the lawmakers appreciated the enforcement problems inherent in the policies they had devised. First, the laws required the federal and state governments to confront economically and politically powerful industries as an adversary. No established tradition of business–government consultation facilitated a less confrontational alternative, as it did abroad. Second, the agency charged with confronting these powerful interests was new and untested. The EPA never had adequate personnel or funding to carry out its responsibilities effectively, and its inevitable mistakes cast doubt on environmental regulation itself. Third, specific provisions, notably the auto emissions standards for 1975, set very strict standards in an attempt to force industry to develop and use technologies that were still untested and undeveloped. Senator Muskie conceded to a Michigan colleague that the deadline might have to be extended if the automakers genuinely could not develop equipment in time to meet the deadline.[59]

Fourth, and most important, the laws required centralized policy in a government structure still internally fragmented and dominated by policymaking institutions capable of sabotaging the EPA's strategies. Frustration with past policy failures caused legislators to include several provisions that forced the EPA to confront subnational governments and industry, but by 1977 Congress redesigned the laws to protect constituents from the consequences of these confrontations. Key court decisions often prevented a more conciliatory approach. In turn, local courts undermined EPA authority by exempting particular targets from regulation. In such cases the EPA was compelled to pronounce strict standards it was not allowed to enforce—a result that frequently thrust the EPA into a no-win situation that exhausted its energy and eroded its legitimacy. Environmentalists and industrialists distrusted it in equal measure, leaving it with no stable constituency support.

Auto emissions. Ruckelshaus's plans to improve air quality centered on strictly enforcing the emissions deadlines imposed on the auto industry. He anticipated being more flexible in requiring states to impose more controversial restrictions on automobile traffic in cities. The U.S. Supreme Court frustrated the first part of this strategy in February 1973, when it ordered the EPA to reconsider its decision to enforce the emissions deadlines. Two months later Ruckelshaus agreed to suspend some of the emissions standards for a year. By the fall, the shortage of oil made

Congress more willing to delay pollution enforcement, in the interest of oil conservation. The following spring Congress suspended the standards for two years, and the EPA subsequently delayed them for another year. Amendments to the Clean Air Act in 1977 delayed the deadline until the early 1980s, when they finally took effect.[60]

In twenty-five of the largest urban areas air quality standards could be achieved only by modifying cars that were already in use and inspecting them annually, by improving mass transit, or by limiting driving. Two court cases (*Riverside* v. *Ruckelshaus,* November 1972, and *National Resources Defense Council* v. *Environmental Protection Agency,* February 1973) prohibited any delay in implementing local transportation control plans. Under a court order in the *Riverside* case the EPA announced that gasoline would have to be rationed in the Los Angeles area and other drastic measures would have to be taken to reduce driving by 82 percent for several months each year. To meet their deadlines, the EPA estimated that more than three dozen cities would have to implement similar controls. As an EPA official put it, "The public reaction was one of utter disbelief . . . It was immediately clear that achieving the objectives of the Clean Air Act would require changes that touched citizens in their daily lives."[61] The EPA rapidly lost credibility when it threatened to impose stringent measures but in private signaled that it would not actually force draconian solutions.[62]

Stationary sources. The Clean Air Act required states to develop strict regulations of their industries within a nine-month period. Understaffed and underfunded state air pollution agencies "generally developed very simple plans using very simple methods" that ignored the problems of economic efficiency, uncertainty, and growth. Responding to the groundswell of environmental concern in 1971–1972, state elected officials pressed for relatively strict State Implementation Plans (SIPs). Industry began to challenge the legitimacy of the SIPs, to defy compliance orders, and to challenge the SIPs in court.[63] In a short time the states began to relax their regulations. In 1974 the Massachusetts legislature passed an industry lobbyists' bill relaxing the state's SIP. North Carolina weakened its SIP after one house of the legislature passed a bill to prevent the state's environmental laws from being more restrictive than those of any other state.[64]

Enforcement of the state implementation plans, especially in the most difficult cases, clearly required EPA intervention. State enforcement agencies had little ability to police their regulations adequately (one study estimated that "inspectors would have to perform anywhere from three to thirty inspections daily just to inspect each source annually"). These agencies often needed cooperation by elected state attorneys general to bring an action against a violator. State legislatures cut the budgets of overaggressive agencies and occasionally transferred over-zealous officials.[65]

State governments did not take up the EPA's offer to proceed on their own in prosecuting violators. Daunted by the prospect of taking on big corporations, states preferred to hand the problem over to the EPA. The reasons for this were recounted by an EPA official to Senator Muskie's subcommittee in 1979:

> . . . these [civil and criminal actions] include the largest, most complicated (sometimes most recalcitrant) sources . . . These included the deadline-violating large power plants, steel mills, pulp and paper mills, chemical plants, etc. . . . Analysis indicates that 510 of the 609 facilities designated for civil actions (84%) and all of the 5 designated for criminal actions were left by the states for federal . . . action . . . [W]ith a few notable exceptions, almost all the largest and most difficult sources were left to EPA and the Department of Justice. I call this to the attention of the Committee not to criticize the States, but to indicate the essentiality [sic] of a strong, active federal presence in enforcement if the large sources are to be made to comply and national consistency achieved. It is often very controversial for the federal government to enforce against these sources, but if we do not, no one will.[66]

And often, no one did. Some state enforcement officials believed that the EPA was not aggressive enough. A Massachusetts official complained that the EPA was not as aggressive in starting legal actions against violators as was his own agency.[67]

Water pollution. In 1970 the Council on Environmental Quality persuaded the EPA to adopt a clever and heavily interventionist approach to water pollution control. Under the plan, the EPA would require polluters to obtain a permit to discharge wastes, using authority established in the Refuse Act of 1899. Most of the Nixon administration agencies supported the strategy, including the Commerce Department, which viewed it as a more predictable process than the aggregate outcome of individual lawsuits.[68] But within eighteen months, twenty thousand permit applications flooded the EPA, making a mockery of an apparently good idea (a court decision rendered this approach moot in 1972).[69]

The EPA had more success in limiting discharges from large industrial sources under the 1972 Clean Water Act, but at the cost of generating significant conflict with industry. By 1975, 150 lawsuits had been filed against the agency, and by 1976 requests for formal hearings were filed in 1 out of 10 cases. The law provided that states could assume authority for regulating water pollution, and twenty-six had done so by 1975.

Funding for municipal wastewater treatment slowed after it became entangled in conflict between Congress and the president. Nixon impounded $9 billion, hoping that the courts would strike down congressional legislation requiring the cities to spend money for wastewater treatment. The courts did so. Construction of new plants was behind schedule by 1977, when only about half of the cities met the statutory standards.[70]

Congress reacts to the EPA. By the mid-1970s, strict rules and complicated enforcement had created almost insurmountable political problems . Industries and state and local governments expected their legislators to protect them from bearing the costs of environmental laws. When Congress amended the statutes in 1977, it reduced the stringency of some standards, increased the EPA's authority to enforce remaining standards, and added provisions that allowed their constituents to avoid some of the consequences of individual EPA regulations. Automobile exhaust standards were delayed until 1980–1981, "healthy" air quality achievement was postponed until the middle 1980s, and the goal of "zero discharge" of water pollutants was abandoned until the 1990s. The Clean Air Act amendments permitted the EPA and Transportation Department to cut off grants to noncomplying jurisdictions. Amendments to the Clean Water Act set additional standards for 129 toxic pollutants. At the same time, state and local interests gained some leverage with the EPA. Governors were given the power to suspend any transportation controls that required gasoline rationing, parking controls, or limited access to cities. States received more responsibility for water treatment facilities and wastewater management.[71]

By 1980 Congress added new laws addressing the "second generation" of environmental problems. Widespread toxic waste contamination became the leading environmental issue of the 1980s. The discovery of toxic wastes in Love Canal, New York and Times Beach, Missouri, forced families to abandon their homes. Hundreds of toxic waste accidents occurred each year in the 1980s, and the EPA identified over 20,000 toxic waste sites in the United States by 1985. In December 1984, more than 2,500 residents in the area of Bhopal, India, died after a cloud of methyl isocyanate, a toxic gas, escaped from a nearby Union Carbide factory.[72]

In legislation passed before the 1980s, the states were given a primary role in implementing hazardous waste policies, but they could defer to the national government if they felt that large enforcement effort were necessary. The EPA moved slowly to execute the Toxic Substances Control Act of 1976, the Resource Conservation and Recovery Act of 1976 (a law that regulated hazardous waste disposal), and the "Superfund" of 1980 (a law that created a federal fund for cleaning up toxic waste sites such as Love Canal and Times Beach). Regulations for the 1976 act were not finalized until 1980, for example.[73]

In the interim, forty-four states began to regulate hazardous waste. However, the states' political will and ability to control the serious environmental threat posed by hazardous waste varied widely. By the early 1980s there was an inverse relationship between the amount of a state's budget that was committed to environmental quality and the number of toxic waste sites identified in the state. Political scientist Bruce Williams suggested that "[t]hese figures might even indicate that hazardous waste site operators are drawn to states that spend little on regulation, since the absence of such oversight would make site operation easier and cheaper."[74]

Qualified Success and Political Vulnerability

Considering the political problems faced by the EPA, and in light of the growth of industrial production (which increased 50 percent between 1965 and 1980), of cities and of driving, it would be remarkable if air and water quality did not deteriorate further in the 1970s and 1980s.[75] Instead, regulation resulted in measurable environmental improvement after the early 1970s. The concentration of lead in the air fell appreciably after 1970, and carbon monoxide and sulfur dioxide concentrations also declined. Airborne particulate levels held steady through the 1970s but diminished during the recession of the early 1980s, as did ozone, which fell briefly but began to rise again in 1983.[76] The sharp reductions in emissions by automobiles built since 1972 account for much of the improvement in air quality.

Achievements in water quality up to 1980 are harder to discern. Still, water quality improved from 1963 to 1972, and between 1972 and 1980 most pollutants stayed at about the same level or declined. Some lakes and rivers once given up for "dead," such as Lake Erie, were partially restored. Samples of freshwater fish show significant declines in toxic chemicals such as DDT and PCBs since 1970. Manufacture of both these chemicals is banned through federal legislation.[77]

In every instance in which the EPA has had to work through states or local governments, progress has been slower. By the 1977 target date, only one in five industrial sources of water pollution (enforcement through SIPs) and three out of seven municipalities had met the goals of using the "best practicable technology" for reducing wastes. Since the EPA had limited personnel to enforce the laws and since it had to devote much of its time and energy to litigation (much of it initiated by cities and states), it often could not identify violations at all. It often negotiated standards with individual polluters to save time. The compromises did not always benefit the environment. Firms in Virginia negotiated agreements that, in effect, permitted them to increase the amount of waste they could dump into nearby waters. From 1977 to 1980, fines amounted to $69.3 million, or about 0.1 percent of compliance costs.[78]

The U.S. approach to environmental regulation guaranteed that, however successful it was in some respects, it would remain constantly vulnerable to political attack. In his study comparing British and American environmental policy, David Vogel concluded that:

> The fact that many American environmental regulations have been written in such a way that they cannot be enforced means that government officials, unlike those in Britain, receive no credit for enforcing them in a flexible manner . . . While British industrialists attribute their government's system of flexible enforcement to the 'good sense' of their nation's officials, the American business community tends to attribute the 'regulatory relief' granted them by either Congress, regulatory agencies, or the courts as to their own lobbying and litigations skills. Rather than getting credit for being 'reasonable,' the government is blamed for enacting 'unrealistic' regulations in the first place . . . the economics of enforcement may be similar in both nations, but the political and legal context in which they take place differs markedly.[79]

When Ronald Reagan was elected president in 1980, the percentage of Americans who believed that the nation was spending too much on environmental protection was at its highest level since opinion polls began asking systematic questions about the environment.

THE REAGAN ADMINISTRATION'S ENVIRONMENTAL POLICY

As a presidential candidate Reagan promised to liberate American industry from "excessive" environmental regulations. He even redefined the concept of "environment" to include "economic prosperity," and then argued that because antipollution laws reduce profits they harm the environment. During his campaign and early in his administration, he took little interest in environmental policy (as conventionally defined) except when sympathizing with complaints by industrialists.[80] Conservative policy thinktanks and organizations such as the Heritage Foundation conceded the "unquestioned" need for a national environmental agency and admitted that "remarkable progress has been achieved" in water and air pollution control since the early 1960s. But the foundation attacked "crippling and costly EPA regulation," inept management, overcentralization, and excessively costly pollution remedies.[81] The Reagan administration agreed with this analysis, and it soon reduced the federal government's ability to regulate the environment and increased the states' discretion in environmental policy.

Reducing Federal Capacity to Regulate the Environment

Reagan officials singled out the Council on Environmental Quality, the Environmental Protection Agency, and the Office of Surface Mining for budget cuts in 1981. As Table 10.2 shows, the EPA budget had gone up in every presidential administration until the 1980s and had increased as a share of all federal spending until it leveled off in the Carter years. Congress cut environmental spending even more than the administration requested. In constant dollars (controlled for inflation), the EPA enforcement budget dropped by 28 percent between 1981 and 1984, and research and development funding fell 39 percent between 1980 and 1984.

Amendments to the Clean Water Act significantly reduced authorization levels for state and local wastewater treatment facilities. In the wake of strong criticisms that the Superfund program was moving far too slowly to clean up hazardous waste sites, the Reagan administration deflected criticism by requesting a significant real increase in authorizations for the Fund. After 1983 Congress resisted additional cuts proposed for other environmental programs. For example, the 1985 administration request for the EPA represented an 8 percent reduction from 1981, but Congress restored EPA funding almost to 1981 levels.[82]

Table 10.2. *Environmental Protection Agency[a] budget, selected years, 1962–1989*

Fiscal Year	Outlays ($ millions)	Percentage of Total Federal Outlays
1962	70	0.1%
1965	134	0.1
1969	303	0.2
1975	2,531	0.8
1977	4,365	1.1
1981	5,242	0.8
1982	5,081	0.7
1983	4,312	0.5
1984	4,076	0.5
1985	4,490	0.5
1986	4,867	0.5
1987	4,904	0.5
1988[b]	4,853	0.5
1989[b]	5,127	0.5

[a] Prior to 1971, figures include functions later transferred to the EPA.
[b] Estimate
Source: Executive Office of the President, Office of Management and Budget, *Historical Tables, Budget of the United States Government, Fiscal Year 1989* (Washington, DC: GPO, 1988), Tables 4.1, 4.2.

Reagan appointed administrators who sympathized with industry's view that environmental policy should be deregulated and decentralized. The first Reagan-appointed EPA head, Ann Burford (Ann Gorsuch until her marriage in 1983), had been a lawyer with Mountain Bell Telephone Company, a Colorado state legislator, and a vocal critic of environmental regulation. James Watt, appointed as the Secretary of the Interior, had been a Colorado lawyer spearheading the "Sagebrush Rebellion," a movement by officials in a dozen western states to force the federal government to relax its regulation of federally owned lands so that cattle, mining, mineral, and real estate companies could more easily profit from their use. The White House fired the entire staff of the Council on Environmental Quality, slashed its budget by 72 percent, and appointed a smaller staff of inexperienced Reagan loyalists.[83] A reduction in the size of the research staff at the EPA caused it to rely increasingly on data provided by the industries it regulated. The Office of Surface Mining closed seventeen of thirty-seven field offices and all five of its regional offices. Personnel in the Denver office were told that they could resign, retire, accept termination, or relocate to Casper, Wyoming.[84]

The effort to reduce environmental enforcement began immediately after the inauguration, when President Reagan rescinded several rules approved by the Carter administration. Deregulation was manifested in three ways. First, fewer new regulations went into effect. Since Burford agreed with the goal of deregulation, she put forward very few new rules during her tenure. Her successors discovered that even modest regulations were challenged by the Office of Management and Budget. Second, enforcement was reduced. The EPA's production of civil suits and administrative orders dropped 50 percent from 1981 to 1983, and water quality enforcement dropped 40 percent after a memorandum directed officials to avoid confrontational settlements.[85]

Third, the EPA experimented with new regulatory ideas. The "bubble" concept set limits for a facility (such as an entire factory rather than each smokestack) and allowed each firm to decide how it would reduce pollution. The EPA also extended the idea of the pollution "offset" (initiated by the Carter administration in 1980) that "permits firms to sell or trade 'rights' to emit pollutants to other companies so that new sources of pollution are permitted as older facilities are abandoned without exceeding environmental standards."[86]

The pollution offset produced some potentially controversial results. For example, late in 1986, when the EPA approved the state of Missouri's implementation plan for ozone emissions in the St. Louis area, corporations, including Monsanto Chemical company, Anheuser-Busch, and General Motors, had "banked" hundreds of tons of pollution rights that they planned to use for factory expansion or to sell to other companies.[87]

Ironically, industrial self-interest sometimes clashed with lax environmental enforcement. After the EPA issued a proposal to relax standards for lead in gasoline, large refiners such as Mobil and Exxon protested that, since they had invested huge sums in equipment to meet the stringent standards, the proposals would only benefit their competitors. Subsequently the EPA announced that it planned to tighten its lead standards.[88] In 1985, the major chemical companies called for stricter federal controls on toxic chemical air emissions. A senior vice-president of Monsanto attributed the change to public concern in the wake of the disaster in Bhopal, India, that had occurred three months earlier, saying that the public "simply does not have faith that the chemical industry will regulate itself in the public interest . . . we need public support in which to operate."[89] Chemical company executives also feared that some states would enact stricter regulations.

Environmental Federalism

Burford believed that the EPA had allowed the states too little discretion and had "developed horrendously complicated regulations that were simply unnecessary, that nine times out of ten just made states madder than hell, and they couldn't follow."[90] Under her direction the EPA almost routinely approved states' requests for more autonomy. By 1983 the number of states authorized to prevent the deterioration of air quality increased from sixteen to twenty-six and those authorized to manage hazardous waste programs increased from eighteen to thirty-four.[91] Though the Interior Department had approved strip mining regulations for only eleven of the twenty-four largest coal-producing states by early 1981, all had been approved by August 1982. The speedy approval of state plans by an EPA staff that had been sharply reduced in size raised questions about whether federal officials had looked at the state proposals at all.[92]

Decentralization does not inevitably result in less effective pollution control. Some states have experimented with new regulations and battled the Reagan administration's efforts to relax environmental standards.[93] California's pioneering automobile pollution laws, relatively extensive land use controls, and its Coastal Commission provide models of effective, enduring environmental policy at the state level.[94] Wisconsin also applied creative solutions in regulating pulp and paper mills that are important to the state's economy.[95] State environmental initiatives include hazardous waste disposal and clean-up programs (twenty-nine states), laws banning nonreturnable beverage containers (nine states), and laws prohibiting water quality degradation (nine states).[96]

But in the *aggregate* and in combination with budget cuts, "environmental federalism" severely weakened environmental management. First, since 45 percent of the states' budgets for air and water quality and 69 percent of their hazardous waste budgets came from federal funds, increased responsibility along with reduced funding meant that states were unlikely to maintain their environmental efforts. In fiscal year 1982, the federal government contributed 58 percent of the average state's overall environmental program budget, ranging from a low of 24 percent in California to a high of 80 percent in Rhode Island, Montana, and Connecticut. A survey taken among budget staff in thirty-one states found that only one state was replacing federal cuts in pesticide enforcement grants, two were making up for reductions in wastewater treatment grants, three were replacing lost federal funds in water pollution control grants, four were allocating state funds to compensate for reductions in air pollution control grants, and six were replacing cuts in hazardous waste management grants.[97]

Where states experimented with economic incentives as an alternative to regulation, as in issuing "reclamation performance bonds" meant to give mining companies an incentive to restore stripped lands, severe underfinancing caused these programs to have little effect.[98] Combined with the recession of 1982–1983, which severely strained state budgets, disparities in state environmental efforts became more pronounced. Between fiscal years 1979 and 1984, the real value of state, local, and other funding for air pollution decreased by 6 percent.[99]

Interstate pollution problems became more difficult to solve under these circumstances. The "acid rain" issue best illustrates the problem. States in the Ohio River valley and the middle Atlantic region have frequently permitted industries to construct "tall" smokestacks as an alternative to much more expensive "scrubbers." Such smokestacks disperse sulfur dioxide and other pollutants across a wider area, thus reducing local concentrations of air pollution. However, winds high in the atmosphere often transport these pollutants hundreds of miles away, where they return to earth in the form of acidic precipitation. This acid rain sterilizes lakes and forests, and the problem has reached crisis proportions in New England and Canada. Not surprisingly, state regulatory agencies in the midwestern states "have been extremely reluctant to require, or even to suggest, that existing industries with tall stacks install alternative technologies."[100]

Decentralized policy has raised the level of interstate competition, "leaving some states increasingly vulnerable to being played off against others with more lax standards . . . [w]ithout federal requirements and EPA enforcement to support them."[101] In 1987 a federal regulator privately agreed with an assessment by environmental groups that the EPA "just stopped requiring states" to demonstrate that they had attained air quality goals. "Since we have not pressured the states, the states have not pressured industry."[102]

Environmental Stalemate after 1983

Criticism of the Reagan administration's environmental enforcement reached a crescendo early in 1983. Evidence suggested secret collusion between private industry and the EPA. Agency records showed that EPA officials had held thirty meetings with representatives of the lead and petroleum industries before devising standards for leaded gasoline but had not met with public health officials or sought data on the effects of lead on health.[103] Superfund administrator Rita Lavelle was fired after documents were published that indicated frequent meetings with businesses affected by EPA regulations, including her former employer, Aerojet General Corporation, itself accused by the state of California of illegally dumping thousands of gallons of toxic waste. Lavelle complained of another EPA official that he was "alienating . . . the primary constituency of this administration, big business."[104] Burford resigned amid much controversy in March 1983. James Watt resigned later in the year, after a series of controversial remarks.

In the wake of Burford's resignation, the Reagan administration attempted to restore public confidence in the EPA by appointing William Ruckelshaus, who had been the agency's first director in 1970. Ruckelshaus and his successor, Lee Thomas, restored some of the morale at the EPA, but they did not reverse decentralization and deregulation. Ruckelshaus found that the White House still opposed increases in the EPA budget and in grants for wastewater treatment. His recommendations on acid rain policy were blocked by the cabinet in late 1983, and he was unable to win a restoration of the EPA budget to 1981 levels.[105]

By 1987 environmental policy had reached a stalemate. Environmental regulation was not relaxed further, and in some areas it was strengthened. With toxic wastes causing widespread concern, Congress renewed the Superfund and increased its authorization to $8.5 billion for five years. Although President Reagan protested the measure because it imposed additional taxes on business (especially on the chemical and petroleum industries), he signed it less than three weeks before the 1986 congressional election.[106] When Congress enacted a reauthorization of the Clean Water Act in 1986, Reagan vetoed the measure. Reintroduced as HR1 when the new Congress met in January 1987, the bill again was passed by overwhelming margins and again was vetoed. The veto was overridden by a 93 percent vote in the House and an 86 percent margin in the Senate. However, the law reauthorized the grants program at the reduced levels established by the budget cuts of 1981.[107] The EPA began to reassert its regulatory role in 1987, when it issued standards for microscopic pollutants and charged Bethlehem Steel with violating air pollution limits (however, few staff members in the EPA expected the agency to impose penalties on steel companies). The EPA also developed new methods for negotiating agreements between environmentalists and industrial concerns. But these initiatives did little to reduce congressional distrust of the Reagan EPA.[108]

THE UNCERTAIN STATUS OF ENVIRONMENTAL REGULATION

Unlike civil rights, welfare, education, or other policies that were well established in the states before the New Deal legitimized national activism, environmental policy is almost entirely a product of an era when Americans expected the national government to exert policy leadership. Even in this case, however, the inheritance of an incoherent policymaking structure dictated strategies of policy design and enforcement. The slow response by most states to environmental concerns led Congress to enact laws that in principle established far-reaching federal power. In practice, however, enforcement proved to be uncertain, complicated, and expensive.

Despite these problems, environmental laws produced measurable positive results, especially in reducing air pollution. The controversies provoked by their enforcement methods, however, contributed to their partial dismantling through deregulation and decentralization in 1981 and 1982. Only overwhelming public opposition and the ability of Congress to prevent further erosion of environmental statutes prevented the Reagan administration from going further in dismantling the national government's involvement in environmental regulation.

NOTES

1. David Vogel, *National Styles of Regulation: Environmental Policy in Great Britain and the United States* (Ithaca, NY: Cornell University Press, 1986), 164. Other cross-national comparisons come to similar conclusions. Cf. Lennart Lundquist in *The Hare and the Tortoise: Clean Air Policies in the United States and Sweden* (Ann Arbor: University of Michigan Press, 1980), and Cynthia H. Enloe, *The Politics of Pollution in a Comparative Perspective: Ecology and Power in Four Nations* (New York: David McKay, 1975).
2. Vogel, *National Styles of Regulation*, 164. See the excellent discussions of the gap between regulatory law and regulatory enforcement in Michael D. Reagan, *Regulation: The Politics of Policy* (Boston: Little, Brown, 1987), and Eugene Bardach and Robert A. Kagan, *Going By the Book: The Problem of Regulatory Unreasonableness* (Philadelphia: Temple University Press, 1982).
3. Rachel Carson, *Silent Spring* (Boston: Houghton Mifflin, 1972), 1–2.
4. John C. Maloney and Lynn Slovonsky, "The Pollution Issue: A Survey of Editorial Judgements," in Leslie L. Roos, Jr., ed., *The Politics of Ecosuicide* (New York: Holt, Rinehart and Winston, 1971), 64–78.

5. J. Clarence Davies III, *The Politics of Pollution* (New York: Pegasus, 1970), 79.

6. Robert Cameron Mitchell, "Public Opinion and Environmental Politics in the 1970s and 1980s," in Norman J. Vig and Michael E. Kraft, eds., *Environmental Policy in the 1980s: Reagan's New Agenda* (Washington, DC: Congressional Quarterly, 1984), 58–64.

7. *St. Louis Post-Dispatch*, 4 January 1940, p. 1, 25 February 1940, pp. 1, 4, 26 March 1940, p. 6, and 8 April 1940, p. 1; Charles O. Jones, *Clean Air: The Policies and Politics of Pollution Control* (Pittsburgh: University of Pittsburgh Press, 1975), 23.

8. Matthew Crenson, *The Un-Politics of Air Pollution: A Study of Non-Decisionmaking in the Cities*, (Baltimore: Johns Hopkins University Press, 1971), 35–82.

9. Richard B. Stewart, "Pyramids of Sacrifice? Problems of Federalism in Mandating State Implementation of National Environmental Policy," *Yale Law Review* 86:6 (May 1977), 1196 ff.

10. James E. Krier and Edmund Ursin, *Pollution and Policy: A Case Essay on California and Federal Experience with Motor Vehicle Air Pollution, 1940–1975* (Berkeley: University of California Press, 1977), 57–61.

11. Randall B. Ripley, "Congress and Clean Air: The Issue of Enforcement, 1963," in Frederic N. Cleaveland, ed., *Congress and Urban Problems* (Washington, DC: Brookings, 1969), 226; Comments by Congressman William C. Cramer (Republican of Florida) in *Congressional Record* 3 May 1961, H7167.

12. Quoted in Jones, *Clean Air*, 28.

13. Gary C. Bryner, *Bureaucratic Discretion: Law and Policy in Federal Agencies* (New York: Pergamon Press, 1987), 110.

14. Bruce A. Ackerman and William T. Hassler, *Clean Coal/Dirty Air, Or How the Clean Air Act Became a Multibillion-Dollar Bail-Out for High Sulfur Coal Producers and What Should Be Done About It* (New Haven, CT: Yale University Press, 1981).

15. Robert V. Bartlett, *The Reserve Mining Controversy: Science, Technology, and Environmental Quality* (Bloomington: Indiana University Press, 1980), 59–64.

16. R. Shep Melnick, *Regulation and the Courts: The Case of the Clean Air Act* (Washington, DC: Brookings, 1983), 355.

17. Ibid., 71–81, 217–9.

18. Davies, *The Politics of Pollution*, 96–7.

19. U.S. Congress, Senate, Committee on Public Works, Subcommittee on Air and Water Pollution, *Air Pollution Control* (Washington, DC: GPO, 1963), 42.

20. Davies, *The Politics of Pollution*, 38.

21. *Water Pollution Control Act of 1948*, Public Law 80-845.

22. M. Kent Jennings, "Legislative Politics and Water Pollution Control, 1956–1961," in Frederic N. Cleaveland, ed., *Congress and Urban Problems* (Washington, DC: Brookings, 1969), 74. On Taft, see James T. Patterson, *Mr. Republican: A Biography of Robert A. Taft* (Boston: Houghton Mifflin, 1972).

23. Davies, *The Politics of Pollution*, 109–10, 214–5.

24. Jennings, "Legislative Politics and Water Pollution Control," 74–86.

25. Ibid., 86–91; "Veto of Bill to Amend the Federal Water Pollution Control Act, February 23, 1960, *Papers of the Presidents of the United States: Dwight David Eisenhower, 1960–1961* (Washington, DC: GPO, 1961), 208–9.

26. Davies, *The Politics of Pollution*, 51.

27. James L. Sundquist, *Politics and Policy: The Eisenhower, Kennedy and Johnson Years* (Washington, DC: Brookings, 1969), 331–2.

28. U.S. Congress, Senate, *Air Pollution Control*, 42.

29. *Congressional Record*, 5 May 1961, H7166.

30. Jennings, "Legislative Politics and Water Pollution Control," 95–101.

31. Ripley, "Congress and Clean Air," 248.

32. U.S. Congress, Senate, *Air Pollution Control*, 47, 51–2.

33. Ibid., 259–78; Jones, *Clean Air*, 73–6; Sundquist, *Politics and Policy*, 351–5.

34. Sundquist, *Politics and Policy*, 362; Lyndon Baines Johnson, *The Vantage Point: Perspectives on the Presidency, 1963–1969* (New York: Holt, Rinehart and Winston, 1971), 337–8.

35. U.S. Congress, House Committee on Public Works, *Water Quality Act of 1965*, House Report 89-215 (March 31, 1965), 10.

36. *Congressional Quarterly Almanac, 1965* (Washington, DC: Congressional Quarterly, 1966), 743–50.

37. Sundquist, *Politics and Policy*, 365–7.

38. Walter A. Rosenbaum, *The Politics of Environmental Concern* (New York: Praeger, 1973), 141.

39. Ibid., 173.

40. Davies, *The Politics of Pollution*, 114.

41. *Congressional Quarterly Almanac, 1965*, 780–6.

42. U.S. Congress, Senate, Committee on Public Works, Subcommittee on Air and Water Pollution, *Hearings on Air Pollution—1967*, Part 1 (Washington, DC: GPO, 1967), 403.

43. Davies, *The Politics of Pollution*, 54; Jones, *Clean Air*, 67–8; *Congressional Quarterly Almanac, 1967* (Washington, DC: Congressional Quarterly, 1968), 875–86.

44. Quoted in Jones, *Clean Air*, 123.

45. Jones, *Clean Air*, 130–1.

46. See *Congressional Record*, 10 June 1970, pp. H19204–5, and the statement on environmental policy by President Richard Nixon, February 10, 1970, *Congressional Quarterly Almanac, 1970* (Washington, DC: Congressional Quarterly, 1971), 22A–24A.

47. Jones, *Clean Air*, 178; John C. Whitaker, *Striking a Balance: Environment and Natural Resources Policy in the Nixon-Ford Years* (Washington, DC: American Enterprise Institute, 1976), 27.

48. Helen Ingram, "The Political Rationality of Innovation: The Clean Air Act of 1970," in Ann F. Friedlaender, ed., *Approaches to Controlling Air Pollution* (Cambridge, MA: MIT Press, 1978), 24.

49. Lawrence J. White, "The Automobile Industry," in Walter Adams, ed., *The Structure of American Industry*, 5th ed. (New York: Macmillan, 1977), 196; Rosenbaum, *The Politics of Environmental Concern*, 127.

50. Whitaker, *Striking a Balance*, 34, 40.

51. Rosenbaum, *The Politics of Environmental Concern*, 117–22; *Congressional Quarterly Almanac, 1969* (Washington, DC: Congressional Quarterly, 1970), 525–7.

52. Ibid., 54–5; Rosenbaum, *The Politics of Environmental Concern*, 122–4.

53. U.S. Congress, House, Committee on Interstate and Foreign Commerce, *Clean Air Amendments of 1970*, Report 91-1146 (Washington, DC: GPO, 1970); Helen M. Ingram and Dean E. Mann, "Environmental Policy: From Innovation to Implementation," in Theodore J. Lowi and Alan Stone, eds., *Nationalizing Government: Public Policies in America* (Beverly Hills: Sage, 1978), 133.

54. Jones, *Clean Air*, 175–210.

55. Helen M. Ingram and Dean E. Mann, "Preserving the Clean Water Act: The Appearance of Environmental Victory," in Norman J. Vig and Michael E. Kraft, eds. *Environmental Policy in the 1980s: Reagan's New Agenda* (Washington, DC: Congressional Quarterly, 1984), 262.

56. *Congressional Quarterly Almanac, 1972* (Washington, DC: Congressional Quarterly, 1973), 708–22.

57. Marc J. Roberts and Susan O. Farrell, "The Political Economy of Implementation: The Clean Air Act and Stationary Sources," in Ann Friedlaender, ed., *Approaches to Controlling Air Pollution* (Cambridge, MA: MIT Press, 1978), 152.

58. *Congressional Record*, 10 June 1970, H19204–13.

59. Ibid., 21 September 1970, S39202–7.

60. Lundquist, *The Hare and the Tortoise*, 132–42.
61. John Quarles, *Cleaning Up America: An Insider's View of the Environmental Protection Agency* (Boston: Houghton Mifflin, 1976), 201–11.
62. Arnold M. Howitt, *Managing Federalism: Studies in Intergovernmental Relations* (Washington, DC: Congressional Quarterly, 1984), 107–80.
63. Roberts and Farrell, "The Political Economy of Implementation," 158–9.
64. Ibid., 159–60. Cf. U.S. General Accounting Office, *Assessment of Federal and State Enforcement for Control of Air Pollution from Stationary Sources* (Washington, DC: GPO, 1973).
65. Roberts and Farrell, "The Political Economy of Implementation," 165.
66. Statement of Marvin B. Durning in U.S. Congress, Senate, Committee on Environment and Public Works, Subcommittee on Environmental Pollution, *Enforcement of Environmental Regulations* (Washington, DC: GPO, 1979), 213–4.
67. Charles Corkin II, "Comment," in Ann Friedlaender, ed., *Approaches to Controlling Air Pollution* (Cambridge, MA: MIT Press, 1978), 188–98.
68. Quarles, *Cleaning Up America*, 97–101.
69. Allen V. Kneese and Charles L. Schultze, *Pollution, Prices, and Public Policy* (Washington, DC: Brookings, 1975), 39–40.
70. Stewart, "Pyramids of Sacrifice?," 1197; Ingram and Mann, "Environmental Policy," 140–7.
71. Alfred Marcus, "Environmental Protection Agency," in James Q. Wilson, ed., *The Politics of Regulation* (New York: Basic Books, 1980), 296–7; Ingram and Mann, "Preserving the Clean Water Act," 262.
72. Walter A. Rosenbaum, *Environmental Politics and Policy* (Washington, DC: Congressional Quarterly, 1985), 79–81, 198.
73. Steven Cohen, "Defusing the Toxic Time Bomb: Federal Hazardous Waste Programs," in Norman J. Vig and Michael E. Kraft, eds., *Environmental Policy in the 1980s: Reagan's New Agenda* (Washington, DC: Congressional Quarterly, 1984), 279.
74. Bruce A. Williams, "Bounding Behavior: Economic Regulation in the American States," in Virginia Gray, Herbert Jacob, and Kenneth N. Vines, eds., *Politics in the American States*, 4th ed. (Boston: Little, Brown, 1982), 365–7.
75. John E. Schwarz, *America's Hidden Success: A Reassessment of Twenty Years of Public Policy From Kennedy to Reagan*, rev. ed. (New York: Norton, 1987), 55–6.
76. Council on Environmental Quality, *Environmental Quality, 1984* (Washington: GPO, 1985), 583; Kenneth J. Meier, *Regulation: Politics, Bureaucracy, and Economics* (New York: St. Martin's Press, 1985), 155.
77. Schwarz, *America's Hidden Success*, 56–8; Council on Environmental Quality, *Environmental Quality, 1984*, 599.
78. Meier, *Regulation*, 158, 197.
79. Vogel, *National Styles of Regulation*, 180.
80. Michael E. Kraft, "The 1980 Presidential Campaign," in Norman J. Vig and Michael E. Kraft, eds., *Environmental Policy in the 1980s: Reagan's New Agenda* (Washington, DC: Congressional Quarterly, 1984), 32–8; Lou Cannon, *Reagan* (New York: G.P. Putnam, 1982), 287, 369.
81. Louis J. Cordia, "Environmental Protection Agency," in Charles L. Heatherly, ed., *Mandate for Leadership: Policy Management in a Conservative Administration* (Washington, DC: Heritage Foundation, 1980), 969–74.
82. U.S. Congress, House, Committee on the Budget, *A Review of President Reagan's Budget Recommendations, 1981–1985* (Washington, DC: GPO, 1984), 120–9.
83. Richard N. L. Andrews, "Deregulation: The Failure at EPA," in Norman J. Vig and Michael E. Kraft, eds., *Environmental Policy in the 1980s: Reagan's New Agenda* (Washington, DC: Congressional Quarterly, 1984), 166.
84. Rosenbaum, *Environmental Politics and Policy*, 247–8.

85. Andrews, "Deregulation: The Failure at EPA," 165, 171

86. Bryner, *Bureaucratic Discretion*, 111.

87. Martha Sirk, "Ozone Better; U.S. Lifts Freeze," *St. Louis Post-Dispatch*, 9 November 1986, p. 4C.

88. Robert A. Leone, *Who Profits? Winners, Losers, and Government Regulation* (New York: Basic Books, 1986), 37–40.

89. Philip Shabecoff, "Companies Say Toxic Emissions Need U.S. Curb," *New York Times*, 27 March 1985, 1.

90. Anne Burford with John Greenya, *Are You Tough Enough?* (New York: McGraw-Hill, 1986), 65.

91. Andrews, "Deregulation: The Failure at EPA," 172.

92. Barbara S. Webber and David J. Webber, "Promoting Economic Incentives for Environmental Protection in the Surface Mining Control and Reclamation Act of 1977: An Analysis of the Design and Implementation of Reclamation Performance Bonds," *Natural Resources Journal* 25:2 (April 1985), 391–2.

93. John Naisbitt, *Megatrends: Ten New Directions Transforming Our Lives* (New York: Warner, 1982), 105.

94. Daniel Mazmanian and Paul A. Sabatier, *Implementation and Public Policy* (Glenview, IL: Scott, Foresman, 1983), 218–63.

95. T. H. Tietenberg, "Uncommon Sense: The Program to Reform Pollution Control Policy," in Leonard W. Weiss and Michael W. Klass, eds., *Regulatory Reform: What Actually Happened* (Boston: Little, Brown, 1986), 297.

96. Scott Ridley, *The State of the States, 1987* (Washington, DC: Fund for Renewable Energy and the Environment, 1987).

97. James P. Lester, "New Federalism and Environmental Policy," *Publius: The Journal of Federalism* 16:1 (Winter 1986), 149–65.

98. Webber and Webber, "Promoting Economic Incentives for Environmental Protection in the Surface Mining Control and Reclamation Act of 1977," 406–10.

99. Ridley, *The State of the States.*

100. Rosenbaum, *Environmental Politics and Policy*, 20, 135–6.

101. Andrews, "Deregulation: The Failure at EPA," 172–3.

102. Claudia H. Deutsch, "The Pollution Hounds Get Ready to Pounce," *New York Times*, 6 September 1987, 6F.

103. Richard J. Tobin, "Revising the Clean Air Act: Legislative Failure and Administrative Success," in Norman J. Vig and Michael E. Kraft, eds., *Environmental Policy in the 1980s: Reagan's New Agenda* (Washington, DC: Congressional Quarterly, 1984), 237.

104. Susan J. Tolchin and Martin Tolchin, *Dismantling America: The Rush to Deregulate* (New York: Oxford University Press, 1985), 101–2; Burford, *Are You Tough Enough?*, 179.

105. Andrews, "Deregulation: The Failure at EPA," 178.

106. *Congressional Quarterly Almanac, 1986* (Washington, DC: Congressional Quarterly, 1987), 111–20; Rochelle L. Stanfield, "Stewing Over Superfund," *National Journal* 8 August 1987, 2030–2.

107. *Congressional Quarterly Weekly Report* 8 November 1986, 2874 and 7 February 1987, 170.

108. Deutsch, "The Pollution Hounds Get Ready to Pounce;" Rochelle L. Stanfield, "Toxics and Trust," *National Journal* 16 April 1988, 1040.

Chapter 11

POLICY PERFORMANCE AND STRUCTURAL REFORM

THE CONSERVATIVE ARGUMENT FOR ENHANCING STATE
POLICYMAKING CONTROL

In 1981, President Ronald Reagan told the National Conference of
State Legislatures that

> . . . today the Federal government takes too much taxes from the people,
> too much authority from the States, too much liberty with the Constitution
> . . . the steady flow of power and tax dollars to Washington has something
> to do with the fact that things don't seem to work anymore. The Federal
> government is overloaded, musclebound, if you will, having assumed
> more responsibilities than it can properly manage . . . the Federal Govern-
> ment is so far removed from the people that Members of Congress spend
> less time legislating than cutting through bureaucratic redtape for their
> constituents.[1]

In this statement, Reagan summarized the two conventional jus-
tifications for a "new" federalism: that state governments *respond* better
to citizens than does the federal government and that state-run policies
perform better than federal policies. Based on these claims, Reagan committed his "heart and soul" to transferring policy to the state governments.

Reagan's case for a "new" federalism coincided with an apparently
rising public dissatisfaction regarding the responsiveness and com-
petence of the national government. In 1972, 39 percent of Americans
surveyed said that they got more for their money from the federal
government than from state and local governments. Seven years later,
only 29 percent expressed the same relative satisfaction with federal

354

performance.[2] A 1981 Gallup poll found that 64 percent of Americans thought that power should be concentrated in state governments rather than at the federal level and 67 percent believed that "the state government is more efficient than the federal government in administering social programs and in better understanding the real needs of the people."[3]

Was the Reagan administration's "new" federalism likely to increase the responsiveness and performance of American public policy? Or was the appeal to federalism a beguiling "Trojan horse" that concealed a conservative agenda in the guise of a populist rhetoric?

This chapter critically examines and rejects claims that American state policies under current conditions respond better to popular preferences or perform better than federal policies. In nearly all cases, state policy is superior to national policy only if one defines "good" policy as *conservative* policy—that is, less activist, less redistributive, and less regulatory. Despite its rhetoric, the Reagan administration did not enhance policy performance or responsiveness. Instead, it reduced government capacity and coherence in policy areas outside the conservative agenda. In effect, the Reagan administration sought a "new" federalism that would strengthen the structure of policy restraint.

We believe that a genuinely new federalism can shift the bias of the American policymaking structure to facilitate both policy capacity and coherence. We very briefly outline how this could be accomplished, in the conclusion to this chapter.

ARE THE STATES MORE RESPONSIVE THAN THE FEDERAL GOVERNMENT?

The Virtue of Local Control

American folklore romanticizes the tradition of direct, local participation in community decisions. Civics texts used in the schools and media coverage of political events extoll the New England town meeting as pure American "grassroots" democracy.[4] Political idealists as different from one another as Thomas Jefferson, the progressive jurist Louis Brandeis, the New Deal administrator David Lilienthal, and the "new left" theorists of the 1960s and 1970s articulated the view that only local government facilitates genuine democracy in the sense of direct participation in collective public decisions. Jefferson wrote that citizens could learn about democracy by observing the fragmentation of native Americans into small tribes because such decentralization allowed members to share responsibility for governing themselves.[5]

American democratic theorists have often quoted Jefferson in insisting that autonomous state governments are indispensable to responsive government. These theorists argue their case by making three principal claims. First, state governments prevent despotic rule at the national level. Second, states are more responsive than the distant national government to citizens' needs. Third, states multiply the number of avenues for citizen participation in the policy process.

Though America's founders argued about how strong the central government should be, they agreed that autonomous state governments would prevent the emergence of oppressive national power. Madison's essays in *The Federalist* argued that state governments would protect against the exercise of arbitrary power by the national government because "different governments will control each other, at the same time that each will be controlled by itself." A majority would have fewer chances to abuse the rights of a minority in a government so divided. Indeed, the larger the society, the less likely such a majority could act, so that "[I]n the United States . . . a coalition of a majority of the whole society could seldom take place on any other principles than those of justice and the general good . . ."[6] Jefferson similarly argued that the states were the "true barriers of our liberty" against an absolutist national government and the "surest bulwarks against antirepublican tendencies." President Reagan quoted Jefferson to make the same point in 1986.[7]

The founders viewed state governments not only as a "bulwark" against despotism but also as necessary for preserving democracy. Madison believed that state and local governments should undertake most public endeavors because citizens were closer to these governments and they therefore could exert more control. He thought citizens would also be more familiar with politics in their states and communities:

> the first and most natural attachment of the people will be to the governments of their respective states . . . By superintending the care of these, all the more domestic and personal interests of the people will be regulated and provided for. With the affairs of these, the people will be more familiarly and minutely conversant. And with the members of these will a greater proportion of the people have the ties of personal acquaintance and friendship, and of family and party attachments; on the side of these, therefore, the popular bias may well be expected most strongly to incline.[8]

In his book *Democracy in America* (1835 and 1840), French author and traveller Alexis de Tocqueville marveled at the vigor of American democracy, which he attributed to the independent role of the state governments. The national government managed foreign and military affairs, while the states fostered local democracy: "One can hardly imagine how much this division of sovereignty contributes to the well-being of each of the States . . . In these small communities, which are never agitated by the desire of self-aggrandizement or the care of self-defense, all public authority and private energy are turned towards internal improvements." Americans were "happy and free as a small people, and glorious and strong as a great nation."[9]

In the twentieth century, many state governments expanded direct participation in taxing, budgeting, and policymaking through the processes of initiative, referendum, and recall. In 1988, thirty-seven states provided for referenda in which state laws passed by the legislature may be referred to voters before going into effect. Twenty-one states permitted the initiative by which a citizen petition may place a proposed state law on the ballot to be enacted or rejected by the electorate. Fifteen states allowed recall elections, which voters can utilize to remove elected state officials from office. In contrast, federal laws contain no provisions for direct citizen involvement in policymaking.[10]

Federal programs passed during the New Deal and the Great Society years created additional avenues for policy participation at the state and local levels. David E. Lilienthal, the chief architect and administrator of the New Deal's Tennessee Valley Authority (TVA), promised that the TVA would meld the benefits of a large organization with the responsiveness of "grassroots" decisionmaking. He specifically invoked de Tocqueville when he explained why the TVA relied so heavily on state "universities and extension services, local and State planning commissions, State conservation boards, chambers of commerce, [and] boards of health . . ."[11]

The 1964 Economic Opportunity Act required the participation by residents of impoverished communities in antipoverty programs. The Bureau of the Budget supported these community action agencies as a way to "target" antipoverty funds (see Chapter 7), but the architects of community action viewed the agencies as vehicles for mobilizing community participation, cohesiveness and autonomy. As Lyndon Johnson later explained, "the plan . . . was based on one of the oldest ideas of our democracy, as old as the New England town meeting—self-determination at the local level."[12]

Federal laws often have expanded citizen involvement in state and local decisions. The national government frequently requires citizen and group participation as a condition for receiving grants. Congress chartered local chambers of commerce and encouraged the spread of local farm bureaus before World War I. Beginning with the Economic Opportunity Act of the 1960s, many federal domestic grants programs specifically required state and local governments to open up the policymaking process. Statutes that required direct citizen participation included the Coastal Zone Management Act of 1972, the Headstart Economic Opportunity and Community Partnership Act of 1974, the Housing and Community Development Act of 1974, and the Regional Development Act of 1975. By 1978, federal agencies managed 155 different domestic grant programs that required citizen participation, and these programs accounted for 80 percent of federal grant expenditures in fiscal year 1977. Fifty-five grant programs required public hearings in planning, project application, or program development. Local officials believed that these requirements had a significant impact on the development of new grant proposals, local budgetary priorities, and the continuation of projects after grants expire.[13]

The Reagan administration amplified the claims that decentralized policy is best as it went about dismantling many of the New Deal and the Great Society programs. Unlike Roosevelt and Johnson, who used federal programs to create new state and local policymaking institutions, Reagan believed that policy should be turned over to existing state and local governments. For example, the administration asserted that state legislatures were potentially far more responsive to citizens than the U.S. Congress. Reagan's Domestic Policy Council argued that members of Congress "are frequently less than well-informed of local conditions or needs," while "State legislatures generally contain fewer members, are more knowledgeable of local conditions, and are less pressed for time than Congress."[14] Other proponents of devolution have added the assertion that local media are better able to report on the state legislature than on the U.S. Congress, so that "most voters would be more informed about an issue if addressed by the state legislature than if the same issues were addressed by Washington."[15]

The Ambiguity of State and Local Government Responsiveness

These are serious problems with the argument that state and local governments facilitate more participation and are more responsive to citizens' desires than the national government. James Madison long ago asserted the view that centralized decisionmaking involves a greater diversity of political interests and that more inclusive governments are less easily captured by single interests than are smaller political jurisdictions. This principle has been reformulated more recently by political scientist Grant McConnell:

> In a small community there will probably be fewer different interests— economic, religious, ethnic, or other—than in a large community. Thus it may happen that a single economic interest, such as a particular farm product or a particular industry, is overwhelmingly the largest in the community . . . Thus, for example, the importance of dairy farmers will be greater in a rural county than in the state of New York at large, and the power of an oil company will be greater in Baton Rouge than in Washing-

ton, D.C. If decisions relating to dairy farming can be put in the hands of the counties and those relating to the oil industry in the hands of the states, the power of both interests will be much greater than if such decisions were put in the hands of the nation as a whole.[16]

A political system in which power is distributed to small constituencies works against two types of interests. The system diminishes the influence of minority political interests that are distributed evenly across jurisdictions. A decentralized system also diminishes the power of the relatively small numbers of people dedicated to the collective good (or the "public interest"), since they "may have no effect in small constituencies and, if they are to succeed, must have the larger numbers of a big constituency from which to draw enough people with the time, money, and drive to work for a cause the benefits of which will be shared by all."[17]

Substantial evidence contradicts the view that the states are more familiar, accessible, or responsive to American citizens than is the national government. First, citizens know and care less about state and local government. Virtually all American adults can name the U.S. president. Eighty-nine percent can name their state's governor, and 70 percent can name their mayor. While 46 percent can identify their U.S. representative and 39 percent know the names of their U.S. senators, only 28 percent can name their state senator.[18]

Citizens participate less in significant state and local than in national elections. In 1976 and 1980, for example, the turnout in gubernatorial elections averaged 56 percent (fractionally larger than the 55 percent who voted for president), but it dropped to less than 42 percent in the "off-year" (i.e., nonpresidential) election years of 1974 and 1978.[19] A study of state initiatives and referenda discovered that fewer voters cast ballots for direct legislation than for state offices. Citizens who vote on direct legislation are unrepresentative of the electorate at large because the more-educated and higher-income voters disproportionately turn out, compared to other elections.[20]

Political analysts observe that small jurisdictions are more vulnerable to intense, targeted pressures and the loss of popular control than are large jurisdictions. At the state level, business influence tends to dominate policymaking.[21] Interest group power can work in two ways. First, a group may be influential in one or a few states and dominate policy relevant to its interests. While Wisconsin is viewed as one of the most progressive of the American states, for example, its powerful dairy industry for many years successfully lobbied for state laws to limit the consumption of oleomargarine in the state.

Second, an interest outside the state can mobilize resources to target the policymaking process in that state. The Chemical Manufacturers'

Association responded to the deregulation of the chemical industry in the early 1980s by creating a new office of state affairs. This office tracked state regulatory legislation on a computer and focused lobbying resources on such states as Michigan, New York, Texas, California, and Massachusetts, the states believed most likely to enact new regulations opposed by the industry.[22]

States do less than the federal government to limit resource disparities in the political process, and they may be particularly vulnerable to targeted pressures. In the early 1980s, only ten states limited expenditures for state campaigns and only a third provided some public financing of campaigns. Half the states had placed no limits on contributions to political campaigns and of the rest, eighteen had "relatively limited restrictions."[23] Like many large states, California had no law limiting the contributions of political action committees (PACs) to candidates for the California state legislature and other state offices in 1982. PACs are exceptionally well-organized in California. For example, PACs gave 53 percent of the campaign money received by candidates for state office in the eighteen months preceding the June primary election. In contrast, PACs provided 31 percent of the money received by candidates for the U.S. House of Representatives in the 1982 elections and 18 percent of the contributions for candidates for the U.S. Senate.[24] We have too little information to conclude that PACs are more influential at the state level than in Congress, but at the very least, the California experience suggests that state legislatures are extremely vulnerable to the influence of PACs.[25]

Political leaders also expect that small jurisdictions can be manipulated, and they make decisions based on that premise. For example, following Walter Mondale's loss in the 1984 presidential election, southern Democratic party leaders successfully lobbied southern states to hold their 1988 presidential primaries on the same day (March 8, or "Super Tuesday"). As former Virginia governor Charles Robb explained, the Democrats were concerned that primary elections on separate days in small states such as New Hampshire "are small tests that are predictable and can be manipulated." The regional primary would be less vulnerable to "single-interest groups" capable of targeting their resources and more likely to elevate debate to a "national purpose agenda."[26]

Neither evidence nor logic consistently supports the claim that enhanced state policy autonomy improves government responsiveness in the United States. The romantic ideal of the participatory town meeting bears little resemblance to the complex process of policymaking in American states in the 1980s. Indeed, one could argue that the states offer the *least* responsive level of government. All of them are too large and heterogeneous to be considered a political "community" in the sense of the New England town or an American city,[27] but most are too small to provide an arena for minority political interests to wield significant influence or to mirror American society in the aggregate.

Since devolving governmental authority to the states does not necessarily lead to more democratic government (and it often leads to less), any claim that state policymaking is superior to national policymaking must rest on the assumption that state governments are more efficient and effective than the federal government in implementing policy.

ARE THE STATES MORE EFFICIENT AND EFFECTIVE THAN THE NATIONAL GOVERNMENT?

The Efficiency and Effectiveness of Decentralized Policy

Before the mid-1960s, states' rights advocates rarely claimed that state government policy performance was better than federal policy performance. Despite the oft-stated assertion that state officials' "practical experience" resulted in policy designs superior to programs based on "the theories . . . of an elite few in Washington,"[28] state and local governments were frequently considered more antiquated, amateurish, parochial, and prone to corruption than the federal government.[29] Most reformers believed that the federal government could manage policy more effectively than the state governments, with the exception of a few progressive states with highly professionalized administrators and legislatures. They argued that its size enabled the federal government to develop superior expertise and to achieve economies of scale that could reduce the costs of policy implementation. It often was said that the federal government could achieve levels of professionalization, planning, comprehensiveness, and fairness that were impossible to attain where policies were left to the states. Drawing on such analyses, NBC newscaster David Brinkley observed in 1966 that "the states are pretty much disappearing as a political force. They're almost through. I think in another generation they will be, politically speaking, just about insignificant."[30]

Criticisms of federal performance as well as fading public confidence in the federal government caused policy analysts to reconsider the relative efficiency of national and state governments through the late 1960s and the 1970s. By the time Ronald Reagan assumed the presidency in 1981, critics of "overcentralization" inside and outside the White House offered five principal reasons why the transfer of power to the states would improve policy performance. First, they said, the federal government's size leads to inefficiencies that offset any advantages gained from "economies of scale." Second, the superior responsiveness of smaller governments allegedly permits them to adapt policies more quickly, specifically tailored to citizens' needs. Third, it was claimed that state and local policy control maximizes intergovernmental "competition," instilling a concern for performance in public officials. Fourth, states were said to be social policy "laboratories" in which innovative policy experiments are tried out, improved, and then copied by other states. Finally, beginning in the mid-1960s state governments grew much more capable of policy management and thus, went the argument, they could now can be trusted with more policy responsibility.

The inefficiency of large governments. Disappointed with the apparent failures of social programs, many scholars examined the problem of "implementation" in the 1970s and 1980s. Most of these analysts concluded that the federal government was too large and too detached from local circumstances to manage social programs effectively. Policy overcentralization doomed many well-intentioned initiatives to failure. In a study of the U.S. Economic Development Administration's attempt to stimulate the economic revitalization of Oakland, California, political scientists Jeffrey Pressman and Aaron Wildavsky observed that "obstruction, delay, red tape, overlapping, duplication, vacillation, hesitation" typified this and most other federal social programs.[31]

In a later book, Wildavsky expanded on this theme and ascribed the federal failure to solve such problems as crime, poverty, and education to the inherent flaws of central planning and objective-setting. He argued that in a complex world, social problems are complex, little understood, and unresponsive to uniform, centrally controlled policies imposed on a national scale. Federal policymakers cannot understand or know the variations in local conditions that make one solution or another appropriate. Thus, the "quality of [government] service declines with increasing size."[32]

Robert Dahl concluded that any large centralized organization is inefficient and encounters serious difficulties when it attempts policy innovation. Centralized control requires accurate information about units located at the base of the bureaucratic pyramid, but information may "jam up" at the top of the organization because so many different units are reporting to it. As information passes upward through layer after layer of hierarchy, the information is also likely to become distorted. Applied to federal policy, these observations suggest that federal policymakers necessarily make judgments based on incomplete and inaccurate information and are likely to err.[33]

Charles Lindblom noted that this jamming and distortion reduces the ability of a centralized policy system to discover all the decision alternatives, predict all the outcomes, and anticipate all the problems of a centrally imposed policy. Difficulties of coordination, communication failure, and information overload all diminish the value of centralized problem solving. The wider variety of views expressed in centralized decisionmaking makes it difficult for a government to establish priorities on which to act and reduces the likelihood that government will respond to fundamental and divisive social problems at all.[34]

The adaptability of decentralized policy. Wildavsky and other critics of centralized policy have asserted that decentralized policies are more efficient because they respond better to citizens. Because state and local officials are closer to citizens, they are less likely to make policy "mistakes" and will discover much sooner than national officials when a policy is "failing." Moreover, their "mistakes" affect fewer people. Wildavsky observed that the "crazy-quilt pattern of interaction" caused by policy decentralization often "generates more information on preferences, imposes fewer costs, inculcates more dynamism, and leads to more integrative solutions."[35]

Martin Landau has argued that complex and little-understood social problems such as poverty and crime require complex, multiple, and independent channels of social problem solving and information gathering. Uniform national policy is inappropriate under these circumstances. Instead, successful policy will be characterized by the redundancy, duplication, and overlap characteristic of the U.S. federal system.[36]

The Reagan administration's Domestic Policy Council concluded in 1986 that the national government cannot tailor policy to the individual needs of the states and that its attempts to do so creates inefficiencies in domestic policy implementation. According to the Policy Council,

> The federal 55 mile-per-hour speed rule . . . may be desirable in urban States and substantially reduce accidents there, but in rural States such as Idaho or Wyoming limiting speed to 55 miles per hour may be unwanted and counterproductive. Likewise, the nation-wide minimum wage and overtime provisions of the Fair Labor Standards Act overlook the large local differences in the cost of living and labor markets. Similar examples abound.[37]

In this view, policies that cannot respond to important local differences cannot succeed as well as policies that are flexible; only state discretion can improve policy flexibility.

Political scientist John Kirlin has linked these arguments together by expanding the meaning of performance to embrace the political system rather than a single policy. According to Kirlin, even if the federal government could efficiently deliver services, too much reliance on the distant national government erodes citizen participation and confidence in all levels of government. Kirlin asserts that more state control can make policy more visible and legitimate. The concept of performance "should be replaced, or at least complemented, by analyses focusing on the capacity of the political system." Federalism enhances this capacity because states pursue many different policy strategies, because they make difficult trade-offs among policy choices, and because "they are still the vehicles by which . . . 'humanizing' political action . . . can occur."[38]

Public choice: the benefits of policy competition. "Public choice" theorists, who apply economic reasoning to policy problems, go a step further by theorizing that decentralization forces governments to improve policy performance by competing to please citizens (who are viewed as "customers" of different governments). Decentralization creates a kind of "market" for public services that enhances both responsiveness and performance. The "market" for sanitation, police, education, or other government services should be viewed much like the market for consumer goods and services. A government that imposes a uniform, centralized policy is much like a business firm that possesses monopoly power. In contrast, when policy is divided among a number of jurisdictions, the process is more like a competitive market in which jurisdictional competition ensures efficiency and consumer (i.e., resident) sovereignty.[39] The conclusion is that instead of being forced to accept centralized policy, the public should have a chance to choose among the services offered by different governmental units.

From this perspective, decentralization enhances public choice by providing citizens the freedom to move from one jurisdiction to another. The prospect of losing constituents to other jurisdictions forces state and local governments to be responsive to citizen-consumer demands. James Buchanan and Gordon Tullock have stated that "If the individual can have available to him several political units organizing the same collective activity, he can take this into account" and decide to move to a more compatible jurisdiction rather than try to persuade "his stubborn fellow citizens to agree with him" on changing policy.[40] An individual or family that dislikes the schools, police, fire department, social services, or tax rates in one jurisdiction can freely move to another, where the mix of taxes and services are judged as more suitable. Rather than relying on centralized bureaucracies, cities and states can use this market opportunity creatively. For example, different police departments could bid against one another to provide protection to a suburban village or town. A city sanitation department might be forced to bid against a private company for a contract to collect refuse in a city.[41]

The Reagan administration has applied "public choice" theory by encouraging state and local governments to compete against one another for residents and business. To replace federal grants-in-aid, cities are exhorted to compete for business investment.[42] In 1986 the Domestic Policy Council expanded this advice to all social policy areas:

When the size of government is kept as localized as possible, there is the potential that jurisdictions will compete against one another in the kinds of public goods they provide, the kinds of regulation of private activity they permit, and the way they tax their citizens . . . Ill-conceived public policy over the long-run leads to an exodus of business and talented individuals; the State's tax base erodes and its infrastructure deteriorates. States are thus strongly encouraged to rectify misguided public policy in order to maintain fiscal health and to enhance their appeal to potential residents.[43]

The council singled out Delaware as an example of a state that produced "a lively marketplace for the way people and firms wish to be governed." Delaware has very relaxed municipal incorporation laws and low corporate tax rates. In contrast, "injurious national policy cannot be escaped by flight to a different State" so that ill-conceived (i.e., overly liberal) national polices do not have the same self-correcting mechanisms as state policies.[44]

States as social laboratories. Proponents of state policy autonomy argue that state governments should enjoy the freedom to test alternative solutions to public problems. Before the 1930s, political progressives such as Supreme Court Justice Louis Brandeis often argued that American federalism permitted progressive states to serve as "social laboratories" that developed effective remedies for public problems later adapted by other states and often by the federal government. In the Supreme Court decision *New State Ice Co.* v. *Liebmann,* decided in 1932, Justice Brandeis wrote an oft-cited formulation of this argument:

The economic and social sciences are largely uncharted seas . . . There must be power in the States and the Nation to remold, through experimentation, our economic practices and institutions to meet changing social and economic needs . . . It is one of the happy incidents of the federal system that a single courageous state may, if its citizens choose, serve as a laboratory; and try novel social and economic experiments without risk to the rest of the country.[45]

Brandeis and his contemporaries frequently pointed out that states such as Wisconsin and New York had developed model legislation that subsequently diffused to other states. Wisconsin, for example, demonstrated that a state could enact an income tax and levy an unemployment insurance tax on employers without provoking a mass exodus of industry and jobs. New York's factory legislation of the period from 1911 to 1914 provides a similar illustration.

The concept of states as social laboratories remains alluring today and is used to counterbalance the charge that the states are inherently conservative. Widely read social commentators such as John Naisbitt assert that the states have revived "their traditional function as the laboratories of democracy, experimenting with society's most intractable problems." Like many observers, Naisbitt is impressed by some states' willingness to regulate the environment more strictly than the federal government.[46]

The Reagan Domestic Policy Council justified state policy control on the ground that it would enhance such experimentation and independence. Stating that "the science of government is the science of experiment," the council argued that "the examples of constructive state experimentation are legion." In recent years states have tried out such educational reforms as merit pay for teachers, teacher certification, and equalizing formulas for spending per pupil. States have also pioneered "no-fault" automobile insurance laws, banking laws to permit regionalized operations, and telephone, occupational, and insurance deregulation, and changes to labor relations, welfare, and criminal sentencing law. "The important point," said the Domestic Policy Council, "is that the States, as laboratories for testing public policies, can experiment with novel, risky, even exotic, approaches to their problems without threatening the nation as a whole."[47]

Throughout this book we have cited examples of state innovations, noting that state policies frequently have served as models for national programs. Among these examples were mother's aid, unemployment insurance, fair housing laws, air pollution statutes, and equalization formulas for financing public education.

Recent improvements in state capacity. Historically, the amateurism and petty politics that characterized many state governments undermined arguments in favor of policy decentralization. Until the mid-1960s most analysts noted that California, Minnesota, New York, and other "progressive" states constituted the exception and not the rule. More typically, state governments operated under antiquated constitutions suited to a society of rural farmers. State legislatures met for brief sessions, usually every other year, and legislators and governors often were amateurs interested in politics mostly for personal or political gain. Patronage workers, with little expertise or interest in policy innovation or efficient implementation, dominated state bureaucracies.

Changes in the fiscal and administrative capacity of state governments in the 1960s and 1970s enabled proponents of decentralization to argue that the states had become more trustworthy and as capable of effective program management as the federal government. Political scientist Ira Sharkansky argued in 1969 that "too many people malign the states unjustly."[48] In the 1960s, Supreme Court decisions such as *Baker* v. *Carr* (1962) and *Wesberry* v. *Sanders* (1964) forced the states to apportion legislative districts equally, giving urban residents their fair share of representatives in legislative policymaking.

The executive director of the Council of State Governments claimed by the mid-1980s that "a revolution—albeit a quiet one—has transformed the states." He said that state government could now formulate and implement modern social policies. Legislatures had all been reapportioned to represent city and suburban populations as well as rural legislative districts. A large majority of the states had longer legislative sessions than in the past, with larger staffs to assist in lawmaking. Governors served longer terms, had more power and additional staff. State civil servants and judges were more competent and professional.

Our book has detailed the growth of state and local capacity measured in terms of taxes, spending, and personnel. Most states had adopted modern tax systems, with nine states enacting new income taxes for the first time between 1959 and 1970.[49] Many states delegated significant powers of "home rule" to local governments, and a few permitted cities to levy income taxes on their residents.[50]

The Biases of State Policy Performance

These arguments seem reasonable, but as is true for claims about the superior responsiveness of state governments, their immediate plausibility masks serious logical and evidentiary flaws. For instance, the claim that the states now have achieved the capacity to implement creative public policies assumes that the states will use their capacity in a neutral manner—that is, that state policy innovations and administration are as likely to be politically "progressive" as they are likely to be conservative. Our book has demonstrated that this assumption is not accurate. First, the states' individual and collective ability to pursue policy goals is inherently more limited than the federal government's. Second, the states' ability to pursue "progressive" policies is much more severely restricted than their ability to pursue conservative policies.

Though the states have become "modernized" in the past generation, a modernized government is not the same as an activist government. Reforms since the 1960s have increased the states' ability to cope with social problems, but they have not changed most states' fundamental resistance to redistributive and regulatory policies. In fact, many of the reforms "modernizing" the states imposed new limits on government capacity. Some of the changes created new barriers to policy activism, while others reinforced state fiscal conservatism and disparities among the states.

Modernization and limited state capacity. Many of the state management and budget reforms celebrated by proponents of a new federalism are expressly designed to limit the expansion of government effort. For example, forty-three states provide for "item veto," which permits a governor to veto portions of legislation (including individual appropriations) rather than an entire law or budget. Of these states, eleven allow the governor unilaterally to reduce spending on individual items. Undoubtedly this power is sometimes used to veto "pork-barrel" legislation. Evidence suggests that the line-item veto has a relatively modest effect on the size of state budgets. Nevertheless, the line-item veto is a power that can be used to *cut* effort by limiting spending but cannot be used to redistribute funds or to allocate additional money.

A few states have developed innovative devices for limiting spending. For example, Maryland and West Virginia permit the legislature no power to increase the governor's budget proposal, but these states allow the legislature to cut the executive budget. (Nebraska law achieves a similar effect by requiring a three-fifths vote to increase the governor's budget.) Alabama voters in 1985 passed a "budget isolation" amendment to the state constitution. This provision tied the passage of all new programs to the approval of the entire state budget.[51]

States also have developed laws that, in principle, make public regulation more difficult to impose and sustain. Forty-four states in the mid-1980s had enacted some form of "sunset" legislation that terminates government agencies unless they are explicitly renewed by the legislature. The eleven states with the most comprehensive sunset laws (e.g., Texas, Delaware, Arizona, and Alabama) tended to be the states with low taxes, meager social expenditures, and good "business climates." Forty-one states also added legislative oversight of individual administrative rules. Although courts have ruled that the "legislative veto" (the practice of a legislature voiding an agency rule) is unconstitutional, some states have found legal ways to exercise this power. Iowa voters, for example, approved a constitutional amendment providing for a legislative veto in 1985.[52] Though evidence of the effectiveness of these provisions remains lacking, their aim is undeniably to limit, but not to enhance, government capacity.

Some state regulatory agencies overtly benefit state businesses by limiting competition, so that a sunset law may, in principle, work against the interests of businesses within a state. But it is obvious that these laws are more likely to affect newer agencies with less well organized political support (such as environmental agencies) than older, more entrenched administrative units.

"Home rule" and other laws have increased the capacity of local governments to become active policymakers, but other state laws have counteracted this delegation of power by imposing severe limits on local government financial capacity. California voters in 1978 and Massachusetts voters two years later enacted propositions that reduced property taxes and made it difficult for state and local governments to increase taxes. Between 1976 and 1980, eighteen states enacted legal limits on the growth of taxes, expenditures, or both. In these cases state law played its traditional role of limiting the policy options available to local government.

Resource disparities and limited state capacity. Continuing inequality of resources among the states fosters a "beggar thy neighbor" competition for business that acts as an automatic policy drag in the U.S. system. State reforms of the past twenty-five years have sometimes increased these inequalities. For example, the tax limitation amendments pioneered by the states created greater differences between rich and poor states. Several of the states that limited revenue growth, "including Utah, Missouri, South Carolina, Tennessee and Texas, rank in the lowest third of states in tax burdens and tend to have regressive tax structures."[53] In the 1980s, the states vary tremendously in their ability to raise revenues. Income per capita is much higher in some states than in others, so that a state with the same income tax rate as its neighbors can collect fewer revenues because its overall income is lower.

The gap between the revenue generating *capacity* of the poorest and richest states grew wider in the 1980s. The Advisory Commission on Intergovernmental Relations (ACIR) has developed a measure of tax capacity that combines property, retail sales, income, and minerals taxes. This indicator shows how different the states' ability to raise money would be if all applied an identical set of tax rates. Table 11.1 shows that in 1985 there would have been a substantial disparity among the states' ability to raise revenue, even if all of them taxed at the same rates, and that the disparity had grown since 1975. The standard deviation, a statistic that measures the degree to which the states depart from the national average, grew from a 17 percent variation from the mean in 1975, to 39 percent in 1981 (a year in which high oil prices drastically increased the potential revenues of oil-rich states), and dropped to 29 percent variation in 1985. As shown in Table 11.1, the revenue-generating ability of the least well-off states remained virtually the same from 1975 to 1981, but the revenue-generating ability of several states blessed with healthier economies improved in the same period.[54] It is important to keep in mind that the limited capacity to raise revenue is a condition over which such states as Alabama, Mississippi, and Arkansas have little control.

An enhanced fiscal capacity does not necessarily lead to generous policies, it only creates the possibility of doing so. For instance, its superior ability to generate revenue did not encourage so conservative a state as Texas actually to increase its governmental revenue (or to raise the level of assistance to its least well-off citizens, as was shown in Table 7.5). In energy-rich states, higher energy prices in the 1970s did not move historically conservative state governments to more policy effort.

Most states inhibit their ability to raise revenues even during prosperous times by relying heavily on inflexible or regressive taxes that place the heaviest tax burden on the people least able to pay taxes. The states still derive half their revenue (49 percent, down from 58 percent in 1957) from sales taxes, the least flexible type of tax. Thus, revenue varies

Table 11.1. *Tax capacity*[a] *of selected states, 1975–1985*

Seven states with the least ability to levy taxes, 1985	1985 per capita Tax Capacity	Index		
		1985	1981	1975
Mississippi	$ 972.43	69	72	70
Arkansas	1,038.81	74	82	78
Alabama	1,056.85	75	75	77
South Carolina	1,081.68	77	75	77
West Virginia	1,085.74	77	90	89
Idaho	1,099.75	78	87	89
Kentucky	1,101.28	78	82	85

Seven states with the greatest ability to levy taxes, 1985	1985 per capita Tax Capacity	Index		
		1985	1981	1975
Alaska	3,648.29	259	324	155
Wyoming	2,380.33	169	216	154
Nevada	2,054.18	146	148	145
Connecticut	1,782.92	127	110	110
Delaware	1,733.07	123	111	125
California	1,691.83	120	115	110
Colorado	1,662.90	118	113	106
Fifty-state average	1,408.06	100	100	100
Standard deviation[b]	408.30	29	39	17

[a]A measure of what each state would raise if it used an identical set of taxes

[b]A measure of how widely the fifty states' tax capacity varies. This statistic was calculated by the authors.

Source: Advisory Commission on Intergovernmental Relations, *Measuring State Fiscal Capacity,* 1987 edition (Washington, DC: ACIR. 1987),70, 130, 134.

kaleidoscopically from year to year and from state to state. An economic recession caused tax revenues to fall by more than 19 percent in Alaska but to increase by 19 percent in Washington in 1983, for example.[55] States indisputably rely more heavily on income taxes now than they did in the 1950s. Income taxes have increased from 18 percent of state tax collections in 1957 to 37 percent in 1983.[56] Though state tax systems are more flexible now than they were in 1960, Susan B. Hansen emphasizes that "state revenue [flexibility] has affected state spending only *within limits*" (emphasis in original). Instead, federal aid explains most of the growth in state activism.[57]

Federal grants-in-aid have increased the amount of funds available to each state, but they have not significantly reduced interstate resource disparities. Only one-seventh of grant formulas have explicitly included criteria that involved the redistribution of aid to needy areas. Instead, many grant programs have distributed federal funds based on population instead of on demand or need. In the mid-1970s, the wealthiest states actually received the most grants per capita.[58]

Interstate policy competition and limited state capacity. Because of continuing resource disparities and because federal grant programs did little to equalize state revenues, interstate competition for business continued to set an upper limit on state policy effort throughout the 1970s.[59] In that decade, many states, especially in the Sunbelt, aggressively tried to entice corporations to relocate within their borders by fine-tuning the policies that might contribute to a good "business climate." In mid-1975, the Fantus Company, a consulting firm that provides estimates of "business climate" to employers, estimated the relative business climate of the forty-eight contiguous states based on fifteen criteria (Table 11.2). States with low taxes (especially on corporations), restrictive labor laws, niggardly public assistance, and small government debt were scored as having the most favorable environments for business.

Two-thirds of the states with the best business climates (according to these measures) were former Confederate states with a record of conservatism in most areas of social policy. In contrast, many of the "worst" states—including New York, California, and Massachusetts—have been

Table 11.2. *States with the "best" and "worst" business climates, 1975*

"Best" Climates	Score[a]	"Worst" Climates	Score[a]
Texas	192	New York	628
Alabama	210	California	581
Virginia	214	Massachusetts	547
South Dakota	230	Michigan	532
South Carolina	236	Delaware	520
North Carolina	239.5	Connecticut	516.5
Florida	244	Pennsylvania	506
Arkansas	248	Minnesota	505.5
Indiana	251	Oregon	499
Utah	279	Washington	495
North Dakota	286	Vermont	489
Mississippi	287	New Jersey	483

[a]The score represents an index based on fifteen criteria; a lower score indicates a better business climate.

Source: Philip L. Rones, "Moving to the Sun: Regional Job Growth, 1968 to 1978," *Monthly Labor Review* 103:3 (March 1980), 15.

regarded as "progressive" states that have (in the past) pioneered new social policies. It is important to note that business climate does not predict a state's economic prosperity. In the 1970s Indiana lost manufacturing jobs despite its high "business climate" ranking, and California prospered despite a poor ranking.

State officials everywhere *perceive* business climate as a fundamental policy concern, regardless of the shaky link between business climate and actual economic growth.[60] Political leaders in all parts of the country ascribed the Sunbelt's prosperity to its perceived political conservatism. Pressures on policymakers in states with the "worst" business climates intensified. Public officials in Illinois and New York warned that they were losing jobs and industry to states with lower taxes, fewer services, and fewer protections for unions.[61] Accordingly, most states since 1966 have changed tax laws and offered a variety of subsidies in an effort to attract industry. Thus, though only eleven states had corporate income tax exemptions for new or expanded businesses in 1966, twenty-five states had such exemptions by 1983. Similarly, the number of states offering tax breaks for business inventories more than doubled, to forty-four, since 1966; the number offering state loans for equipment and machinery tripled, to twenty-four; and the number offering tax exemptions for land or capital improvement almost tripled, to thirty.[62]

Despite strapped budgets and in the wake of tax revolts, the states invested ever-increasing sums to lure business in the early 1980s.[63] Economic development expenditures by individual states ranged from $511,400 to $30,812,000 by 1981–1982, leading analysts to conclude that "the commitment of state funds is substantial, and even the states at the lower end of the expenditure scale tend to make economic development a high priority, as measured by the proportion of available resources committed to this purpose."[64] For example, the state of Mississippi in 1981 authorized local governments to issue industrial revenue bonds (amounting to nearly $114 million), industrial revenue notes ($3.6 million), taxable industrial revenue bonds ($54 million), tax-exempt general obligation bonds, and small business loan guarantees (in a fund capitalized at $3 million). Mississippi spent an additional $450,000 on "customized" training for employers and provided numerous tax deductions, exemptions, and abatements for private employers. Every state developed a similar package of business lures.[65]

By the mid-1980s interstate competition to attract business, and the jobs and taxes that accompany it, imposed significant limits on officials' willingness to use government as an active tool for regulating business or redistributing resources. According to the executive director of the Advisory Commission on Intergovernmental Relations:

In this case, economic development is one of those nice fuzzy terms to gloss over bitter interstate competition for investors' dollars. In fact, I cannot recall a time in the last thirty years when state leaders evinced greater interest than they do now about the need to attract and to hold business investment . . . The last two major recessions and the rise of the footloose multinational and multistate firms have caused state leaders to become acutely sensitive to the need to create "a favorable business climate." Although this concern for economic development has been used to justify larger appropriations for physical infrastructure and, in some cases education, more often than not it has prompted state officials to pursue conservative tax policies.[66]

Interstate competition does not *cause* conservative policies. The key word is "tendency"; states tend to be cautious in such an atmosphere, though they vary, as they always have.

In this context, it is remarkable that some states still pioneer in policies that regulate business or that provide more social benefits to citizens. California's environmental legislation serves as a model for regulating natural resources within a state. Missouri's early childhood education program drew international interest in the late 1980s. Massachusetts' guarantee of health insurance to all its citizens in 1988 was discussed as a prototype for national legislation.

Moreover, as Ann Bowman and Richard Kearney point out, many of the states showed surprising budgetary resilience in the wake of federal budget cuts in the 1980s. State spending on education across all the states increased by 62 percent between 1978 and 1983, during a period of often severe fiscal strain in state government.[67] Many states restored or at least absorbed some of the deep cuts in social program grants effected in 1981. It should be noted that programs that served the middle class seemed much more resistant to state budget cuts than programs for the poor.

Corporate lobbying at the state level increased dramatically in the 1980s, an indication of the growing importance of state laws to business.[68] In some cases states protect economic interests within their borders to the disadvantage of large corporations. The Texas Railroad Commission historically limited the operations of large oil companies in order to protect thousands of Texans who derive income from oil royalties. Ohio passed a law in 1986 designed to protect its manufacturing corporations from hostile takeovers by out-of-state companies. According to lawyers in that state, the statute "could allow [company] directors to turn down a takeover bid of several dollars a share over the market price on the ground that the potential acquirer might shut down factories, lay off thousands of workers and devastate communities."[69] A few other states, including Delaware, have followed Ohio's lead.

At the same time, Florida's effort to impose a new sales tax on services showed where there is a line that must not be crossed when taxing businesses. On July 1, 1987, the state of Florida implemented a new tax that included collecting revenues on the sale of advertising to national corporations. Under intense lobbying pressure from "the biggest guns of corporate America," and with the state electorate generally unconvinced of its need, Florida's governor reversed his earlier support for the law, called for its repeal, and asked for a $1 billion cut in state services. The Florida legislature repealed the tax on December 10 and replaced the lost revenue by increasing the state's sales tax from 5 to 6 percent. Many observers believed that the failure of Florida's experiment would have a "chilling effect" on other states.[70]

State experimentation and limited state capacity. If the states engage in policy experimentation, their experments usually entail little economic or political risk. More often than not, the states as "social laboratories" limit themselves to politically neutral or conservative social policy experiments. The states tend to enact programs that appear to be immediately cost-effective, that do not redistribute from propertied interests to nonpropertied interests, and that improve "business climate." During every period of policy activism, state innovations that met these criteria have spread rapidly. Innovations that did not meet these criteria spread much more slowly or died out entirely.

Labor market policy illustrates the point. Even the most progressive American states have lagged behind Britain and other West European democracies in policies designed to protect, train, and employ workers. In the Progressive Era, American states passed relatively modest laws that abrogated employers' defenses in worker injury lawsuits, and nine states specified that the legal working age started at fourteen. By 1920, thirty states had limited a child's workday to eight hours. Stimulated by the war effort and by federal grants, forty-one states still funded free public employment offices in 1920, but federal withdrawal of funding caused that number to shrivel to twenty-four by 1930. Until Wisconsin enacted such a law in 1932, no state experimented with unemployment insurance, and only in 1935, with the Social Security Act imminent, did other states follow Wisconsin's lead. By the outbreak of World War II, less than half of the states set a minimum legal age of 16 for factory work. With industrial dislocation on the rise in the 1960s and 1970s, Britain and other European nations required employers to notify their workers in advance of a move or shutdown. In the United States, only Maine, Wisconsin, Hawaii, and the Virgin Islands had enacted mandatory notification laws of any kind by the time Congress approved a national notification law in July 1988.[71]

The development of unemployment insurance illustrates the conservative effects that the U.S. system exerts on state "policy laboratories." The Wisconsin model of unemployment insurance strongly influenced the design of the national Social Security Act, with lasting consequences that make American unemployment insurance unique among capitalist democracies. By relying almost entirely on employer contributions, the U.S. system gives business a proprietary interest in the program. American unemployment compensation requires an unusually long waiting period in order to establish eligibility for benefits. Unlike European systems, which replace a larger percentage of wages for the lowest-paid workers, American compensation has no element of redistribution.

Finally, states' emphasis on balanced budgets and minimal taxes causes American unemployment insurance to be perennially underfinanced, so that demands on state funds peak during recessions—at exactly the time that states can least afford to increase spending. In contrast to nations in which unemployment insurance is a tool for stabilizing the economy, the American system works against economic planning and undermines economic stabilization policies.[72]

Even in other federal systems, subunits enjoy enough autonomy and sufficiently equalized resources that they can conduct bolder policy experiments than the American states. For example, only one American state experimented with a very limited public health insurance program before the enactment of Medicaid (California provided medical aid to the needy in the early 1960s). No state experimented with a "negative income" tax before, during, or after the debates on such proposals in the Nixon and Carter administrations. In contrast, the Canadian province of Saskatchewan enacted a public health insurance program in 1944 and a negative income tax plan in 1973. (Ontario, Canada's most populous province, also experimented with the negative income tax.[73])

The U.S. government usually must act as a catalyst to encourage the diffusion of state experiments. Before the Social Security Act, only nine states had merit systems covering welfare administrators; between the enactment of the federal social security law and 1940, all the rest of the states added such a provision.[74] The "grants strategy" of the 1960s and 1970s must be understood as such an effort, and one that doomed many federal programs to appear inefficient and ineffective.

National government ineffectiveness reconsidered. Research in the United States and abroad confirms that most large, centrally controlled organizations encounter the problems of control, coordination, and communication that Dahl, Lindblom, Wildavsky, and other policy analysts have identified. National policy control is difficult and cumbersome. In the United States, the national administration of policy is most problematic precisely when implementation strategies involve states and localities.

American federalism makes the national government appear especially inept because it works against straightforward, centrally managed programs in which administrators have the authority to make key decisions, such as how to distribute funds, who will receive benefits, and what punishments will be meted out for violating regulations. The system favors policy designs in which decisionmaking authority is delegated to state and local officials or private firms beyond the reach of federal officials; yet these federal officials nevertheless are held ultimately accountable for program outcomes.

In sum, the evidence suggests that under current circumstances state policy performance is "superior" to federal performance *only in the sense that state policy performance in the aggregate is usually more conservative* than federal policy performance. Most states are reluctant to try new policies unless they are guaranteed to reduce government cost or to attract business.

REAGAN'S "NEW" FEDERALISM AS THE OLD CONSERVATISM

Despite its rhetoric extolling the states and local control as the means of achieving policy accountability and efficiency, the Reagan administration's programs came *at the expense of* responsiveness and performance. The administration reduced federal requirements for participatory policymaking and shifted remaining participation requirements toward business and away from local community groups. The block grant programs created in 1981 contained very weak participation requirements, *except when these enhanced business influence*. For example, the Job Training Partnership Act of 1982 required a business majority on the "Private Industry Councils" that controlled program decisions in administrative regions.

Many changes hurt the nonprofit agencies and groups most responsive to and close to the poor. Local nonprofit organizations that serve the poor, such as legal aid, employment and training, and social services agencies all experienced above-average reductions in government support (and because their clients are disproportionately poor, they could make up less of the funding gap through fees and charges).[75]

The Reagan administration's cuts in federal aid worsened revenue disparities between the states. State tax expert Susan Hansen predicted in 1983 that "cutbacks in federal aid should be a highly effective means to limit state government growth,"[76] although the economic recovery after 1983 permitted more state budget growth than expected. The executive director of the Advisory Commission on Intergovernmental Relations observed that many of the state tax increases of the early 1980s were made on a short-term basis and were driven by fiscal desperation. He saw little evidence that state governments would let public sector spending grow at a rate faster than the economy.[77] A Princeton University study indicated that domestic spending had reached a "plateau" in the 1980s. Of fourteen states studied, five largely replaced the Reagan budget cuts, eight had partially replaced the cuts, and one made "little or no response" to federal budget cuts. The traditionally conservative states replaced federal cuts the least, since "the character of this response varied according to the political ideology and the fiscal condition of the state."[78]

By accentuating revenue disparities and state self-reliance, the Reagan administration intensified interstate competition for investment. In some cases, it explicitly armed the states with economic weapons for this conflict. For example, federal job training programs in the 1960s and 1970s were intended to serve the hard-core unemployed by making such individuals more attractive to potential employers. The Reagan administration transformed these programs into a "block grant," with increased state control and business influence over the types of training provided and the selection of trainees. As a result, the emphasis in this "federal" job training program turned to "customizing" workers to business needs, often as part of a package of tax breaks, bonds, and other incentives designed to lure or to keep business in a jurisdiction. Missouri and other states moved state job training administration from state social services departments to state economic development offices.[79]

Reagan-era reforms made it difficult for states to increase spending on programs unless they seemed directly connected to economic growth. Welfare reforms that encouraged cost savings and permitted states to experiment with "workfare," but not a guaranteed minimum income, exemplified this trend. The administration provided the state policy "laboratories" the incentive *to produce only conservative outcomes.*

It is important to note that the Reagan administration was far more closely wedded to its ideology of "less government" than it was to decentralization *per se.* Usually, decentralization efficiently served the administration's conservative ideology. But when this turned out not to be the case, the goal of decentralization was abandoned. The administration argued that states' rights stopped where business was threatened. According to Assistant Attorney General Charles J. Cooper, "Interstate commerce is something that is inherently national and not an appropriate subject for 50 different laboratory experiments."[80] In the cases of interstate trucking, nuclear power, and offshore oil exploration (to name a few), the administration subordinated federalism to the national protection of business. When state and local officials opposed the administration, Reagan officials moved to preempt their authority.[81]

UNIFORMITY VERSUS VARIATION: THE BASIC ISSUE IN A FEDERAL SYSTEM

There are two fundamental policy questions in any federal political system. First, how much *discretion* over policy will states be allowed? If the states have wide discretion, then civil rights, welfare, education, environmental, or urban policies will inevitably vary from state to state. Policy performance and responsiveness will vary. If the states are allowed no discretion, they must conform (in principle) to standards set by the central government and merely administer policies set forth by national officials. This is almost never the case, for as Aaron Wildavsky has aptly put the issue, "uniformity is antithetical to federalism":

> The existence of states free to disagree with one another and with the central government inevitably leads to differentiation. Yet differ states must if they are to do more than obey central directives. Were there to be a change in values toward equality of condition, therefore, the political culture that undergirds federalism would fall apart. You can have a belief in equality of opportunity to be different, but you cannot have a belief in equality of results to be the same and still have a federal system.[82]

Wildavsky has concluded that "federalism means inequality." If this is so, then for policies to become uniform, "federalism" must be eclipsed or weakened.

The second fundamental question involves resource disparities. Will the states have *approximately comparable resources* to conduct policy? If the states differ significantly in wealth and potential tax revenues, they will behave much like business firms in a competitive market. The most desperate, marginal competitors will cut costs in every way possible to attract business. In the private sector such competition leads marginal firms to lower wages, to permit unsafe working conditions, and to engage in a variety of unsavory business practices called "unfair competition." Among states, this competition causes marginal (i.e., poor) states to cut taxes and services to levels that endanger or impoverish their citizens. In both cases, their better-off competitors feel pressured to follow suit, and in the absence of legal limitations they more or less do so. A policy system so arranged militates against improvements in responsiveness and performance above a level believed necessary to prevent a potent political reaction.

In our view the United States lacks the level of policy responsiveness and performance it should have because progressive policy experiments are made unlikely, and they spread slowly, if at all, when they are undertaken. We endorse Robert Dahl's conclusions about inequality: "Disparities of income and wealth confer extraordinary advantages and disadvantages. The distribution of advantages and disadvantages is often arbitrary, capricious, unmerited, and unjust, and in virtually all advanced countries no longer tolerable."[83] It is especially so in the United States, where income distribution is measurably more unequal than in most Western European democracies.[84]

In the policymaking system as it exists in the United States, how could the tendency toward extreme policy restraint be changed?

Nationalizing Basic Protections

While professing faith in decentralized policy, most Americans take for granted that some protections and rights should be granted equally to all citizens. In this century, the list of such protections in several nations has expanded beyond procedural guarantees and now embraces basic necessities required for personal growth. As R. H. Tawney put it, "equality of opportunity . . . depends, not merely on the absence of disabilities, but on the presence of abilities."[85] These abilities include employment, health, income support for those who cannot work, and education. Some policies designed to provide these basic governmental protections should be nationalized in the United States, and the ability of state and local governments to provide highly unequal policies should be curbed when policies providing basic protections remain de-centralized.

Reducing Interstate Economic Competition

The engine that drives the federal system in the direction of con-servative policy results is the competition among states for a share of national economic growth. Such competition maximizes the leverage of business to bargain for lower taxes and less public policy effort. Federal regulations could drastically reduce the proclivity (and ability) of states and cities to create poverty in the public sector even in the midst of private plenty. Several changes would accomplish this. For example, the federal tax code could be amended to prohibit states from issuing tax-free industrial development or industrial revenue boards for private business purposes. States and their dependent governments could be prohibited from granting tax abatements, tax holidays, or other devices to escape taxation.[86] The right of states to weaken labor unions through right-to-work laws could be withdrawn.

Equalizing Jurisdictional Capacity

If resources were equalized across the states, they would be more likely to produce progressive policy outcomes, though variations would still exist because of cultural, economic, and historical differences that have shaped the various states' responses to social problems. Even if Mississippi had possessed the revenues and budgets of a Massachusetts or Wisconsin early in this century, for example, its policies still would have differed substantially. But a different federal system would have moderated Mississippi's conservatism and permitted such states as Wisconsin and Massachusetts to experiment with a wider range of redistributive and regulatory policies. The states might have become genuine policy laboratories for conducting progressive policy experiments. No other major federal policy system does so little to equalize resources.

The West German Basic Law requires that the national government promote uniform living conditions across the Laender, and national law requires the equalization of state and local governments' revenue base. In 1978 this equalization requirement raised the revenue of the poorest Laender to 95 percent of the national average and reduced the revenue differences of the richest and poorest Laender from a ratio of 1:1.24 to 1:1.07.[87] Australia's national government began to provide special grants to poor states in 1910 and in 1933 it created the Commonwealth Grants Commission, "the most highly developed system of fiscal capacity equalization in any federal country." Canada has equalized fiscal resources since 1957. While oil-rich Saskatchewan received $62 (Canadian) in equalization grants per capita in 1980, Newfoundland received $494 per capita.[88] A similar program of revenue equalization among American states, and a required equalization among American general purpose governments, would significantly change the direction of state experimentation. It is a reform so fundamental that it may require a constitutional guarantee, as in West Germany and, more recently, Canada.

POLICYMAKING IN A COMPLEX POLITICAL SYSTEM

Policymaking processes should be designed to preserve some of the advantages of a complex, decentralized policymaking structure and at the same time introduce the possibility of enacting and implementing public policy with the necessary capacity and coherence to realize its purposes. Excessively centralized policies breed self-sustaining bureaucracies that are difficult to change, as any examination of the Department of Defense will reveal. At the same time, the demands of modern society for tractable, corrigible policies make extreme fragmentation of the policy process often clearly inappropriate and—as in the case of pollution control—potentially deadly. Reforms that try to centralize all decisionmaking in the interests of efficiency are doomed to failure. At the same time, a policymaking structure that gives up the idea of equity and efficiency makes policy success nearly impossible.

NOTES

1. Ronald Reagan, "National Conference of State Legislatures: Remarks at the Annual Convention in Atlanta, Georgia, July 30, 1981," *Weekly Compilation of Presidential Documents,* 3 August 1981.
2. Daniel J. Elazar, *American Federalism: A View from the States,* 2d ed. (New York: Harper & Row, 1984), 249–50.
3. Virginia Gray, "Politics and Policy in the American States," in Virginia Gray, Herbert Jacob, and Kenneth N. Vines, eds., *Politics in the American States,* 4th ed. (Boston: Little, Brown, 1982), 24; Carl W. Stenberg, "States Under the Spotlight: An Intergovernmental View," *Public Administration Review* 45:2 (March/April 1985), 319–26.
4. Grant McConnell, *Private Power and American Democracy* (New York: Alfred A. Knopf, 1966), 91–101. Cf. "American Scene: Participatory Democracy," *Time,* 13 April 1970, 34.
5. Thomas Jefferson to J. Taylor, 1816, in Saul K. Padover, ed., *Thomas Jefferson on Democracy* (New York: Appleton-Century-Crofts, 1939), 39–41. For a selection of "new left" views on participatory democracy, see Terrence E. Cook and Patrick M. Morgan, *Participatory Democracy* (San Francisco: Canfield, 1971).
6. James Madison, Federalist 51, in the *Federalist Papers* (New York: Mentor, 1961).
7. Jefferson to De Tracy, 1811, in Padover, *Thomas Jefferson on Democracy,* 52–3.
8. James Madison, Federalist 46, in the *Federalist Papers.*
9. Alexis de Tocqueville, *Democracy in America,* trans. and ed. Richard D. Heffner (New York: Mentor, 1956), 84–5.
10. Council of State Governments, *Book of the States, 1988–1989,* (Lexington, KY: Council of State Governments, 1988), 217–20.
11. Philip Selznick, *TVA and the Grass Roots: A Study in the Sociology of Formal Organization* (Berkeley: University of California Press, 1949), 25, 60–1.
12. Lyndon Johnson, *The Vantage Point: Perspectives of the Presidency, 1963–1969* (New York: Holt, Rinehart, and Winston, 1971), 74. Some of the "poverty warriors" had a more radical vision of the community action agencies as institutions that would challenge public and private power structures in urban areas; cf. Dennis R. Judd, *The Politics of American Cities: Private Power and Public Policy,* 3d ed. (Glenview, IL, and Boston: Scott, Foresman/Little, Brown: 1988), 314–8.
13. Advisory Commission on Intergovernmental Relations, *Citizen Participation in the American Federal System* (Washington, DC: GPO, 1980), 111–3. Note that in practice, such federally mandated participation overrepresents consumers and direct beneficiaries of services and underrepresents low-income groups and other citizens (132–42).
14. Domestic Policy Council, Working Group on Federalism, "The Status of Federalism in America," (unpublished mimeo, November 1986), 56.
15. Bruce Fein, "Where Has the New Federalism Gone?" *St. Louis Post-Dispatch,* 15 October 1986, 3C.

16. McConnell, *Private Power and American Democracy*, 104–5. Pluralist David B. Truman explained, "[g]roups that would be rather obscure or weak under a unitary arrangement may hold advantageous positions in the State governments . . .," *The Governmental Process: Political Interests and Public Opinion* (New York: Alfred A. Knopf, 1953), 323.

17. McConnell, *Private Power and American Democracy*, 109. Cf. Amitai Etzioni, "The Fallacy of Decentralization," *Nation* 25 August 1969, 145–7.

18. Robert Erickson, Norman Luttbeg, and Kent Tedlin, *American Public Opinion: Its Origins, Content, and Impact*, 3d ed. (New York: Macmillan, 1988), 42.

19. John F. Bibby, Cornelius P. Cotter, James L. Gibson, and Robert J. Huckshorn, "Parties in State Politics," in Virginia Gray, Herbert Jacob, and Kenneth N. Vines, eds., *Politics in the American States: A Comparative Analysis*, 4th ed. (Boston: Little, Brown, 1983), 64. Kenneth Newton finds a similar patterns in citizen participation across large and small local governments in Britain, "Is Small Really So Beautiful? Is Big Really So Ugly? Size, Effectiveness, and Democracy in Local Government," *Political Studies* 30:2 (June 1982), 190–206.

20. David B. Magleby, *Direct Legislation: Voting on Ballot Propositions in the United States* (Baltimore: Johns Hopkins University Press, 1984), 86, 104.

21. L. Harmon Zeigler, "Interest Groups in the States," in Virginia Gray, Herbert Jacob, and Kenneth N. Vines, eds., *Politics in the American States: A Comparative Analysis*, 4th ed. (Boston: Little, Brown, 1983), 99.

22. Daniel W. Gottlieb, "Business Mobilizes as States Begin to Move in the Regulatory Vacuum," *National Journal* 31 July 1982, 1340–3.

23. Alan R. Gitelson, M. Margaret Conway, and Frank B. Feigart, *American Political Parties: Stability and Change* (Boston: Houghton Mifflin, 1984), 210.

24. Timothy D. Schellhardt, "Corporate PACs Turning Attention to the States as Deregulation Gains," *Wall Street Journal*, 28 October 1982, p. 31; Roger H. Davidson and Walter J. Oleszek, *Congress and Its Members*, 2d ed. (Washington, DC: Congressional Quarterly, 1985), 67

25. Frank J. Sorauf, *Money in American Elections* (Glenview, IL, and Boston: Scott, Foresman/Little, Brown, 1988), 285–96.

26. Harold W. Stanley and Charles D. Hadley, "The Southern Presidential Primary: Regional Intentions with National Implications," *Publius* 17:3 (Summer 1987), 83–100; Phil Gailey, "Some Second Thoughts on 'Super Tuesday,' " *New York Times*, 25 March 1987, 10.

27. Norton E. Long, "The Three Communities," in Marylin Gittell, eds., *State Politics and the New Federalism* (New York: Longman, 1986), 138–47.

28. Fein, "Where Has the New Federalism Gone?"

29. Etzioni, "The Fallacy of Decentralization."

30. J. F. Fixx, "An Anniversary Talk with Huntley and Brinkley," *McCall's* October 1966, 176, as cited in Terry Sanford, *Storm Over the States* (New York: McGraw-Hill, 1967), 37.

31. Jeffrey L. Pressman and Aaron B. Wildavsky, *Implementation* (Berkeley: University of California Press, 1973).

32. Aaron B. Wildavsky, *Speaking Truth to Power: The Art and Craft of Policy Analysis* (Boston: Little, Brown, 1979), 150–2.

33. Robert A. Dahl, *Dilemmas of Pluralist Democracy: Autonomy vs. Control* (New Haven, CT: Yale University Press, 1982), 103–4.

34. Charles E. Lindblom, *Politics and Markets: The World's Political-Economic Systems* (New York: Basic Books, 1977), 66–70.

35. Wildavsky, *Speaking Truth to Power*, 152.

36. Martin Landau, "Federalism, Redundancy, and System Reliability," in Daniel Elazar, ed., *The Federal Polity* (New Brunswick, NJ: Transaction Press, 1974), 173–96.

37. Domestic Policy Council, "The Status of Federalism in America," 57.

38. John J. Kirlin, "A Political Perspective," in Trudi C. Miller, ed., *Public Sector Performance: A Conceptual Turning Point* (Baltimore: Johns Hopkins University Press, 1984), 182–7.

39. Charles M. Tiebout, "A Pure Theory of Local Expenditures," *Journal of Political Economy* 64:5 (October 1956), 416–24; Dennis Epple and Allan Zelenitz, "The Implications of Competition among Jurisdictions: Does Tiebout Need Politics?," *Journal of Political Economy* 89:6 (1981), 1197–1217.

40. James M. Buchanan and Gordon Tullock, *The Calculus of Consent: Logical Foundations of Constitutional Democracy* (Ann Arbor: University of Michigan Press, 1962), 114.

41. Vincent Ostrom, *The Intellectual Crisis in American Public Administration* (University, AL: University of Alabama Press, 1974), esp. 114–30.

42. Dennis R. Judd and David Brian Robertson, "Urban Revitalization in the U.S.: Prisoner of the Federal System," in Michael Parkinson, Bernard Foley, and Dennis R. Judd, eds., *Urban Economic Development in the United States and Britain* (Manchester, England: Manchester University Press, 1988), 9–26.

43. Domestic Policy Council, "The Status of Federalism in America," 55–6.

44. Ibid.

45. Quoted in Lewis J. Paper, *Brandeis* (Secaucus, NJ: Citadel Press, 1983), 330–1.

46. John Naisbitt, *Megatrends: Ten New Directions Transforming Our Lives* (New York: Warner, 1982), 105. See David Osborne, *Laboratories of Democracy* (Cambridge, MA: Harvard Business School Press, 1988).

47. Domestic Policy Council, "The Status of Federalism in America," 52–5.

48. Ira Sharkansky, *The Maligned States: Policy Accomplishments, Problems, and Opportunities* (New York: McGraw-Hill, 1972), 153.

49. Ibid., 63–8.

50. Stenberg, "States Under the Spotlight" and Mavis Mann Reeves, "Looking Again at State Capacity," in Robert J. Dilger, ed., *American Intergovernmental Relations Today: Perspectives and Controversies* (Englewood Cliffs, NJ: Prentice-Hall, 1986), 143–69.

51. Council of State Governments, *Book of the States, 1984–85* (Lexington, KY: CSG, 1985), 112–5, 244–5; and *Book of the States, 1988–89* (Lexington, KY: CSG, 1988), 9-40, 113–4.

52. Council of State Governments, *Book of the States, 1988–89*, 133–7.

53. Susan B. Hansen, "Extraction: The Politics of State Taxation," in Virginia Gray, Herbert Jacob, and Kenneth N. Vines, eds., *Politics in the American States: A Comparative Analysis* (Boston: Little, Brown, 1983), 441–9.

54. Advisory Commission on Intergovernmental Relations, *1983 Tax Capacity of the States* (Washington, DC: ACIR, 1986), 8, 66.

55. Council of State Governments, *Book of the States, 1984–85*, 342.

56. Ibid.; see Jeffrey R. Henig, *Public Policy and Federalism: Issues in State and Local Politics* (New York: St. Martin's Press, 1985), 36.

57. Hansen, "Extraction," 440.

58. R. Douglas Arnold, "The Local Roots of Domestic Policy," in Thomas E. Mann and Norman J. Ornstein, eds., *The New Congress* (Washington, DC: American Enterprise Institute, 1981), 268.

59. Ann O'M. Bowman and Richard C. Kearney, *The Resurgence of the States* (Englewood Cliffs, NJ: Prentice Hall, 1986), 35–7.

60. Philip L. Rones, "Moving to the Sun: Regional Job Growth, 1968 to 1978," *Monthly Labor Review* 103:3 (March 1980), 15. Studies conclude that transportation, wage levels, productivity of labor, and proximity to markets tend to be more important to business' locational decisions than tax breaks; cf. Thomas R. Plant and Joseph E. Pluta, "Business Climate, Taxes and Expenditures, and State Industrial Growth in the United States," *Southern Economic Journal* 50:1 (July 1983), 99–119.

61. Robert Goodman, *The Last Entrepreneurs: America's Regional Wars for Jobs and Dollars* (Boston: South End Press, 1979).
62. Mel Dubnick and Lynne Holt, "Industrial Policy and the States," *Publius: The Journal of Federalism* 15:1 (Winter 1985), 113–29.
63. Bowman and Kearney, *The Resurgence of the States*, 188–203.
64. National Association of State Development Agencies et al., *Directory of Incentives for Business Investment and Development in the United States: A State-By-State Guide* (Washington, DC: Urban Institute Press, 1983), 3.
65. Ibid., 350–8.
66. John Shannon, "Federal and State-Local Spenders Go Their Separate Ways," in Robert Jay Dilger, ed., *American Intergovernmental Relations Today: Perspectives and Controversies* (Englewood Cliffs, NJ: Prentice-Hall, 1986), 178.
67. Bowman and Kearney, *The Resurgence of the States*, 214.
68. W. John Moore, "Have Smarts, Will Travel," *National Journal* 28 November 1987, 3020–4.
69. Steven Greenhouse, "Ohio's Tough Takeover Curb," *New York Times*, 16 December 1986, 30.
70. Gary Klott, "States Study Florida Actions," *New York Times*, 29 September 1987, 34; Jon Nordheimer, "Florida Legislators Vote to Repeal Tax on Advertising and Services," *New York Times*, 11 December 1987, 1.
71. David Brian Robertson, "Governing and Jobs: America's Business-Centered Labor Market Policy," *Polity* 20:3 (Spring 1988), 426–56; Carol Matlack, "Forewarning," *National Journal*, 11 June 1988; Elizabeth Wehr, "Senate OK's Advance Notice of Plant Closings," *Congressional Quarterly Weekly Report* 9 July 1988, 1919–20; Elizabeth Wehr, "Trade, Plant-Closing Bills Win Strong House Backing," *Congressional Quarterly Weekly Report* 16 July 1988, 1991–2.
72. Robertson, "Governing and Jobs"; Edward Harpham, "Federalism, Keynesianism, and the Transformation of Unemployment Insurance in the United States," in Douglas E. Ashford and E. W. Kelley, eds., *Nationalizing Social Security in Europe and America* (Greenwich, CT: JAI Press, 1986).
73. Christopher Leman, *The Collapse of Welfare Reform: Political Institutions, Policy, and the Poor in Canada and the United States* (Cambridge, MA: MIT Press, 1980), 119. Cf. Jacqueline S. Ismael, *The Canadian Welfare State: Evolution and Transition* (Edmunton: University of Alberta Press, 1987).
74. Virginia Gray, "Innovation in the States: A Diffusion Study," *American Political Science Review* 68:4 (December 1973), 1174–85. Susan Welch and Kay Thompson, "Impact of Federal Incentives on State Policy Innovation," *American Journal of Political Science* 24:4 (November 1980), 715–29. Cf. Dennis R. Judd, "The States in the Federal System," in Stuart S. Nagel, ed., *Encyclopedia of Policy Studies* (New York: Marcel Dekker, 1983), 238.
75. Lester M. Salamon, "Nonprofit Organizations: The Lost Opportunity," in John L. Palmer and Isabel V. Sawhill, eds., *The Reagan Record: An Assessment of America's Changing Domestic Priorities* (Cambridge, MA: Ballinger, 1984), 278–84.
76. Hansen, "Extraction," 440.
77. Shannon, "Federal and State-Local Spenders Go Their Separate Ways," 178.
78. Richard P. Nathan, "Institutional Change Under Reagan," in John L. Palmer, ed., *Perspectives on the Reagan Years* (Washington, DC: Urban Institute Press, 1986), 139.
79. Robertson, "Governing and Jobs."
80. Charles J. Cooper, "Can States Act Without Federal Permission?" *New York Times*, 16 November 1986, E5.
81. Art Levine, "Easing of State-Local Regulatory Burden Leaves Some Pleased, Others Grumbling," *National Journal* 4 August 1984, 1464.

82. Aaron Wildavsky, "Federalism Means Inequality: Political Geometry, Political Sociology, and Political Culture," in Robert T. Golembiewski and Aaron Wildavsky, eds., *The Costs of Federalism* (New Brunswick, NJ: Transaction Press, 1984), 57.
83. Dahl, *Dilemmas of Pluralist Democracy*, 117.
84. Benjamin I. Page, *Who Gets What from Government* (Berkeley: University of California Press, 1983), 190–1.
85. R. H. Tawney, *Equality* (London: Unwin, 1931), 103.
86. Barry Bluestone and Bennett Harrison, *The Deindustrialization of America: Plant Community Abandonment, and the Dismantling of Basic Industry* (New York: Colophon Books, 1982).
87. Arthur B. Gunlicks, "Financing Local Governments in the German Federal System," in J. Edwin Benton and David R. Morgan, eds., *Intergovernmental Relations and Public Policy* (New York: Greenwood Press, 1986), 84–5.
87. Advisory Commission on Intergovernmental Relations, *Studies in Comparative Federalism: Australia, Canada, the United States and West Germany* (Washington, DC: ACIR, 1981), 48–62.

INDEX